A DREAMING FOR THE WITCHES

The Recreation of the *Dobunni* Primal Myth

Stephen J. Yeates

Oxbow Books

Published by
Oxbow Books, Oxford, UK

ISBN 978-1-84217-358-9

A CIP record for this book is available from the British Library

This book is available direct from

Oxbow Books, Oxford, UK
(Phone: 01865-241249; Fax: 01865-794449)

and

The David Brown Book Company
PO Box 511, Oakville, CT 06779, USA
(Phone: 860-945-9329; Fax: 860-945-9468)

or from our website
www.oxbowbooks.com

Front cover: St Bartholomew's, Churchdown Hill (photograph S. Yeates), and the relief of Mercury and Mater (photograph Courtesy of Gloucester City Museum and Art Gallery)

Back cover: sunrise over Oxenton Hill (photograph S. Yeates), and the Birdlip Bowl (photograph S. Yeates, Courtesy of Gloucester City Museum and Art Gallery)

Frontispiece: a relief of the sacred genius, from the Ashcroft area of Cirencester (Photograph the late M. B. Cookson)

Printed in Great Britain by
Information Press, Eynsham

For David and Sandrine for all their help and support

To Tony

Stephen Yeates.
24/6/09.

Contents

List of Figures   vi
Acknowledgements   xii

1   In the Beginning there was Anthropology   1

2   Pantheons   29

3   Interpretatio   56

4   The Flora and Fauna of the Earth   78

5   The Divine Couple from the Shakespeare Inn   137

6   Sacred Places   170

7   Tribal Legends and the Holy Grail   201

     Appendix: Potential Periods of River-name Changes (for Chapter 4)   209

Bibliography   211

Index   226

List of Figures

1   A map showing the Iron-Age tribal groups of the Iberian Peninsula (drawing S. Yeates)

2   A map showing the Iron-Age tribal groups of Gaul, based on coinage distribution, and the later Episcopal sees, derived from the *civitas* territories (drawing S. Yeates)

3   A map showing the Iron-Age tribal groups of Hibernia as mentioned by Ptolemy in the second century AD (drawing S. Yeates)

4   A map showing the Iron-Age tribal groups of Northern Britain, based predominantly on the accounts of Tacitus. Those tribal names marked by a grey circle are considered to have been Caledonian tribes (drawing S. Yeates)

5   A map of the Iron-Age tribal groups of Southern Britain, based on Iron-Age coin distribution, and the known locations of certain *civitas* towns (drawing S. Yeates)

6   A map showing the area of Britain which has produced *Dobunnic* Iron-Age coinage and is, therefore, associated with the tribal territory of that group. The black dots represent major coin hoards (drawing S. Yeates)

7   A map showing the distribution of Iron-Age currency bars in southern Britain. The spit shaped bars, produced from Forest of Dean and Kingswood iron ore, can be seen to have a distribution confined primarily to the territory associated with the *Dobunni* tribe (drawing S. Yeates)

8   A map showing the distribution of the reliefs showing the *Mater* and Mercury (black circles), which can be interpreted as the mother and father of the *Dobunni*. The reliefs from Wellow and Aldsworth (shown as crosses) have also been included because they also show these deities. The Wellow relief shows them either side of another female deity; while the Aldsworth relief shows a divine couple in which the mother may be shown as Minerva (a protectress). The Kenchester (black square) inscription has also been inserted, with the light grey shading indicating territory which was almost certainly part of the *Dobunnic* territory (drawing S. Yeates)

9   A map showing the areas which were probably lost from the *civitas* of the *Dobunni/* Kingdom of the *Hwicce* between AD 410 and *c.* 800 AD, with all the relevant locations marked. The area of the See of Worcester, which is equated to the eleventh century kingdom of the *Hwicce*, is marked in grey (drawing S. Yeates)

10 A Cornelian intaglio (in iron ring) depicting the god Apollo leaning against a column, behind which is the Delphic tripod. In his hand he holds his sacred laurel branch (gem damaged at this point), the intaglio is from Gadara in Jordon (photograph Robert Wilkins, Institute of Archaeology Oxford)

11 A bronze statuette from Richborough, Kent, of Vulcan the smith god (photograph Robert Wilkins, Institute of Archaeology archive, source Martin Henig)

12 a) An early engraving by Samuel Lysons showing a Cornelian intaglio, depicting Jupiter, from Bourton-on-the-Water, Gloucestershire (drawing S. Lysons). b) An

impression taken from a Cornelian intaglio depicting an image of Jupiter seated and holding an eagle, from Bath (Institute of Archaeology archive, University of Oxford)

13   A Cornelian intaglio from Bampton, near Norwich, Norfolk, depicting the goddess Minerva (photograph Robert Wilkins, Institute of Archaeology archive, source Martin Henig)

14   A Cornelian intaglio from the Snettisham Roman jeweller's hoard, Norfolk, depicting Diana with bow and arrow and hunting dogs (photograph M. Maaskant-Kleibrink, Institute of Archaeology archive, source Martin Henig)

15   A bronze statuette from Earith, Huntingdonshire, of Mars the god in Roman military garb (photograph Institute of Archaeology archive, Oxford)

16   A bronze statuette depicting Mars nude but helmeted; from Foss Dyke near Lincoln (photograph Institute of Archaeology archive, Oxford)

17   A bronze figurine of Venus from Colchester, Essex (photograph Institute of Archaeology archive, Oxford)

18   A bronze figurine of Mercury, from the Thames at London Bridge (photograph Institute of Archaeology archive, Oxford)

19   An impression taken from a red Jasper intaglio depicting the god Bacchus, or *Liber Pater*, found in the Roman small town of Cambridge (photograph Robert Wilkins, Institute of Archaeology archive, source Martin Henig)

20   The pediment of the temple of *Sulis Minerva* at Bath showing the Gorgon's head in its oak-leaf wreath (photograph by the late M. B. Cookson, Institute of Archaeology London).

21   A plan of the temple of West Hill, Uley, Gloucestershire, showing where the line of the sunrise would have been located on the festival of Mercury on the 15th May (drawing S. Yeates).

22   A map of the *parochia* of Marden-cum-Sutton with the major archaeological features marked (drawing S. Yeates).

23   A relief of the sacred *genius*, from the Ashcroft area of Cirencester, wearing a mural crown. He is presumably *Corinius* the representation of the Roman town (photograph by the late M. B. Cookson, Institute of Archaeology, London, held at the Institute of Archaeology, Oxford).

24   An impression from a red Jasper intaglio showing Antioch-on-the-Orontes. The original gem is set in the crozier of Archbishop Hubert Walter, Canterbury Cathedral (photograph Robert Wilkins, Institute of Archaeology archive, source Martin Henig)

25   The proposed location of the Romano-British province, inferred by Tacitus in the first century AD, as one of the regions of Britain in which a Germanic language was spoke. This would explain why this area became called the Saxon Shore (drawing S. Yeates)

26   A further proposed location of the Romano-British province which may have been part of the area in which a Germanic language was spoken, according to Tacitus. This area became associated with the Anglian territories (drawing S. Yeates)

27   A map of the divine river-names in and around the *Dobunnic* territory starting with the letter A (drawing S. Yeates)

28   A drawing of the Roman altar from Siddington on which the name inscribed upon it may have been *Amimonedum* (drawing S. Yeates)

29 A map of the divine river-names in and around the *Dobunnic* territory starting with the letter B (drawing S. Yeates)

30 A map showing the *parochiae* of Evesham and Fladbury in Worcestershire. Evesham's territory was associated with the *Badesæte* (drawing S. Yeates)

31 A map of the divine river-names in and around the *Dobunnic* territory starting with the letter C (drawing S. Yeates)

32 The relief from a well at Lower Slaughter which shows the *genii cucullati* alongside a figure, wearing a tunic, in the place of *Cuda*. In the pediment design of the relief are two birds, either side of a rosette, which are considered to be pigeons (photograph Gloucester City Museum and Art Gallery)

33 A map of the divine river-names in and around the *Dobunnic* territory starting with the letter E (drawing S. Yeates)

34 A map of the divine river-names in and around the *Dobunnic* territory starting with the letter G (drawing S. Yeates)

35 A relief showing the images of two goddesses standing alongside Mercury. Mercury (see chapter 5) can be identified as the tribal god of the *Dobunni*, while the Fortuna replaces of the tribal goddess. The central goddess, who wears a mural crown, may well be the city *Tyche* of Gloucester, *Gleva* (photograph by the late M. B. Cookson, Institute of Archaeology London, held at the Institute of Archaeology, Oxford)

36 A map of the divine river-names in and around the *Dobunnic* territory starting with the letter I (drawing S. Yeates)

37 A map of the divine river-names in and around the *Dobunnic* territory starting with the letter L (drawing S. Yeates)

38 A map of the divine river-names in and around the *Dobunnic* territory starting with the letters M and O (drawing S. Yeates)

39 A map of the divine river-names in and around the *Dobunnic* territory starting with the letter S (drawing S. Yeates)

40 Chepstow Castle, a site where a relief of Venus and the nymphs has been recognised re-set into the wall of the Norman great hall. The castle is in a location which would have been ideal as a shrine for the mouth of the river Wye (photograph S. Yeates)

41 A map of the divine river-names in and around the *Dobunnic* territory starting with the letter T (drawing S. Yeates)

42 A map of the divine river-names in and around the *Dobunnic* territory starting with the letter V (drawing S. Yeates)

43 A map showing the *parochia* of Worcester and the territories of the folk-groups *Crohhæme* and *Weogorena* (drawing S. Yeates)

44 A map showing the *civitates*, which almost certainly lay in the province of *Britannia Prima*; those which may have belonged to that territory are also shown (drawing S. Yeates)

45 A plan of Cirencester showing the probable location of the temple of the Capitoline triad (drawing S. Yeates)

46 The relief of Mercury and the mother, found in 1857, from Northgate Street, Gloucester. This has the best surviving image of the mother goddess of the *Dobunni*.

In it she holds a ladle above a bucket or circular vessel (photograph used by kind permission of Gloucester City Museum and Art Gallery)

47   The relief of Mercury and the mother, found in 1960, in excavations at the Cross, Gloucester (photograph used by kind permission of Gloucester City Museum and Art Gallery)

48   A map showing the location of the main shrines in the Gloucester environs (drawing S. Yeates)

49   The relief showing Mercury and the mother from the Leauses site in Cirencester (photograph by the late M. B. Cookson, photograph held by the Institute of Archaeology, Oxford)

50   The relief of Mercury recovered from the Leauses in Cirencester in 1862 (photograph by the late M. B. Cookson, photograph held by the Institute of Archaeology, Oxford).

51   The relief showing the *Matres* from the Leauses site in Cirencester. This shows the consort of Mercury in a triple representation (photograph by the late M. B. Cookson, photograph held by the Institute of Archaeology, Oxford)

52   The relief of Mercury and the *Mater* recovered at Bath from excavations at the Great Bath (photograph used by kind permission of The Roman Baths, Bath and North East Somerset Council)

53   The relief of Mercury recovered in Bath from excavations at the Great Bath (photograph used by kind permission of The Roman Baths, Bath and North East Somerset Council)

54   A map of the Roman town of Bath showing the relationship between the temple of *Sulis Minerva*, who personified the springs and the town, and the probable shrine of Mercury and *Mater* (drawing S. Yeates)

55   A sketch of the relief of Mercury and the *Mater* recovered from Nettleton in 1912 (drawing S. Yeates)

56   A sketch of the relief of Mercury with two goddesses, from Wellow in Somerset (drawing S. Yeates)

57   The relief of Mercury and consort from Aldsworth, in which the goddess is portrayed as Minerva and is, in this guise perhaps, a representation of the goddess as protector (photograph Robert Wilkins, Institute of Archaeology archive, source Martin Henig)

58   The burial goods from the Birdlip Cemetery, including basin and mirror (photogaph used by permission of the Gloucester City Museum and Art Gallery)

59   The skyline of Barrow Wake, on Birdlip Hill, the major recognised burial place of the *Dobunni* elite (photograph S. Yeates)

60   The major hill-fort on Bredon Hill, Worcestershire (photograph S. J. Yeates)

61   The line of the hills which lie around the north-east edge of the Vale of Gloucester (photograph S. Yeates)

62   A map of the Severn valley showing the location of the rich late Iron-Age burials at Crickley and Birdlip, and the other unusual but undated burials at Leckhampton Hill and Nottingham Hill. The grey areas indicate the lines of scarp slope along the Cotswold Edge and outliers, the Forest of Dean, Malverns, Mendips, and Wyre Forest. The enclosed circular valley lies to the north-east of Gloucester and is highlighted in black (drawing S. Yeates)

63 An image of the cockerel can be seen on this *Dobunnic* silver coin unit, called today the Cotswold Cock. On one side the coin has a female head with moon symbolism and a small horse; on the other is a triple tailed horse, with the hooked beak of a bird above and the cockerel's head between the legs of the horse (photograph courtesy of Chris Rudd and Liz Cottam)

64 An image of the cockerel can be seen on this *Dobunnic* silver coin unit, now called the Cotswold Eagle. The coin has a female head with moon symbolism on one side, and the triple tailed horse, with the cockerel's head between the horse's legs, on the other (photograph courtesy of Chris Rudd and Liz Cottam)

65 A map showing the locations of the *Wonders of Britain* as listed by Nennius (drawing S. Yeates)

66 A map of the known thermal springs in the area around the Bristol Avon (drawing S. Yeates)

67 The sacred spring at Bath being excavated under the auspices of Prof. Barry Cunliffe. The walls that surround the spring were described by Nennius in the eighth century AD (photograph Robert Wilkins, Institute of Archaeology archive, source Barry Cunliffe)

68 A map showing the *parochia* of Caerwent and the location of the Whirlypools along the River Troggy (drawing S. Yeates)

69 A picture of the Severn in flood during the 1980s near Wainlode, with the Malvern Hills in the background (photograph S. Yeates)

70 The penannular brooch (of Irish type) recovered from the sacred spring at Bath. The images depicted represent local mythological tales found in the The Mabinogion and associated with Gloucester. The salmon being pulled from the water was thought to be the oldest living creature in the world (photographs Robert Wilkins, Institute of Archaeology archive, source Barry Cunliffe)

71 The image of a pollard Ash tree used as a tribal emblem on the *Dobunnic* gold coinage unit of Anted Rig. The pollard ash-tree is shown on one side, while the triple tailed horse is seen on the other below the legend of Anted and a wheel below (photograph courtesy of Chris Rudd and Liz Cottam)

72 The *parochia* of Gloucester, showing the locations of Roman Gloucester and the minster, along with the four Iron-Age hill-forts located in and around the *parochia* (drawing S. Yeates)

73 The sunlight shining on the face of Cooper's Hill in the period just after the Vernal Equinox (photograph S. Yeates)

74 The earthworks and buildings at Witcombe Roman Villa which lie above a spring, the probable source of the *Gleva* (Horsebere). This stream and the mythical lake gave their name to the city and people of Gloucester (photograph S. Yeates)

75 A sketch plan of Witcombe Roman Villa and shrine above the spring of the *Gleva* (drawing S. Yeates)

76 The mound which is considered to be the location of a temple set above the Tile Well at the source of the Horsebere Brook (photograph S. Yeates)

77 The artificial mound, forming part of the Iron Age rampart or built over the rampart, which is claimed by tradition (and supported by the surviving evidence) to have been the location of an important pre-Christian shrine (photograph S. Yeates)

78   A plan of the Iron-Age hill-fort on Churchdown Hill showing the main locations of mythical traditions (drawing S. Yeates)

79   A photograph of the Saddle Hill, which is the major horn-work of the Iron-Age entrance way into the fort. It is through this gate that the fairy funeral was claimed to enter into the depths of the hill (photograph S. Yeates)

80   A glass intaglio, from Gadar in Jordan, depicting two deities, Hera (Juno) and Tyche (Fortuna) closely associated with a sacrilised mountain, Mount Argaeus, in Asia Minor. The horse below must also have been associated with the Mount Argaeus cult (photograph Robert Wilkins, Institute of Archaeology Oxford)

81   A map showing the most significant Arthurian sites located in the West Country and Wales (drawing S. Yeates)

82   A view of Caerleon a site claimed in the majority of British medieval tales as Arthur's seat of power; the legionary amphitheatre was known as Arthur's Round Table (photograph S. Yeates)

83   The abbey of Glastonbury, Somerset; the claimed burial site of King Arthur. The Tor, considered the location of the Isle of Avalon, can be seen framed by the abbey ruins (photograph S. Yeates)

84   The Skirrid (Ysgyryd Fawr) and the Sugar Loaf on the eastern edge of the Black Mountains. On the former is a cairn known as Arthur's Chest (photograph S. Yeates)

Acknowledgements

I would like to thank David Yeates, Martin Henig, Helen Lewis, and David Price for reading through various parts of this work, and David Bland for helping with the aerial photographs. Thank you also to the Gloucester City Museum and Art Gallery, Corinium Museum, The Roman Baths Museum at Bath, The Institute of Archaeology at Oxford (especially Martin Henig and Barry Cunliffe), and also Chris Rudd and Liz Cottam for the use of photographs and access to the archaeological material. Ideas often develop from conversations, debate and even casual remarks and here I would like to thank Chris Rudd for pointing out the Cockerel on the coinage of the *Dobunni* and also Tony Davis for making me realise that the syllable breaks in the name *Dobunni* could be arranged in a different way. Finally I would like to thank various publishers for the use of English translations of Greek and Latin texts and other authors' views: Harvard University Press, Phillimore, Oxford University Press, Princeton University Press, and Thames and Hudson.

Chapter 1

In the Beginning there was Anthropology

The word Dreaming is at the heart of the title of this work for two reasons: first because it is intrinsically linked to creation ideas (concerning for example those of aboriginal Australians), and secondly to underscore the highly speculative nature of this book, which explores Welsh legend and folk traditions, relating to the area around Gloucester and hence to the *Dobunni*. In general, the beliefs and world-views of Europe's pre-Christian peoples, especially those concerning their origins, are poorly understood, with only a few being recreated from the fragments of knowledge still available. Ancient Europeans' descriptions of their origins have been preserved in some traditional mythological accounts, in material remains, and through comments in ethnographic texts.

Problems with the interpretation of pre-Christian religion stem from the retention of certain out-dated views and a lack of proper scientific investigation; also the field has been distorted by fanciful claims and interpretations. Some of these have seized the popular imagination and have tainted more serious attempts to understand this field. For example, Eric Von Daniken informed us in *Chariots of the Gods* (1969) that many of the world's major religious sites were produced by spacemen with superior technology; earlier in *The Old Straight Track*, Alfred Watkins (1925) proposed that all religious sites in Britain were set out on straight lines; and Guy Underwood in *Patterns of the Past* (1969) suggested there are specific types of unexplained energy forces running through the ground which cannot be measured or explained scientifically. Another example of this pseudo-archaeology is enshrined in the Zodiac circles (Maltwood 1964; 1982), where vast figures are claimed to have been imposed on the landscape. Unlike these examples, this book attempts to discuss pre-Christian religion in a far more grounded way, looking at myth and folk-tradition in an attempt to marry these to the archaeological data. The works mentioned above, to a large extent, fall outside the academic field, even though some of the authors may have started off in an academic context (for example Alfred Watkins and his work with the *Woolhope Naturalists' Field Club* (1918–20; 1923; 1924; 1928; 1931; 1931; 1932)). Archaeological data on religion derives from inscriptions and symbolic depictions and the interpretation of artefacts and structures, along with a reliance on anthropology. Here I will show that it is possible to gain insight into pre-Christian creation myths in Britain and Gaul through archaeological assessment and river name onomastics.

Anthropology and Folklore

Anthropology provides much of the theory which underlies past understandings of religious activity. During the nineteenth and early twentieth centuries there was increasing interest in European and British native mythological traditions. This gave rise to such works as *The Golden Bough* (Frazer 1922), along with the more popularist *Archaic England* (Bayley 1919). These attempted to bring together various strands and ideas from diverse locations and centuries in the belief that they could determine certain traits as being universally human, and which could thus explain certain aspects of religious and cultural activity in pre- or proto-historic times. The work of Frazer is seen as one of four great works of Victorian-Edwardian ethnography which attempted to put forward a theoretical understanding of religion (Morris 1987, 91–106), the others being Müller (1889), Spencer (1876) and Tylor (1913). Behind these works there was an attempt to explain religion as an intellectual aberration. Müller accepted that a belief in divinity was an attribute common to mankind, and that this, along with language, formed a basis for ethnic identity. He interpreted the religion of the *Vedic* scriptures as an early example of the origins of religion. Spencer attempted to organise all existing scientific knowledge to provide a basis for the understanding of the entire world, and his work and ideas of progress and evolution influenced Darwin. He discussed the distinction between magic and religion, and the notion that cultures move from polytheism to monotheism as knowledge increases. Tylor was the first to define anthropology as the study of culture in which he included: knowledge, beliefs, arts, morals, laws, and customs; besides other attributes. He gave voice to the ancient idea of the savage, barbaric and civilised, and claimed that elements of recent religion and ritual were capable of throwing light on the past. Tylor also developed the idea of animism as a means of explaining religion, and discussed or tried to explain, the notion of magic. Frazer (1922), the last of these intellectuals, produced a work which is difficult to evaluate. He published three treatises of which the last, *The Golden Bough*, is an encyclopaedic study of religion in twelve volumes. This brings together much folklore and anthropology of the Classical World, taking its main theme from the killing of the priest of Diana at her sanctuary of *Nemi* in Italy by his successor. Frazer tried to explain the traditions which underpinned this rite. Besides this there are other accounts of human folk-tradition from as far a-field as India, Africa, Australia and America, which he drew upon in an attempt to explain the Classical World. Frazer adopted ideas of Science, Magic and Religion, along with evolutionary ideas from Spencer's and Tylor's earlier works. These studies took data from all over the world and often used them out of context to create a general scheme. These scholars all viewed human culture as evolutionary and approached religion with an empiricist bias. Of these influential works it is the latter with which we are most concerned here, particularly how it influenced later ideas on the nature of religion in pre-Christian Britain. Hutton (1996, 409) noted that Frazer's interpretations of the ritual cycle of pre-Christian beliefs have hung like a ghost over all later studies.

There were also studies of folk beliefs aimed at understanding Britain's past, such as Harold Bayley's *Archaic England* (1919) and Lewis Spence's *The Mysteries of Britain or the Secret Rites and Traditions of Ancient Britain Restored* (1931). These were probably influenced by the claims of Iolo Morganwg, an influential researcher but also forger of

Welsh folklore. He is perhaps another reason why many researchers have treated this subject with caution. Such works can stimulate the imagination but, ultimately, much of the combined information leaves a great deal to be desired, although one must consider that they were works of a specific time. For example, the first paragraph of *Archaic England* reads:

> *'This book is an application of the jigsaw system to certain archaeological problems which under the ordinary detached methods of the specialist have proved insoluble. Fragments of evidence are drawn as occasion warrants from history, fairy-tale, philosophy, legend, folklore – in fact from any quarter whence the required piece unmistakably fulfils the missing space. It is this mental medley with all the defects, and some, I trust of the attractions, of a mosaic.'*

From *Archaic England* by Harold Bayley

That all of these fields should be fitted together to provide some view of the British past is to be applauded, but for them to fit together properly they require structure, which requires an understanding of time and place, something archaeologists would describe as a 'context', which in some respects Bayley lacks.

John Rhys (1901) also discussed some of these ideas in his *Celtic Folklore*, which presents an approach that is more palatable to modern discussions of myth and place-name association. The work of Rhys was grounded in a locality, Wales, and in an important set of texts, which included the Mabinogion. He became one of the leading Celtic academics of his day, and some, if not all, of his philology came to be employed within the later work of Kenneth Jackson (1953), whose *Language and History in Early Britain* still provides the main list of philological changes in British language.

Some of the ideas discussed in *The Golden Bough* became problematic, for example in the work of Margaret Murray (1921), who considered the history of pagan cults in Western Europe. Trained initially as an Egyptologist, Murry gained her initial reputation from an attempt to document the theory that the Great Witch Hunts of the medieval period were an attempt to persecute the surviving remnants of an ancient cult that had survived the introduction of Christianity. Other historians had mooted this idea previously (for example Jules Michelet and Charles Godfrey Leland (Hutton 1996, 423)). However, Murray was the first to try to document the idea properly. Her ideas were accepted by some and rejected by others, but Murray became increasingly influential in the Folklore Society (for example Charlotte Burne (1917, 453)). In 1934 Murray noted that the *sheela na gig* was an ancient fertility figure which had been carved onto medieval churches in Western Europe. This led to Lady Raglan (Hutton 1991, 308–316) developing further ideas on Jack in the Green and the Green Man. It was only in the 1970s and 1980s that some of the ideas put forward by Murray were, to a certain degree, dismissed; for example by Simpson (1994, 89–96). A more recent suggestion, by Weir and Jerman (1986), was that medieval carvings, like the *sheela na gigs*, were intended to deter medieval people from sexual impropriety.

A number of works have looked at the ritual processes of the year, and there have been various discussions on how the quarter days recorded in early Irish texts related to other areas of the 'Celtic World' (for example Chadwick, Ross, Laing, Aldhouse-Green, Graham Webster and Jane Webster). The Irish quarter days were pastoral festivals and included the following: Imbolc on the 2nd February, which became Candlemas; Beltene on the 1st May, later May Day; Lughnasad on the 1st August, Christianised as Lammas; and finally Samhain on the 1st November, which was transformed into the Christian festival of the dead called All Hallows or All Souls. It has been suggested that the Irish quarter day festivals were practiced across Britain and Gaul. There is circumstantial evidence that the festival of Lugh was held on the 1st August at Lyon or *Lugdunum*, the fortress of *Lugos*. This festival was transformed into a festival of the Imperial Cult, under Augustus, in 12 BC (Green 1992, 136). The existence of this festival is the reason the eighth month is now known as August. Hutton (1996) rejected this theory of the universal practice of the quarter days and pointed to the Coligny calendar, found in southern Gaul (Rhys 1910), which did not feature the quarter days as part of a Gallic system of ritual life. It has also been pointed out that the ancient monuments of the Neolithic and Bronze Age period have no real alignments with the Irish quarter days, but focus mainly on the solstices, of Midsummer and Midwinter. Hutton sensibly pointed out that it would not seem appropriate to expect all of the tribal groups across Gaul, Britain and Ireland to have carried out the same seasonal rituals. He also made the valid point (Hutton 1996, 416) that the early and later medieval periods saw a gradual elaboration and development of religious, municipal, and courtly ritual:

> 'The distinction here, however, is that the 'Old Religion' which is being sought in this exercise is not a putative one concealed in the shades of pagan antiquity, but a well-documented one which was brought to an end only four to five centuries ago.'

45w from p. 416 from Stations of the Sun: A History of the Ritual Year in Britain
by Ronald Hutton (1996) free permission

Hutton concluded that the seasonal cycles of the ritual year were timeless and would keep throwing up the same types of seasonal association and desires within humanity.

Even though there are major problems with the earlier works, it has become apparent that, due to developments in archaeology and landscape studies (for example Derks (1998, 134–144), and Yeates (2006a; 2008b)) some of the old lines of enquiry should be revisited. Derks (1998, 134–144) determined that there was a connection between landscape features and the names of gods in what was Northern Gaul and that, following in the steps of Bayley (1919), these were homonyms. His work is based on recent advances in understanding of the data, the inscriptions, and philology.

The focus of this research is the *Dobunni* tribe, the people who occupied an area of Britain centred on Worcestershire and Gloucestershire in the Iron Age. The tribe were called later the *Hwicce*, the Old English word which developed into the modern English witch (Yeates 2008b, 136–146). We are now able to bring back to life certain of the ideas and myths which formed the basis of their religious world-view, by drawing on information from a number of areas normally regarded as distinct, including theology, archaeology, onomastics and anthropology. Onomastics is the study of place-names, while anthropology is the study of human culture. Some anthropologists may produce ethnographies, studies of specific ethnic groups or peoples. Ethnographies can deal with many different aspects of society including economy, day to day life, and religion.

In this book we will concentrate on studies of religious activities and ideas, especially tribal creation myths. Ethnographic studies of primal myths are common, particularly in studies of peoples in Africa, North and South America, Asia and Oceania, where certain peoples have, until recently existed as discrete ethnic groups whose primal myth was still recorded in some form (for example orally). In Europe in historic times ritual activities had become more homogenised over time, and the many discrete ethnic groups had become much more difficult to discern as nation states came to prominence in place of the old tribal systems. However, archaeologists have determined the extent of the old tribal territories and provided names for these lost peoples of Europe, and to what extent they have survived. Discussions from material culture remains depend upon the extent to which relevant material culture was used as part of religious activity and the survival of these remains. Temple sites and religious artefacts, such as altars and reliefs, can, however, provide good data for a sustained and meaningful debate, as will be seen below.

The Old Tribes of Western Europe

The old tribal groups of Europe were first described by the Greek and Roman Historians, who can also be termed in some cases Ethnographers. Surviving examples include the works of: Herodotus, Caesar, Strabo, Dio Cassius, and Diodorus Siculus, to mention but a few. Hesiod, in the *Catalogue* (fr.150 22ff.m–w), probably provided the first surviving record describing the people who lived north of the Alps, calling them simply *Hyperboreans* (Hornblower and Spawforth 1996, 736). In *c.* 460 Aeschylus informed us that the river Danube rose in the territory of the *Hyperboreans* (Weir Smyth 1922, *Prometheus Bound*). *Hyperborean* is obviously a very general term used to describe groups of people who lived in an area about which the authors knew very little **beyond the North Wind**. In the late sixth century BC Himilco, in reference to a trip up the Atlantic coastline of Europe, stated that part of that land was inhabited by Celts (Rackham 1938, ii.169–171). Herodotus (Godley 1926, II.33; Godley 1938, IV.49), in *c.* 490 BC, referred to Celts as living around the source of the Danube, or *Ister*, and also along the Atlantic Coast beyond the Pillars of Hercules. In a secondary source Hecatus (*c.* 540–475 BC) is said to have informed us that the Celts lived inland from the town of Massalia, thus placing this group of people in what is now central France and the Rhône valley.

The Celts were also mentioned by later writers like Aristotle, Plato, Heraclides of Pontus, Theopompus, Ephorus, Pytheas, and Xenophon, and in the anonymous text *Periplus*. In many of these texts there is evidence that the Celts were stereotyped for Greek literary consumption. Pytheas of Marseille (Jones 1923, 4.2), *c.* 330 BC, mentioned the *Pretannic Isles* (Britain) which lay to the north of the Celtic lands. It was only from the late third century BC that more detailed descriptions were given. Cato's *Origines*, written in *c.* 140 BC, was a book that dealt with the origins of the Italian cities. He located a number of 'Celtic' tribes, including, the *Volcae* in southern France, and the *Salassi, Lepontii,* and *Cenomani* in northern Italy. Polybius (Paton 1922; Paton 1922), in his historical studies of the rise of Rome from 220 BC to 168 BC, provided the first of the surviving accounts of the Celts. He sailed along the Atlantic coast, visited Spain, Gaul and the Alps, along with Sardis and Alexandria. He was the first to list the Celtiberian

tribes of central Spain. Apollodorus Athemaeus (*On the gods Chronicle*) in the mid second
century BC mentioned Roman alliances with the *Arverni* and the *Aedui*. The fact that
the work of Poseidonius of Apameia, of the late second and early first century BC,
is now lost is unfortunate as it was probably one of the earliest and most important
texts, concerning the tribes of the north-west provinces written; it has, however, been
reconstructed partially (Tierney 1960, 189–275) from passages in Caesar's and other
writers which drew on his work, but this can never be as good as the original. The
major plagiarist of Poseidonius, from which scholars have attempted to reconstruct it,
was Diodorus Siculus, in *c.* 60 BC.

    In the first century BC it was Sallust who was first known to have made a distinction
between the Germanic tribes and the Celts (Rolfe 1931, *Catiline, Jugurtha, Historiae*),
although there is some suggestion that he just derived this from Poseidonius. It is
possible that at some time in the future the work could be recovered from amongst the
documents which are being excavated from a town villa called the *Villa of the Papyri* in
Herculaneum (Neuerburg 1975). Here, many ancient Greek and Latin texts apparently lost
in antiquity survive as charred manuscripts awaiting excavation and then decipherment
as the scientific techniques designed to recover this information have improved. Caesar
(Edwards 1963, i.1), *c.* 50 BC, continued with the Germanic/Celtic distinction, but also
made another between the Celts and the *Belgae*. He also wrote about the tribal groupings
of Gaul and Germany in more detail than had been done previously. The first distinct
British tribal group to be mentioned was the *Trinovantes*, while it is assumed that
Cassivellaunus was king of the *Catuvellauni* who were mentioned slightly later. Cicero
(Gardner 1958, 563, 624), at about the same time, mentioned certain tribal groups in Gaul,
for example the *Helvii* and *Helvettii* of Transalpine Gaul. Much of this was in the context
of Caesar's conquest of that territory. Livy (Foster 1924, 116–119) wrote his History in
the first century BC, giving some indication of the existence of some of the *Gallic* tribal
groups in the fourth and fifth century BC, especially the *Bituriges Cubi*, who, it seems,
were at the centre of a tribal federation. The tribes listed as forming part of this included:
Bituriges, Arverni, Senones, Haedui, Ambarri, Carnutes, and *Aulerci*. This historical data is
now supported archaeologically with evidence of a large town, dating from that period,
under the later city of Bourges (Collis 2003, 169–170; Ralston 2006, 166). Nepos, in the
late first century BC attempted to write a history of certain *Gallic* tribes. Dio Cassius
(Cary 1924, 417), in the early third century AD, also wrote a history in which certain
Gallic and British tribes were mentioned. It was here that the first known reference to the
tribal group called the *Dobunni* was mentioned (here called *Bodunni*) apparently under
the supremacy of the *Catuvellauni*. In the second century AD, Ptolemy (Ptolemaeus 1966)
produced his geography identifying a number of towns and relating them to specific
tribal groups. There are other sources besides these but to summarise we can say that
the major ethnographic sources were the works of Posidonius, Polybius, and Caesar.
These historians were not, however, impartial recorders of the events that occurred in
Europe in the proto-historic and early historic periods, but were playing to a Roman
audience and, so, wrote accordingly. For the vast majority of the tribal groups in Europe
a religious discourse, as part of an ethnography, was never recorded. For others they are
extremely fragmentary and written from an external, and non-objective, viewpoint.

    In both Britain and Gaul the approximate extent of some tribal territories is known from studies of Iron-Age coinage distribution, research on which has been conducted on both sides of the English Channel. In Britain, a pioneer was Derek Allen (1944, 1–46) who found that, in south-east Britain, coinage distribution defined discrete topographical areas, which he associated with named tribal groups. Some of the Iron-Age coinage in Gaul and Britain contains the name of the tribal group, for example that of the *Catuvellauni*, while some does not. Sometimes tribal names are found on other types of archaeological material. The name of the *Helvettii* has been found scratched on a piece of pottery from the north-west Alpine area of Italy, at Mantua, dated *c.* 300 BC; this lies roughly in the land of their later known territory (Collis 2003, 114). Further references to groups of indigenous peoples from throughout the period of the Roman Empire have been found in inscriptions; for instance two Yorkshire tombstones, one being the memorial of a *Cornovian* woman found at Ilkley (RIB(I) 1995, no.639), the other to a *Dobunnic* Woman found at Templeborough (RIB(I) 1995, no.621). However, there is no systematic epigraphic record, and the distribution patterns cannot be used in the same way that coinage distribution can be. It is now apparent that the ethnic political landscape of the tribal groups of Gaul had become more or less formalised by the fifth century BC (Collis 2003, 169). The *Bituriges Cubi* of Central Gaul, for example, are known, from historical texts, to have existed as a powerful political entity some 200 years before coinage production started in the second century BC. The situation in Britain is less clear, however, and views that the tribal groups of Britain had only organised a formalised structure prior to the Roman invasion is probably not correct. The *Catuvellauni* are known to have lived in the Chiltern and Fen areas prior to the invasion and it is apparent that certain cults relating to the cohesion of the *Dobunni* tribe go back before this date (Yeates 2006a; 2007, 55–69; 2008b, 137–146). In the case of the *Silures* the distribution of late Bronze-Age metalwork is considered to be the first indication that this tribal area started to acquire a more formal structure (Gwilt 2004, 111–139) as this covers the area of Glamorgan and Gwent which was later associated with the tribe. Archaeologists often have to be innovative in order to interpret underlying social structures and settlement patterns from fragmentary surviving material remains, and to comprehend how and when the tribal systems of Western Europe coalesced into larger, more formalised, groups.

The tribal names recorded in Spain, in Gaul and in Britain, are a roll-call giving us an insight into our past. From Celt-iberian historic sources refer to the *Saefes*, the *Derybraces*, the *Ascones*, the *Cerretes*, the *Ilergetes*, and the *Indicetes,* to name but a few (see Figure 1). In Gaul there were the *Helvetii*, the *Allobroges*, the *Sequani*, and the *Aedui*, who were initially an ally to Rome but who later rallied the Gauls against Rome. Often named tribes include the *Arverni*, with their famous leader *Vercingetorix*, the *Bituriges Cubi*, the *Carnutes* who reputedly lived at the heart of Gaul, and the *Veneti* who had their fleet decimated by Caesar (Edwards 1963, III.16). Amongst the *Belgae* were the *Mediomatrici*, the *Remi*, the *Treveri*, and the *Eburones*, and in modern day Germany there were the *Sugambri*, and the *Ubii* (see Figure 2).

In Ireland the tribes recorded in *c.* AD 90 (see Figure 3) included the *Darni*, the *Pictes*, the *Monaigh* (who lived in what is now Ulster), the *Dumnonii* in Connaught, the *Gangani* and *Iverni* (who lived in Munster), and the *Cauci*, the *Brigantes* and the *Menapii* (who hailed from Leinster).

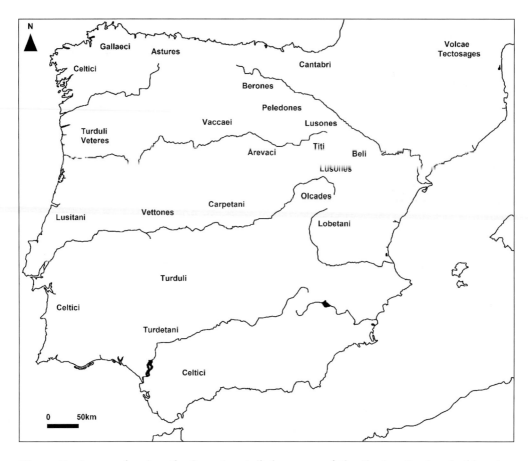

Figure 1: A map showing the Iron-Age tribal groups of the Iberian Peninsula (drawing S. Yeates)

In Britain many tribes are known through ethnographic study, as well as ancient historical accounts and Roman period inscriptions. In Scotland the *Caledones* lived. This term described a number of tribal groups: the *Caereni*, the *Carnonacae*, the *Decantae*, the *Creones*, the *Vacomagi* and the *Taezali*, all of the Uplands, and the *Damnonii*, the *Votadini*, the *Selgovae*, and the *Novantae* of the Lowlands (see Figure 4). In the alleged *Belgic* areas of southern Britain were the *Cantiaci*, the *Catuvellauni*, the *Trinovantes* (who were conquered by the *Catuvellauni*), the *Atrebates*, the *Regni* and the *Belgae* (who are considered to have originated as part of the *Atrebates* of Berkshire). The *Durotriges* are also considered to have had a *Belgic* association by some. In what is now Eastern England lived the *Iceni*, who occupied East Anglia; and the *Corieltauvi* of the East Midlands. The *Parisi* occupied the East Riding of Yorkshire, and the *Brigantes* Western Yorkshire, while the *Carvetii* resided in Cumberland. In Wales and the Marches were the *Ordovices*, the *Cornovii*, the *Demetae*, the *Decangli*, and the *Silures*. In south-west England lived the *Dumnonii* (see Figure 5). The *Dobunni* lived in the lower Severn Valley and the adjacent

Figure 2: A map showing the Iron-Age tribal groups of Gaul, based on coinage distribution, and the later Episcopal sees, derived from the civitas territories (drawing S. Yeates)

hills. It is important to determine what the names of these peoples mean, as these were the names which these ethnic groups used for themselves, or others used to describe them and to define the territories that they occupied. Each and every one of these tribes undoubtedly had its own creation myth. These were probably based on local factors derived from the local landscape as well as a broader underlying framework.

In Gaul the network of cathedrals and *vicus* churches (a *vicus* was a political division of a *civitas* or tribal area), as written down in the sixth century AD, also gives us an indication of the extent of Iron-Age tribal territories. *Civitates* were established by the

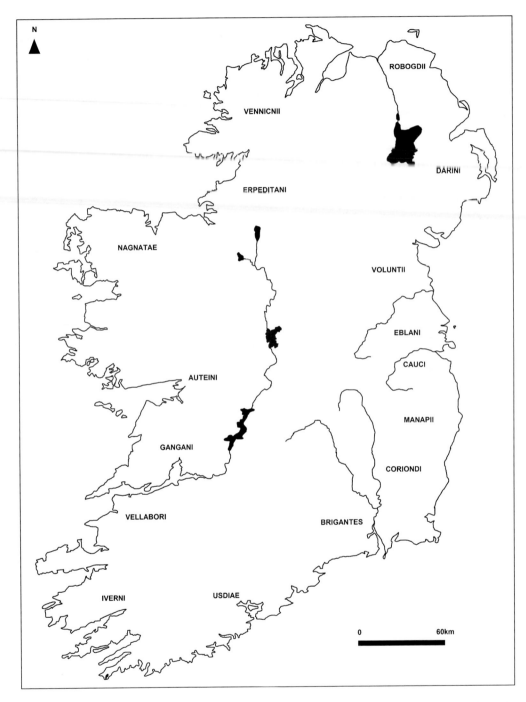

Figure 3: A map showing the Iron-Age tribal groups of Hibernia as mentioned by Ptolemy in the second century AD (drawing S. Yeates)

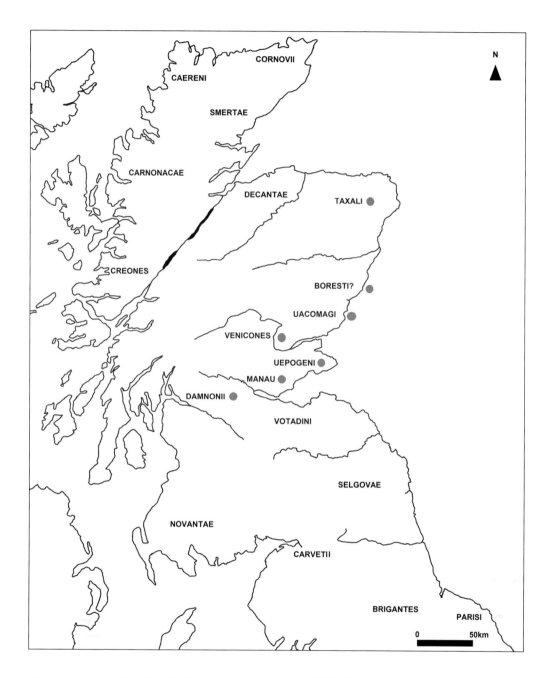

Figure 4: A map showing the Iron-Age tribal groups of Northern Britain, based predominantly on the accounts of Tacitus. Those tribal names marked by a grey circle are considered to have been Caledonian tribes (drawing S. Yeates)

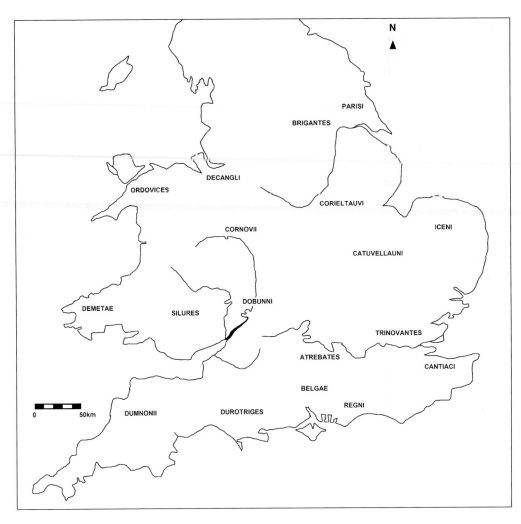

Figure 5: A map of the Iron-Age tribal groups of Southern Britain, based on Iron-Age coin distribution and the known locations of certain civitas towns (drawing S. Yeates)

Romans for these tribal groups, whose organisational structure survived the Roman invasion. Some named groups, such as the *Eburones*, did not survive as they were harshly treated by the Romans and their land given to other German tribes. In the Christian era Roman archbishoprics were generally coterminous with the late Roman provinces of Gaul. Below this each *civitas*, and so each tribal group, had its bishopric (Giot, Guigon *et al*. 2003, 107–108). Due to the conservative nature of the early Church, and the means by which it accrued and retained power, the imprint of political Roman Gaul survived well into the historic period. Some changes to diocesan boundaries occurred between the Roman period and the French Revolution, including the amalgamation of some dioceses, mainly due to population movements. Some alterations also occurred in the medieval period, especially in 1317–18, when a number of new dioceses were carved out by the Catholic hierarchy, based at Avignon. Further changes occurred between the sixteenth and eighteenth centuries, mainly in the north of France following the Spanish occupation. These changes are, however, well documented and it is easy, with one or two local exceptions, to recreate the original diocesan organisation. In Britain, however, it is believed that the Roman archbishoprics did not survive, and it is less clear how the tribal system was preserved in the Roman diocesan organisation and, if it was, how long it was used by the 'Celtic' Church; that is the remnants of the Church left behind following the end of Roman rule. There are indications, especially in the west, but also in the east of Britain, that some of the prehistoric tribal areas also became *civitas* territories during the Roman period and then emerged as early medieval kingdoms (Dark 1994). The traditions may have differed from those in Gaul, but the underlying argument, that the cohesion of the basic folk-groups predisposed this structure, is still valid. There is, however, much debate concerning the extent to which Christianity survived in Britain at the end of the Roman period and what percentage of the population was Christian. On the one hand, Frend (1955, 1–18; 1992, 121–131) and Watts (1991; 1998), have claimed that Christian presence was not strong and that the Roman authorities did not actively pursue reform of the religious systems; on the other hand, Thomas (1981), Henig (2002; 2008, 189–204) and Petts (2003) have claimed that there probably was a survival of Christianity and Christian structures. Aspects of Christian development and survival have been touched on in other works (Yeates 2006a; 2008b), and will also be considered in certain aspects in this work, such as *interpretatio* in Chapter 3. It is possible that in some areas the imprint of *vicus* church territorial organisation may have survived (Yeates 2006a, i.57–66). Certain political units or kingdoms took their names from older groups, for example, the *Cantiaci* in Kent, the *Dumnonii* in Devon, and the *Demetae* in Dyfed. Even in these territories it is possible that the sub-Roman church may have had a diocesan structure which mirrored the earlier *civitas* territories, especially for Saint David's and the *Demetae civitas*, and the See of Glamorgan (later Llandaff) and the *Silures civitas*.

The Dobunni and the Hwicce

The change from pre-Roman Iron-Age tribal group to sub-Roman kingdom has only been illustrated satisfactorily for the *Dobunni* (Yeates 2006a; 2008b), who emerged as a much reduced tribal unit called the *Hwicce*. When this tribal group originated is difficult to determine, and may never be known satisfactorily. To gain even a vague understanding it is essential to identify characteristic aspects of tribal structure, something that has always been seen as unstable due to shifting settlement patterns. In reality societies may not have altered as rapidly as certain archaeologists believe, and there is some evidence that tribal traditions become ingrained and survived over long periods.

The Iron Age and Roman clues to the nature of the *Dobunni* have already been discussed by Yeates (2005; 2006a; 2007, 55–69; 2008b) and Moore (2006). In the Iron-Age coins and currency bars were produced and both of these can be associated with

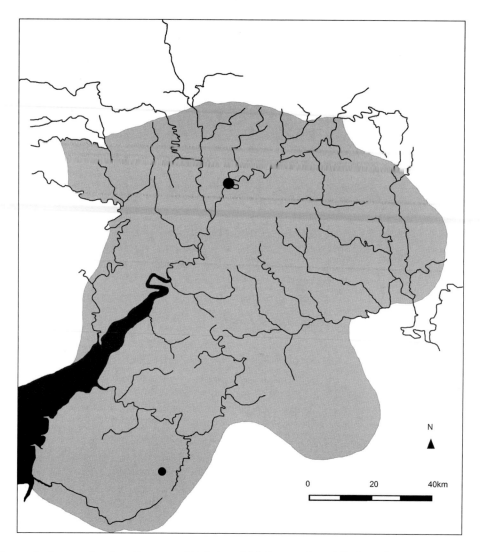

Figure 6: A map showing the area of Britain which has produced Dobunnic Iron-Age coinage and is, therefore, associated with the tribal territory of that group. The black dots represent major coins hoards (drawing S. Yeates)

Dobunni traditions and territory. The distribution of *Dobunnic* coinage is seen as a good indicator of the extent of their territory at the end of the Iron Age (van Arsdell and de Jersey 1994), stretching as it did from Hereford to the Cherwell, in Oxfordshire, and from the central Arden to the Brue (see Figure 6). The use of currency bars in later Iron-Age societies in Britain has been known about for some time, and it is evident that the distribution of spit shaped currency bars, produced from iron supplies in the Forest of Dean and Kingswood areas, covered predominantly a territory associated with the *Dobunni* (see Figure 7). The debate on what exactly these currency bars were and what

Figure 7: A map showing the distribution of Iron-Age currency bars in southern Britain. The spit shaped bars, produced from Forest of Dean and Kingswood iron ore, can be seen to have a distribution confined primarily to the territory associated with the Dobunni tribe (drawing S. Yeates)

they were used for has developed over a period of 2000 years. Caesar (Edwards 1963, V.12.4) claimed that iron ingots, of a fixed weight, were used as a form of currency.

The Roman sculptural reliefs of the probable *Dobunnic* tribal god and goddess, whose cult object was a **sacred vessel**, along with inscriptions referring to them and the tribe, are also distributed within the area covered by *Dobunnic* Iron-Age coinage (Yeates 2006a; 2007, 55–69) (see Figure 8). It is apparent that the presence of the **sacred vessel** led to the Old English tribal name of this folk-group, the *Hwicce* (Yeates 2008b, 1–8, 137–146). By looking at the use of this name, and the *Dobunni* references, it is possible

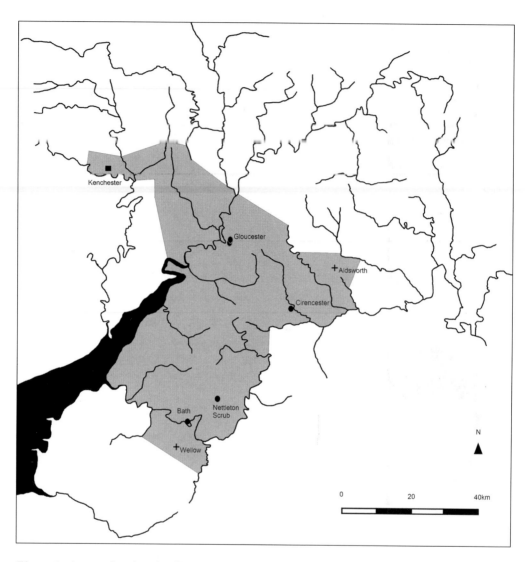

Figure 8: A map showing the distribution of the reliefs showing the Mater and Mercury (black circles), which can be interpreted as the mother and father of the Dobunni. The reliefs from Wellow and Aldsworth (shown as crosses) have also been included because they also show these deities. The Wellow relief shows them either side of another female deity; while the Aldsworth relief shows a divine couple in which the mother may be shown as Minerva (a protectress). The Kenchester (black square) inscription has also been inserted, with the light grey shading indicating territory which was almost certainly part of the Dobunnic territory (drawing S. Yeates)

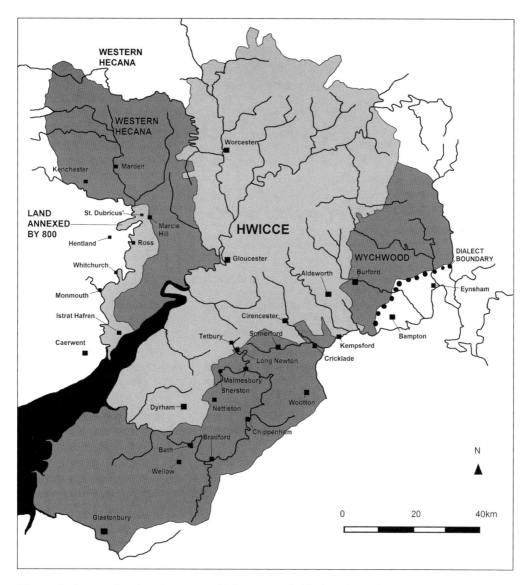

Figure 9: A map showing the areas which were probably lost from the civitas of the Dobunni/ Kingdom of the Hwicce between AD 410 and c. 800 AD, with all the relevant locations marked. The area of the See of Worcester, which is equated to the eleventh century kingdom of the Hwicce, is marked in grey (drawing S. Yeates)

to determine that the *Dobunni* tribal area went through a period of contraction in the post-Roman period; a number of dates and processes can be used to demonstrate this (see Figure 9). Previous studies have been controversial due to the strongly supported theories concerning Anglo-Saxon migration in the fifth and sixth centuries AD. Two recent studies have, however, found these historical academic traditions wanting. The first of these is a genetic study (Oppenheimer 2006) which suggested that Anglo-Saxon migrants in this period only account for 5.5% of the DNA of the surviving British population. The second is a cultural study of the *Dobunni* and *Hwicce* which explained many long-term aspects of their culture (Yeates 2006a; 2008b). The following paragraphs contain a series of statements which refer to the territory of the *Hwicce*; it must be noted, however, that from *c.* AD 630 the *Hwicce* became a sub-kingdom of Mercia and some of the statements concerning boundary locations must be understood in the context of Mercian territory and not just as *Hwiccian* territory.

An inscription on a milestone erected by the **R(es) P(ublica) C(ivitatis) D(obunnorum)**, dating to the reign of Emperor Numerian AD 283–4 (RIB(I) 1995, no.2250) from Kenchester, Hereford, indicates that the central Herefordshire plains originated as part of the *Dobunnic* territory. White (2007, 100) has suggested that a second *civitas* territory was carved out of the larger territory sometime in the Romano-British period. This territory, if it did exist, was later called the *Magonsæte* but may originally have been called the *Western Hecana* (Sims-Williams 1990, 40–42). This group must have been west of some other group and the only territory it is west of is that of the *Hwicce*. John of Worcester in, *Chronicon ex Chronicis*, claimed that Worcester was the ancient metropolis of the *Hwicce* and *Magonsæte* (Pretty 1989, 171–183); implying that there was some connection or association between the two groups. That the identities of these peoples were entwined in a common past would explain why, in a charter of 1012 x 1056, Bishop Athelstan of Hereford had to demarcate the two territories (Finberg 1972, 225–227).

It is possible to suggest where the boundary between the *Dobunni* and the *Silures* lay. The *Silures* were a neighbouring Iron-Age tribe whose territory was centred on Gwent and Glamorgan. There are a number of pieces of evidence that allow us to associate certain locations with the early medieval territory of the *Glywysinga*, a territory which developed from the Roman *civitas* of the *Silures*. The names Much Marcle and Marcle Hill contain the Old English word *mære*, **a boundary** or **border**, which refers to an ancient boundary (Coplestone-Crow 1989, 141) that must have run between the *Dobunni* (later *Hwicce*) and the *Silures* (later *Glywysinga*). Charters from the Book of Llandaff refer to grants of land, and the establishment of churches, in and around the area of the Lower Wye; thus indicating that parts of this territory were controlled by the *Silures-Glywysinga*. These charters, by some considered problematic, include one, for *Istrat Hafren* (associated with the Tidenham area), of *c.* AD 700 thus suggesting that the church in this territory was under the control of the *Glywysinga* and its kings (Finberg 1972, no.7; Davies 1979, no.174b (56)). The church in the Tidenham area was still claimed as being under the control of Glamorgan in AD 878 (Finberg 1972, no.81; Davies 1979, no.229b (121)). It is possible, through research, to show that the probable *parochiae* of major Welsh church foundations often occupied land on either side of the Wye, thus indicating that the fixing of the Wye as a boundary river below Hereford was probably a late development. These major Welsh churches were known collectively as clas churches, a Welsh term which can be equated with the English Minster. They were probably established at: Monmouth, Whitchurch, Ross, and Hentland; all in the vicinity of the Wye. The *parochia* of Monmouth contained land in the lower valley of the Monnow as well as land adjacent to it in the Forest of Dean. The *parochia* of Whitchurch was located in the land around the Lower Garron and also extended into the north facing valleys of the Forest of Dean. The *parochia* of Ross lay predominantly on land associated with the topographical area called the Forest of Dean in the valleys of the Rudhall and Coughton Brooks, but also included land on the opposite side of the Wye. The *parochia* of Hentland was predominantly on the west side of the river Wye, but also included some land on the east side. Three of these places had associations with Llandaff Charters (Davies 1979, no.145, 175, 186b), namely Monmouth, Whitchurch, and Hentland, and almost certainly fell under the influence of the See of Glamorgan. The fifth and sixth centuries AD in Wales is recognised as an age of saints, many of whom were associated with the foundation of churches. One of these legendary saints was *Dubricus* and, although there are arguments over the authenticity of some of the claims, dedications to this saint in Herefordshire are often seen as a means of identifying areas which were under the influence of the See of Glamorgan. The *parochia* of Woolhope-cum-Fownhope has a chapel in its parish dedicated to Saint *Dubricus* (Caley and Hunter 1817, 27–28) and so would, presumably, have been under the influence of Glamorgan, which later became the See of Llandaff. We also have a number of other clues to say where the boundary between these two tribes lay. The land which lay immediately to the east of the Wye must have been annexed to Mercia, or to a province of Mercia, by the reign of Offa. The valleys whose rivers flowed from the Forest of Dean to the east were probably *Dobunnic* territory.

In the east and south-east the *Dobunni-Hwicce* were bordered by the *Catuvellauni* and the *Atrebates* and their successor kingdoms. In Oxfordshire there are further indications that territory was lost by the *Hwicce* to these successor kingdoms. In AD 840 the Bishop of the *Hwicce*, at Worcester, was granted land in Wychwood (Gelling 1979, no. 264), a name derived from the tribal name *Hwicce* (Gelling 1954, ii.386); this suggests that this area was not then under *Hwiccian* ownership, and that the charter granting rights in the Wychwood may have been an attempt to appease the annexation of the territory. The territory was probably part of a Middle Anglian kingdom, perhaps part of South Mercia. The place-names of Oxfordshire shows an ancient linguistic division which runs along the south edge of the Cotswolds; the areas around Bampton and Eynsham had a Saxon dialect, while those around Burford and Shipton-under-Wychwood had a Mercian one (Gelling 1953, i.xix). This is perhaps roughly the area where we would expect to see the divide between the *Dobunni-Hwicce* and the *Gewisse*, who were later known as the West Saxons (and whose early capital was at Dorchester-on-Thames).

For Wiltshire there is also evidence to support alterations in the political boundaries between the *Dobunni-Hwicce*, and the *Atrebates* and the *Durotriges* and their successor kingdoms. The date at which West Saxon influence was first felt in the Severn valley has been placed at AD 577 when forces from the towns of Bath, Gloucester and Cirencester were claimed to have been defeated in a battle at Dyrham in what is now southern Gloucestershire. The date, and even the veracity, of the battle of Dyrham have been increasingly questioned. The event seems to have occurred too far to the west, at a date when other West Saxon activity was confined to the area around the Upper Thames valley. Bassett (2000, 107–118) noticed that the information given contradicts that given by Bede, who had a more neutral political position. Sims-Williams (1983, 33) considered the entry concerning Dyrham to have been forged, in an attempt to enhance West Saxon claims to territory in Wiltshire. The West Saxons were involved in another battle, at Bradford-on-Avon, in AD 652 (Morris 1973, 230) and was confusingly listed as being fought against the Mercians or Welsh. This may indicate that much of north-west Wiltshire was still under Mercian and possibly *Hwiccian* control at this time, and it is perhaps the case that if the battle of Dyrham did occur it was probably fifty years or so after the date given in the Anglo-Saxon Chronicle. The *Hwicce* in AD 603 was considered by Bede to have been part of the British Church (Colgrave and Mynors 1969, II.2), a factor which makes the Bradford account understandable. Some, however, consider the use of the term *Hwicce* at this date by Bede to be problematic. The *Hwiccians* were British (Welsh) but under Mercian over-lordship. There exists a series of charters from *c.* AD 675–685, drawn up by the Mercian lords, which suggest that Mercia's sub-kingdom of the *Hwicce* had control in the area of north-west Wiltshire. These charters refer to Wotton, Long Newton, Tetbury, and Somerford Keynes, in Gloucestershire and Wiltshire (Finberg 1964, no.182, 183, 184). Only one grant, of AD 675 concerning Malmesbury, was drawn up by a West Saxon king and this stands at odds with the others (Finberg 1964, no.181). This charter is, however, probably a forgery. The authentic charters of *c.* AD 680 for Newton, and Somerford Keynes led Jackson (1864, 19) to the conclusion that, at an early date, the land between Malmesbury, Cricklade, and Cirencester was in the kingdom of Mercia (hence the *Hwicce*) and not Wessex, and that the River Avon was possibly the boundary between the two. There seems to have been a view amongst antiquarians, for example Brompton, that Cirencester and Chippenham were cities of the 'Wiccians' (Colt Hoare 1819, 103), and that the Cotswold part of Wiltshire was traditionally seen as *Hwiccian*. This view became unfashionable in the Victorian period and after. It seems likely that land in north Wiltshire was lost to the *Hwicce* between 700 and 800 AD, and there is also an assumption that the battle between the West Saxons and *Hwicce*, which occurred after the *Hwiccians* crossed the Thames at Kempsford in AD 800 (Bately 1986, 40), was associated with the loss of territory. The area around Sherston remained *Hwiccian* territory until AD 1016 when a battle occurred there (Darlington and McGurk 1995, *Worcester, Chron.* 486–487). One must assume that this had been transferred by AD 1086 as, in the *Domesday Book*, the manor was recorded as being part of Wiltshire (Thorn and Thorn 1979, 1.23g, 27.24). The boundary between Wiltshire and Gloucestershire, which later marked the boundary between the kingdoms of Mercia (*Hwicce*) and Wessex can, from the historical texts, be seen to have moved northwards and westwards as Wessex or the West Saxon kingdom became more powerful. Onomastic studies suggest that Kemble was an old name and that it is probably related to the Welsh *cyfyl*, the **border** (Watts 2004, 339); hence referring to the border between the *Dobunni* and the *Atrebates*; and later between the *Hwicce* and the *Gewisse*. This interpretation becomes problematic, however, when one considers the distribution of *Dobunnic* and *Atrebatic* coins, and the Anglo-Saxon charter evidence. As the name of a topographical forest located in the upper Thames Valley Kemble is more likely to have been a name related to a divinity (Yeates 2008b, 18–19).

In the South of the territory *Dobunnic* issues dominate coin distribution in the Mendips and it has been suggested that the River Brue originally marked the southern boundary of the tribe (Cunliffe 1991, 170), where they bordered the *Durotriges*. That parts of north Somerset lay in the *Dobunni* territory is evident from the reliefs of the mother goddess, and her consort Mercury, at Bath and Wellow (Yeates 2008b, 137–146). It is possible that Glastonbury, with its legendary liminal status, reflects an ancient boundary. This land had presumably been lost to the *Dobunni* by *c.* AD 600, according to the *Chartularum Saxonicum*, when land at Glastonbury was granted by the king of the *Dumnonii* (Hill 1914, 15; Carley 1988, 2). Bath may have remained in *Hwiccian* territory until *c.* AD 970 (Taylor 1900, 129–161), as supported by charters which show that the minster at Bath was founded by the *Hwiccian* king Osric in AD 675 x 676 (Finberg 1964, no.355). Mercian (*Hwiccian*) control within North Somerset is supported by a charter of AD 781, when the bishop of Worcester relinquished control of the minster at Bath to King Offa (Finberg 1972, no.228). This agreement included land to the south of the Avon. The date at which *Hwiccian* territory in the Mendips was transferred to the West Saxon kings was probably in the reign of Alfred the Great, *c.* AD 890. It was in his reign, or immediately after, that we find Bath being turned into a burh town in the defense of the realm.

From the surviving data it is apparent that the *Hwicce*, as a successor kingdom to the *Dobunni civitas*, had gone through a process of contraction (see Figure 9). In the west the new entity, the *Magonsæte*, was carved out of the territory, probably also with parts of the *Cornovian* territory. In the east Wychwood proclaims its past territorial association, and linguistic differences are noted in place-names, which give an idea of where the territorial boundary ran. In Wiltshire indications are that a large part of the territory was annexed from the *Hwicce*, and one can make similar claims for Northern Somerset.

Limited Archaeological Views of Past Religion

Attempts by archaeologists to recreate religious activity have been limited. Christopher Hawkes (1954, 155–168), in *A View from the Old World,* suggested that any attempt to recreate ancient religion was impossible and, as a result, developed his ladder of inference. Since then discussion on ancient religious activity has varied from period to period and country to country. There are different approaches with respect to the understanding of religion in the pre-historic and historic periods. One relies on the interpretation of material culture, helped by anthropological theory; the other is restricted to the textual sources. Archaeologists do, to some extent write about ritual activity of past communities; for example, through the structured use of space in the landscape and in buildings, or the reasons for the occurrence of bones on an archaeological site. Hawkes's initial pessimism may have been ill-founded and there are some arguments now being advanced which may provide a context in which we can better understand ritualised activity.

One of the more interesting attempts to explain the ritual and beliefs of a past British society was *Ancestral Geographies of the Neolithic: Landscape, Monuments and Memory* by Mark Edmonds (1999), which contains a consideration of the tombs and the causewayed camps that were the major archaeological features of the early Neolithic. Each of these structures would have had a mass of meaning and been associated with a multitude of stories, relating the history of the peoples who built them. The stories associated with these sites, however, are remembered no longer. Also considered to be important was the significance of kinship, ancestry, and the other forms of affiliation which would have been associated with these monuments; these notions are assumed through anthropology as it is impossible to excavate such affiliations unless recorded. The Neolithic monuments of Britain have been the subject of many hypotheses and much interpretation, most of which concerns a sacred world which continued to evolve until the middle of the Bronze Age. No structural framework has yet been developed to demonstrate how the societies of the Neolithic influenced the later tribal affiliations of the Bronze Age or Iron Age.

There seems to have been a fundamental change in the society of southern and central Britain during the Bronze Age (Darvill 1987, 108–132). The major debates in middle and late Bronze-Age archaeology concern the altering settlement patterns, metal working, and finally the deposition of metal into rivers. These all had an impact on the basis of political power and have led to the idea that changes were occurring due to exchange networks being created through political and marriage alliances linked to changes in those having power over land and agricultural production (Thomas 1989, 263–286). Major changes in burial practice started to take place in the middle Bronze Age and continued into the later Bronze Age. There were variations in how these practices manifested themselves in different parts of Britain, Ireland, and the Continent; thus regional studies are extremely important.

There is a tendency in Britain for the regional model of the Wessex Downlands to be imposed at a national level for both the later Bronze Age and the Iron Age; this is mainly because it has the best-preserved archaeology. In the southern chalklands of Britain there was the development of hill-forts, of major lowland settlements, and the division of the landscape for agricultural purposes (Bradley, Entwistle *et al.* 1994).

In the northern midlands the archaeology dominated by burials was also replaced in the middle and later Bronze Age. Here, there was a trend which saw the development of hill-top enclosures, which later developed into hill-forts (Mullin 2003, 72–78), for example Old Oswestry. There was also an increase in the numbers of large lowland settlements. Similar trends are evident for the south-west Midlands of the later *Dobunni* homelands, although here the best excavated and understood sites occur on the gravel terraces on the north side of the Thames, for example Shorncote Quarry (Brossler, Gocher *et al.* 2002, 37–87) and Eynsham (Pike 1992, 46–47; Blair 1994, 63; Barclay, Boyle *et al.* 2001, 105–162). It is recognised that there was also a development of hill-forts from smaller settlements along the Welsh Marches (Olding 2000, 51–55), but it is also apparent that the land division that occurred in the late Bronze Age chalklands did not happen here.

Further debates on ritual activity have included discussion of the use of space in domestic locations; for example, the universal theory put forward by Mike Parker-Pearson with respect to the use of Late Bronze-Age and Iron-Age round houses (1996, 117–132). Certain spaces are considered to have been designed for specific activities; such as, cooking and living on the south side of the round house, and sleeping on the north side of the structure. It has been claimed that all of the houses followed the same orientation, mostly towards the east. In reality this produces a false model of homogenous 'Celtic' house in a unified 'Celtic' world (Moore 2006, 82) that was never present in reality. Moore also showed that, of the 180 Iron-Age round-houses in the

Dobunnic territory for which the orientation could be worked out, only 110 faced the south-east, which does not conform to the ideas set out above. Though facing the south-east may have been usual there were other factors which one needs to consider, for example prevailing wind direction.

Other debates have considered the use of space in settlement patterns and of house designs within or around the edges of the *Dobunnic* territory. Clarke produced a theoretical model which looked at Glastonbury Lake village (1972, 801–869). This considered how space was used in the village and if houses were paired in any way. Much more extensive work was carried out on the design and layout of Iron-Age settlements by Hingley (1984, 72–88). He produced complex models which incorporated ideas of structured deposition. These discussions were roundly criticised by Moore (2006, 82–88, 102), who suggested that structured deposition did not, in itself, represent the cosmological beliefs of a folk-group and that it was not clear how social space and settlement could be equated to social organisation or cosmological ideology. In many settlements the survival rate has not been especially good and part of the evidence for the constant building on space may have been lost.

Through the course of the later Bronze Age there was, in much of western Europe, deposition of metal artefacts, such as swords, shields, and axes, into a variety of dry and wet places (Barber 2003, 43–53). Discussions of these deposits initially categorised the hoards as personal or merchant in origin, although the actual situation is now seen as being much more complex. In recent years there has been more interest in the deposition of weaponry into wet places, such as rivers, lakes, and marshes (Bradley 1990, especially 98–99). The work by Bradley focused on the south of Britain and highlighted certain rivers such as the Thames, the Witham, and the Nene. Bradley (1988, 258), for the first time, distinguished the deposition of single finds, being treated as a potential loss, and that of hoards, which were always treated as votive. He also determined that there was a high degree of variation. At Flag Fenn, in Cambridgeshire, a large wooden platform was constructed in the marshland of the Nene valley (Pryor 1991; Barber 2003, 68–69), from which objects were deposited into the water. The objects recovered from this site date from *c.* 1300 BC to *c.* 300 BC. In the northern Midlands the deposits of the middle Bronze Age are dominated by axes (75%), and many of these occur in dry locations. There is, however, still a significant number that occurred in the upper Severn and in the wetlands of Shropshire (Mullin 2003, 93–103). This activity continued in that area in the late Bronze Age; it has been claimed that wetland deposits such as these predominate in areas which did not have iron ore. In the area of the *Dobunni* two different types of place were being used, predominantly for the deposition of bronze objects, watersheds and rivers. Other water-related places which are known to have been venerated are: lakes, marshes and, probably, the sea. Ritual deposition has been found at all such locations. The deposition of Bronze Age axes, spears, and swords in rivers or streams is also known from Meare Heath, in the Somerset Levels. Other depositions are known from Herefordshire, at sites along the River Eign, and in Worcestershire and Gloucestershire, at locations along the Severn (Kempsey, Astley, Chaddesley Corbett, and Westbury-on-Trym), in the Isbourne (Sedgeberrow), and in a brook at Harvington (VCH(Wo1) 1901, 193). In the Cotswold, an axe has been recovered from a stream at Batsford (Terry 1953, 150). A votive hoard has been found in the

Bristol Avon at Melksham in Wiltshire, where the objects were deliberately mutilated (Fowler and Miles 1971, 20). It is difficult to categorise these deposits, but it is possible that there may have been two types of deposition. The first concerned those in watery places, the second the deposition of hoards on watersheds. That deposition stopped in the Bronze Age cannot be categorically demonstrated as Iron-Age objects have been recovered from the Thames at Stanton Harcourt (O.SMR 2370), Oxfordshire, and from near the confluences of the Evenlode and Thames (VCH(Ox1) 1939, 264), and the Churn and Thames (Cricklade).

Deposition into water continued into the Iron Age and Roman period. Two of the chief sites showing this phenomenon are in continental Europe, including the renowned La Tène site on lake Neuchâtel, Switzerland (Brunaux 1988, 42–43), and the sacred lake at Toulouse (Rankin 1987, 99). In the former, a whole range of middle to late Iron-Age material came to light one summer in the 1800s when, due to dry conditions, the level of the lake dropped. The majority of the metalwork is dated from *c.* 250–120 BC (Shipley, Vanderspoel *et al.* 2006, 494). Iron-Age votive deposits into watery contexts are known from Britain, Ireland and other parts of the continent; however, the finds are less well preserved.

One example of a deposition from the Roman period is the head of a bronze statue of Claudius or Nero recovered from the river Alde, Suffolk; probably deposited after *Boudica's* attack and ransacking of Colchester (Huskinson 1994, no.23). At a later date the head of an over life size bronze statue of Hadrian was deposited in the River Thames at London (Toynbee 1964, 6, 50–51). It appears that ritual deposition in water was still being carried out at that time, and a symbol of the new power structure was possibly being offered to appease the old spirits of the water. The deposition of objects into water on a scale far larger than had previously been seen may represent a change in peoples' cosmological paradigm but this, at present, is a point of conjecture. The worship of rivers seems to have been important in the Roman period (Yeates 2008b, 30–58), when many rivers and other water-based locations were deified. Other places that have been identified as places of ritual deposition include shafts and wells (Ross 1968, 255–285). Wells seems to have been an extremely important feature at Roman period river shrines (Yeates 2008b, 30–58).

There have been numerous debates on the deposition of burials from across Britain and the Continent; these can be catalogued chronologically and regionally. The changes in settlement and apparent belief systems which affected the Bronze Age, and the increasing emphasis on settlement patterns and ritual deposition into water also affected burial practices (Brück 1995, 245–277). In these traditions there seems to have been a new set of beliefs emerging which affected the way the dead were viewed; with the dead becoming strong symbols of liminality, continuity, identity, and renewal. Regional variation is a key factor in all of the main areas of study. For the northern Midlands there is growing evidence that the reuse of earlier monuments was significant in the middle and late Bronze Age (Mullin 2003, 19–23). In some cases there is evidence for the construction of smaller cairns and also the placing of bodies in watery contexts.

Certain theoreticians have claimed that the ancestor cult of the Iron Age never died out. For example, Woodward (1993, 1–7) suggested that the random distribution of human bones on Iron-Age sites was similar to the later cult of the Saints in the early medieval period. In this activity human bones were left on display for a variety of reasons – usually, because the dead person was a member of an elite, or a venerable or heroic fighter. The practice of displaying human bones probably meant that some sort of veneration was occurring; however, whether the veneration was of ancestors, or their symbolic replacements, is not readily discernible. For Gaul it is generally accepted that the cults of gods and local-spirits were replaced, in the Christian context, by those of Saints (Brown 1981), and that local Christianity conflated the two deliberately on the uptake of the new religion. As such, the veneration of saints' bones could well have been a continuation of earlier ancestor veneration rites.

Real Archaeological and Historical Indicators of Religion

Even such insights as these only reveal a vague idea of the beliefs of our prehistoric ancestors. Unless one is extremely careful it would be very easy to garner a few clues that seem to point in a particular direction but one which further thought and new evidence could quickly dismiss. This would be especially true when attempting to reach back to the primal myths. The aim of this work is to move away from the idea that the cosmology of a tribe can be ascertained through the analysis of the depositional process in a round house or a settlement. In the late Iron Age there were new emergent material cultures which mean that the religion and religious beliefs of the *Dobunni* can be discussed in a different way. The tribe occupies a unique position in the map of archaeological and historical traditions. First, it was one of a group of southern tribes which produced late Iron-Age coinage. Second, the tribe has one of the best groups of surviving sculptures from any tribal group in Britain. Finally, although the shires of this tribal area lie in England, in the Roman and sub-Roman period it formed part of a province called *Britannia Prima*, and it was this province which gives rise to the historical and textual traditions which we now associate with Wales.

Only for the Roman period do we find artefacts and messages which could explain aspects of creation myths. There are many examples of temple-complexes from Roman-period *Britannia*, *Gallia* and *Germania*; which used mainly Greco-Roman, Romano-Celtic, or simple cella designs. Some of these complexes had their origins in the Iron Age; those which did were invariably in rural sites in geographical locations of specific interest. Those temples constructed in towns or semi-urban centres were mostly new religious sites constructed to serve communities that had relocated in the landscape. Examples of Gaulish Iron-Age temple sites include: Ribemont-sur-Ancre, Gournay-sur-Aronde, Mirebaeu and Saint-Maur (Brunaux 1988, 11–24); those in Britain include the Hayling Island and Uley Shrines. These sites are associated with specific types of sculptured stone work, including altars and reliefs. These reliefs have been discussed in many works, including *Pagan Celtic Britain* (Ross 1967), *Symbol and Image in Celtic Religious Art* (Green 1989), *Religion in Roman Britain* (Henig 1984), and *Gods, Temples and Ritual Practices* (Derks 1998). These use as their source material various Roman sculpture (Espérandieu 1907; 1908; 1910; 1911; 1915; 1918; 1922; 1925; 1928; 1938; Cunliffe and Fulford 1982; Brewer 1986; Henig 1993a; 2004). From these syntheses a number of general religious and symbolic themes have been recognised, including: the severed head, the mother goddess, the divine couple, and ritual sacrifice, as well as many others. However, these are broad syntheses and the way in which they mix and match information from different tribal areas is problematic. By considering the local aspect, by looking at each tribal group separately, further revelations can be made and new ideas encountered. It is only through such contextualisation that it will be possible to infer anything concerning primal myths of any specific tribal groups of Western Europe.

Texts, hinting at aspects of the European primal myths, have survived, but these are often mixtures of different oral traditions compiled over long time periods with much subsequent reworking. Many gods were mentioned by Greco-Roman authors and quite a number are concealed in medieval Irish and Welsh texts. Some of the texts, such as those from Ireland, have received considerable analysis but those of Wales, primarily the Mabinogion, have received relatively less attention; it is evident that a number of important deities are concealed in the lines of the texts (Yeates 2006a; 2008b). Complementary to these sources are inscriptions recovered from throughout the Roman Empire. When all of this information is looked at together it is possible to determine the names of some four hundred native deities from the north-west provinces of the Roman Empire. If these then turn up in a textual source we may have a hint at some of their stories, but invariably many are missing.

The Migration period, when hordes of Angles, Saxons and Jutes allegedly arrived in Britain from the east, is often seen as a time of great discontinuity in English history; the same is not, however, true for Welsh history. This distinction was emphasised by the texts of Bede, which discussed the movement of people from what is now northern Germany and Denmark into the east of Britain (Colgrave and Mynors 1969, I.14–16, 20). Bede described the 'plundering foe' and the Angles, Saxons and Jutes as hoards of people crowding the shore. After this there was a response by the local British and a recovery, under the leadership of Ambrosius Aurilius. Later, the Saxons and the Picts joined forces to attack the British. These tales have been used to suggest that the British population was displaced westwards. The fact that there were cultural connections between the new arrivals and the pre-existing populations is more apparent. DNA analysis has drastically questioned such arguments. There are even problems concerning when certain German peoples moved to Britain; many probably did, as *foederati*, in the Roman period. The basic claims of Bede's texts (who drew on earlier claims of Gildas) were pushed during the Victorian period; skulls were measured and analysed in an attempt to support the basic premise. This was followed by the development of a linguistic framework (Jackson 1953). This suggested that many of the pre-Old English names in the 'invaded' landscape were lost at this time. The model for the introduction of Old English was based on the analysis of river-names. This linguistic framework has been challenged in *River-names, Celtic and Old English: their dual medieval and post-medieval personalities* (Yeates 2006b, 63–81), which showed that, during the Middle Ages, rivers often had an ancient 'Celtic' name in addition to their English name, and that both occurred alongside each other until the sixteenth century, when cartographers set about mapping the landscape and standardising the names of natural features, at which time many of the ancient names were lost. If this is true then Jackson's hypothesis was based on an inaccurate assumption of the date at which these names changed. The subject of language is an important factor when considering elements of pre-Christian religion in Britain and the framework suggested by Jackson and its problems will be returned to in Chapter 4. The invasion tradition is also being challenged through scientific analysis of Migration Period burial material, and modern DNA population studies (Oppenheimer 2006), to mention but a few areas of present controversy. These problems led to the suggestion that continuity of the Iron-Age and Roman tribal groups into the sub-Roman period was much more likely than previously thought. Dark (1994) suggested that the pre-Roman territories developed into the *civitas* territories of the Roman province, which corresponded roughly to the territories which emerged in the early medieval period, extrapolating from the development of the Kentish kingdom, the county of Devon, and the kingdom of Dyfed, among others, where the place-name continued, albeit in a philologically developed form. But does this mean that the civil power structures followed suit? The kingdom of Kent took its name from the *Cantiaci*, as did the *civitas* capitol of the Roman province, Canterbury, **the fortification of the Cantiaci or Cantwara** (Watts 2004, 114). The county of Devon derived its name from the *Dumnonii* (Watts 2004, 186), and the kingdom of Dyfed derived its name from the tribal name *Demetae* (Owen and Morgan 2007, 133). There are, therefore, grounds to consider that there was a continuity of peoples and power structures in each of these areas and that the native British population absorbed groups of incoming settlers. However, only in the case of the *Dobunni* and the *Hwicce* has any real association yet been shown between the Iron-Age group and the early medieval group (Yeates 2006a; 2008b). The continuity which bridged the Migration Period becomes clearer once an understanding of each group's religious belief systems is acquired. In the case of the *Dobunni* and *Hwicce*, place-name changes seem to continue to reference the religious imagery and stories which existed previously and described a sacred landscape. These studies have shown, for the first time, that there was a process of Germanic *Interpretatio* (that is, the association of a deity of Germanic origin with one of British origin) at work. This means also that, it is possible to start thinking about what tribal creation myths there might have been, what religious structures existed, and what the pantheon of each tribe could have been. The idea of a pantheon will be discussed in Chapter 2 and that of *interpretatio* is developed in Chapter 3. The earlier chapters grapple with wider issues in the north-west provinces of the Roman Empire while the later chapters focus on what can be interpreted or hypothesised for the *Dobunni* specifically.

There are means through which we can identify the tribal groups of later prehistory in Britain and in Gaul. For instance, we can use coinage distribution and the development of ecclesiastical structures. Names were given to these tribal groups by ancient ethnographers, geographers, travellers and military, and sometimes these are supported by inscriptions. To go from this evidence to an understanding of a group's religious concepts is, however, difficult and largely depends on the material available today, and the context of that material. Complications due to the effects of migration, especially in the post-Roman world, have probably been over-played, but they must still be borne in mind.

Conclusion

Victorian anthropologists set up the notion that we could eventually work out what made pre-Christian religion in Britain operate. There were many caveats and side spurs to this debate, some of which ran down blind alleys. We can now start to define some of these traditions with respect to at least one tribal group, the *Dobunni-Hwicce*, and even gain an indication of how their territory receded. With respect to overcoming Hawkes's ladder of inference (1954, 155–168), archaeologists still have a problem in bridging the gap between evidence and theory in relating use of space to ancient cosmological and common views. It is only from the Roman period, and perhaps the later Iron Age that we can start to discuss certain specific aspects of the mythological traditions in Britain. The key to explaining much of what we can determine on these issues is recorded in the textual traditions of *Britannia Prima*, the forerunner of parts of early medieval Wales.

Chapter 2

Pantheons

The pantheon of gods is a common theme; we know it best from the Greek and Roman worlds. How these developed is not always clear but it is probable that they derived from prehistoric beliefs, and are part of a long accumulation of knowledge. In these developing beliefs it is possible to recognise the evolution of the gods individually and the wider stories and relationships which developed around them. The traditions probably developed at a later date in northern Europe; although we do not know this for sure it fits into the view that sees southern Europe as the innovator, if only because its art, architecture, and literature survived better than that in northern Europe. Thus, southern Europeans are seen as having exported their material culture and presumably their beliefs.

In some religious belief systems there has been a concerted effort to ensure that written records of the tenets were kept. The best known examples are the Jewish religion, (from which Christianity and Islam developed) and Hindu traditions. Other religions were also recorded, for example those of the Greek and Roman worlds, in poems, inscriptions, and legislative tracts. This also happened for the Scandinavian Eddas and, on the fringes of the Celtic world, sagas and tales containing a number of mythological components. Of course, it is only through the advent of writing that these practices began.

Generally, the religious beliefs of north-west Europe were not written down, or if they were then the records have not survived. If we consider what Caesar (Edwards 1963, VI.14) said about literacy and religion we are left with the notion that no religious creed was ever recorded in tangible form.

> *"Reports say that in the schools of the druids they learn by heart a great number of verses, and therefore some persons remain twenty years under training. And they do not think it proper to commit these utterances to writing, although in almost all other matters, and in their public and private accounts, they make use of Greek letters."*
>
> Reprinted by permission of the publishers and Trustees of the Loeb Classical Library from *I. Caesar: The Gallic War*, Loeb Classical Library Vol. 72, translated by H. J. Edwards, Cambridge, Mass.: Harvard University Press, © 1917, by the President and Fellows of Harvard College. The Loeb Classical Library ® is a registered trademark of the President and Fellows of Harvard College

What we are left with are a few generalisations, from ethnographers such as Caesar, Diodorus Siculus, and Ammianus Marcellinus, which hint at the framework of a belief system. These classical writers recognised that the druids, and hence the belief system, had a religious philosophy very similar to the views of *Pythagoras* (see Chapter 5). This was a Greek philosophy, or mysticism, which was most widely discussed in the surviving texts of Aristotle (Tredennick 1933). This philosophy had views on the soul, and the size of the universe, as well as other aspects.

PANTHEONS: GREEK

The Greek traditions are the oldest mythological ideas to survive, in a textual context, in Europe; consequently, they are perceived as a common European heritage. Due to the antiquity of the record, Greek mythology is often seen as a source for comparing and contrasting other European and Middle Eastern traditions. This religious culture grew over many centuries and was added to from many sources; we can see this process occurring for the pantheon as a whole, and also with some of the individual deities. It is considered that a process of religious unification could have taken place in the Bronze Age, when a veneer was added to the philosophies and stories of a number of more localised cults, probably under political influence (Dickinson 1994, 278, 282). A number of the well known deities have names which can be read on the Linear B tablets; yet a number of the deities that they mention: *Diwija*, *Marineus*, and *Komawenteia*, for example, have disappeared completely from later Classical sources (Chadwick 1976, 95, 99; Dickinson 1994, 291). This process of accumulation can be recognised in some of the Greek primal myths (see Chapter 5).

At the time of the classical Greek and Roman worlds pantheons were common; with each of the gods in the group ruling over a specific aspect of the natural world: the landscape, the sky, the sea, the otherworld, crafts, and also, the emotions. These gods and goddesses are often well-known; in the Classical Greek pantheon there were twelve principal ones elevated above other divinities. The development of the pantheon of twelve and their relationship to the titans has been used to suggest that certain mythological traditions originated from specific invasion cycles and cultural dominance in Greece. The reason for listing these divinities here is; first, to obtain an idea of how the Greek pantheon survived; and second, how this group of deities interacted with the Roman gods (who will be discussed later) and ultimately how they, in turn, effected the Gallic and British provinces.

Zeus

Zeus, whose name is sometimes given as **bright** or **clear sky** (Harvey 1984, 453–454; Shipley, Vanderspoel et al. 2006, 960), is regarded as the only Greek god the meaning of whose name is considered transparent; he has often been paraded as a key example of Indo-European philology (Burkert 1985, 125–131). His name is equated with the Indic sky god *Dyaus pitar*, the Roman *Diespiter* or *Jupiter* (*Juppiter*), the Umbrian *Iuve* or *Jove*, the Germanic *Tiw* or *Tye*, the Illyrian *Dei*, the Hittite *ᴰSius*, who had a common proto-Indo-European origin as **dyeus* (Mallory 1989, 128). The root of the name also provides the Latin *dues*, **god**, and *dies*, **day**, thus Zeus's name informs us that he was the god of the **luminous day sky**. The origins of the god are obscure, and his Indic equivalent, *Dyaus*, was overshadowed by more important gods. Assuming that there was just one origin for this god, in Europe he took on the attributes of a weather god, and this was generally how he was perceived across the continent. The perceived common origins of his name point to the movement of an idea, not necessarily to the movement of peoples.

Zeus's name has been identified on Linear B tablets, indicating that his cult was known in the Mycenaean Bronze Age (Chadwick 1976, 95, 99; Dickinson 1994, 291) in *c.* 1300 BC. The god's name has also been recognised on Minoan Linear B tablets from Knossos (Burkert 1985, 43–44). He and Poseidon, were the only two gods whose worship can be inferred as being widespread at that date. It is considered that there was a month named after Zeus, *Zeus Diktaios*, although the tablet on which this is recorded was damaged. The name is also believed to have originated in oral form in the Bronze Age and it was here that Zeus's association with the weather was first documented (Burkert 1985, 126–127). Homer referred to the ruler of the gods as: **the cloud gatherer, the dark clouded, the thunderer on high**, and **the hurler of thunderbolts**. It was at this time that the eagle was first recognised as the god's totem bird. Although his name and those of other deities are known from that period it should not be assumed that their cults were identical with those that survived into the Classical Hellenistic period, as there was a dark age between these two periods in which certain traditions became obscure. One possible aspect of the cult which may have disappeared in this period is the presence of a goddess called *Diwija*, whose name was derived from the same linguistic origins as Zeus (Burkert 1985, 44). This goddess was worshipped in temples in her own right. Knowing that the god was first recognised in the Bronze Age and was documented in the Classical World does not mean that the whole of Zeus's development is clear, as the path of this concept is not fully recorded.

The tales of Zeus that have survived are numerous. There are rival claims that he was born in Crete and in Arcadia, and then brought to Crete, where he was fed by the goat *Amalthea* (Harvey 1984, 453–454). Cretan traditions concerning his childhood describe a band of warriors (the *Kouretes*) dancing with shields around the infant. These traditions seem to have developed from rituals on Ida in which Zeus was re-born every year in the embers of a great fire (Burkert 1985, 127). The legend in which he overthrew *Kronos* has parallels with a number of Hittite and Mesopotamian myths (Shipley, Vanderspoel et al. 2006, 960). He was not only the greatest of the Greek deities but was often seen as the key divinity, his worship being associated with the overthrow of previous religious systems in the Greek peninsula (see *Kronos* later). Zeus was originally accounted in numerous legends in which he had many wives; eventually, with the advent of the Greek monogamous society, he ended up with one, Hera. He was, nevertheless, often unfaithful to her; for example, with Metis, Demeter, *Leto*, and Maia. This may have been because Zeus was a conflated version of the consort of a number of local goddesses, a similar arrangement to that which the Romans perhaps found when they invaded Gaul and Britain. The overthrow of *Kronos* loomed large in the mythological traditions which surrounded Zeus, and the idea persisted that he, in turn, would be overthrown. From this developed the stories of Metis and Athena, and of the sea goddess *Thetis* who Zeus had to deny (Burkert 1985, 127).

Why temples were built to divinities in certain locations can never properly be resolved, and this is much the same for Zeus as for other deities. Some of his temples were probably established on mountains where storm clouds gathered, such as Mount *Lykaion* in Arcadia, *Oros* on Aegina, and Mount Ida near Troy (Burkert 1985, 126). Mount Olympus is the location of another sanctuary; Olympus is believed to mean **sky** and so the mountains became associated with Zeus initially and later became a home to all of the gods, although still Zeus's main site of worship. One could perhaps surmise that the title *Olympos* was the name of a pre Bronze-Age sky god onto which the cult of Zeus was welded, perhaps leading to the epithet Olympian Zeus. One of Zeus's epithets was *Kataibates*, descending, and it is this title that was used in temples where lightning had struck the ground (Tomlinson 1976, 56–64). The earliest recognised religious features in the sanctuary at Olympus seem to have been an ash altar, dated by its material culture to the tenth century BC, and an enclosure for a sacred grove. When the site first became used for the worship of Zeus is not known precisely, but the sanctuary lies below a conical shaped hill known as the *Hill of Kronos*. It was perhaps events that took place at this sanctuary which provided the tale of Zeus overthrowing his father *Kronos*. The structure of the tale, with the overthrow of the titans, may have been imported but *Kronos* was probably a local component inserted into this story. Other well known sanctuaries to Zeus have been identified at *Nemea*, and at Dodona, where there was an oracle (Shipley, Vanderspoel et al. 2006, 960). His worship later made its way to Sicily (Italy or Graeco Major) where he is known to have had a dedication at *Akragas*.

Hera

Hera was the sister and consort of Zeus and was the goddess of women and wives, and the protectress of marriage (Harvey 1984, 200–201). Her name is not understood in the same philological manner as Zeus's, and one suggestion concerning its origin is that it is derived from the word *hora*, **season**; an allusion to a female who was ripe for marriage (Burkert 1985, 131).

Her name, like Zeus's, was recorded on Linear B tablets of the Mycenaean Bronze Age (Chadwick 1976, 95, 99; Dickinson 1994, 291). Homer also gave some indication that some of the traditions which we associate with Hera may go back to the Bronze Age (Burkert 1985, 132–133). Tradition has it that Hera first rejected Zeus (Shipley, Vanderspoel et al. 2006, 418) and an account is given of a divinely consummated marriage with Zeus in the temple precinct on Mount Ida (Burkert 1985, 132–134) in which Zeus transformed into a Cuckoo and landed in the goddess's lap (Shipley, Vanderspoel et al. 2006, 418). One female aspect that, it has been suggested, Hera lacked was motherhood; she was often characterised by her jealousy of her husband and her hatred of his paramours and their offspring. Hera was associated with actions and tales in which the cycle of life was brought into deep crisis before being reborn. She was often associated with a cow and white cows were sacrificed to her (Shipley, Vanderspoel et al. 2006, 418).

Legend has it that she was born on Samos, where a large temple was constructed in her honour (Harvey 1984, 200–201). This temple was probably constructed in *c.* 800 BC (Burkert 1985, 131, 135). Further temples were erected at *Perachora*, where two statues of the goddess were erected, one to *Hera Akraia* and the other to *Hera Limenia*. Temples were also constructed at river sites, one near the estuary of the Sele River, and another on the River Imbrasos. That on the Imbrasos was associated with her wedding; the sanctuary by the river was called *Parthenios*, maiden. Hera was also worshipped in

Boeotia, in her temple at Plataea. Here, a wedding festival, *Daedala,* was celebrated, where a wooden image was made of a bride. There were also two statues; one to the bride, the other to the goddess fulfilled. It is interesting that the name Plataea is an Indo-European name for the earth mother.

The *Heraion/Heraeum*, Hera's major shrine, is located on the eastern side of the Argive plain, to the south-east of Mycenae (Tomlinson 1976, 90–92). Homer recognised Hera as an important pre-Hellenic goddess of the Argive region, but no physical evidence has yet been found at the Argive site to date her cult back into the Bronze Age, although it probably originated then. The sanctuary is located where springs rise up from the base of a mountain on the edge of the plain. The most prominent feature amongst the ruins is the terrace, with a monumental wall dated to the eighth or seventh centuries BC. The nature of the wall indicates that it was constructed in a location already used for the worship of this goddess, but this has not been proven categorically. Little remains of the temple but it was probably constructed of unbaked brick and wooden columns; also indicative of an earlier origin than the eighth century BC. Her classical sanctuary was redeveloped in the mid-fifth century BC. Physical evidence indicates that this goddess's cult originated in the Argive Plain so the claims of her birth in Samos provide a further twist in her development.

Poseidon

Zeus's brother Poseidon was lord of the sea, earthquakes, horses, horsemen, and horse races (Harvey 1984, 343; Shipley, Vanderspoel et al. 2006, 710). Archaeological investigation has confirmed that Poseidon's name was recorded in the Mycenaean Linear B texts (Chadwick 1976, 95, 99; Dickinson 1994, 291). Thus, he had pre-Hellenic origins, *c.* 1300 BC. In Mycenaean Greece he was called *Poseidaon,* and in Dorian areas *Poteidan* (Burkert 1985, 44, 136). The first part of his name is considered to be derived from *potei,* **lord**. The Linear B texts, as they did with Zeus, indicated that there was a goddess who bore a female name of the god, *Posidaeja,* and one could also consider that the Bronze-Age goddess *Potnia*, mistress, may also have her name linked to Poseidon. Linear B sources indicate that Poseidon was the chief god worshipped in Bronze Age Pylos (Burkert 1985, 44, 136); this is further supported in the accounts by Homer. The early textual sources even provided a list of offerings to be made to the god.

Like Zeus, Poseidon also had a totem animal, which in his case was the horse. He was associated with a Horse Spring, *Hippou Krene*, which arose from the ground where the first horse hit the ground with his hoof (Burkert 1985, 138). It is also known that horses were drowned to him in the whirlpool at Argos. He also had a number of epithets; these included: Poseidon *Hippios* (**horse**) which associated him with a horse cult, and Poseidon *Taureos* (**bull**). Many tales evolved concerning his exploits. He, like Zeus, had many consorts: *Amphitrite* (his wife), *Ge,* Medusa, and Demeter (Harvey 1984, 343). In some of these tales there are further associations with horses, for example Pegasus the winged horse who sprang from the blood of Medusa. There are important aspects which surround Poseidon and his role as progenitor of many peoples and ancestral lines; including the *Aeolos* and the *Boeotos.* In Athens he was associated with *Erechtheos,* the divine king, from whom the Athenian tribe were descended.

Poseidon's principle sanctuary in the Bronze Age was at Pylos while in the Classical period known temples were located at Isthmia, near Corinth, at *Mycalē* (Tomlinson 1976, 93–96), on Cape Sunium, and at Tainaron (Burkert 1985, 136–137; Shipley, Vanderspoel et al. 2006, 710). The temples of Poseidon were considered to have been locations at which escaped slaves could take refuge (Shipley, Vanderspoel et al. 2006, 710). There also seems to be evidence to suggest that he was associated with certain seasonal cycles. One tradition was the seasonal tunny-fish hunt in which tridents were used and the first offerings were given to the lord of the sea (Burkert 1985, 136–137).

Hades

Hades, the last of Zeus's brothers whose name means **unseen** (Harvey 1984, 193), was depicted as grim and terrible, but was considered a just god. His origins are considered to be as an earth god, associated with fertility and the bounty of the land. The antiquity of his worship is, however, not attested in the same way as for his male siblings. Where his cult did occur he was often known by different names: *Plouton*, *Klymenos*, and *Eubouleus* being some examples (Shipley, Vanderspoel et al. 2006, 410). The name *Plouton*, means **wealth**, and in this guise he was associated with the wealth of the earth. It is probably for this reason that he participated in the legends of Demeter. In various works, including Homer's (Murray and Wyatt 1999, XV) and Apollodoros's (Frazer 1921, I, III) we are informed that, after the overthrow of the Titans, the three brothers drew lots to deal out their share of the spoils. It was to Hades that the realm of the earth and underworld fell.

Hades shared his name with the underworld, which was the land of the dead (Harvey 1984, 193; Shipley, Vanderspoel et al. 2006, 410). Notions of what this world represented varied over time; altering with the accumulation of knowledge of the natural world. In the *Iliad*, Hades was a realm to the west, beyond the stream of *Oceanos*. In later interpretations it was described as being below ground and accessible through a number of chasms. The otherworld contained a number of regions: the plain of *Asphodel*, the *Elysium* Fields, and *Tartarus*. The last was a place of punishment for those who were enemies of the gods. We also hear of the rivers of the underworld: *Styx, Acheron, Kokytus, Phlegethon*, and *Lethe* (see Chapter 4).

Demeter

Demeter, worshipped as the goddess of the corn (Harvey 1984, 138), was portrayed constantly with sheaves and wreaths, and was symbolically called on as the separator of the fruit from the chaff. In the Dorian and *Aeolic* dialects she was called *Damater*; the latter part of her name meaning *mother* (Burkert 1985, 159–161). The name has often been interpreted as Earth Mother, which is incorrect, or corn mother, which does also not work linguistically. Burkert inferred that her cult was old and widespread yet offered no reference to her name in the Linear B texts. One possibility, which is worth considering, is that the <De-> of Demeter derived from the same root as Zeus, and that she was the goddess *Diwija*. Hence, the corn only grew under the auspices of the **mother of the bright skies**. Though Hera is given as Zeus's usual consort the goddess Demeter is known as the mother of *Persephone*; her son *Plutos* is claimed to have been conceived in a corn-field.

Traditionally, Demeter was claimed to be the daughter of *Kronos* and *Rhea*, and the sister of Zeus, Poseidon, Hades-Plouton, Hera, and Hestia (Shipley, Vanderspoel *et al.* 2006, 266); unlike the other gods she did not live on Mount Olympus. It was Demeter's relationship with her daughter *Persephone,* or in Attic *Pherephatta,* which was crucial, and at the root of our ability to understand this goddess (Harvey 1984, 138; Burkert 1985, 159–161). Persephone was also known as *Kore,* and with her mother was referred to as the *Demeteres,* the Two Goddesses. The tale was not incorporated into most of the mainstream Greek texts, but was included at an early date in the Homeric Hymn to Demeter. In the story *Kore* went to the edge of the world to pick flowers; while doing this the ground opened up and Hades-Aidoneus rode out on a chariot and took her to his realm. In her sorrow and anger Demeter wandered across the world in an attempt to find her daughter; in doing this she prevented the earth from giving up her fruits. The most significant sites accounted in this tale were on Sicily. Demeter was worshipped at *Eleusis* near Athens, which was one of the locations mentioned in her wanderings. It was here that the Eleusinian mysteries were invented and were carried out in her honour. These tales hint at the antiquity of myths in which deities wandered the landscape and initiated traditions at certain places (see Chapter 4). The outcome of the tale is that *Kore* was allowed to leave Hades, but she also had to taste the pomegranate, and, as a result, was forced to return periodically to the underworld. Thus it became necessary for the corn goddess to be appeased so that the order of the natural world could commence. This tale was used to explain why the earth became barren every winter, when Demeter withdrew her benefits in grief for the loss of her daughter. The story can be interpreted in two ways, one as an allegory of the cycles of the natural world; the other, which Burkert preferred, to refer to a double existence (in summer and winter) as *Kore's* rape had disrupted the previous cycle. The story has parallels with the Sumerian-Babylonian myth of the *Katabasis,* and the Hittite myth of *Telepinu.* Neither, however, is a complete match, and the Greek version is, in some ways, a combination of both traditions. The process of *Kore* being carried away by Hades was ambivalent; was it death or marriage. *Kore* was a symbol of the corn or wheat which was placed in the earth. Demeter's daughter *Persephone,* alias *Kore,* was associated with festivals in November; her emblem was three poppy heads (Harvey 1984, 138).

Hestia

Hestia, was categorised as one of the lesser gods of the Greek pantheon. In the Hymn of Aphrodite she was deemed to be one of daughters of *Kronos* and *Rhea* (Harvey 1984, 208; Burkert 1985, 170). In Ionian she was called *Histie,* a name which referred to the hearth at the centre of the home and family. She was worshipped in each home at the hearth and also at the *Prytanēum,* where a sacred fire was kindled in her honour, at each town hall. In each *polis* (city) there was a *prytaneion* (temple of Hestia) which stood at the centre of the settlement; while the hearth at Delphi was often seen as the hearth of Greece.

Athena

Athena is one of the Greek goddesses who can be used to show how persistent religious ideas could be in Greece (Harvey 1984, 55). Her name was written as either *Athenaia,* Ionian *Athenaie,* or Attic *Athena* (Burkert 1985, 139). It is unclear if the city is named after the goddess, or visa versa, but it has been suggested that since *–ene* is a Greek place-name ending then the city was probably named first.

Athena is seen as having had, from analysis of mythical tales and archaeological evidence, pre-Hellenic origins. The reference in the Linear B texts from Knossos was to *atana potinija*; this can be translated as mistress of *At(h)ana* (Burkert 1985, 139), hence she was the goddess or *pallas* (**maiden**), of the city. The interpretation of this name implies that place-names were given first and that the personification of the place developed afterwards.

Like other Greek deities a range of stories and traditions have survived. The story of her birth is seen as an attempt to reconcile the traditions of this goddess with that of the new Hellenic order, as personified by Zeus (Burkert 1985, 140–143). In this tale she has either been described as the daughter of Metis (**wisdom**) and Zeus, or sometimes of Zeus alone. In the usual version of the tale, Zeus, in fear that his position would be usurped, swallowed Metis when he found out that she was pregnant. Zeus later had a severe pain in his head and, to relieve him of suffering, Hephaistos struck him over the head with an Axe. It was from the resulting wound that Athena was born. Athena thus had a special place amongst the gods in that she alone was born of Zeus. As his prize, Hephaistos attempted to rape Athena, his semen fell on the ground and the king *Erichthonios/Erechtheos* was born. Athena fought with Poseidon for control of the city in which her temple and cult centre were founded on the Acropolis. In some of her early legends there is a sense of a primitive warlike ferocity; for example in the killing of a monstrous goat to create her *aegis*, and in the killing of the giant *Pallas* to provide parts of her clothing. Her totem animal was the little owl, found on the Acropolis, and the olive tree was also considered sacred to her.

There is reason to believe that Athena was worshipped, on the hill above the city that bears her name, as early as the Bronze Age (Tomlinson 1976, 78–90), although physical evidence occurs only for the eighth or seventh centuries BC. Nevertheless, there are signs of Bronze-Age fortifications on the hilltop. The nature of the entrance onto the hill may have been determined by the form of earlier late Bronze-Age defences; the earliest known temple was destroyed in the Persian Wars and was eventually replaced by the surviving structure. Temples were not only erected to her in Athens, but also in fortresses at Argos, Sparta, Gortyn, Lindos, Larisa, Thessaly, and Ilion (Burkert 1985, 140). It was in her role as the goddess of the city of Athens that she was represented as an armed maiden.

Ares

Ares (Harvey 1984, 40) was called a son of Zeus and Hera and the god of war or warlike frenzy. The name Ares is an ancient abstract noun, meaning **throng of battle** or **war** (Burkert 1985, 169–170). It is derived from *areios*, and was a recognised early epithet for Zeus *Areios*, Athena *Areia*, and Aphrodite *Areia*. This tradition goes back to the Bronze Age when there were references to Hermaes *Areias*. In Athens there is an *Ares pagos*, the hill of Ares.

He did not play an important role in the Greek myths, the earliest descriptions being in Homer where he was a warrior who stirred up *Phobos* (**fear**) and *Deimos* (**terror**), the horses which pulled his war chariot (Burkert 1985, 169–170). Often, in fights he came off second best. Perhaps one of the most important legendary traditions concerning him is that of the foundation of Thebes. In this tale Ares's son *Kadmos* married *Harmonia*, the daughter of Aphrodite and Ares. *Kadmos* was later killed (so that his teeth could be sown and the earth-born warriors could arise as the children of Ares), but the anarchy of war frenzy eventually gave way to the harmony required for the foundation of the city. Ares found later significance at Athens due to the importance of the Roman cult of Mars *Ulator*; in this we can see a way in which the traditional Roman world affected the Greek world.

Apollo

Apollo (Harvey 1984, 34) is seen as one of the more recent introductions to the Greek religious traditions (see Figure 10). He had three cult centres: Delphi, Delos, and Didyma. Two of these operated as major regional foci (Delphi and Delos) which acted as means of diffusing his cult throughout the Aegean world; which had occurred by *c*. 700 BC (Burkert 1985, 143–145). There is no clear indication, from Linear B texts, that Apollo was a god worshipped in the Bronze Age, but it is apparent that some of his divine attributes were evident in certain cultural activities (medicine, music, and archery) and may ultimately have given rise to his cult. The three component parts which are considered to have come together to form the cult of Apollo were: a Dorian one, a Cretan one and a Syro-Hittite one. The Dorian component, the earliest name *Apellon*, was associated with the word *apellai*, a name applied to tribal gatherings in northern Greece. These gatherings were associated with male coming of age ceremonies. From Crete there is evidence to suggest that the cult of Apollo had taken over that of a Bronze Age god called *Paiawon*, whose name produced the word *paean*, the name of Apollo's cult hymn. Semitic traditions explain the imagery of Apollo, and these may have originated with a god called *Rešep*, who had a bow and was associated with a stag. Evidence of *Rešep's* worship

Figure 10: A Cornelian intaglio (in iron ring) depicting the god Apollo leaning against a column behind which is the Delphic tripod. In his hand he holds his sacred laurel branch (gem damaged at this point), from Gadara in Jordon (photograph Robert Wilkins, Institute of Archaeology Oxford)

in dark age Cyprus and Greece is known and, at *Amyklai,* a sanctuary to Apollo lies in a town which shares its name with *Rešep (A)mukal.* It has been argued that youthful renewal, the banishment of disease, and the arrow-bearing guardian were all brought together in the form of Apollo.

He was, according to myth, born at Delos, along with his sister Artemis. As a result the island became sacred to them (Harvey 1984, 34). This story, perhaps like Athena's, points to a new idea being introduced and hence a rewriting of the older traditions. The island of Delos is a small inhospitable place with no springs or rivers, yet the population of the Cyclades seem to have developed the location as a shrine in the late Bronze Age (Tomlinson 1976, 64, 71–77). It is thought that the original deity worshipped on the island was female of which Artemis may be a later Hellenised form (Burkert 1985, 144). It has even been conjectured that the festivals of *Karneia Hyakinthia* and *Daphnephhoria* were initially celebrated without Apollo. The first recognised temple built on Delos was by the *Naxians* in the seventh century AD (Tomlinson 1976, 64, 71–77). At Delphi Apollo was seen as an intruder or usurper and it is unlikely that he arrived before the end of the Bronze Age. He slew the Python at Delphi to establish his own cult centre, and became a god of prophecy. The sanctuary had previously been considered to be dedicated to the earth-mother.

Artemis

Artemis, the sister of Apollo, and daughter of Zeus and *Leto* (Harvey 1984, 52), was the goddess of the wilderness and hunting. She was linked to the moon and attended to by nymphs. Her name probably derives from *Arte-,* **bear.** She is considered to have had one of the oldest and most widespread cults in the Greek world (Burkert 1985, 149–151), although it has not been confirmed that her name was present in the Linear B texts. In the Iliad she was referred to as *potnia theron,* mistress of the animals. In Greek culture she became a symbol of virginity and birth, and was also associated with female initiation and coming of age. She was associated with the **bear;** her temple servants in Athens being called **bears.** Female initiation ceremonies which formed part of the rituals of the Artemis cult took place at Brouron, near Athens, where a bear sacred to Artemis was killed by Attic youths.

Her most famous cult centre was at Ephesus so she has been seen as a goddess with Asiatic origins. Her image was probably brought from *Tauris* (Harvey 1984, 52). Artemis is important for understanding the origins of a number of traditions, and their connections with place-names, and deification of the landscape, and its population with the names of flora and fauna (see Chapter 4).

Hermes

Hermes took his name from a heap of stones, a *herma* (Burkert 1985, 156–158). The basic concepts concerning him, however, accrued over a long period of time, for Hermes was another of the Hellenic gods whose name was present in the Mycenaean Linear B tablets; in the form *Hermaias* (Chadwick 1976, 95, 99; Dickinson 1994, 291). The name also occurred in the Doric form, *Herman,* and in an Ionian-Attic form of Hermes (Burkert 1985, 156–158). Though the name occurred in Bronze Age texts it is not apparent that he had evolved at that time into the god we recognise from the Classical World. In these texts he was the embodiment of the herm or the territorial boundary. In some traditions these markers originated as boundary or clearance cairns. In some places it became common to place wooden phalli on top of the cairns. Philological discussions of the name Hermes have looked for more complicated explanations; for example, *hermēneia*, **explanation**, and *hermēneus*, **interpreter** (Kerényi 1986); these may, however, be later backformations from the simpler association that is now generally accepted.

Hermes's domain was luck, wealth, merchants and thieves and, in some areas of Greece, fertility. He was also portrayed as the messenger of the gods, and the conductor of souls to Hades (Burkert 1985, 158). Besides this he was the god of sleep and dreams (Kerényi 1986). There is nothing in the *Iliad* to suggest that he was responsible for guiding souls, being solely concerned with the violation of boundaries and laws. It was in the Odyssey where Hermes called the souls of the dead away to the underworld. In the Hymn of Hermes there is a sense that this god, like others, may have belonged to the pre-Hellenic world, his mother being a goddess bound to the Arcadian landscape.

From his origins in the Bronze Age as a god of boundaries, his role developed quickly. In the Greek dark ages the ideas of a trickster and a messenger became conflated, developing possibly from the idea of boundary transgression (Burkert 1985, 157–158). Hermes was another child of Zeus, but this time by *Maia*; he was born on Mont *Cyllēne* in Arcadia (Harvey 1984, 205). He made a lyre on the day of his birth from the shell of a tortoise, and drove away the cattle of Apollo, who, insulted, turned up in a rage and had to be pacified with the gift of the lyre (Evelyn-White 1982, 324–360, 362–404).

Aphrodite

The origins of the name of Aphrodite are obscure; one recent suggestion, however, is that it is derived from the word *aphros*, **sea foam** (Shipley, Vanderspoel *et al.* 2006. 56). It is considered that her worship was probably introduced from the east and that she was borrowed from the Semetic, or more precisely, the Phoenician peoples (Burkert 1985, 152–155). The reason for this is that there was much in her worship which was associated with, or similar to, the worship of the goddess *Ishtar-Astarte*, the divine consort of heaven. These traditions included a cult of sexuality, androgyny, the sacrifice of doves, the use of incense, ideas of a warrior goddess, and also prostitution. Aphrodite's non-Greek origin has been confirmed by her absence from the Mycenaean texts. The worship of Aphrodite is considered to have been introduced to the Greek world through *Paphos,* on Cyprus, an area with which she was associated in the Odyssey. It is known, from archaeological evidence, that Phoenician colonisation occurred there in the ninth century BC, during the Greek dark ages, and that in *c.* 800 BC a temple to *Astarte* was built at Kition. A further cult centre of the goddess grew up at *Amathus*.

The legends concerning her origins and offspring are numerous and not consistent, perhaps pointing to her late arrival in the Greek pantheon and possible association with a number of minor regional deities. Although Aphrodite did not occur in the Linear B texts, she had been introduced by the time of Homer (Burkert 1985, 153–155). This could have been due to a late oral reworking of these passages (or she had usurped an earlier goddess). In Homer's texts she was claimed to be a daughter of Zeus (and *Dione*); according to Hesiod (Harvey 1984, 33), however, she was formed in the foam of the sea; tales which described the genitals of *Ouranos* being severed and thrown into the sea,

Aphrodite was formed in the foam of the waves and came ashore on Cyprus. Aphrodite's role may have changed over time; in Homer's works she was the liberty that lied in nature and at this stage there was no recognition of the marriage to Hephaistos (Kerényi 1979, 56–61); this relationship only appearing in the Odyssey. In the Iliad she was one of the three goddesses (along with Hera and Athena) amongst whom *Paris* had to choose the most beautiful (Burkert 1985, 153–154). In another tale her infidelity was revealed when her husband, Hephaistos, caught her in a net with Ares, much to the amusement of the other gods. Sacrifices had to be made to her at marriage nuptials in Sparta, where she was known as Aphrodite Hera (Harvey 1984, 33). A temple was constructed to her on Mont *Eryx* in Sicily. On Lesbos her name was a homonym of the river *Aphrodisios*. The widespread nature of her cult indicates that her cult spread rapidly; one could suggest that if the name Aphrodite was used as a river name then she could have started as a nymph whose role was transformed when amalgamated with *Ishtar-Astarte*.

Hephaistos

Hephaistos shared his name with *Hephaistias*, a town on Lesbos, which had a non-Greek population until the sixth century BC (Burkert 1985, 167–168). The god may have had his origins in the fire festivals of the island, which were associated with the kindling of fire and its distribution; thus he could have an intimate relationship with fire. He also had an association with the activity of smith craft. The significance of metalworking activity became associated with kingship and religion in the Bronze Age and the Iron Age.

In the mythological traditions the accounts of Hephaistos are not considerable and it is considered that this was due to his association with Athena and Athens. He was, in some traditions, the father of the sacred king *Erichthonios*, which gave him his place amongst the twelve gods (Burkert 1985, 167–168). It was this role which saw the erection of a temple to him on the high ground above the Athenian Agora in *c.* 450 BC (Camp 1986, 82–87). The smith god was, in many traditions, represented as being lame, the Aegean traditions were no different and an explanation has been put forward to explain this; his imperfection being

Figure 11: A bronze statuette from Richborough, Kent, of Vulcan the smith god (photograph Robert Wilkins, Institute of Archaeology archive, source Martin Henig)

caused by his birth to Hera alone (Burkert 1985, 167–168). In the earliest known traditions he was married to *Charis* (**Grace**) and it was only in later ones that he wed Aphrodite. In the Roman world Hephaistos became associated with Vulcan, god of fire and black-smiths (see Figure 11).

Dionysos

Views on the meaning of the name and, even on the origins, have changed over time; Dionysus was the god of wine and intoxicated ecstasy. The earliest arguments for his non-Greek origins were put forward in a Thesis by Erwin Rhode and based on statements from Herodotus that Dionysos was a late addition to the Greek mythological pantheon. It was considered that he was introduced from Thessaly (Harvey 1984, 147–148; Burkert 1985, 162–163). In other claims he originated in Thrace or Phrygia (Otto 1981, 52). However, Dionysus was attested to on the Linear B tablets from Pylos and at the shrine of *Ayia Irini,* on Keos, where he was associated with a wine cult (Burkert 1985, 162). At the latter sanctuary activity can be traced from the fifteenth century BC to the time of Classical Greece, thus indicating the longevity and continuity of his worship in Hellenistic culture. Four types of festival were held in his honour. One of these, the *Older Dionysia,* must have predated the Ionian migration period.

The name Dionysus (and its variations *Deunysos* and *Zonnysos*) is difficult to interpret but it is probable that it contains the name Zeus, *Dios Dionysos,* **Zeus's son Dionysos** (Burkert 1985, 162–163). The associated cult names: *Semele* (his mother), *Bacchus* (the votary and alternative divine name), *thyrsos* (sacred wand), *thimbos,* and *dithyrambos* (cult hym) are all regarded as non-Greek words. Greek traditions associated Dionysos with Phrygia and Lydia, both Asia Minor kingdoms of the eighth to sixth century BC. It is probably not now possible to resolve the origins and the originating languages of these names.

There is very little surviving heroic poetry concerning Dionysos, the only one being the Hymn of Dionysos (Burkert 1985, 163). He was born at Thebes, a child of Zeus and *Semele;* his mother was consumed by a thunderbolt, and his father rescued him (Harvey 1984, 147–148). Some of the accounts indicate that he was twice born; after being snatched from his mother he was stitched up in his father's thigh to complete his term (Shipley, Vanderspoel *et al.* 2006, 117–118). Hermes took the infant to *Nysa,* where he grew up. Hera pursued him relentlessly, in her jealousy, forcing madness onto him and his followers. Madness was, besides wine, a major part of his cult (Burkert 1985, 162–165). Tradition claims that Dionysos first revealed the art of viticulture to *Ikarios,* a peasant from Attica. He was slain by other peasants who thought he had poisoned them, and was found hanged by his daughter *Erigone.* The tale was associated with the festival of the *Anthesteria,* as are the traditional associations with his wife *Ariadne.*

Eileithyia

The goddess *Eileithyia* was classed as one of the lesser gods, but there is evidence that she was worshipped from Mycenaean times in the cave of *Amnisos* (Burkert 1985, 170–171). Her name is derived from the verb *Eleuthyia,* **the coming,** thus she was the goddess of childbirth.

Conclusions and Kronos

The stories of these deities represent the long process of knowledge accrual within the main cultural group (the Greeks, their ancestors, and their offspring) and the importation of cultural ideas (of which those most noted are from Asia). There is also an indication that the religious activity of cities (Athens for example) could skew unexpectedly the development of these religious systems. It is normally easier to confirm the longevity of the cults of female deities, such as Hera and Athena, than those of the male divinities, such as Apollo. Interpretation of the Linear B texts has transformed our understanding of many of these deities. Some of the deities are now perceived as being of Greek origin, being pre-Hellenic and recorded in Mycenaean texts, while others are seen as being brought in from Asia Minor. Six of the deities (five classed as twelve of the major gods) were considered the offspring of *Kronos* (Harvey 1984, 125–126), a titan who represented a golden age, and whose once important status was overthrown by invading forces or changing attitudes and beliefs within Greece. *Kronos* can, therefore, be seen as pre-Hellenic and associated with earthquakes and volcanic eruptions.

PANTHEONS: ROMAN

Most Greek deities were given their counterpart in the Roman world, due to a process of Greco-Roman *interpretatio*. The date at which the exchange of ideas between the Greek and Roman main-lands is not known but the earliest indication that the Greek language and letters were known on the Italian peninsula comes from the Iron-Age cemetery of Osteria dell'Osa (20 kilometres east of Rome) from tomb 482 (Wiseman 2004, 13). The word ΕΥΟΙΝ, or ΕΥΛΙΝ, was recorded on a locally made pottery vessel deposited in *c.* 800 BC at the latest, but possibly some two hundred years earlier. This actually represents the earliest documented use of the Greek language. The Etruscans especially are known to have emulated the Olympian pantheon, although there were differences in the ways in which goddesses were viewed (Shipley, Vanderspoel *et al.* 2006, 331). The nature and extent of Greco-Roman *interpretatio* are perhaps most evident in the later Classical period; in such works as the creation poems of Ovid, where certain aspects of Roman religion were welded with the allegedly older traditions of Italy. It was the Roman gods which were introduced into Gaul and Britain and which were associated, in various ways, with the deities of the peoples who were found there.

Jupiter

The Greek Zeus was equated with Jupiter; both were lords of the **sky** or **the bright day** (see above). An alternative Italian name of Umbrian origin for the god was *Jove*. The exact mechanism by which Jupiter reached Italy remains unknown. Rome was in existence, from recent archaeological assessments, in the ninth or tenth century BC (Wiseman 2008, 1–2, 155–157). At this time there was a major settlement and a major cemetery down by the Tiber; in *c.* 875 BC the cemetery site was moved to a location on the Esquiline Hill. When these communities took up the worship of Jupiter is not known, but there is a tale, alluded to by the likes of Varro and Livy, that *Numa*, a *pontifices*, summoned Jupiter down to the Aventine Hill to negotiate what should be sacrificed to him to expiate the power of his thunder and lightning.

As the Greek world grew, and became more integrated, the image associated with Zeus must have become standardised and homogenised. The same must also have been true of Jupiter in Italy; and these images became standardised throughout the Roman Empire (see Figures 12a and b). Jupiter does seem to contain elements of Roman origin; he was a god of the sky, and lightning, but was also connected with the grape harvest and sowing (Harvey 1984, 232). In Italy Jupiter obtained many epithets and one has to consider whether these were regional gods, or just different titles for the same god: *Lūcetius* (**light**), *Feretrius* (**bond or union of the community**), and *Stator* (**victory**). The temple of *Jupiter Feretrius* was claimed to have been the oldest temple in the city of Rome. He was considered to have been a state god before the introduction of Greek elements to his cult, and to have already been associated with the oak tree and the eagle. There is evidence that Jupiter was worshipped with other gods: with Mars and *Quirinus* for whom there was a priest called the *flamen Dialis*, and also, from the sixth century BC, with Juno and Minerva (Shipley, Vanderspoel *et al.* 2006, 480). The development of the Capitoline tradition (with Juno and Minerva) is also considered to have taken place before the introduction of major Greek influence. In this context he was known as Jupiter *Capitolinus*. Festivals associated with Jupiter include the 13th September (dedication of the Capitoline temple), the 15th October (*Feretrius*) and the 13th November. When Jupiter was introduced to Gaul and Britain he already had a standardised image; the representations of the god at that time being simply exported to the new Roman provinces. Both Zeus and Jupiter acquired an important position at the head of a group of nominally equal deities.

a

b

Figure 12: a) An early engraving by Samuel Lysons showing a Cornelian intaglio, depicting Jupiter, from Bourton-on-the-Water, Gloucestershire (drawing S. Lysons). b) An impression take from a Cornelian intaglio depicting an image of Jupiter seated and holding an eagle, from Bath (Institute of Archaeology archive, University of Oxford)

Juno

Alongside Zeus/Jupiter was his consort Hera, in the Greek world, or Juno, in the Roman one. They became conflated because of their association with similar male gods. Juno was also associated with childbirth and women in general. In these parings we find the divine marriage, a subject which will be returned to later. Her name derived from a word the etymology of which is **youth** (Shipley, Vanderspoel *et al.* 2006, 480).

Juno, like Jupiter, is considered to have been of Italian origin (Harvey 1984, 232). She has been identified with a number of Italian peoples: the *Sabines*, the *Oscans*, the *Latins*, the *Umbrians*, and the *Etruscans*. Juno was identified with the Etruscan goddess *Uni* (Shipley, Vanderspoel *et al.* 2006, 480). The Italian origins of the goddess and her pre Hellenic development are indicated by the Capitoline traditions which were already evident by the sixth century BC. She was also given a number of epithets, including *Lucetia*, and *Lucina* (**bright light**), and was often associated with the moon. A further epithet was *Monēta* (**giver of counsel**), the source of the word money. Her festivals included the *Matronalia* (1st March), the *Sospita* (1st February), the *Monetia* (1st September) and the *Sororia* (1st October) (Shipley, Vanderspoel *et al.* 2006, 480). Her sacred animals were geese; because of this a sacred gaggle was kept in Rome. These birds awoke the city in 390 BC when there was a threat of a nocturnal Gallic attack on the city (Foster 1984, V.47.4). In one tradition she was the sole parent of the god Mars, whose children founded the city of Rome.

Minerva

Minerva, the Italian goddess of wisdom, became associated with the Greek Athena, and originated in the lands of the *Etruscans* or *Faliscans* (Shipley, Vanderspoel *et al.* 2006, 582). She was a goddess of storms, thunder and lightning, and tempests, besides being a goddess of artificers and trade guilds (Harvey 1984, 275). The latter associations are considered to provide the basis of her name which means **remembrance**, indicating intelligence. Her major festival was on the 19th March which was called the *Quinquatrus*; the festival of artisans.

Athena and Minerva have different names and different origins, yet they were conflated, most likely due to their similar images (see Figure 13). Juno and Minerva, along with Jupiter, became closely associated as the members of the Capitoline triad by the sixth century BC (Shipley, Vanderspoel *et al.* 2006, 582). How the three deities came to form this group is, however, still a subject for debate. The Capitoline triad could have been based on the idea of the divine couple with the female component split into two separate identities; the mother

Figure 13: A Cornelian intaglio from Bampton, near Norwich, Norfolk, depicting the goddess Minerva (photograph Robert Wilkins, Institute of Archaeology archive, source Martin Henig)

and the protectress. Hence, Minerva, in her masculine warrior attire, could have been placed in the triad to represent protective attributes, which probably once also applied to Juno. The Capitoline traditions were extremely significant. The ideas contained within it could have equated with ideas already in existence in the British and Gallic worlds or they affected significantly these ideas.

Neptune

Neptune was regarded by some as a god of ancient Italian origin (Harvey 1984, 286) of which little is known. However, his origins may be far older and a suggestion has been made that he is associated with the Indic *Apam Napat*, **grandson** or **nephew of the water**, and also the Irish *Nechtain* (Mallory 1989, 129–130). The two European versions contain the word **neptos*, **grandson** or **nephew**, and are both associated with water (the sea and a sacred well). Neptune was worshipped in Italy at the *Neptūnālia* on the 23rd July (Harvey 1984, 286). By the time he was first documented he seems to have been fully conflated with his Greek counterpart, Poseidon, and also associated with horses and the sea. Thus there are similar ideas and comparable images.

Pluto

Pluto, the **wealth giver**, had an even more obscure origin than Neptune (Harvey 1984, 337). His name is considered to be of Greek origin, referring to the bounty of the earth. It is possible that the god was an introduction from Greece or that he had an association with the deity first recorded in Greece as *Plutos*, **wealth**. He was named as the child of Demeter (and presumably Zeus) and was conceived on a ploughed corn field (Burkert 1985, 159). There are, perhaps, parallels with the god Mars *Nodens*, in Britain, whose name meant **he who takes possession of** (Tolkien 1932, 132–137).

Ceres

The goddess Ceres is considered to have originated in Italy and to have been associated with the generative power (growth) of nature and the earth (Harvey 1984, 97). The root of her name **ker*, means **to grow**, and is found in the Latin word *crescere*, **to increase** (Shipley, Vanderspoel *et al.* 2006, 180–181). She was associated with the growth of the young wheat; accounts of her tales were given by Ovid (Frazer 1989, iv.681) and Virgil (Rushton Fairclough 1999, i.338–50).

Her cult was found in its earliest forms in the territory of the *Oscans*. Her priests were known as *flamines* and were considered to have been part of an archaic order (Shipley, Vanderspoel *et al.* 2006, 180–181). Her festival, the *Cereālia,* was held from the 12th to the 19th April. There was a further festival in January associated with the act of sowing, when she was worshipped alongside *Tellus* (**earth**). Her temple in Rome was founded in the fifth century BC, but her cult soon obtained a Greek character when she became associated with Demeter. The dedication of this temple, on the Aventine, was to Ceres, Liber and *Libera* (who were associated with their Greek counterparts: Demeter, Dionysos, and *Kore*).

Vesta

Vesta, the goddess of the hearth (Harvey 1984, 446), was worshipped in every household,

Figure 14: A Cornelian intaglio from the Snettisham Roman jeweller's hoard, Norfolk, depicting Diana with bow and arrow and hunting dogs (photograph M. Maaskant-Kleibrink, Institute of Archaeology archive, source Martin Henig)

and a fire was kept burning for her in her state temple, by the Vestals. The fire was only extinguished, by ceremony, on the 1st March, the beginning of the New Year. The flames are believed to have represented the king of Rome. Though she shared the name and attributes of the Greek Hestia the two goddesses seem to have retained their individuality and the specific cultural attributes which reflected their countries of origin. Specific festivals called the *Vestālia* were held in the goddess's honour in June, when offerings were made by the matrons of Rome.

Diana

Diana was another Latin goddess who had a temple in Rome from the earliest times (Harvey 1984, 143–144; Shipley, Vanderspoel *et al.* 2006, 271). It is thought that she was originally a goddess of the wild and the wilderness (see Figure 14). The association with the goddess Artemis seems to have occurred at an early date and so major Greek components developed within her cult. It is considered that this connection gave Diana her association with the moon. Her cult was mainly adhered to amongst the plebeian classes, and seems to have been focused on the Italian territories of Latium, Sabine, and Campania.

Her most famous cult site was that at *Nemi*, or *Aricia*, which Frazer exploited for his haunting work *The Golden Bough* (Chapter 1). At that shrine she had a male consort called *Virbius*, the god of the forest, and there was also a priest called the *Rex Nemorensis* (**king of the grove**), a position which was filled by a runaway priest (Shipley, Vanderspoel *et al.* 2006, 271). Another important shrine associated with this goddess was on *Mount Tifata*, near *Capua*. It is considered that her temples were always constructed in peripheral locations.

Mars

Mars is considered to have had Italian origins, but the etymology of his name is uncertain (Shipley, Vanderspoel *et al.* 2006, 558). He is believed to have originated as a spirit of vegetation and, according to Cato (Hooper and Ash 1934, lxxxiii/87, cxli/121–3), was particularly revered by farmers. In one tale there was an offering to Mars Silvanus in the forest; in another, an offering to Mars to protect the harvest of crops and grapes and to ward off pestilence.

In the state religious mechanism Mars was primarily a god of war (Harvey 1984, 260–261), with the wolf as his sacred animal (for typical images see Figures 15 and 16).

He obtained a parental role in the development of Rome, being a child of Jupiter, and the father of *Romulus* and *Remus* (Shipley, Vanderspoel *et al.* 2006, 558). Like other Roman gods he was also given a number of epithets, including *Grādīvus* (**he who marches out**) and *Ulator* (**avenger**), and, became associated with Ares. In the guise of Mars *Ulator* he took his place as one of the ancestors of the Julian-Augustan imperial line and a temple was built in his honour in the new forum complex.

Mars was also worshipped in Rome along with Jupiter and *Quirinus* where they formed a divine triad (Shipley, Vanderspoel *et al.* 2006, 558). Shield-carrying festivals took place in the 19th March at the *Quinquatrus* (when the military season opened). Horse racing festivals were also staged, when a horse was sacrificed in his honour; this took place on the 15th October with the *Salii* procession. There were also chariot races in February and March. At his festival of the *Suovetaurīlia,* an ox, a sheep, and pigs were sacrificed.

Figure 15: A bronze statuette from Earith, Huntingdonshire, of Mars the god in Roman military garb (photograph Institute of Archaeology archive, Oxford)

Figure 16: A bronze statuette depicting Mars nude but helmeted; from Foss Dyke near Lincoln (photograph Institute of Archaeology archive, Oxford)

Venus

Venus probably took her name from an unattested noun (Shipley, Vanderspoel *et al.* 2006, 924), which became anthropomorphised by the fourth century BC (Figure 17). It was about that time that she became associated with Aphrodite. In Rome she was seen as one of the ancestral goddesses of Rome, more specifically of the Julian-Augustan line as Venus *Genetrix* (**the ancestor**). The major redevelopment of the *forum*, which was started under Caesar, included a temple dedicated to her.

Mercury

Mercury was the Roman god of trade (Harvey 1984, 267); his name was derived from the Latin noun *Merx*, **commodity**, and the verb *mercari*, **to buy** (Shipley, Vanderspoel *et al.* 2006, 572). Mercury is thought to be an adaptation of Hermes mediated perhaps with the Etruscan god *Turmus*, whose complex character was altered (Figure 18).

The worship of Mercury has been attested from the 15th May 495 BC when a temple

Figure 17: A bronze figurine of Venus from Colchester, Essex (photograph Institute of Archaeology archive, Oxford))

Figure 18: A bronze figurine of Mercury, from the Thames at London Bridge (photograph Institute of Archaeology archive, Oxford))

was established for a guild of merchants in the city (Shipley, Vanderspoel *et al.* 2006, 572). His cult was only sporadically encountered in the Empire and only became popular in the Gallic and Germanic provinces.

Silvanus

Silvanus was worshipped widely around Italy and the Roman Empire (Shipley, Vanderspoel *et al.* 2006, 824). He was not adopted as a god of state, his cult mainly being taken up by the lower classes, possibly because of his rural origins. The name is derived from the word *silva*, **woodland**, and so he was god of the forest, and the embodiment of trees and shrubs. Literary sources claimed that his origins went back to the beginning of Rome. He rarely turned up in mythological traditions and no genealogical origin is extant. The only surviving story gives an account of the god killing a stag belonging to *Cyparissus*.

Bacchus or Liber Pater

The Greek god Dionysos was known in the Roman world by his alternative name *Bacchus* (*Bakchos*) and was also equated with the Italian fertility god *Liber Pater* (Shipley, Vanderspoel *et al.* 2006, 117). The Italian name of the god is indicative of **freedom** (Wiseman 2008, 84–86), he gave man wine which freed them from their cares, mysteries which freed the soul from morality, and the power to free the seed in sexual union (Figure 19). The word *libertas* means political freedom. His festival, the *Liberalia*, was held on the 17th March (when free speech was upheld); the festival was probably seen as important from the time of the expulsion of *Tarquin*. To the plebians the festival was important because of its association with freedom, but to the ruling families it was seen as anarchic. Thus, in the second century BC, the senate suppressed the cult of *Liber*; the ritual of which was considered to have included stage performance. The association with Dionysos was first encountered from the fifth century BC.

Figure 19: An impression taken from a red Jasper intaglio depicting the god Bacchus or Liber Pater, found in the Roman small town of Cambridge (photograph Robert Wilkins, Institute of Archaeology archive, source Martin Henig)

Janus

The two headed god Janus was the Roman god of the doorway, or transition, his name being derived from *ianus*, **gateway**, and *ianua*, **door** (Shipley, Vanderspoel *et al.* 2006, 471). He is considered to have been an old Italian god and was first known from being portrayed on Roman coinage from the third century BC. In myth he was regarded as an archaic king who received *Saturnus* from Greece.

Conclusions and Saturnus

It is known that the Romans drew parallels between their gods and those of the Greek world. It is also true, however, that there were indigenous Italian gods, many from ethnic Italian groups, for example the Etruscans, and some associated directly with Rome and Latium. There are also indications that traditions around Rome played an important part in the development of wider Italian traditions. *Saturnus* for example was associated with the Greek titan *Kronos* (Harvey 1984, 384; Wiseman 2004, 32–33; Shipley, Vanderspoel *et al.* 2006, 789) and his cult was extremely Hellenised. The name was considered previously to be derived from the Latin word *satus*, **sowing**, but this is now thought unlikely.

Saturnus, the father of Jupiter, was claimed to have fled from his son to found a settlement on the Capitoline Hill in Latium (Wiseman 2004, 32–33). His cult was limited and focused on Rome, where his temple stood on the Capitoline Hill. It contained the *aerarium* of the Roman people as well as the laws passed by the senate. His cult statue was portrayed in shackles and also used traits of *Kronos*. He was reputed to have ruled over a golden age but, like *Kronos*, was reckoned to have devoured his children. His major festival was the *Saturnālia*, celebrated from the 17th to the 19th December. It was associated with the sowing of crops, presents, and the lighting of candles (and is seen as a fore-runner of Christmas). Initially, human sacrifice was associated with this festival; it was brought to an end by Heracles and his Argive followers, who settled on the Palatine Hill. It is possible that, in the traditions associated with *Saturnus* and *Kronos*, there is an allusion to the winter solstice and the death and rebirth of the sun. The association with the winter solstice may also have been because of *Saturnus's* association with sowing and agriculture, which probably occurred in the days after his festival. There are a number of variations of tales concerning him (Harvey 1984, 384) as *Saturnus* was, in certain texts, considered a consort of *Ops* and the father of *Picus* (the **woodpecker**).

It seems that the group of gods formed as a result of the growing influence of certain ethnic groups, leading to political and cultural interaction and, eventually, to harmonisation and the sharing of divinities by the wider group; thus leading to the pantheon that we know today. Though one can argue about the extent of Greek influence one can not deny that it existed. This shows that there was an evolving development of knowledge and ideas, which was constantly being added to and manipulated. Ovid (Miller and Goold 1977) emphasised this fact because he took it upon himself to retell what was known of classical mythology.

PANTHEON: GERMANIC

In the Germanic world the idea of a pantheon also existed, but our evidence for this is from a much later date. Tacitus (Hutton, Ogilvie *et al.* 1970, *Germania*), in the first century AD, mentioned a range of deities but he did not indicate how the different deities related to each other, if at all. The gods recorded in the Icelandic sagas originated from at least two sources as there are two distinct sets of divinities; called the *Aesir* and the *Vanir*. Where each of these groups arose is not known but it was probably within different folk-groups. Through the interaction of these two groups it is likely that new ideas, myths, and tales arose. The Icelandic records are rather late in date, but they have served, correctly or incorrectly, to provide a framework for the Germanic traditions as a whole. Snorri mentioned the *Aesir*, a group which included most of the gods, and the *Vanir*: *Njord*, *Freyr* and *Freyja*. The *Vanir* are known to be quite old, as the name *Njord* is derived from *Nerthus*, as mentioned by Tacitus (Ellis Davidson 1964, 94–95). *Nerthus* was an earth goddess worshipped by a Germanic tribal group. *Njord*, however, does not show many of her attributes. Strangely, it was the offspring of *Njord*, *Freyr* and *Freyja*, who exhibited the attributes which Tacitus attributed to *Nerthus*. Amongst the *Aesir*, Snorri identified twelve main gods (Ellis Davidson 1964, 28–30). Odin, the son of *Bor*, was the chief deity. He had two brothers *Vili* and *Ve*. He was known by a number of names: the one-eyed, the god of the hanged, the god of cargoes, and the father of battle. He also had a number of sons, fathered with various partners. These included Thor, the god of thunder; Balder, the bold and beautiful; and Hoder, the blind god. Others include *Loki*, *Bragi*, *Heimdaill*, *Ull*, and *Hoenir*. There were also a number of goddesses, including: *Frigg*, Odin's wife; *Skadi*, the wife of *Njord*; *Bragi's* wife *Idun*; and *Nanna*, the wife of *Balder*. The pantheon's evolution is apparent in the development of *Nerthus* into *Njord*. Also, behind these traditions are indications of the once mighty sky god, *Tiw*, who is believed to have been usurped in the same way *Kronos* was. What the exact mechanisms for these changing oral traditions were is not known but one can, perhaps, suggest that they were based on cultural interactions between groups in a specific location, followed by the exportation of the ideas. Once taken abroad by wandering mercenaries further interaction, with other groups, would have occurred.

PANTHEON: CELTIC AND BRITTONIC

More analysis has been carried out on the Irish textual material than on the Welsh. The Irish texts are, also, far older and much better preserved. In these tales the divinities form part of hierarchies. Much of the present synthesis on the Irish historic and mythological tales derives from the work of O'Rahilly (1946). More recent analyses have concluded that the tales were compiled from oral and, by definition, older sources; and then amalgamated with contemporary medieval traditions. Therefore, they can not be taken as indications of, or interpretation of, Iron-Age society (Aitchison 1994), and consequently Iron-Age religion, at face value, although there are many clues. This makes it difficult to interpret themes; including those which hint at the existence of a tribal pantheon. Such a pantheon may have come into existence in prehistory, but it may also have been a product of early medieval Ireland when it attempted to draw parallels with other societies, such as the Romans and the Greeks. It is also possible that the pantheon may not represent a pan-Irish tradition but one which originated as the folk tradition of a particular tribe, and which was, subsequently, used by all Irish peoples. If this did occur then deities associated with other groups may have been lost. A diverse group of eclectic deities could have arisen as the political interactions between the ethnic groups in Ireland increased; with the ideas of the unified group of gods being bound up with the traditions of the high kings and the claimed common political origins needed to bring political cohesion to a larger pan-Irish populace.

The ideas from the Greek, Roman, and Germanic worlds, especially the use of a pantheon, have influenced what is perceived to have happened in north-west Europe.

In Irish traditions there are accounts of a group called the *Tuatha de Danann*, the tribe of the god or goddess *Don* (O'Rahilly 1946, 308–317). These gods are encountered in a number of Irish tales, including the migration cycles which accounted for the formation of the Irish population and described how the people came to live there with the gods; chief of whom was the *Dagda*. Other gods known from Irish mythology include the '*tri deo Danonn*': *Brian*, *Iuchar*, and *Iucharba*. They are variously described as the sons of *Tuirill Piccrom*, *Delbaeth*, or *Bres*; and were the three gods who provided weapons for the *Tuatha de Danann*. *Lug*, or *Lugh*, also listed as a member of this group, was probably cognate with the continental *Lugos*, although like Jupiter and Zeus the name and ideas may have derived from a common linguistic base. Another of the gods, *Nuadha*, has been equated with the Welsh *Nudd*, and with the British *Nodens*. The same arguments applied to *Lugos* would also apply to this god. Other divine names of Irish origin include: *Goibnia*, *Dian Cécht*, *Credne*, *Luchta*, *Ogma*, *Mórrígan*, and *Dinann*. Some of these deities can be equated with deities found in continental inscriptions, while others can not. Although we have an account of an Irish pantheon there are a number of things which are unclear about it; including the antiquity of its development and the fact that many of the gods were present at earlier dates elsewhere in Europe. It is also not apparent that this pantheon can be attributed to any other Celtic or Brittonic groups, as some of the attributes are specifically Irish in character. Thus it can not be seen at present as a pan-Celtic pantheon.

In Britain and on the Continent (Gaul, Germany and the Low Countries) over 400 named native deities are known from inscriptions; a number of these are known from more than one tribal area. Even though we know about these deities it has been claimed within Classical traditions that the Celts (and Britons) worshipped natural forces and had no notion of a pantheon like the Greco-Roman one (Rankin 1987, 260). In *c.* 278 BC they were regarded as never having seen deities portrayed in human form. A few of the deities will be mentioned briefly here as they indicate a wider distribution than has hitherto been realised. Some will be more fully discussed in later chapters. These deities include the goddesses *Nehalennia* and, more importantly, *Epona*. How widely these goddesses were worshipped is not known as there are problems with the conflation of images? Other gods that have been named are: *Mars Camulos*, who was recognised and worshipped amongst the *Remi* in Gaul, and was also recognised in the land of the *Trinovantes* at Colchester, *Camulodunum* (Rivet and Smith 1979, 294–295), and at Southwark (Tomlin and Hassall 2003, 364, no.5); and *Cocidius*, worshipped at the east and west ends of Hadrian's Wall (Charlton and Mitcheson 1983, 143–153) in the territories of the *Carvetti*, and the *Selgovae*. Further examples of deities, recognised and worshipped in disparate places, can also be offered. As yet it is not possible to determine how traditions concerning these deities came about. The tribes in northern Europe used a variation of either the common Celtic or the common Germanic language or a mixture. It would have been the case, therefore, that, even if gods developed in separate regions, they were likely, given that they represented similar natural features, to have had similar names. Even if they developed in this way, further conflation would have harmonised still further the names and associated images. This could have happened under the influence of the druids, or possibly under that of the Romans. Alternatively, it could have occurred when one ethnic group held sway over another; for example, the *Biteriges* of modern Bourges and Berry controlled, according to Livy in his *History*, a number of other groups around them under King *Ambigatus* (Foster 1984, v.xxxiv). The importance of Bourges in the fifth century BC is now being identified archaeologically, as a significant and wealthy urban settlement has recently been discovered (Collis 2003, 169–170). Its prominence was such that traditions which emanated from it may have become associated with all or many of the Celtic and Belgic peoples. We know that the Celtic and British tribes had many gods; the problem is how they were used and recognised. Is it possible to recognise a group of gods used in a homogenous fashion? The evidence that there was a common father of the gods recognised by the Celtic or British tribes is in a statement by Caesar (Edwards 1963, vi.18):

> *'The Gauls affirm that they are all descended from a common father, Dis, and say that this is the tradition of the Druids.'*
>
> Reprinted by permission of the publishers and Trustees of the Loeb Classical Library from *I. Caesar: The Gallic War*, Loeb Classical Library Vol. 72, translated by H. J. Edwards, Cambridge, Mass.: Harvard University Press, © 1917, by the President and Fellows of Harvard College. The Loeb Classical Library ® is a registered trademark of the President and Fellows of Harvard College

Dis was regarded as a god of the Underworld, but apart from this statement we know very little about him, and we do not know if this is the name which both the Gauls and the Britons used. It is this statement which suggests that there was a wider cultural understanding amongst the peoples of north-west Europe, but again the associations and significance of the statement are unknown. What we know of *Dis* is extremely obscure and it is possible that much information concerning this god, perhaps even his proper name, have become lost in translation. The name is believed to have been associated with the Old Irish *díth*, **death** or **destruction** (Rankin 1987, 265). *Dis* has also been associated with the gods *Sucellus* (de Vries 1963, 89) and *Cernunnos* (Ross 1967, 212). It is possible; however, that Caesar was referring here to Jupiter as *Diespiter* and that he was casting Gaulish religion in the same light as that of the Romans. There has been a suggestion also that the insular form of *Sucellus* is possibly *Goibniu* or *Govannon*, but this would be hard to sustain at present (Rankin 1987, 265).

As stated above the Irish material is different from the Continental material as it contains later alterations. Because of this it could be worth exploring the Irish goddess *Macha* in more detail to ascertain how some of these deities may have operated in places, totems, and mythological traditions. She is sometimes portrayed as one goddess, while in other contexts is in triple form (Green 1992, 138). These are common British and Continental themes as will be seen throughout this work. *Macha* was associated with the crow as well as the horse, which has led to her being equated with the continental *Epona*. Besides this she was a deity associated with a specific place; her name being a homonym of *Emhain Macha*. Her character has been incorporated into three tales of the Irish mythical cycles. In the first story she was the wife of *Nemedh*, the leader of the third invasion cycle. In the second she ruled Ireland as a warrior and established the site of *Emhain Macha*. In the third she was the divine bride, associated with horses. *Crunnchu*, her husband, boasted that his wife could outrun the king's horses; thus *Macha* was forced to compete, when heavily pregnant. She won the race, gave birth on the finish line, and died, cursing the Ulstermen. Two of these stories, and her cultural associations, show that the tradition of the localised deity of the place, the triple mothers of the folk-group of that place, and hence the derived descent from this group existed in Ireland and was probably not a product of Roman religious traditions. *Emhain* means twins, and the ancient site of *Emhain Macha* is considered, by archaeologists, to be located at Navan Fort (Raftery 1994, 74–79); it has been excavated on two occasions. The second excavation uncovered a structure, considered to be religious in nature, with a diameter of 37m; a cairn 2.8m high was constructed within an earlier wooden building. If this is the religious site of *Emhain Macha*, as archaeologists believe, named after the horse goddess *Macha* and her offspring, then it would be natural to wonder about the connection between the two, and to consider if this was part of a shrine to that goddess. The cairn may well have been a podium for a shrine. It can, perhaps, not be proved but the use of the site for her worship seems the most likely explanation.

A DOBUNNIC PANTHEON

In earlier studies (Yeates 2006a; 2008b) there was an attempt to start formulating a religious structure based on the archaeological and historical accounts of the religion of the *Dobunni*. This identified deities of specific locations, for example the Cotswold Hills in the form of *Cuda*, or the River Severn in the form of *Sabrina*. It was recognised that the rivers and their homonym deities became associated with specific groups of people. Besides this it was also apparent that the *Dobunni* had a number of gods associated with certain social activities. These gods of social action would initially, within each tribal group, have been associated with certain narratives. Amongst the *Dobunni* the hunter-god, lord of the animals, was *Cunomaglos*, lord of the *Nemeton* (Yeates 2008b, 107–116). There are also hints of a war god called *Cocca* (Yeates 2008b, 102–106), and a mining god called *Nodens* (Yeates 2008b, 90–101). How all of these were related to each other and how they were ordered into a pantheon is, at present, not apparent but might, if we are lucky enough to identify them, be concealed in some surviving medieval texts.

The only recognised texts at present are from two passages in the *Mabinogion* concerning the father and mother and *Modron* and *Mabon*. In the tale of *How Culhwch won Olwen* (Jones and Jones 1974, 125) we are informed:

> *"Salmon of Llyn Llyw, I have come to thee if thou knowest aught concerning Mabon the son of Modron, who was taken away at three nights old from his mother?"*
>
> From *The Mabinogion* (1844) by Lady Charlotte Guest, p.300

Here *Modron* is seen as begetting *Mabon*. *Modron* is known to be derived from the divine name *Matrona*, but in the land of the *Dobunni* the name may have been associated with the *Matres* or *Mater*, who are known to have been worshipped amongst that tribe, in single or triple form. In the tale of *Peredur son of Efrawg* (Jones and Jones 1974, 198) the following is mentioned:

> *"Nine sorceresses are here, my soul, of the sorceresses of Gloucester, and their father and their mother are with them;"*
>
> From *The Mabinogion* (1838) by Lady Charlotte Guest, p.323

These passages seem to be all that remain of the stories describing the pantheon which may have underlied the religious traditions of the *Dobunni*; the divine couple of the father (who can be equated with *Mercury*) and the mother (who can be associated with *Mater* or *Modron*) with their child *Mabon* or *Maponus*. *Mabon* may have played different roles in each cultural group, as there is a further *Mabon* referred to as the son of *Mellt* (**lightning**) and *Gware* golden-hair (Jones and Jones 1974, 129). This simple triangle of deities, which is recognisable from the Roman and early medieval sources, is perhaps comparable to the evidence known from Bronze Age Greece, where there is evidence of a divine couple and a son: Zeus, Hera, and *Drimios* the son of Zeus (Burkert 1985, 46).

There are also references to *Nudd* being the father of certain peoples in the Mabinogion but, as yet, they can not be contextualised. Other gods, for example: *Cor(o)s*, *Blatonos*, and *Cunomaglos* are only mentioned briefly (see Chapter 4), while a group of deities was claimed to have resided at Hereford (Jones and Jones 1974, 43–44). There is also no indication as to whether the neighbouring tribal groups recognised the same pantheon, had variations on these groups, or had completely different groups.

CONCLUSIONS

The nature of the pantheon has been discussed for Greece, Rome, and more briefly for Germany and the Western provinces, for a number of reasons. Firstly, to show the longevity of development of Greek and Roman deities and how these evolving characters fitted into a wider web of beliefs. Secondly, to show a cultural group developed, what we consider to be, a pantheon. This was a long drawn-out process of knowledge accumulation. We may not appreciate this but in many respects we are simply picking up the final result in the development of a religious cultural system. The native religions of the north-west provinces did have many gods; as evident in Gaul and Britain through inscriptions, and in later Irish and Welsh traditions. When deities were named in inscriptions it probably meant that they were recognised widely and by more than one tribe. Also, within each tribal area more than one god was probably worshipped. Only three deities can, at present, be placed back into the structured framework of a *Dobunnic* Pantheon: the Father (alias Mercury), *Mater* or *Modron* and *Maponus* or *Mabon*; although we do know the names of other deities. In addition to this it would be useful to consider other aspects of ritual development. During the Roman period these areas probably reworked their traditions into a wider cultural context (the Empire) which included the Roman gods. Archaeologists tend to imply that this action was a process of imposed religious beliefs, but this may not have been the case and Roman traditions may mask Gallic gods, with the stories and metaphors already employed only being reformed organically if the Roman deities offered new and improved elements which could enhance the native deities.

It is not, at present, possible to say how influential and widespread the cult associated with the druids was in pre-Roman society. Part of the reason for this is the fragmentary tribal system and the fact that we can not easily determine if all tribes adhered to the rules, or whether this was Roman political propaganda to make the tribal groups seem more unified. Some aspects of the religion were strongly focused on the tribe, while others were related to social action, such as warfare and hunting.

Chapter 3

Interpretatio

The means by which older religious traditions were maintained alongside newer ones is worthy of consideration; in order to assess the possibility that Roman traditions adapted earlier ones, and to understand how those customs were further altered in the fifth century alleged AD Migration Period, when some peoples of Germanic origin are thought to have settled in Britain and introduced some of their beliefs and traditions. Imposition of tradition often happens without too much difficulty because there are often a number of underlying common factors in a process of acculturation, when two different cultures are fused to produce a new one. How would these traditions have been viewed and adapted, if at all, following the introduction of Christianity? How can we identify the stratification of information available in early medieval Christian texts and how much of this material can be considered to pre-date the texts themselves? The process of one culture assimilating another was given the name 'Interpretatio' by Tacitus (Hutton, Ogilvie *et al.* 1970, *Germania* 43.3–5), and was also used by later historians and archaeologists.

The construction of religious beliefs and traditions was a process of continual change just as certain oral tales were handed down and altered at each iteration. Much work has been conducted on analysing traditions of oral origin, for example those in Homer (Sherratt 1992, 145–165) and on the Irish material (Aitchison 1994). We will return to these traditions and tales later, but it is fair to say that the gods, like the tales, were being transformed and altered by similar processes (Chapter 2).

INTERPRETATIO GRAECA

In discussing the notion of the Greek and Roman pantheons it is evident that the Roman world is usually interpreted as drawing heavily, for its religious and cosmological understanding, from what had originated in Ancient Greece. One can see that there was a process of pairing of deities; some of whom had a logical process of association, while others did not. The Greek gods had a long tradition of worship which can be traced back to the Bronze Age; for example: Hera and Athena. There is also the notion that some of these deities were brought in from surrounding areas; such as Thessaly. This hints at a process of *interpretatio* and an interplay of local deities and divinities which had taken on a larger merged role. It wa mostly deities such as Apollo and, incorrectly, Dionysos who, it has been claimed, had a later origin or were subject to intensive re-development; one could suspect that it was often goddesses who were more resilient to change than gods, though this may be more apparent than real following the identification of Dionysos on the Bronze-Age Linear B texts (see Chapter 2).

The Romans are usually considered to have used the process of *interpretatio Graeca* to an unprecedented level, although this tradition is now being challenged and it is evident that there was a process in Italy, as elsewhere in which native traditions continued alongside newly imported ones (Wiseman 2004). From these a new hybrid religious culture emerged. In respect of the god Apollo, associated as he was with light, healing and the bright sun, the image and name were taken on wholesale; this suggests that the Romans had no comparable god to stand in opposition to him.

INTERPRETATIO ROMANA

From the work of Tacitus, and Roman period inscriptions, it has become apparent that when the Romans entered a territory they employed a process, referred to today as *interpretatio*, to absorb the local religion into the mainstream Roman culture. In a discussion presented by Tacitus, the divine twins worshipped by a Germanic tribe called the *Naharvali* became associated with the Greek twins Castor and Pollux even though, in their native tradition, they were called the *Alci*. The passage reads (Hutton, Ogilvie *et al.* 1970, *Germania* 43.3–5):

> *"It will be sufficient to have named the strongest: these are the Harii, Helvecones, Manimi, Helisii, Naharvali. Among the Naharvali is shown a grove, the seat of a prehistoric ritual: a priest presides in female dress; but according to the Roman interpretation the gods recorded in this fashion are Castor and Pollux: that at least is spirit of the godhead here recognised, whose name is the Alci."*

> Reprinted by permission of the publishers and Trustees of the Loeb Classical Library from *V. Tacitus: Germania*, Loeb Classical Library Vol. 35, translated by M. Hutton, rev. R. M. Ogilvie, Cambridge, Mass.: Harvard University Press, © 1914, rev. 1970, by the President and Fellows of Harvard College. The Loeb Classical Library ® is a registered trademark of the President and Fellows of Harvard College

Here we see the use of the phrase *Interpretatione Romana*. It is evident from this passage, and an earlier one found in the work of Caesar, that this was not just an invention of Tacitus, but a far older tradition, relating to the cultural mix of Rome and Greece, as stated above. All Tacitus provided was a name for the process which was being observed. Caesar (Edwards 1963, VI.17) discussed the deities of Gaul as if they were Roman gods:

> *"Among the gods, they most worship Mercury. There are numerous images of him; they declare him the inventor of all arts, the guide for every road and journey, and they deem him to have the greatest influence for all money-making and traffic. After him they set Apollo, Mars, Jupiter, and Minerva. Of these deities they have almost the same idea as all other nations: Apollo drives away disease, Minerva supplies the first principles of art and crafts, Jupiter holds the empire of heaven, Mars controls war."*

> Reprinted by permission of the publishers and Trustees of the Loeb Classical Library from *I. Caesar: The Gallic War*, Loeb Classical Library Vol. 72, translated by H. J. Edwards, Cambridge, Mass.: Harvard University Press, © 1917, by the President and Fellows of Harvard College. The Loeb Classical Library ® is a registered trademark of the President and Fellows of Harvard College

This confirms that they did not see the deities of other peoples as anything other than versions of their own deities, but that they wholeheartedly equated these new deities with their own gods who had familiar forms and roles.

This process of *Interpretatio Romana* has been discussed, primarily by Jane Webster (1995a, 153–161; 1995b, 175–183). These explored the epigraphic evidence for the pairing of Celtic deities with Roman gods, and also the pairing of Roman and Celtic gods as divine couples. Webster saw *interpretatio* as a post-Conquest discourse which was created in a world of unequal powers, the Roman conqueror and the subjugated. Associated with this argument was the idea that Celtic deities were polyvalent, which means that they embodied a whole series of ideas and actions. This meant that paired god-names, for example *Cocidius Mars* and *Cocidius Silvanus*, could vary from context to context. In the first example the native northern god *Cocidius* was paired with the Roman god Mars, who represented aspects of war or agriculture, and was also the presiding god of Rome. In the second he was associated with *Silvanus* a god of woodland. There are a number of questions concerning who exactly was doing the *interpretatio*; the Roman or the native. Some of the associations may have been made on a poor understanding of the deities concerned. When considering the process of *interpretatio* it became apparent that the naming tradition was part of the process of *interpretatio*; however, the view that *interpretatio* played a part in the pairing of divine couples has to be reconsidered. This discussion will suggest that the divine couples probably already existed, and that in certain cases, for example amongst the *Dobunni*, it was the whole image of the god which was replaced, although not necessarily the underlying meaning (see Chapter 5).

The process of *interpretatio* is evident for the Roman period in the territory of the *Dobunni*, but was probably more complex than has previously been recognised. In a previous work (Yeates 2008b) I noted that during the alleged Anglo-Saxon migration period there was also a process of *Germanic Interpretatio* taking place. This indicates that if communities were stable, as discussed in my *Religion, community, and territory*, any incoming group could bring their new religious beliefs into the equation and fuse them, to a lesser or greater degree, with the pre-existing religion. Alternatively, the incoming culture could be subsumed by the culture of the established group. Such stable communities must have existed, as certain pre-Old English folk-names, for example the *Weogorena* and *Salenses*, survived the migration period.

A number of Tud, or folk-groups, developed in similar ways (Yeates 2006a). These groups produced the same underlying settlement patterns in the Iron Age, through the Roman period, and into the early medieval period. The classic settlement pattern for these folk-groups is evident in central Gloucestershire; two examples, those from the minster territories of Gloucester and Winchcombe, can be mentioned briefly here. Each of these has the same archaeological settlement features which show a development along the river Horsebere Brook (which must originally have been the *Gleva*) and the Hailes Brook (originally the *Salia*). The mechanism for this development was religious belief systems which reflected the physical aspects of the settlements with respect to their named landscape. These ideas need to be explored further and it will become evident that the process was just one of building onto that which already existed in each area.

In the Roman period the names of the pre-existing divinities were caught up in the process of Roman *interpretatio*. Webster pointed out that the power relationships which caused the conflation of native deity with Roman god are not always evident, unless the order of the names used is itself an indication. In the foremost example known from the region it was the Celtic, or Brittonic, name which occurred first, while for the others it was the Latin representative who came first. *Interpretatio* is evident at a number of temple sites in the area; the most recorded example is from Bath, where the goddess *Sulis* was worshipped. She was known by her native name, and was equated with the Roman goddess Minerva. It is possible that Minerva was chosen as an alternative, because she was also a sky goddess or, perhaps more significantly, because, in one of her guises, she was a healing goddess, as *Minerva Medica*. The image of the goddess in the cult statue is of a goddess with a Roman image. This, in itself, is unusual as the general trend for Celtic deities was to portray them in native costume. It is often difficult to see how the native culture related to the incoming Roman traditions. The name implies that the Brittonic character was more important, but the image suggests that she was consumed totally by Roman traditions. The sculpture of the temple also reveals a mixture of Roman and Celtic imagery (Henig 1999, 419–425); this is perhaps best exemplified by the image on the pediment of the temple, the head of a Celtic gorgon surrounded by oak leaves (see Figure 20). The worship of *Sulis Minerva* was associated with a specific natural feature, the three hot springs at Bath, for which no recognised pre-Roman human representation existed. This may, however, be due to a lack of evidence as late Iron-Age bronzes of female deities have been recovered in the *Dobunnic* area, at Aust and Henley Wood.

A second example of *interpretatio* can be found in the *Dobunnic* area in and around the Severn estuary. On the Forest of Dean's south-east escarpment, at Lydney Park, are the remains of an Iron Age hill-fort, in which survive the significant remains of a Roman temple (Wheeler and Wheeler 1932). In the temple, evidence has been found for its dedication to the god *Nodens*, whose native name means **to acquire possession of**, and who has been associated with the Roman god Mars, whose name preceded *Nodens's*. Reinterpretation of the cult of this god's attributes has suggested that this was not a temple primarily associated with a healing cult, but with the mining industry of the Forest of Dean, hence the name. A number of images have been found at the temple, but none have been specifically associated with *Nodens*. As with *Sulis*, however, there was a natural reason why the site was chosen for the temple, in this case, the mineral deposits of the region. By associating *Nodens* with iron mining in the Forest of Dean (Yeates 2008b, 90–101) one can start to gain some idea of the process of *interpretatio* occurring between the natural resources and the deity. Minerals were considered to have been living entities; so it is possible that, as the iron ores were believed to have a living root like a tree as expressed by Ovid (Miller and Goold 1977, *Meta.* v.316, vii.204; Miller 1984, *Meta.* xii.810, xiv.713) and Virgil (Goold 1999, *Aen.* i.66, iii.688), Mars was being venerated, in his original context as an agricultural deity. These beliefs are also, perhaps, indicated by the deposition of Roman coin hoards in the Forest of Dean area which were placed at the ends of exhausted mines or scowles. In the light of research currently in progress the tradition in the Mendips and in South Wales contained the notion that it was good to give something back to replenish the root, in the same way that apple trees are still wassailed with cider. Conversely, Mars may also have been

Figure 20: The pediment of the temple of Sulis Minerva at Bath showing the Gorgon's head in its oak-leaf wreath (photograph by the late M. B. Cookson, Institute of Archæology London).

shown in his guise as a war god as iron was an important component in the production of weaponry.

A further example is the hunter god *Cunomaglos*, who was equated with the Graeco-Roman god Apollo (Wedlake 1982, 135–136). The name of the Roman god was recorded first in this example also. The god *Cunomaglos* can also be found in Welsh folk-traditions where he is known by his native name alone (Jones and Jones 1974, 69); one could say that he had successfully jettisoned his Roman dedication as if it were a simple veneer. In the Welsh texts he is described as a hunter, with hounds, who overtakes and kills a stag on the banks of the river *Cynfael* (the *Cunomaglos*). Two of the only three rivers known with this apparent name are both in the Cotswolds, and it is possible it was here that his cult originated. The Welsh legends indicate that the god *Cynfael* presided over a river, but he was more complex than this. The temple at Nettleton Scrubb, where a dedication to him has been found, had two votive wells, or pits, in front of it. Besides this there was a platform which extended over the Broadwater Brook. In early medieval charters the brook was known as the *Alor broke* in AD 944 (Gover, Mawer *et al.* 1939, 4) but it must surely have been known as the *Cunomaglos* in the Roman period and before. By referring to the Welsh texts it is appropriate to associate the god with the common images of the Cotswold Hunter God, with his three animals; a hare, a dog, and a stag. The god was occasionally portrayed in a naked form but more often is Romanised, with a tunic and a Phrygian cap. The cap is usually seen as a Roman import as there is no evidence that it was part of an indigenous traditional dress. The continuation of the Celtic name in Welsh contexts indicates that the associations attached during the Roman period were shallower than previously thought.

Although *interpretatio* is seen as a Roman process which is particularly apparent from the recording of names in epigraphy, it made itself evident in different ways and places. Other evidence for *interpretatio* may possibly be found at the shrine of Uley. The god of the temple was Mercury; his image occurs on all of the reliefs and his name is also present on some curse tablets (Henig 1993b, 88–101). On one of the curse tablets the name Mars was used instead of Mercury, but the name had been deleted and replaced by Mercury. It is not known if this was confusion of an individual or an endemic confusion of the cult itself; that the native god, whose name is hinted at but not given precisely, may have been associated with more than one Roman god. The native name can only be surmised from the recording of a place-name on one of the curse tablets (Tomlin 1993, 113–130). Further possible occasions where *interpretatio* could have taken place were the days associated with cult festivals. Certain Greco-Roman temples were aligned so that the sun would illuminate the cult statue on a specific cult festival. The feast day of the Roman god Mercury, as recalled in Ovid's *Fasti* (Frazer 1989, v.90, 103–104, 671, 690), was on the 15th May. The month of May was sacred to his mother *Maia*, after whom the month was named. The sun did not shine on the cult statue of this day, which is about 35° to the north of east, but it does shine into the temple on a series of days at the end of April (17° north of east) into the beginning of May (27° north of east). There is a further period where the sunrise would also shine on the face of the cult statue at the end of July and into the beginning of August (see Figure 21). Although the temple was not aligned to the exact day associated with Mercury, but it is possible that Mercury had the nearest festival to the relevant native festival; perhaps the festival was Beltene (1st May), allegedly one of the two Celtic festivals in which the souls of the dead could cross over to the otherworld (Forcey 1998, 87–98), or Lughnasad (1st August). It is, therefore, possible that there was an association between the day on which the native and Roman deities were venerated. This indicates a further reason why divinities may have been associated with each other; that they shared a common time for a festivals and had associated ideas.

One can further surmise that there was a process of *interpretatio* at work with the possible deification of the river Glyme (Yeates 2008b, 54–55); a name derived from a Celtic word meaning *bright* (Gelling 1953, i.7). Around the source of the river much archaeological material has been found in a scatter of debris covering 2ha. One of the artefacts recovered was a head of the Roman god Jupiter, lord of the bright skies. The religious sculpture from this scatter, found around a spring site at the source of a minor Cotswold river, indicates that this was probably a shrine site of a native god. These associations imply that some of these deities had form before the Roman period, even if that form was not a human one. In this case, it is possible to hypothesise that the god

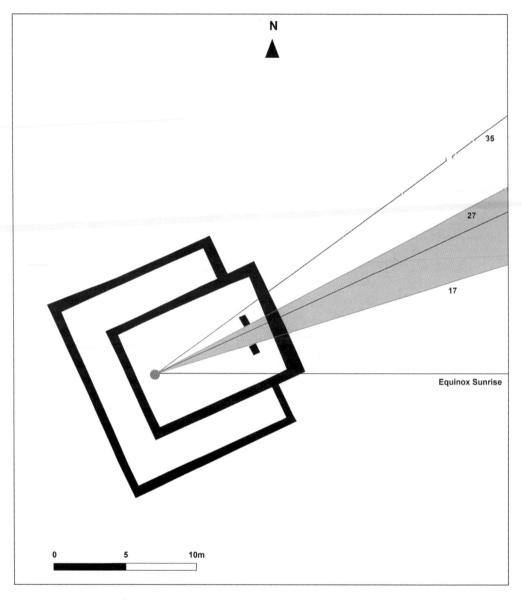

Figure 21: A plan of the temple of West Hill, Uley, Gloucestershire, showing where the line of the sunrise would have been located on the festival of Mercury on the 15th May (drawing S. Yeates).

worshipped at this shrine site was a deity hypothetically called *Jupiter Glimos*, even if this is not yet provable from inscriptions, as suggested by the surviving topographic names and sculpture.

INTERPRETATIO GERMANIA

It has been determined that there was a further process of *interpretatio* in the religious activity of the migration period of the fifth to sixth centuries, and possibly into the seventh century AD (Yeates 2008b, 116, 145). This process was possibly post-migration and apparent when certain Roman period reliefs are contextualised. It was evident that the reliefs of the *Dobunnic* tribal mother were used to provide the name *Hwicce*. The goddess was associated with her cauldron, and also occurred in triple form. Such images could then have been associated with the *Wyrd* or *Norns* of Germanic and Scandinavian origins. This gave rise to the association of the tribe with the **sacred vessel**, and also meant that these people became known as the *wicce* or witches (Chapter 5). The incoming population groups were thus trying to equate the deity, who was widely known in the region, with ideas that had been developed in their own cosmology. In this case it can be seen that, not only was there a process of *interpretatio*, but that it was taking place in the same way in which the Roman process occurred. This is not the only goddess who can be recognised as having had a re-evaluation or re-definition in the migration period or after. There are others, and the fact that these cases exist should impact on our understanding of the nature of the migration, or perceived migration, which saw the establishment of the English state.

From place-name and archaeological evidence it is apparent that the goddess *Cuda* was still recognised as *Codes* and that she still retained her own name, albeit in a masculine form, during the migration period (Yeates 2004, 1–8; 2006a; 2006b, 63–81; 2007, 55–69; 2008b) The tribal goddess, termed *mater* in the Roman period and *Modron* (**the mother**) in the Mabinogion texts (Jones and Jones 1974, 125), also occurred in triple form in the Roman period as the *Matres* (**the mothers**). The recognition of these goddesses in the early medieval period shows that they were being added to in a new cultural mix which was being created in the Cotswold region and South Wales.

After studying the religion of the region it became evident that there had also been a process of Germanic, and even later Christian, *interpretatio* of the god *Cunomaglos* (already discussed for the Roman period and with respect to the Welsh texts). Although, on the one hand, the hunter-god can be recognised as a river-god he also became a symbolic god of social action. The location of a number of his temples can be recognised on the Iron-Age woodland banks of the *nemetons* (**the sacred groves** in which the large topographical regions were deified); thus he became associated with the social action of hunting in the *nemetons*. The names of these woodland banks changed over time, although the names always retained a recognisable central theme, hunting. In Old English the Iron-Age banks in Wychwood became known as the Grim's Dyke; *Grim* being another name for the Germanic god Woden. The Forest of Arden bank runs across a hill called *Grymshill*, and so must also have become associated with Woden (Gelling 2006, 7). It was this god who took part in a mythical hunt of the souls of men. The changing names of the nemetons showed that the god was evolving with the new social order. The last change of name saw some of the dykes in the Forest of Arden referred to as the Hob Ditch Causeway, and of course Hob is a name for the devil; who also hunted down the souls of men. So, with the Forest of Arden *nemeton* there was a process of *Interpretatio Germania* and a later Christian *interpretatio*. This shows us that there was a process of adaptation and re-definition at work, not only in the Roman period but also in the sub-Roman period and later in the medieval period with the adoption of the new faith.

These are probably not the only examples of *Interpretatio Germania*, as a number of place-names in the region are known to derive from the names of Germanic gods, these include: the Oxfordshire Tews (Gelling 1954, ii.288); the Warwickshire hill of Tysoe ; and *Tyesmere* (Sims-Williams 1990, 73) which all conceal a reference to *Tiw*; the village of Withington in Gloucestershire, which refers to the heroic figure *Widia* ; Wendel's Cliff, near Bishop's Cleeve ; and other *Grim* names. On the northern edge of the territory and perhaps just outside there is the place name Wednesbury which contains the name of the god Woden (Watts 2004, 658) Here the Germanic god's name is associated with a hill-fort In the heart of the Forest of Arden. Many of the Germanic divine names across England were listed by Gelling (1987, 99–114), but no consideration was given by her of their potential for understanding *interpretatio*. Sims-Williams (1990, 73–74) noted that the names of Germanic gods occurred primarily on the boundaries of the *Hwicce*, and were peripheral in the Christian realm. Alternatively, it has been noted, in opposition to Sims-Williams's argument, that there was a concentration of such pagan-names in the Tamworth area (the seat of Mercian royal power). This implies that the Anglian elite of Mercia recognised these gods, and had their shrines built close to their royal centre, and that these gods were not worshipped widely beyond this social class. Sims-Williams's ideas underestimated the survival of Celtic-Brittonic names which refer to deities.

In the parish of Tew antiquaries, excavations in 1817 and 1852, claimed the existence of a Roman period temple, now lost (Pearson 1909, 11–13), the dedication of which is unknown. *Tiw* was a sky god, as accounted in the last chapter, who has been associated with Jupiter and Zeus, as their names are all derived from a common source. It is not; however, possible to equate this name with a temple dedicated to Jupiter, and the site at Glyme is perhaps too far away for this association. The Tews lie on a ridge between two streams, both of which seem to have lost their original Celtic names. The hill at Tysoe, meaning the nook of land of *Tiw*, is associated with the cutting of a red horse, the antiquity of which is unknown, onto the hill-side (Petrie 1926; Miller 1965; Sims-Williams 1990, 74). The name *Tyesmere*, refers to the pool of *Tiw*, which was located on a ridge of high ground to the south of King's Norton (Sims-Williams 1990, 73–74).

Of the other two folk-figures or gods mentioned above *Widia* gave his name to a hill near to Withington, Gloucestershire, and also to the village . The site became important in national debates about the Anglo-Saxon migration period because it was the example used by H. P. R. Finberg (1955) to show that the migrating Anglo-Saxons had not wiped out the pre-existing British peoples or driven them into Wales, and that some of their traditions and landscape use had survived. Though Finberg did not prove this categorically he did eventually manage to change the debates in archaeology and history. Withington was the site of an early medieval minster foundation (Finberg 1972, no.5), and there is evidence of earlier buildings in the churchyard and in the neighbouring rectory garden; what these structures were, is not known. As the village is recognised as having taken its name from a Germanic godling this hints strongly that the site may be that of a pagan temple. The fact that the buildings were of stone suggests that they could have been Roman period religious buildings. This, however, would still have to be confirmed by systematic excavation.

It can also be suggested that a process of *Interpretatio Germania* occurred in the case of Wendel's Cliff, on the West face of Cleeve Hill, as it was recorded in the form *Wendel*, on an Anglo-Saxon charter for Bishop's Cleeve . The cliff lies below a bivallate hill-fort, which has been badly damaged on the one side by quarrying, and has never been excavated. The association between hill-forts and shrines, coupled with the cliffs below the fort being associated with a Germanic godling, strongly suggests the potential existence of an earlier shrine. Unfortunately this may have been quarried away. In Sweden an important boat burial was recovered from *Vendel* (Owen-Crocker 1981, 102), and it is evident that the names *Vendel* and *Wendel* are derived from a similar source. The same name *Wændel* was used as a component of place-names such as Wandsworth in Surrey (Gover, Mawer *et al.* 1934, 36) and Wensdon in Bedfordshire (Mawer and Stenton 1926, 114–115), besides *Wændelescumb* in Berkshire, and *Wendlesbiri* in Hertfordshire; the last of these being a hill-fort. The name, allegedly derived from the Old German name *Wandil* or *Wendil*, must equate with the Norse name *Vandill*, regarded as the name of a sea-king and giant. The name has also occurred as a component part of *Orvandill*, from the Old German *Aurivandala*, **the dawn**. In the *Helgakviða Hundingsbana* (*ii.34*) there is a reference to *Vandill's* shrine. All of these names must also be associated with the Germanic *Vandilo*, a mythological person from whom the Vandals derived their name. In mythology *Orvandrill* the giant was caught in a net, with one toe poking outside; this toe then got frost bite, was broken off, and became the morning star (Branston 1957, 124–126). The association of the name with the dawn or morning star is significant in the Gloucestershire example of the name as Cleeve Hill lies on the east side of the Vale of Gloucester, and for any settlement in the valley, would have been in the direction in which one would see the dawn and the morning star. There may be, therefore, a geographic determinism underlying the tale and, it is possible that the Germanic Giant possibly replaced an earlier figure associated with the tradition.

The name *Grim,* it was noted, was significant on the long boundaries in the wooded landscapes forming the *nemetons* and may have derived from an association with the mythical hunt. There are at least two cases where the name *Grim* may have been used to represent a pre-English divinity. The Romano-Celtic temple which existed at Coleshill (Magilton 2006, 1–231) is known to have been located on a hill, later called Grimstock, that was initially known as *Grimscot* (Gelling 2006, 5–7). It is of interest because it shows that an alternative name for the god Woden was associated with a temple location. The name was, therefore, being used in a more specific way than one would imagine. This place-name is important as it also shows that the word *cote*, **cottage**, was associated with Roman buildings, hence the name is **Grim's cottage**. The same association may perhaps be made at the Worcestershire village of Grimley. Here the remains of a Roman enclosure show up as a cropmark. It has three ditches and has previously been interpreted as a fortlet (1956, 130). Excavations have confirmed that it is Roman (Hurst, Pearson *et al.* 1995; Cook 1996, 351) in date; the place-name, however, may suggest that this was the location of a temple enclosure near the confluence of the Grimley Brook and the river Severn. The name of the village is derived from *Grim*; associated with a spectre or goblin in early interpretations . In AD 841 the name was *Grimanlea(ge)*, the clearing of Grim, while in AD 969 it was *Grimsetne gemære*, the boundary of the **dwellers of Grim**. The later name is important as it implies that the temple was associated with a localised folk group and the focus for veneration may have been the Grimley Brook. The name *Grymeshyll* occurred in AD 816 at Hallow, to the south of Grimley, and this location may also be significant. No previous religious significance has been attached to Grimley, not even the recognition that it was a pagan shrine, but it is feasible that *Grim*, in these cases, was being associated directly with Mercury, the Roman god with which he is normally associated. There may also have been a connection with the major barrow cemetery which lay to the west of Grimley village.

What these traditions tend to indicate is that, even in the alleged Anglo-Saxon migration period, a process of amalgamation of the old and new ideas was taking place. It is possible to suggest, however, that these traditions and gods may have been used in specific ways; for example, masking the tales or the environmental observations of the previous culture.

INTERPRETATIO CHRISTIANIA

The process of Christian *interpretatio* is extremely complex and seems to have occured on many different levels and in many different ways. First, we can see that deities were transformed into either saints, where they carried on with their divine or miraculous attributes, or were transformed into mythical beings, quite often giants. Second, we have the references that pagan sites were to be Christianised. How this was done, and how we see beyond the basic material evidence is always difficult. Third, natural divinities were transformed into ancestral beings who were placed at the beginning of a genealogy. Fourth, characters were inserted into the romantic myth making of the middle ages: The Mabinogion, Nennius, or Geoffrey of Monmouth's *The History of the Kings of Britain*, to name but a few examples. Finally, and perhaps more significantly, we can see the appropriation of ideas from the earlier religion. These stories mention numerous characters which fitted into specific roles, in a growing process of national tale telling that recreated the old stories but cast them in a new light with the changing ideology. We could also see this with the transformation of Greek traditions where pseudo-scientific observation was constantly making philosophers rewrite their world view and primal myth. Such processes were encountered earlier in the discussion of the development of pantheons.

The initial development of Christianity in the west of England was assessed archaeologically by Thomas in *Christianity in Roman Britain* (1981), but the surviving data is usually only in the form of small objects. Further work has been carried out on the small finds (Mawer 1995), while a wider synthesis was produced by Petts (2003). There are a number of interesting Christian indicators in the *Dobunnic* territory; chi-rho inscriptions from Chedworth Villa (Goodburn 1979, 27–28), a further chi-rho on a lead tank at Wiggington Roman Villa; another on a lead baptismal tank from Bourton-on-the-Water (Donovan 1933, 377–381; 1934a, 99–128; 1934b, 260–265; 1935, 240; Austin 1934, 2–3), and a late Roman Christian ring with a chi-rho symbol recovered from the Andoversford area (Yeates 2008b, 148). Some of the objects claimed to represent the presence of Christianity are ambiguous; for example, an inscription from Bath which complains about the wreckers of the temple (RIB(I) 1995, no.152). The wreckers are often thought to have been Christians but that was not necessarily so. Another example is the remains of a tombstone from Sea Mills with a reference to SPES, *hope* which has been claimed as Christian (Bennett 1985, 61–62). The existence of Christian churches has been claimed, by excavators, on the shrines at Uley (Woodward and Leach 1993, 66–79) and on the Roman villa at Bradford-on-Avon, where a presumably fifth century AD font was found built over a fourth century AD mosaic. Even though these sites may show that Christianity was present in the *Dobunnic* territory some objects provide contradictory evidence. The inscription from Bath records the restoration of the temple; the lead tanks at Bourton-on-the-Water were broken, probably so that they could not be reused in baptism (Doig 2008, 18–19). Such an act was likely a Christian one (which is still carried out) to guard against misuse. The stone at Chedworth on which the chi-rho symbol was carved is considered to have been removed from the *nymphaeum*; although we don't know where these stones were recovered from at the time of their excavation. They do, however, indicate some degree of Christianisation. This shows that religious views were in flux and that Christianity was not yet dominant. An inscription, perhaps from the reign of Julian in *c.* AD 363, from the base of a column from Cirencester, proclaims the reintroduction of the old religion, with a dedication to Jupiter, best and greatest (RIB(I) 1995, no.103). In the Cirencester and Gloucester areas it was probable that the two religions continued alongside each other.

These small objects are not the only indicators of problems with the creation and survival of a Christian tradition; in the area further evidence has been identified at Lydney Temple which has long been noted as an important place for which the evidence was used to indicate a Pagan revival in Britain (Wheeler and Wheeler 1932; Watts 1991; 1998; Frend 1992, 121–131). The terminology here is perhaps misleading and it is perhaps best to regard the two religious traditions of the Roman-native acculturated cults and Christianity as being adhered to alongside each other. Even though the dating of the sequences has been altered (Casey and Hoffman 1999, 81–143), it is still apparent that religious activity continued at the site until quite late, as evidenced by the deposition of a late Roman coin hoard. Views on what happened to these temples, in the Anglo-Saxon migration period in general, are changing; instead of assuming that they were dismantled deliberately they are now seen generally as having gone through a period of decline and decay in much the same way as the villas (Rahtz and Watts 1976, 183–210). The cella at the temple of Henley Wood possibly continued in use after the ambulatory had come down .

It is impossible to know how many Christians there were in the area, but it is probably the case that Christianity was not the dominant religion for some time, despite imperial decrees. That the kingdom, which from AD 603 was called the *Hwicce*, had local Christian elements can also be implied from the writings of Bede (Colgrave and Mynors 1969, EH.ii.2). It is apparent that the earliest Christianity in the region was introduced from the *Silures*, or *Glywysinga*, of South Wales. In South Wales it is apparent that Christian sites were being established at places like Caerwent in the fifth century AD and there seems to have been a series of typical designs for churches, dependent on their hierarchical position. The parishes probably had a major ecclesiastical church and also a major church established at a royal or lordly centre in the area (Gray 1998, 14–24). This type of arrangement is evident in the legendary traditions of *Tatheus*, who established his church at Caerwent, and the king, who established his church at Portskewett (Knight 1971, 29–36;

1993, 1–17). The same apparent arrangement is evident with the churches of Bassaleg and Newport, who had territories which overlapped; both are suspected as having been in existence in the fifth century. At the monastic site of Llangors, *Saint Paulinus* may have founded a monastery at a slightly earlier date (Wade-Evans 1920, 170), though at present this is only conjecture. The analysis of these archaeological sites indicates what form of Christian *interpretatio* was taking place in the *Hwicce* even if it does not explain the intricate relations between the Christian saints and the pre-Christian divinities.

The evidence, which has survived, indicates that the process of Christianisation in the *Hwicce*, and in the territory of the *Magonsæta* (possibly *Western Hecana*), began in the sixth century AD; the earliest known establishment of a permanent church in the region is that at Hereford in AD 540. This site was later chosen for the cathedral church of the *Magonsæta*. Certain medieval documents imply, but do not prove, that a church may have been founded at Gloucester at more or less the same time, in AD 536. The claimed site was near the Southgate; the gate which lay nearest to the site of the Roman basilica, a key location in Roman times for the establishment of early churches. A middle Anglo-Saxon minster was later founded at Gloucester (Finberg 1972, no.1), which may have replaced an earlier church. It was only with this foundation that the church was sited alongside the imperial temple or, more likely, within it. The joint minster of Saint Mary de Lode was also founded on the site of what is considered to have been a Roman temple.

The dates of the establishment of churches at sites such as Glastonbury are often controversial; nevertheless, it is possible that a church was founded there in *c.* AD 600. This date can be supported archaeologically by the recovery of a small cast copper-alloy censer, dated to the late sixth to seventh centuries AD, in 1986 (Bradbury and Croft 1989, 157–185; Rahtz 1991, 33). Legendary traditions claim that Malmesbury also had an early foundation, by an Irish monk (Moffatt 1805, 21). Here again the church was established in a large enclosure, in this case an Iron Age one. At Marden, in Herefordshire, a Celtic bell was found (Mahon 1848, 264; Westwood 1849, 169; Fisher 1926, 330); an object used by the early medieval British Church. The parish at Marden seems to have the classic arrangement of a church founded on a Roman site, and there was also probably a royal centre and church founded at Sutton (see Figure 22). This has the same type of arrangement evident in the parishes of Gwent and implies an earlier foundation than that which can be determined satisfactorily from the archaeological evidence. In Worcestershire, the estate of Hanbury was given to an Irish monk in AD 657 x 674 (Finberg 1972, no.195); this predated the foundation of the see of Worcester, in AD 679. Even though it is possible to recognise that these churches were probably of an early foundation not enough is known of many of them to determine how they related to Roman period shrines, if at all.

A number of place-names contain a word meaning church and, like many place-names, these can be considered to have been developed in a stratified manner. This word is the Latin *eclēsia*, which produced the Welsh *eglwys*, or the old-Irish *egliss*, all meaning church. Eccleswall lies on the ancient Ross parish boundary and may mean **the well on the boundary of the Welsh church's community**. However, this church has a complicated arrangement with that of Linton. The apparent significance of the church at Ross, which was an early ecclesiastical holding, and the church at Linton, which was a known royal centre, follows the hierarchical pattern found in Gwent and tends to

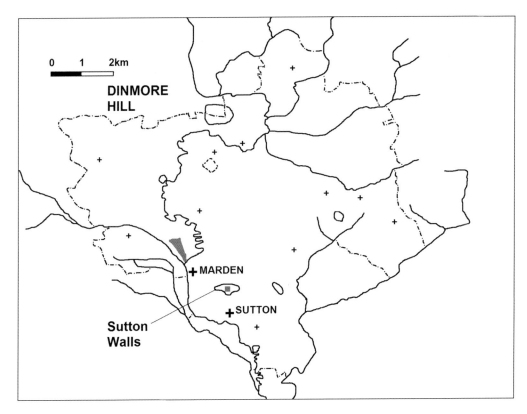

Figure 22: A map of the parochia of Marden-cum-Sutton with the major archaeological features marked (drawing S. Yeates).

indicate that these were British establishments (Knight 1971, 29–36; Knight 1993, 1–17; Gray 1998, 14–24). Exhall was a chapel of Salford Priors, interpreted as **Welsh church on a nook of land**; it lies close to the parish boundary and may simply mean **the hill or nook of land on the boundary of the Welsh church's estate**. A similarly derived name was located on the periphery of the *parochia* of Coventry. If these interpretations are correct then the mother churches of Ross, Salford Priors, and Coventry must also have been founded at an early date. The Eccles Brook lay on the edge of the *parochia* boundary of Worcester Cathedral (Grundy 1928, 103) and it is possibly an indication that a church was in existence prior to AD 679 at Worcester. This may also be the case with Eggleton in Herefordshire which was an estate held by the ecclesiastical centre at Bishop's Frome, the location of another significant mother church.

The foundations of other minsters are not considered to have occurred until the beginning of the eighth century AD, among them Daylesford and Evesham (Finberg 1972, no.13). At Evesham there is a tradition of a vision of three women of whom one was the Virgin Mary (Macray 1863, 8–9, 18). The foundations of such churches started in AD 540 and continued to *c.* AD 730 or later.

When considering the various processes of *interpretatio*, the first concept, the transformation into mythical or mythical historical characters, can be considered as falling into two groups: those which were wholeheartedly embraced by Christianity, and those which were vilified and cast in the role of malign supernatural beings. Of those embraced by Christianity widely the prime example is Saint Bridget or Saint Bride (O'Duinn 2005), formerly *Brigantia*. She was transformed from goddess to saint and continued to reside over the pastoral festival of *Imbolc* (2nd February). It is known from the cartulary of Evesham Abbey that the three mothers were conflated with the Virgin Mary (Smith and Wright 1847, 251). The transformation of pre-Christian deities into Christian saints is also attested in Gaul. Those that became vilified were often conflated with the devil, giants, and wee people. Mention has been made of the development of the hunter-god *Cunomaglos* into Hob or the devil (Yeates 2008b, 107–116) (see above). The gods of Ireland were transformed, in a similar way, into spirits or folk-beings; *Lugh*, for example, became the Lepraucorn. In South Wales many ancient sites are associated with giants; Roman legionary earthworks have been associated with a mythical giant called *Llyon* (Bradney 1923, 185–186), whose origin must be associated with the *genius* of the local Legionary base. Transformations such as these have probably happened on many more occasions than we are aware of. The paucity of such traditions in England is probably due primarily to the survival of the information at hand and to the peculiar way in which the story of the English was redefined and perverted in order to deny the survival of older traditions.

An important part of the process of *interpretatio* was the appropriation of pagan sites and their reuse in a Christian context. We do know that a large number of temple sites were used for the foundation of major churches (Yeates 2008b, 147–156). This reuse was hinted at in Bishop *Milletus's* letter supporting the Christianisation of pagan shrines (Colgrave and Mynors 1969, HE.i.30, ii.13), and also in a reference to *Redwald*, who had a *fanum* or shrine with a Christian altar set alongside that of a pagan god. The king must have been hedging his bets with regards to the afterlife. These activities are accounted in the Anglo-Saxon Chronicles. In Ireland similar traditions, such as when Patrick insisted that the pagan festivals be Christianised (Bieler 1979, I.15 (14)–I.19 (18)), are recorded. The king of Tara was celebrating a pagan festival which saw the extinction of all fires across Meath. This seems to have been a similar event to that practiced in Rome, where the fire of Vesta was extinguished annually on a special day and relit. The new fire was then redistributed around the population. In the Irish case the tradition coincided with Easter, hence the combination of Christian and pagan festivals. The process of Christian *interpretatio* is highlighted by the placing of Christmas on the festival of the birth of *Sol Invictus*, a Middle East cult of the unconquerable sun (Henig 1984, 214). For the *Dobunni* territory there is increasing evidence that a number of churches were founded on the sites of Roman period temples. At one time it was considered that the *Dobunni* may have been exceptional in this respect but it is now becoming apparent that it was a far wider phenomenon and has also been recognised to have occurred in south-east England (Henig 2008, 189–204). *Dobunnic* examples include the Uley Shrines where excavators claimed that, in a late phase probably in the early medieval period, a chapel was built on the remains of the Roman temple (Woodward and Leach 1993, 65–79), mentionoed above. Most of the evidence for this process comes from the major minster church sites. The minster complex at Bath was founded over two temples; the major church of Saint Peter over the tholos of the tribal gods, and the church of Saint Mary de Stalls over the temple of *Sulis Minerva* (Yeates 2008b, 136–146). At Gloucester the major minster was constructed alongside, but initially perhaps over, the probable Imperial temple (Yeates 2008b, 149), while the church of Saint Mary de Lode was probably constructed on a Roman temple site in an island in the river Severn (Bryant and Heighway 2003, 97–178). The church site at Bisley has produced the remains of two Roman altars, found in 1861. The cathedral site at Hereford has produced evidence of a Roman period enclosure under the church (Yeates 2008b, 149, 154). Geophysical survey work at Leominster has produced evidence of a large circular building, described variously as a temple or late Anglo-Saxon rotunda church (Barker and Ranity 2003). This list will probably be expanded as new archaeological data adds to our knowledge.

It is apparent, from earlier studies, that communities had a complex social system and that many ancient sites were continually reused. The fact that hill-forts, standing posts or trees, and *nemetons* also had a religious component, and not just the Romano-Celtic temples, means that there was a diverse range of sites on which the developing Christian religion had to focus and reuse for the establishment of the minsters or mother churches. The key feature of these sites was their boundary wall which became used as a *monastic vallum*. This feature can be identified around temples and hill-forts. That temples were a particular target for conversion into Christian sites is implied from the discussions on Hereford, Gloucester, and Evesham but it can be elaborated. A number of mother churches are known to have been established on religious sites in the area. These sites can be categorised into five groups: large late Bronze-Age settlements, large Iron-Age settlements, large Roman settlements, Iron-Age hill-forts, and Roman period temple sites. In many cases it is known that the large settlements, either of Bronze Age, Iron Age, or Roman date, probably had central enclosures which acted as a religious site. It is also known that Iron-Age hill-forts were associated with temples or shrines (Woodward 1992, 17–26).

The third factor which we can recognise is that there was an appropriation of deities into genealogies. That river and tribal deities were being written into genealogies is evident in at least two examples from outside the area. The Welsh example implies that the tribal deity of the *Demetae* was being incorporated into the genealogical lists as the founder of the royal line. Dumville (1977, 72–104) noted that the royal line of Dyfed claimed descent from *Dimet*; presumably, an eponymous ancestral divinity, whose name was derived from the personification of the *Demetae*. The recording of the name DEMETI on an early medieval stone at Saint Dogmael's, in the form HOGTIVIS FILI DEMETI, shows a tribal name being used as a personal name; again, the reference is probably not so much to a person but to the presiding deity of the people. A further recognisable deity who turns up in Welsh genealogies is *Glywys* or *Gloiu*, who will be discussed more fully later.

Early medieval royal lines in England also claimed descent from gods. The Mercian royal family claimed descent from Woden, *Icel, Cnebba, Cynewald, Crida, Pypba,* and *Penda* (Brooks 1989 159–170, 162–164). Woden has been primarily interpreted as a god, but there are other claims that he was an actual chieftain of a Swedish folk-group (Oppenheimer 2006, 385–391). The primary source for this is in the work of

Saxo Gramaticus, The History of the Danes (Ellis Davidson and Fisher 1996, 25), where there is a reference to a man called Odin who was believed wrongly to be a god. The Mercian royal family was called the *Icelingas*. *Icel* is thought to have been a historical figure but this has not been proven categorically. In the territory of the *Dobunni* and *Hwicce* it was apparent that the smaller folk-groups derived their name from natural features, primarily rivers (Yeates 2008b, 59–89). Hence there were the *Glevenses* or the *Salenses* besides many others. In an assessment of early tribal names across the kingdom of Middlesex it became apparent that some of the folk-group names (Bailey 1989, 108–122), for example the *Beningas*, were derived from natural features; in this case, the etymology is **people of the river Beane**. This hints at similar traditions in the east and west of Britain. The place-name *Gumeninga hearh*, modern Harrow, means the **pagan sanctuary of *Guma's* people**. The interpretation may be slightly misleading as *Guma* may have been the local deity. It is apparent, therefore, that the genealogies that developed in the Later Roman period and in the post-Roman world incorporated the names of deities of rivers and gods of tribes amongst their founders.

The fourth group mentioned above is the insertion or retention of deities in mythical tales; the Arthurian traditions are littered with the remains of historical figures placed alongside once great deities. The mother and the father, *Mabon*, and *Cunomaglos*, all in the Mabinogion, have all been mentioned before. Here I am going to consider the work of Geoffrey of Monmouth, *The Historia Regum Britannie* (Wright 1985) or *The History of the Kings of Britain* (Thorpe 1966), as the work is littered with characters and ideas which are not simply a product of medieval pseudo-history, but use longstanding ideas of spirit of place and the names of divinities out of context. Some of the problems that arise in the study of these texts involve the poor understanding, by those who study the texts, of how pre-Christian traditions functioned in the Roman world and how a large component of this tradition was associated with territory, natural features, and the personification of political units. Some of the historical traits which are found in the work of Geoffrey of Monmouth can be found in the works of people like Tacitus, for example a tribal group taking their name from a god (Hutton, Ogilvie *et al.* 1970, *Germania* 2) hence giving the genealogies cited previously. Thus, Geoffrey of Monmouth may not have considered himself as the originator of his tale, which he may have developed from *Saint Teliau* (Nennius?), a seventh century bishop of Saint Asaph (Coxe 1801, 2.296), but as the interpreter of a number of older traditions.

The first character we have to consider in his works is *Brutus*; we are told specifically that the Island, Britain, had been set aside for him and his followers and that the Island took its name from him (Thorpe 1966, 53). One could consider that this is a creation of the medieval period, but we also know that there are a number of dedications to a female personification of the province of *Britannia*; there is a dedication to the *Matres Brit(annae)* from Winchester (RIB(I) 1995, no.88), and a further dedication to the *Matres Brittiae* on an altar from Xanten (CIL 1908, nos.8631, 8632). The latter inscription is interesting as it is in a truncated form which is more akin to the reference to *Brutus*. If we compare these inscriptions to those referring to German provinces we find that these territories were also personified as a *mater* (RIB(I) 1995, no.88), and that they were also portrayed in the male form of a *genius* (Espérandieu 1922, no.5993). It is feasible, but not categorically provable, that *Brutus* was either a masculinised form of the *Matres*

Brittiae or was derived from a male *genius* which also personified the British province. An element of the idea which underlies this is old even though the newer context into which it was worked may not have been. The stories which precede this could have been taken from the Aenid of Virgil, and also from Caesar's *Gallic War*. The concept which underlies, this of presiding spirits and physical and personal personification of the land, is still associated with: *Locrinus, Kamber,* and *Albanactus* (Thorpe 1966, 56), but here we can presume a medieval invention or reworking and quite clearly something that Geoffrey, or a near contemporary, invented, as it proclaimed the medieval political order of Britain at the time of writing.

Geoffey's next character, which may not have been of his making, was *Corineus, Brutus's* deputy. We are informed that he gave his name to Cornwall (Thorpe 1966, 53). The association with this county may also be a product of the medieval mind, but the name *Corineus* may have originated in Roman Britain or earlier as the presiding spirit of *Corinium,* or Cirencester, and the river Churn. There is a dedication to a sacred *genius* at Cirencester (RIB(I) 1995, no.129) who wore a spiky mural crown (see Figure 23) and can presumably be identified as the presiding spirit of the Roman town (Yeates 2008b, 62, 74–75) . Geoffrey also alluded to the fact that London was previously known by the name *Trinovantum* before it was fortified and called *Kaerlud* (Thorpe 1966, 54–55). This may be an allusion to the site of London being the *civitas capitol* of the *Trinovantes,* and explain why a basilica was constructed at London (Marsden 1987). Previously, the *civitas* capitol of the tribe had been located by academics at Chelmsford, but London is the most plausible city to have had this status.

The third character, which we may have an allusion to, is a lost deity called *Humber,* who drowned in the mouth of the river which later bore his name (Thorpe 1966, 57). The motif of long rivers being born at a spring site and travelling across the landscape before dying in the entrance to the river is common. This process will be mentioned later with respect to the Boyne and the Shannon in Ireland, besides other European rivers, where this type of story was attested at far earlier dates (Chapter 4). This suggests that *Humber* may well have been a Celtic river-name. A further river-deity survives in the form of *Habren,* who drowned in the mouth of the river Severn. In the recording of this name Geoffrey shows his Welsh origins. The river, it was claimed, was named after her (Thorpe 1966, 58). Here again we have the apparent tradition of the deity of the river drowning in the estuary.

The fifth character which we can also recognise as being derived again from an earlier tradition, is *Ebraucus*; the son of *Mempricius* (Thorpe 1966, 59–60). He founded the city of *Kaerebrauc,* the city of *Ebraucus,* on the north bank of the Humber at York. The same character appears in the Mabinogion as *Efrawg,* the father of *Peredur* (Jones and Jones 1974, 183). Geoffrey of Monmouth mentioned that the city was on the Humber; hence it must be the old Celtic name of the Ouse, on which the city of York stands. An inscription from York mentions the *Genius Eboraci* (RIB(I) 1995, no.657). The name is known as a Welsh river-name (Owen and Morgan 2007, 137) besides being that of a deity (see Chapter 4).

Evidence that Geoffrey was aware of certain aspects of the religion of Roman Britain which have subsequently been lost can be seen in his mention of *Bladud* who founded the city of *Kaerbadum* and in reference to the goddess Minerva who was chosen as the

Figure 23: A relief of the sacred genius, from the Ashcroft area of Cirencester, wearing a mural crown. He is presumably Corinius the representation of the Roman town (photograph by the late M. B. Cookson, Institute of Archaeology, London, held at the Institute of Archaeology, Oxford).

tutelary deity of the baths (Thorpe 1966, 61–62, 70). At present we can not contextualise *Bladud* properly but it has been claimed that he encouraged necromancy throughout Britain. There is also an allusion to the temples of Apollo and Concord in the town of *Trinovantum*, which seems to be a reference to London. Currently we have no evidence concerning the existence of these temples but it is possible that archaeological evidence may be found in the future. There are certain notable errors in Geoffrey's work; *Leir* is said to have founded Leicester but the name *Kaerleir* is a purely British name (Thorpe 1966, 62, 67), the name of Leicester in the Roman period was *Ratis* (Rivet and Smith 1979, 443–444); unless *Ratis* was only a part of Leicester's original name.

The next two characters, which can be seen as allusions to British deities, are *Belinus* and *Brennus* (Thorpe 1966, 70–81). The god *Apollo Belenus* is known from Gaul, north Italy, and *Noricum* (Green 1992, 30–31); his cult being mentioned by the classical authors Ausonius (Evelyn-White 1919; Evelyn-White 1921, *Apologeticus* 24.7) and Herodian (Whittaker 1970, viii.3.8) as *Beles*, interpreted as *Belinus*. The other name refers to *Bran*, a raven god (Green 1992, 48–49), whose tale is told as one of the stories in the Mabinogion (Jones and Jones 1974, 25–40) (Chapter 4). There is a passage concerning local knowledge of the Gwent area associating *Belinus* with the city of the Legions (Thorpe 1966, 80). One of the names applied to Lodge Hill Camp is *Belinstock* and the giant *Belinus* was associated with the camp in local tradition (Bradney 1923, 222). Geoffrey is wrong that Caerleon was the capitol of the *Demetae* tribe. *Gorbonianus* (Thorpe 1966, 83) may also have been an allusion to a local deity of the Gwent area and may have been associated with the name Abergavenny.

In the third Chapter of Geoffrey's work we come across a reference to Claudius building a city called *Kaerglou*, or Gloucester (Thorpe 1966, 102), which lay on the banks of the Severn between *Loegria* and Wales. The character who is known alternatively as *Gloius*, *Gloiu*, or *Glywys* turns up in a masculine form in three different medieval texts, of which Geoffrey of Monmouth's account was the last one. It was claimed by Geoffrey that the city took its name from Duke *Gloius*, the son of Claudius, who was granted the duchy of the Welsh. Though one could argue that this reference arose because of the situation in the medieval period; reflecting the control of the dukes of Gloucester in South Wales. It is also feasible that there are older underlying themes in this tale. *Gloius* is recognised to have been a character in the work of Nennius (Morris 1980, 33). Nennius informed us that the rulers of Builth claimed decent from a *Gloiu*, who was responsible for building the city of *Gloiu* (Gloucester) on the river Severn:

> '*son of Vitalinus, son of Gloiu. Bonus, Paul, Mauron and Vitalinus were four brothers, sons of Gloiu, who built the great city on the banks of the river Severn that is called in British Caer Gloiu, in English Gloucester.*'
>
> From *Nennius: British History and The Welsh Annals*, translated by John Morris, © Phillimore, reprinted with kind permission

The ancestral figure of the Silures, or the later *Glywysinga*, was *Glywys* (Savory 1984, 317). As *Glywys* is a recognised philological development from *Glevenses* (folk-name of the people of Gloucester) then it is also possible that there was a connection with this character as well; indeed, aspects of this tradition have been mentioned previously. This is a clear allusion to the personification of the Roman *colonia*, a *tyche* who was transformed into a male figure. We thus have a city with a female founding spirit, being apparently turned into a male one in the Welsh genealogies. However, this ancestral figure was associated specifically with the city on the banks of the river Severn. Gloucester was in a province called *Britannia Prima*. It has been suggested that this province was ruled from Gloucester; hence it would probably have been the seat of a military commander called a *Dux*. That *Glywys* and *Gloiu* (formerly masculine *Glevus* or more likely feminine *Gleva*) appears in the Welsh genealogical lists gives more weight to its position as capitol of this province. In scratching the surface of such medieval texts it becomes apparent that some, if not all, of the ideas in *The History of the Kings of Britain* came from older sources which Geoffrey was reworking.

The characters mentioned here are primarily from the first two Chapters of the work attributed to Geoffrey of Monmouth. Most scholars these days are extremely sceptical of the work; however, it is possible to argue that the text, or certain aspects of it, is more relevant than had previously been though. Geoffrey was not simply creating a fable from his own mind but drawing upon certain surviving fragments of Britain's mythical past. From this we start contextualising some of the characters. There were certain earlier principles which the author was following; the names of kings were associated with the lands over which they ruled in the same way that local *genii* or *matres* presided over Roman provinces. There is also the idea that cities were founded by people who gave their names to the towns, when it is evident to us that these towns were presided over by a spirit of place whose name was often shared with that of a river. There is also the tradition of the name of a river being adopted from that of the person claimed to drown in the estuary of the river. These notions and ideas derived from certain ideas which existed in the Roman period; subsequently the void of prehistory was filled with the names of deities. It is probable that many more of the characters recorded in the first two Chapters of *The History of the Kings of Britain* could be due to such a process; at the moment, however, we do not possess the knowledge to place them in their proper context.

Finally we can recognise the adoption of pre-Christian religious ideas and their incorporation into the romantic medieval tales of the Arthurian tradition. One major component of the Christian process of *interpretatio* which has not been explored is that of the Arthurian myths or the legends of the Grail Quest. It has been recognised for some time through the more popularist, but still academic, works by Loomis (1963) that there is a distinctive pre-Christian or pagan backdrop to these legendary stories and that a Christian veneer has been placed over the top of them. In essence it has been argued that the Christian grail of Joseph of Arimathea originated as a Celtic cauldron or **sacred vessel**. How all this will look when fully developed has not been appreciated, but a good analysis of the major cults which can be recognised in the religious traditions of the *Dobunni* (Yeates 2008b, 137–146) can help.

CONCLUSION

These cases indicate that there was a process at work in which certain aspects of older religions survived; this process occurs due to *interpretatio*. It is first noted for the Roman period when the incoming tradition established in the Roman Empire gave native cults an imperial reworking. There is also evidence that similar traditions developed during the alleged Anglo-Saxon migration period. The process of *interpretatio* continued and enabled the older landscape traditions to be incorporated into the tales of the medieval church where they resurfaced as folk-traditions and folk-characters. There was, therefore, a constant process reconfiguration and reinvention of the mythological past at work. In parts of this process major components of the past could be dropped or considerably re-worked; while other component parts stayed true to earlier parts of the cultural and religious past. How we disentangle the different components is still very difficult and one has to be very cautious about the context of the material. These tales inevitably involve characters who shared their names with certain features in the natural world.

Chapter 4

The Flora and Fauna of the Earth

We now come to considering the mythical characters who shared their names with flora and fauna in creation myths, in folklore, and in traditions in general. This is evident not only from European traditions, but also in accounts from various other parts of the world, discussed here because of the like manner in which disparate cultures often develop similar traits for understanding their landscape. In these traditions cultural creatures are forces of creation and formation and are often the progenitors of population groups.

We will begin by surveying the types of mythical traditions which surround natural features, such as rivers, hills and larger massifs in Europe, and attempt to elucidate the divine names shared with animals, and divinities which are associated with totems. This will be attempted first in a broad European context, including Greece, Italy, Germany, and France, and then more closely in an insular context for Ireland and Britain. Finally, we will focus on the *Dobunnic* territory. To understand these names we first have to comprehend which languages were being spoken in Britain at the time. Certain general themes appear which we will categorise as: animal names, plant names, aspects of light, associations with genealogies, and deaths associated with rivers.

MYTHICAL RIVERS AND BRITISH LANGUAGES

In a number of the European creation myths, there are tales recounting how the Earth was fashioned, the origin of the nymphs, and the moulding of the landscape. This is most evident in the creation myths of Greece, as told in the *Theogony* of Hesiod (Most 2006, 337–370), discussed further in the next Chapter. First the rivers were born of *Tethys* and *Oceanos*, and then they were listed: *Nile, Alpheios, Eridanus, Strymon, Meander, Ister, Phasis, Rhesus, Achelous, Nessus, Rhodius, Haliacmon, Heptaporus, Granicus, Aesepus, Simois, Peneus, Hermus, Caicus, Sangarius, Parthenius, Ladon, Euenus, Aldescus* and *Scamander*. Later, Hesiod tells us that these were not all of the rivers created and that there were some 3000 river nymphs. In other Greek traditions the rivers were accorded specific personifications. The physical evidence for the deification of the rivers is evident in certain cases but less so in others, although their existence is implied. The sanctity of rivers is known from shrines and traditions in the Near East, Greece, Italy, Gaul and even Britain, thus hinting at a common phenomenon across the Near East and Europe, or at least one common in the provinces of the Roman Empire (see Figure 24). From Greece there are accounts of some of these rivers taking on certain characterisations, not always human. The rivers' names probably had some bearing on the way in which the associated mythical entity was perceived.

In the myths of Scandinavia, the world was moulded by the hands of the gods from the remains of Ymir. This implies a different world view, one in which the gods did not inhabit the natural world and did not entirely personify aspects of that world. However, this view is disputed by the fact that specific deities' names were associated with place-names or natural phenomena, for example the god Thor with thunder. The earlier Greek and later Scandinavian views represent the most divergent views evident in Europe: in the former god was nature (pantheism); in the latter god was outside nature and created it (panentheism). It is the former which is more relevant here. As alluded to above, there are indications especially from Tacitus, that the Germanic and Scandinavian traditions changed and that initially they may have been more in accord with the Greek traditions. The reasons why the Greek world-view is, perhaps, more relevant is because it was linked closely to the Roman world-view, and it was into this tradition that Britain was placed culturally. There are perhaps two components which we have to understand: the first is Romanisation with respect to religion, the second is Romanisation with reference to language. Neither of

Figure 24: An impression from a red Jasper intaglio showing Antioch-on-the-Orontes. The original gem is set in the crozier of Archbishop Hubert Walter, Canterbury Cathedral (photograph Robert Wilkins, Institute of Archaeology archive, source Martin Henig)

these have been advanced as major reasons why the Romans were successful in Gaul and Britain and less so in Germany.

Archaeologists discuss the Romanisation of Britain with respect to military and economic aspects, and developing settlements (Millett 1990); or concerning the requirements and will of the ruling elite (Henig 2002). This is the process by which Britain was brought into the Roman World and hence the reason why that world-view prevails. One major component, which has not been elucidated in this debate, is religion. The Romanisation of Gaul and, to a large extent, Britain was successful; attempts to Romanise Germany, however, were seen as a disaster and resulted in the humiliation of the battle of Kalkriese (Wells 2003). Religion, it could be argued, was a major reason for the different results. As noted by Caesar (Edwards 1963, vi.21), the Britons and Gauls had druids or a class of priests, who may have brought about a more conciliatory approach, whereas the Germans did not:

"The Germans differ much from this manner of living. They have no druids to regulate divine worship, no zeal for sacrifices."

The reliability of this statement, or that of any Roman ethnographer, could have been biased politically but we have, at present, no other information in written form to shed light on this matter. The Gauls and Britons had a structured society which included an influential priesthood; this shadows Rome where there were also priesthoods which were, to some extent integrated within the political system. The persecution of the druids is not the issue here; rather that religion had been integrated into society in a specific way.

It is necessary to consider the process of Romanisation and Germanisation of the languages; the Celtic languages were seen as closely related to the Italian languages, but so are the German languages in some linguistic models (Clackson 2007, 9–15), for example: Schleicher's, New Zealand or Pennsylvanian Indo-European language trees. There are, however, a number of problems when assessing which languages were spoken in pre-migration Britain. A framework of linguistic changes was set out by Jackson (1953), although, as discussed above in Chapter 1, there are problems with this framework due to the way river-names were misinterpreted and represented with respect to their use and linguistic origins (Yeates 2006b, 63–81). Jackson's view, which became the general consensus, was that a Celtic or Brittonic language was spoken in pre-migration Britain. The Romans introduced Latin, which was then seen as an official written language. This was subsequently replaced by Old English from the western strain of the Germanic languages. We need to understand these processes, and the problems with our interpretation of them, because so few Roman-period inscriptions survive. A greater emphasis on the origins of river-names offers further clues about which languages were used in Britain at specific times. Oppenheimer (2006) has now questioned the consensual view, believing that migrants from the German countries and the Baltic region had been entering Britain from the Bronze Age, if not before. This is a radical departure from Jackson, but was necessary as a result of modern DNA analysis and greater understanding of the diversity in Old English present in the different regions of Britain. There are also indications from history which support this new view. After reading Tacitus it becomes quite feasible to question the current, widely-held view that Celtic languages were the only ones spoken in Britain; Tacitus mentioned that the *Aestii*, a tribe living on the Baltic, had a language similar to that of the British (Hutton, Ogilvie *et al.* 1970, *Germania* 45). The comment in the Loeb Classic Library translation states that there is no further evidence to support this statement, but should we simply assume that it is false? The statement is normally taken to mean that the people on the Baltic coast spoke a Celtic language, but it may also mean that the people in the east of Britain already spoke a Germanic type of language. Tacitus may have been hinting at a distinct east-west ethnographic split in first century AD Britain, with Celtic languages spoken in the West, and Germanic or Germano-Celtic (perhaps *Belgic*) languages spoken in the East. Recent assessment of the linguistic divisions in the Germanic languages have suggested that the split between Island Germanic (Old English) and Western Germanic had to occur before AD 350 when the Gothic Bible was written (Forster, Polzin *et al.* 2006, 131–137; Oppenheimer 2006, 340–355); hence implying that some form of English was already established by the early fourth century AD. From AD 409 there is a further indication that there was already a strong Germanic component in the south-east of Britain, in the *Notitia Dignitatum* (Rivet and Smith 1979, 216–225). In this work there is a reference to the Saxon shore. This has been interpreted as the command defending the shore that the Saxons were attacking; however, this is at odds with the rest of the document where the commands are named after the areas they occupied. One could argue that Essex, Wessex or the *Gewisse* (around Dorchester-on-Thames and Silchester), Sussex, Kent and *Meonware* (around Winchester) were already an embryonic **Saxon province** formed out of one of the Roman provinces of Britain (see Figure 25). Perhaps to the north of this we could propose another province which spoke another form of Island Germanic, and which incorporated the peoples who became the Angles (see Figure 26). Our understanding of when these languages were introduced, and the historical framework into which they fit, is essential.

ANIMALS IN THE DREAMTIME

When discussing European myths it may also be relevant to look at the myths of peoples from other parts of the world. Frazer's (1922) use of this technique was, perhaps, over-elaborate and too wide-ranging. Often myths were produced from similar ideas that may be a function of peoples' natural way of looking at their surroundings. It is certainly the case that themes often repeat. One important source for us is the dreamtime of the Australian aboriginals. Even though the landscapes of Australia and Europe are very different, and the ways in which spirits were envisaged very different, there are still certain ideas that occurred in both locations. In the aboriginal world there are creatures which wander across the landscape; similar traditions can be found in Europe, with variations occurring principally only in their portrayal. In both traditions there is an attempt to provide the landscape with a meaning encapsulated in a storyline. The fact that it survives better in one place than in the other is due to history, but the fact that it does survive, although in a piecemeal fashion, in Europe means that we can provide ideas about what might have been, even if we cannot confirm them properly.

The Australian aboriginals have a deeply-rooted cultural landscape, in which every feature is explained by a cultural myth. Thus, the landscape is endowed with a 'bibliography' of meaning, channelled into the folk-traditions and beliefs of the people. The creation period of the world was called the Dreaming and was populated by a host of mythical beings or sky heroes. The rock of Uluru is a metaphysical reality for the *Pitjandjara* tribe of the central desert (Cowan 1989). The rock was the site of a battle of two tribes of Sky Heroes; the *Kunia* (**carpet-snake people**) and the *Liru* (**poisonous-snake people**). The *Kunia*, the story goes, journeyed from the east to a sandhill water-hole where Uluru stands today. These people were attacked by the *Liru*, a troublesome tribe of Sky Heroes. Spears were thrown on the invading *Liru* by the *Kunia*, and to this day

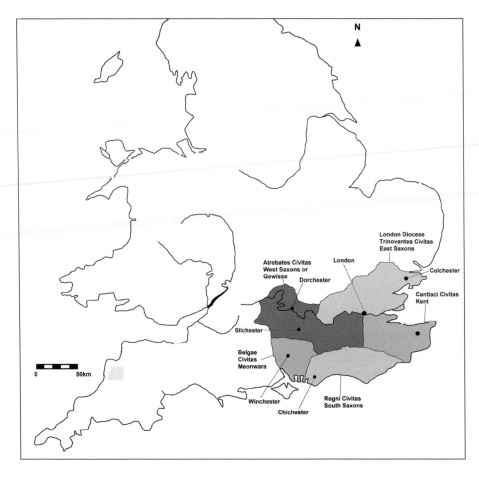

Figure 25: The proposed location of the Romano-British province, inferred by Tacitus in the first century AD, as one of the regions of Britain in which a Germanic language was spoke. This would explain why this area became called the Saxon Shore (drawing S. Yeates)

a number of features, such as desert oaks and sandhills, are supposed to represent the metamorphosed bodies of the invading *Liru*. A *Kunia* woman, called *Minma Bulari*, gave birth to a child, and a cave was created in which there was an entrance to another cave; this symbolised the woman's vulva. Another woman of the same tribe helped her to give birth and her knee marks can still be identified today as a physical natural feature. There was a single-handed combat between the *Liru* leader, *Kulikudjeri*, and a *Kunia* warrior. Both were severely wounded but the blood of the *Kunia* warrior formed the path of a watercourse. The mother of the warrior attacked *Kulikudjeri* with her digging stick and cut off his nose, which is now visible as a huge slab of rock which has sheared off the mass of Uluru. The eyes and nasal passages are marked on the rock, while under the rock are water stains representing the blood of the dying warrior. A second band of

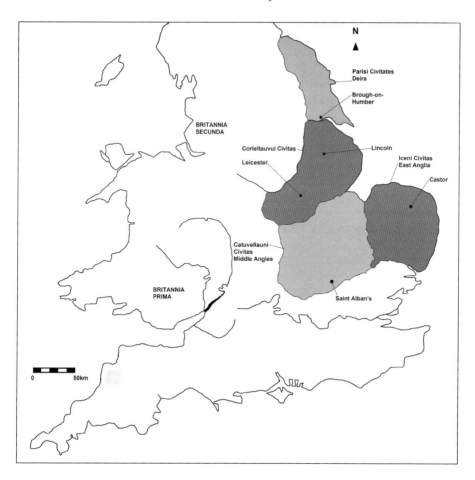

Figure 26: A further proposed location of the Romano-British province which may have been part of the area in which a Germanic language was spoken, according to Tacitus. This area became associated with the Anglian territories (drawing S. Yeates)

Liru attacked the remaining *Kunia*, and a woman fled, leaving her tracks on the rock face. The conflict ended with the withdrawal of the *Liru* warriors, who set off in search of more trouble. The descendents of the *Kunia* people were the *Pitjandjara* tribe of the central desert. Every feature recognised by the *Pitjandjara* tribe has an associated folk-belief which is part of a broader set of actions in which the landscape was moulded by the metamorphosis of the dreamtime spirits.

The myth of the landscape of Uluru is a compact story concerned with a specific topological feature, but one in which the journeys of certain individuals are encountered. In other acts of the Dreamtime there are longer journeys. In these accounts certain Sky Heroes travelled across the landscape creating special features in the primordial earth. The journey of the Rainbow Serpent is one such event and can be found amongst the tales of the *Mirarr* and *Badmardi* tribes. On an escarpment, at *Djuwarr* lagoon the Rainbow Serpent is claimed to have split the rock-face, thus creating a gorge and deep waterfall. The snake disappeared into the pool. Another site where the Rainbow Serpent is claimed to have entered the earth is the Cullymurra waterhole on Cooper Creek in central Australia. To the *Deiri* tribe, this is the hole of life, a location imbued with the power of creation. The Rainbow Serpent is an important being in all of the creation myths of the aboriginal tribes, and so his journeys are always special (Cowan 1989).

Other mythical Australian characters also participated in the Dreamtime and carried out mythical journeys, including *Kolakola*, the red kangaroo, who took a supernatural trek across Australia (Cowan 1989). The series of events recorded in these traditions were actually a celebration of the relationship between man and nature, which gave dignity to the place and, in so doing, created a cogent mythological landscape. The journey of the red kangaroo is thought, to some extent, to represent knowledge of that species which was collected and passed on from generation to generation, in a mythological context. On his journey the animal visited a number of spiritual, and extremely hot, locations and, at one of them, disappeared into the earth.

MYTHIC ANIMALS, PLANTS AND RIVERS IN EUROPE

Having briefly mentioned the aboriginal traditions and gaining from that example a sense of how the land might be imbued with spirits, we can now start discussing the variations in the European traditions that are essential to understanding Iron-Age and Roman period landscapes.

Greece and Asia Minor

In the myths of Greece there was a similar tradition of imbuing the landscape with supernatural beings, and thus giving the landscape a mythology. In the Greek world the landscape was occupied by gods, *genii*, nymphs and other mythical divinities. The Acropolis, for example, contains a temple (the Parthenon) dedicated to the goddess Athena, and there is a tale which accounts how the goddess became associated with this site (Tomlinson 1976, 78–90). This concerned a battle between Athena and Poseidon, who were vying for control of the location; the battle was eventually won by the goddess, as described in Chapter 2. There is also evidence that Hera may also have originated as a topographical or regional divinity of the Argive Plain, also accounted in Chapter 2.

Parallels between the Australian aboriginal traditions of Uluru, and Ancient Greek traditions can be seen in the myths surrounding the sanctuary of the island of Delos. The origins of Apollo and Artemis have already been mentioned in Chapter 2, and various places on Delos were associated with their mythical birth, and their mother *Leto*. The story created a sacred character for Delos (Tomlinson 1976, 71–77), an explanation of why certain features and locations were how they were, and defined how they were to be treated.

In Greek traditions there are a number of personifications of the waters of the region; from *Oceanos* and Poseidon (Harvey 1984, 289, 343), who are treated as titans or gods but who represented the ocean waters, which were thought to surround the earth. Besides this there were local deities of rivers and the nymphs showing that the personification of rivers and springs could have been masculine or feminine. The river-gods were recognised as the ancestors of heroes, and were seen as guardians of the land (Hornblower and Spawforth 1996, 1320). They were often represented as bulls, horses or snakes, and could take on human form.

Achelous

The river *Achelous*, now the Aspropotamos, was associated with a river god and king, he was father of the Sirens (Hornblower and Spawforth 1996, 6; Brewster 1997, 9–14), and often portrayed by Ancient Greek and Roman poets, as horned. A variation on the tale, which was accounted by Hesiod, stated that all rivers were born of *Oceanos* and *Tethys* (Most 2006, 337–370). In one tale, *Achelous* taunted and wrestled with Heracles; he was thrown onto his back, and promptly turned into a serpent. Next, he became a bull and charged at Heracles, who snapped off his right horn, causing *Achelous* to retire (Harvey 1984, 202). Some believe, as Ovid claimed, that it was this horn which became the *cornucopia* when filled with the apples of the *Hesperides* (Brewster 1997, 10–11). In this tale the river was primarily associated with a bull; however, *Achelous* could also shape-shift, taking on other animal forms. The reasons for this are not now apparent, but it could be that the tale tried to explain different aspects of the river, either by season or by location. Confusion may also have arisen, with respect to the river's image, because the god was confused with a tributary which had a different representation. We also see in this legend the association between rivers and the idea of the fertility and the earth, as the snapped horn became the *cornucopia*. This image was used frequently on later reliefs to symbolise fertility and abundance. Pausanias informs us that the *Achelous* was the Greek river which had the most important run of fish (Brewster 1997, 93). The name is also considered to be indicative of any stream or water (GEK 1978, 141).

Acheron

The *Acheron* was considered one of the rivers of the underworld (Hornblower and Spawforth 1996, 6; Brewster 1997, 15–19), represented by a deity who was married to *Gorgyra* and fathered *Askalaphos*. On its banks, beneath the walls of the *Nekyomanteion*, is an oracle of the dead mentioned by Herodotus (Godley 1922, v.92 p113), and it was over this river that the boatman *Charon* ferried the dead. The river was associated with the white poplar which grew along its banks and whose wood was used in sacrificial rites. In Greece, the **white poplar** was called the *Acheroid*, a homonym of the river-name; according to tradition Heracles found such a tree on the banks of the river (GEK 1978, 141). The legend is significant because it hints at a possible reason of why animal or plant names should be associated with specific rivers. In this case the river flowed through a landscape where a specific type of tree, later incorporated into the local culture to serve a specific symbolic function, grew.

Alpheios

The name *Alpheios* is considered by some to mean **whitish**; this is the largest river of the Peloponnese and was also claimed as one of the rivers born of *Oceanos* and *Tethys* (Hornblower and Spawforth 1996, 67–68; Brewster 1997, 80–87). In the Iliad, Homer mentioned that bulls were sacrificed to this river; while in the Homeric Hyme the child Hermes drove the cattle of Apollo to this river to drink. It was this river's waters that

Heracles diverted to cleanse the Augean stables. In later traditions *Alpheios* is claimed to have drowned in the river, which was subsequently named after him. This tradition of naming rivers after drowned heroes seems to be Europe-wide being also found in Ireland and Britain, and, as it occurs in Greek mythology, it can be assumed to have some antiquity. Alpheios's cult was established at Olympia and Sparta. In folk-tradition the river's deity had many amorous encounters, including those with *Arethusa*; he even attempted to rape Artemis. The tributaries of this river are the Arcadian *Ladon*, the *Erymanthus*, and the *Kladeos*. *Alpheios* and *Kladeos* are represented in human form, on the east pediment of the temple at Olympia. No mythology has survived for the *Kladeos*.

Amymone

Amymone is considered to have been a daughter of king *Danaos* of Argos who, when in search of water, threw a dart at a deer only to hit a satyr. Poseidon saved *Amymone* from the satyr, who tried to rape her, and, after lying with her, turned her into a river (Hornblower and Spawforth 1996, 79; Brewster 1997, 59–60). It was also accounted that the hydra lived under a plane tree which grew near the source of the river. The meaning of the name is considered to be **blameless** (Brewster 1997, 59–60), which may be associated with a British river-name.

Aroanios

The river *Aroanios* rises on Mount *Aroanios*, now Chelmos, out of the face of a cliff; and also at a site called *Pegai*, the springs, where it wells up from the ground (Brewster 1997, 72–73). The river was famous in the days of Pausanias in the second half of the second century BC, for having dappled fish which sang like thrushes; although Pausanias admitted that he had never heard them cry. Here we find an association with a specific type of fish, reflecting the idea, already noted in Australia that mythical tradition was a way of imparting knowledge of survival techniques – specifically where one could find certain plants and animals.

Artemis

The goddess Artemis has already been mentioned in Chapter 2, but she requires a mention here too and, like other ancient divinities, seems to have had an origin and association with topographical features. It was noted earlier that the goddess's name was associated with *arte-*, **bear**, and it is also known that her name was borne by *Mount Artemisius* (Brewster 1997, 59). Although she is not identified here as a river-deity, it is apparent that her name is a toponym derived from that of an animal, recognised persistently in aspects of her cult. A more in-depth study of this goddess, and her origins, could indicate how and when the traditions of naming the landscape after animals and plants originated.

Asopos

There are three rivers in Greece called the *Asopos* of which the one rising on Mount Kithairon is the most interesting mythologically in retaining more stories (Brewster 1997, 50–51). *Asopos* was a son of *Oceanos* and *Tethys*; his daughter was *Plataia*, who gave her name to the *Plataians*. Others are claimed as his offspring, but some of the tales are seen as longstanding Boeotian traditions. The name is interpreted as meaning **never silent**.

Asopos

The *Asopos* of Phleius was also a child of *Oceanos* and *Tethys* in some accounts, but of Poseidon and *Pero* in others; in another version it was Zeus and *Eurynome* who were his parents (Brewster 1997, 67–68). His offspring by *Metope* included twenty daughters and two sons, including *Ismenas*, *Pelagon* and *Aegina*. The valley through which the river flows may once have had volcanic outbursts, which may explain the story of the river's confrontation with Zeus. This river draws its water from the Stymphalian Lake through underground passages.

Erasinos

The *Erasinos* issues from a spring in a cavern where there is a building that is now a church, but which may originally have been a *nymphaeum* (Brewster 1997, 61–62). Tradition, along with modern topographers and geologists, has it that the river starts at Lake Stymphalos, the waters of which disappear down a deep chasm.

Erymanthos

The river *Erymanthos* rises on Mount *Lampeia*, which in reality is part of Mount *Erymanthos*, with the river and hill sharing the same name and the same mythological traditions (Brewster 1997, 78–79). This is the second recognised case in ancient Greece where a river and a hill share the same name. These connections between hill names and the names of waters which rise on them is also evident elsewhere in Europe, for example in Britain. Pausanius described statues of the god associated with the river but very little of the myth of the river. The land through which the river flows was associated with tales of Artemis hunting, an account of Heracles hunting a boar, and also an abode for exiled centaurs. The meaning of the name is given as **dividing by lots**.

Eurotas

The river *Eurotas* was incorporated as a mythical character into the kingship and genealogies of the Spartan people (Brewster 1997, 88–92). It was Spartan tradition that games should be held on the banks of the *Eurotas*. In one of these events Apollo threw a discus which killed *Hyakynthos*, to whom a shrine was later built. From the blood that flowed from the wound a flower grew which was like a lily in form, but with one purple flower and another silvery-white in colour. It was on this river that Zeus, in the form of a swan, seduced Leda. The name is translated as **fair flowing**.

Evenos

The *Evenos* was a child of Ares (Brewster 1997, 21–26) and was first recognised as a king. He had a daughter, *Marpessa*, whom he did not wish to get married, and so set tasks in which the suitors would inevitably fail and forfeit their lives. *Idas*, a son of Poseidon, borrowed his father's chariot and eloped with *Marpassa*. *Evenos* pursued the couple and, unable to catch them, threw himself into the river *Lykormas* (**wolf** with suffix), which subsequently bore his name. The valley of the *Evenos* was stalked by a wild boar sent by the goddess Artemis; it was hunted by the *Kalydonian* and first wounded by *Atalanta*. The meaning of the name is given as **controlling the reins**, alluding to chariot reins. The mythological traditions hint at a process, in which river-names associated with animal names were being replaced in, or just before, the classical period. There is also an indication that the drowning traditions were not associated with the older animal names.

Hyllikos

No textual references to the *Hyllikos* survive, but along its banks one of the springs was considered to be unfailing, and there is evidence of shrines along the water course (Brewster 1997, 65–66).

Inachos

The river *Inachos* was punished by Poseidon due to the decision it, and others, reached over which deity should preside over the Argive plain (Brewster 1997, 59–60). The tale explained why the river is dry for parts of the year. The springs which feed the river rise from Mount *Artemesius*, where there is a sanctuary to Artemis. *Inachos* was a child of *Oceanos* and *Tethys* and was, according to tradition, father of *Mycenae* who gave her name to that city, hence he was the primeval ancestor of *Akrisios*, king of the Argive (Wiseman 2004, 25). His other daughter was *Io* who was transformed by Hera into a heifer.

Kephisos (Cephissus), Attica

Kephisos of Attica was one of the river gods, along with *Inachos* and *Asterion*, who arbitrated over a territorial dispute over Argolis between Poseidon and Hera (Hornblower and Spawforth 1996, 312; Brewster 1997, 52–54). He was usually portrayed in the form of a bull, but in some sculpture was represented in human form. This was emphasised by Euripides who called him 'bull-visaged' (Kovacs 1999, *Ion* 1261, p.467). The name is interpreted as **river of gardens**.

Kephisos (Cephissus), Boeotia

The *Kephisos* of Boeotia flows from the Thracian mountains and heads south. This river is referred to in the *Iliad* of Homer and in the Hymn to Apollo (Hornblower and Spawforth 1996, 312; Brewster 1997, 47–49). Here, we find out that a priest resided over a spring at the source of the river. Tradition had it that one of the fountains near the source used to bellow like a bull. The *Kephisos* ravished the nymph *Liriope* and fathered the child *Narcissus*. A spring in the valley was associated with the nymph *Lilaia*, regarded as a child of *Kephisos*, as was *Eteokles*, king of *Orchomenos*. The mythology associated with this river hints at a number of traditions, some of which we can detect in the north-west provinces of the Roman Empire; there is an association with an animal, the bull, the father of a king, and hence, presumably, a royal genealogical line. The tradition concerning the springs and tributaries being the offspring of the rivers we find again with the Rhine in north-west Europe. In some instances the tributaries and springs were nymphs or river goddesses who were ravished by the protagonist to produce further children.

Kokytos

The *Kokytos* is another river of the underworld and is a tributary of the *Acheron* (Brewster 1997, 20). It is known that the river was a stream of Hades, but the tales which accompany it no longer survive.

Kronos

The titan *Kronos* is important when assessing the use of animal and plant names for mythological characters. He gave or received his name from a hill near Olympia; it means **crow**, which is the root of other Greek mythological names, including *Koronea*, *Koronis*, and *Koronus*. The animal-name association is evident in the story of how *Kronos* was overthrown by the new world order of the Olympian gods. This suggests that we are looking at a tradition which originated in the Bronze Age at least, as these myths date to a period prior to the ascendancy of the Olympian gods. There is perhaps an indication here in the replacement of the god with an animal name by Zeus, whose name means the **bright day**, suggestive of the dawn of a new order. From this, it is possible to suggest that the names derived from animals may predate the names associated with light in Greek mythology.

Ladon

The *Ladon* flows from a pool which collects at the base of a perpendicular cliff, and is one of the rivers of Greece which has retained much of its mythological tradition (Brewster 1997, 74–77). It is believed to be fed by the waters of the Phenean Lake. *Ladon's* children included *Daphne*, *Merope*, and *Telpousa* all of whom represented springs and tributaries, or animals and plants along the course of the river. The etymology of the name *Ladon* is given as **he who embraces**.

Neda

The nymph *Neda* was born after *Styx* and *Philyra*, by *Rhea* who struck the ground with a staff, on the slopes of Mount *Lykaion* (Brewster 1997, 95–98). *Neda*, along with *Ithome*, were considered to be the nurses who raised Zeus, one giving her name to the river and the other to a mountain. The Arcadians claimed that Zeus was not raised on Crete but on Mount *Lykaion*, where the *Neda* rises, and that the other nymphs who nursed him were *Theisoa* and *Hago*. The river was honoured by the *Phigalians*, and there is some suggestion that ancient coins depict the river as a god (Roscher 1897–1909, 40, 75f). A tributary of the *Neda* was the *Lymax*, and it was on this river, according to Pausanius (Jones 1935, viii.41.2–6), that Zeus was claimed to have been born. At the confluence of these two rivers, not far from some hot springs, was a sanctuary dedicated to *Eurynome*. The cult statue was anthropomorphic, with the top half human and the lower half a fish. This deity may have represented a local nymph, perhaps a deity associated with a trout before being associated with the *Homeric* and *Hesiodic Eurynome* of north Greece. As a river-nymph, this goddess would presumably have represented one of the river reaches above the confluence, perhaps the *Lymax*, or perhaps just the warm springs.

Orcus

In a discussion on the Vale of Tempe, through which the *Peneios* flows, the latter is described as being joined by a river *Orcus* (Brewster 1997, 35). The word *orcus* means **boar** another Greek river-name associated with an animal name.

Pamisos

Pamisos was mentioned as a god to whom offerings were made and to whom a shrine was established by the king of *Messenia* (Brewster 1997, 93–94). The river was noted by Pausanius for its clear water and abundant fish.

Peneios

The *Peneios* is one of the great rivers of Greece. The deity was born of *Oceanos* and *Tethys* (Brewster 1997, 33–39) and his daughter was *Daphne*. The story of *Duphne* emerges late in Hellenistic traditions, and was used to explain Apollo's association with the bay tree. Indeed, it is claimed that the sacred bay tree of Delphi was grown from a sprig cut from a tree on the banks of the river *Peneios*. The name of the river has been interpreted as meaning **of the thread**.

Scamander

The *Scamander* River is known to have had a special priest, who ruled over the rights associated with the sanctity of that river (Hornblower and Spawforth 1996, 1320).

Selemnos

Selemnos was a shepherd loved by the sea nymph *Argyra* (Brewster 1997, 65–66). When *Selemnos* grew old the nymph no longer visited him and he died of love; out of pity, Aphrodite turned him into a river. This, like a number of Greek traditions, associated the river with a human being who died and was transformed into a natural feature. The waters of the river were considered important for forgetting a lover.

Spercheios

Some of the earliest written evidence for the deification of a European river, which occurs in the work of Homer's *Iliad* (Brewster 1997, 44–46; Murray and Wyatt 1999, 16.174, 176, 23.142, 144), concerns the *Spercheios*. In the tale, Achilles, after the death of *Patroklos*, acclaimed also the river's greatness and stated that he would make a sacrifice to the river of fifty rams. There are also legendary associations with Heracles, but we know less of the deification of the river itself and the image which was associated with it. The river is now known as the Georgopotamos, the **George river**, which indicates that the river-god has now been replaced by a saint.

Styx

Styx was the eldest daughter of *Oceanos*, and wife of *Palla*, and a goddess dreaded by the gods of Olympus (Hornblower and Spawforth 1996, 1450; Brewster 1997, 69–71). The river rises on Mount *Aroanis*, where its water spouts straight over a precipice six hundred feet high. The waters of the river were believed to dissolve glass, stone, pottery and gold. Later Greek and Roman traditions developed the Styx's mythology as a river of Hades where it was considered the lowest river of Tartarus. The etymology of the name is given as **hated** and the legendary traditions are considered to be due to the river's topography.

Tragos

The river *Tragos* is a tributary of the *Ladon*; no mythology survives, but the name has the etymology **he-goat** (Brewster 1997, 77).

Conclusions

When looking at these river-divinities, some common themes emerge. Associations between deities and flora and fauna occurred with some river and hill mythology, but not all. The goddess Artemis and the titan *Kronos* are, perhaps, the key figures here, while Hera and Athena (Chapter 2), are called cow-eyed, and associated with a small eared owl, respectively. *Eurynome* was possibly associated with a fish (possibly a trout), while *Tragos* was referred to as a **he-goat**. The proportion of features with such names is, however, not very high, or obscured, and there may have been a tendency, in the classical period to represent all rivers as bulls, due to changing ideology. In the case of the *Evenos* the river was originally called the *Lykormas*, *Lyko*, which means **wolf**, so it is extremely possible that a number of river-names were lost as Greece entered the Classical period in the seventh or sixth centuries BC. A number of genealogical associations can be identified, usually concerning descent from riverine deities. This probably occurred in Bronze Age or Iron Age contexts, but does not necessarily inform us as to when such traditions were introduced in the north of Europe. In the *Iliad* it seems that the river-gods were once more powerful, as when Zeus summoned the gods to Olympus they also attended. Burkert (1985, 174–175) noted that each city worshipped its river or spring and that the river was accorded a *temenos* and occasionally even a temple. There are indications in Greece that rivers were associated with rituals for coming-of-age for both males and females, and this idea may tie in with river-deities being seen as ancestral figures. Likewise, the idea of a human (or deity) dying in the river and giving his or her name to the river, with the mythical character being shared, was also encountered at an early date. These concepts are also found in north-west Europe; were they introduced with the Roman invasion, or were they already present in some form?

ITALY

Other rivers in mainland Europe, and some on the Mediterranean islands, have also been personified as mythical characters and associated with animals or plants. Their presence in Italy some may argue, represented the expansion of Greek ideas and mythology.

Carna

In the *Fasti*, Ovid (Frazer 1989, vi.101–170) referred to a goddess called *Carna*. He interpreted her name as being equated with *Cardea*, **goddess of hinges**, from the Latin word *cardo*, **a hinge**. Frazer, however, in the footnotes of the Loeb Classical Library version, suggested that her name was associated with the Latin *caro* or *carnis*, meaning **flesh**. Ovid continued to discuss her and, in his song, stated that she originated as a nymph called *Cranaë*. She was portrayed as a divine hunter desired by Janus, who saw her hiding under a rock, caught her, and took her maidenhood. She was associated with a large bird of the night that fed on flesh and also with a rod which was taken from a white-thorn or hawthorn tree. A temple dedicated to her was built on the Caelin Hill in Rome (Wiseman 2004, 161–162). This goddess's name may have developed from an extremely ancient European river-name, like the Greek name *Amymone*; both may be useful when trying to understand the origins of certain British river-names (see below).

Crimissus, Ismenius, Pactolus, and Xanthus

A number of the attributes noted amongst Greek river traditions are also evident for the rivers of Italy; the south of the peninsula had strong ties with mainland Greece and a number of Greek colonies developed there before the rise of the Roman Empire. Such traditions included the representation of the river in animal form and the association of the river with genealogies. In Sicily, for example, it is accounted that *Phoenodamas's* eldest daughter, *Aegesta*, lay with the river *Crimissus*. The river, we are informed in the legend, took on the shape of a dog. The two river-gods *Pactolus* and *Xanthus* are recognised as the progenitors of specific social groups or communities. For other river-gods, such as the *Ismenius*, no tales survive.

Tanais

Tanais, we are informed, rejected the approaches of Aphrodite; in revenge she made him fall in love with his mother, and as a result he drowned himself in a river. So, in Italy there are also stories of humans dying in rivers and giving their names to them. It is possible that the tales represented sacrifices, or offerings, to the river-god.

Tiberinus

The river Tiber rises in a creek in the Apennines near *Aretium* and flows into the Mediterranean near Ostia; like other Italian rivers, it was deified, and bore the name *Tiberinus* (Hornblower and Spawforth 1996, 1522; Wiseman 2004, 31, 288). From ancient texts it is known that the river had two other names: *Rumon*, and *Albula*. In Ovid's *Fasti* (Frazer 1989, v.649–660; Wiseman 2004, 25, 31) the god explains why certain festivities took place at Rome in his honour, for example on the 14th May the *pontifices* and Vestal Virgins presided over 27 straw Argives being thrown into the river from a wooden bridge. The tradition dated back to the third century BC.

Conclusions

The Italians, like the Greeks, associated rivers with animals and trees, and they also had accounts of deaths occurring in rivers, which may hint at sacrificial traditions. Besides this there were also genealogies descending from the deities. In considering the mythology of Rome Wiseman (2004; 2008), showed that certain aspects of the cults were extremely localised and associated with natural features and specific parts of the landscape. Religious devotion was tied to temples at specific locales where specific festivals and rites of passage took place. This has implications on how we understand *interpretatio Romana* in Britain and elsewhere. Only certain aspects of Roman cults could have been exported; for example: the names of gods, the cult of the Emperor, and certain aspects of the Pantheon. What this implies is that in other areas of the Roman Empire the local gods were still essential and that they would have continued to have dominated local aspects of religion, focusing on landscape, rivers and other natural aspects.

GAUL AND GERMANY

In the European traditions looked at so far three main trends are evident and these ideas are also found in other parts of the Roman Empire. The traditions seem to have been repetitive and extremely identifiable. The following list highlights a number of river deities recorded in Gaul and *Germania*, gives their associations with animals and plants, and highlights the use of the *matres* or mothers.

Ancamna

The goddess *Ancamna* was worshipped at the spring sanctuary of Möhn near Trier (Green 1989, 61, 64; Green 1992, 28). She was associated with the gods *Smertrius* and *Lenus*, but no iconography survives.

Atepomarus

The god *Apollo Atepomarus* was worshipped at a number of healing sanctuaries throughout Gaul. Although not associated specifically with a river it is possible that *Atepomarus* presided over springs as these seem to have been an important part of healing cults, especially where the waters had specific properties. The name means **great horse** (Green 1992, 30).

Damona

In certain parts of Gaul, and in other places on the Continent, there is evidence for the worship of a god called *Borvo, Bormo,* or *Bormanus* (Green 1989, 45, 63, 142; Green 1992, 47–48, 75–76). His name signifies the **bubbling spring** and there are a number of images which are believed to depict the god with a cup with water flowing or bubbling over. The god was often depicted at these spring sites with a consort called *Bormana*, who seems to have been a female version of the god, and sometimes with a goddess called *Damona*, who was also paired with the spring god *Apollo Moritasgus*. *Damona* is of interest here because the etymology of her name is **great** or **divine cow**. The goddess is depicted with her head crowned with ears of corn and a serpent curved around her arm. In certain places, such as Bourbonne-les-Bains and in the Charent region, this goddess was invoked alone.

Epona

The goddess *Epona*, whose name means **horse**, was originally worshipped by the *Aedui*, the *Lingones*, the *Mediomatrici* and the *Treveri*, and had a festival on 18th December (Green 1989, 16–24; Green 1992, 90–92). Her cult seems to have spread more widely than those of other Celtic deities with her worship being exported as far as the Balkans; one reason for this extended adoration is that she was adopted by the Roman military. Her image has been found in small domestic shrines, but although her wide distribution is known only the temple at Entraius-sur-Nohain is known to be dedicated to her. The reason for the adoption of her cult was because the images could be appropriated by the Roman cavalry, or at least by its Gallic and Germanic components. Although she became associated with the army, and with horse-breeding, it is apparent, from her association with spring sites at Sainte-Fontaine-de-Freyming in Mosselle and at Allerey in Côte d'Or, where she occurred as a water nymph, that she may have developed as a river deity. At the first of these sites she was worshipped alongside Apollo and *Sirona*. At Hagondange, in the Mosselle, *Epona* was represented in triple form, a classical representation of the mothers. These qualities are often repeated: a connection with springs, a name derived from an animal, and the identification as a mother of a people. They were touched on when the Irish goddess *Macha* was discussed, a distinct tradition located outside the Roman Empire if not necessarily outside its influence. In certain cases it has been suggested that *Epona's* images contain allusions to the after-life and the accompaniment of souls to the otherworld.

Fagus

There is evidence from the Pyrenees of the worship of a god called *Fagus*, meaning **beech** (Green 1989, 153; Green 1992, 93). At Croix d'Oraison in the same region, the remains of a bust, which may represent this deity, were uncovered.

Ianuaria

The goddess *Ianuaria* was known to have been worshipped at the spring-sanctuary at Beire-le-Châtel (Green 1989, 41), where she was also known as the *Deae Ianuariae* a name type associated with the mothers. Once again river deities and genealogical traditions are connected.

Icauna

The remains of a monumental sanctuary with a river shrine dedicated to the goddess *Icauna* (Ekwall 1928, 217–219) is located at the source of the Yonne (Derks 1998, 138). Philologically, the two names are associated and the <c> has been lost; in numerous examples in Britain, however, this is not the case.

Icovellauna

The goddess *Icovellauna* was worshipped at Metz and Trier; at the former she presided over the spring site at Sablon (Green 1989, 50; Green 1992, 125). No images of the goddess have survived, but it is apparent that she was primarily a spring or river goddess as the first part of her name *Ico-*, means **water**. The latter part of the name is considered to be **good** or **better**, but this is not universally accepted (Ellis Evans 1967, 272–277; Rivet and Smith 1979, 271–272).

Loucetius

The deities *Mars Loucetius* and *Nemetona* were worshipped together as part of a divine couple at Bath (Green 1989, 45, 113; Green 1992, 143; RIB(I) 1995, no.140). The context for the inscription, and their exact significance in the *Dobunni* listings of deities, is unknown, but the dedication was made by a citizen of Trier, hence they may have been imported. The couple are known more widely on the continent than in Britain. The etymology of the name is **light** or **bright** and, it has been suggested, is a reference to **lightning** (Ross 1967, 228–229).

Luxovius

This god, *Luxovius*, was worshipped at the spring site of Luxeuil in the Haute-Saône (Green 1989, 45, 46, 163; Green 1992, 50, 136). Little is known of him or his consort, *Bricta*, because they are known only in epigraphic form. The name is also seen as a reference to **light** and he was clearly a local god due to the similarity between the place-name and the divine name.

Matrona

There are many indications from inscriptions that rivers were venerated. Examples include inscriptions referring to the goddess *Matrona* symbol of the river Marne (Green 1992, 140). The remains of a monumental sanctuary dedicated to the goddess have been located at the source of the river (Derks 1998, 138). The name means **divine mother** (Ross 1967, 47). Ross suggested that there must have been a cult legend associating the mother with the river, with the goddess becoming the symbolic representation of the river.

Moccus

The deity *Mercury Moccas* was worshipped amongst the *Lingones* (Green 1989, 113; Green 1992, 149). The name means **pig**, and it is possible that in Britain the name may have been used as a river-name.

Mullo

The god *Mars Mullo* was worshipped widely in Brittany and Normandy (Green 1992, 143–144); his name is thought to be associated with the Latin word *mule* and to mean **horse**. One of the temples dedicated to him, at Craôn was located on a hillock above a confluence of two rivers, a classic location for a river shrine.

Nantosuelta

This goddess, *Nantosuelta*, whose name is usually interpreted as meaning **winding river**, was worshipped as part of a divine couple (Green 1992, 157–158). Her associated images include a beehive and a raven, although neither is known to be represented in her name, and sometimes, due to the imagery, she is regarded as a raven-goddess (Ross 1967, 47). The word *nant-*, meaning **valley**, occurs commonly in Welsh place-names, so the original divine name was probably *Suelta*. Her origins must have been as a localised river-goddess.

Nehalennia

The goddess *Nehalennia* was worshipped at two major sanctuaries on the North Sea coast of the Netherlands and at shrines along certain rivers in the Rhine system, where it was possible to navigate from a coastal trading area (Green 1989, 10–16; Green 1992, 64, 159–160). The name of the goddess is interpreted as meaning **leader** or **steerswoman**. The earliest known sanctuary to her was discovered in 1647 at Domburg, on the island of Walcheren, where some thirty altars were recovered. Since 1970, at a site called Colinjnsplaat, some 120 altars dedicated to this goddess have been brought up from the bed of the sea near the estuary of the East Scheldt River. The site seems to have been called *Ganuenta* and there was certainly a major temple here, all of which was submerged by the rising sea level in the North Sea. The goddess was associated with seafarers, as indicated by the images of ships and dolphins which occur on her altars, but the most common animal depicted was a dog. The goddess was worshipped mainly by the *Morini* tribe, but the dedications on her altars indicate that people travelled from all around the 'Celtic' world to pay homage at her shrines. There is a suggestion that the goddess may have been a personification of the North Sea.

Nemausus

The sanctuary at Nîmes was presided over by the god *Nemausus* (Green 1992, 160). The name is Celto-Ligurian in origin, and his cult centre was expanded and monumentalised in the second century BC during the process of Roman colonisation. The *Nemausicae* were also worshipped at the shrine at Nîmes, and seem to have been the mothers of the people around Nîmes. Here again a classic configuration occurs of god, mother, and folk-group, as noted earlier with *Macha*.

Rhenus

In Germany there is evidence for a god called *Rhenus*, lord of the Rhine, associated with Jupiter and a *genius loci* (Derks 1998, 140–141). On an altar from Strasbourg, the Rhine is considered to be the father of many tributaries. This idea, that the major river was the father or mother or even consort to tributaries and springs within its catchment area was also seen in Greece. The occurrence of this tradition in the north-west of the Empire makes it highly plausible that such traditions were also present in Britain with the Severn and the Thames. This river-name is also known to have been used in northern Italy where it was a tributary of the Po or *Padus* (Hornblower and Spawforth 1996, 1312).

Rura

A votive plaque to the goddess *Rura* has been recovered from a shrine at the confluence of the Roer and Meuse (Derks 1998, 139); it is apparent that this goddess presided over the Roer river.

Segomo

Mars Segomo was worshipped in the form of a horse amongst the *Sequani* (Green 1989, 113), and is known to have been worshipped at Bolards, near Nuits Saint Georges, in Burgundy. He is regarded as a warrior divinity, due to the association with Mars, and even though there is an association with a horse, there is no known connection with a river in the area, although the shrine and settlement lie in a bend of the River Meuzin. In Britain there are, however, two names which are based on the root-word for this god's name, *Segelocum* and *Segontium*, both of which are used with respect to rivers or pools (Rivet and Smith 1979, 453–454). The name is interpreted as meaning **strength** or **vigour** (Ellis Evans 1967, 254–257).

Sequana

Excavations and antiquarian finds from the *Fontes Sequanea* indicate that the goddess of the river Seine was venerated at a healing shrine near the river's source (Green 1992, 102, 188–189; Aldhouse-Green 1999, 1–9). A series of Roman buildings have been identified around the spring; these include a temple and a *nymphaeum* over the spring itself. The sanctuary has produced evidence of wooden and stone carvings, depicting pilgrims and their ailments, along with body parts. These offerings started in the first century BC. The goddess was represented standing in a duck-boat, with the duck holding a berry in its mouth (Espérandieu 1938, no.7676). No derivations of the name are given, but the imagery of the duck may indicate that the latter part of the name *-ana* is the Celtic word for that species.

Sirona

The goddess *Sirona* was worshipped at thermal healing shrines in Gaul at locations such as Neidaldorf, Bitburg, Sainte-Fontaine near Freyming, and Metz (Green 1992, 191–192). The most important sanctuary to her, however, has been excavated at Hochscheid, where the main temple was constructed in the second century AD. This temple has produced much votive material. The name of the goddess has the etymology of **star**.

Souconna

Souconna was worshipped at the sanctuary of Chalon-sur-Saône, and is recognised as the goddess of the river Saône (Green 1989, 40, 161; Green 1992, 196). There is evidence in the vicinity of Chalon, that many Iron-Age objects, for example swords, cauldrons, and cups, were deposited in the river Saône (1994, 147–149).

Sucellus

The god *Sucellus* was worshipped widely across Gaul; his name is interpreted as **good striker** (Green 1992, 200). One of his major shrines occurs on the springs which feed the river Arroux, and it is possible that he may have originated as a spring or river deity, or that he replaced such a deity at that site. This deity will be further discussed in Chapters 5 and 6.

Telo

Telo was the eponymous spirit of Toulon, in the Dordogne. She presided over the sacred springs around which the settlement developed (Green 1992, 208). Three dedications to her are known from nearby Périgueux, where she was associated with another, goddess *Stanna*.

Vesontius

The god *Mars Vesontius* was worshipped at Besançon (Green 1989, 111), and it is from him that the city most probably took its name. Such an association usually hints at the name of the deity being a homonym with a land toponym, usually a river.

Vindonnus

The deity *Apollo Vindonnus* was worshipped at the curative springs of Essarois, near

Châtillon-sur-Seinne in Burgundy (Green 1992, 32). Some of the sculpture from the sanctuary consists of parts of the body, such as arms holding cake or fruit, and plaques with eyes on them. A dedication to *Vindonnus*, recovered from part of the temple pediment also depicts a head with a radiant crown of light. The name may mean *Vindo-onn*, **white ash**.

Vosegus

The Vosges Mountains shared their name with the god *Vosegus*, a woodland deity who personified the range of hills (Green 1992, 220–221; Derke 1990, 136–137). He was worshipped at the sanctuary of Le Donon; it is believed that two of the deities depicted at the site represent him. He was portrayed as a god with a spear, a hunting knife, a chopper, and a wolfskin over his shoulder; he was accompanied by a stag. *Vosegus* carried the fruits of the forest, including acorns and pinecones, in a bag. We know that the name was also applied to rivers, as Lucan noted that a camp was built on the river *Vosegi* (*Vosegus*) to control the warlike *Lingones*, and that it flowed into Lake *Lemmano* (Duff 1967, i.395–400).

Xulsigia

The *Xulsigiae* were a group of local mother goddesses worshipped at a spring site in the vicinity of Trier (Green 1992, 228). The case of *Glanis* and *Glanicae* (Haeussler 2007, 91) suggests that there should also be a singular form, either male or female.

Conclusions

Amongst the Gallic and Germanic river gods a number were associated with animal names, and bright or light names. Certain divine names were associated with animals: *Cernunos*, *Baco*, *Artio* and *Mercury Artaios*. No associations with rivers or springs have been found for these names, although there may have been some. Words which may have been part of river-name components, as they turn up in Gallic personal names, are: **alias* (**alder**), **bosco* (**wood**), *cassano* (**oak**), *eburo* (**yew**), *lisco* (**sedge**), *onn* (**ash**), *banu* (**pig**), *boduo* (**royston crow**), *caruo* (**deer**), *catta* (**bird**), *cattus* (**cat**), *epo* (**horse**), *lucot* (**mouse**), *mand* or *mannus* (**pony**), *matu* (**bear**), *mel* (**honey bee**), *taruo* (**bull**), *volc* (**hawk**), or *verbu* (**amber**) (Ellis Evans 1967, 291–292). Ascertaining further information on the origins of these names is difficult. With respect to certain cults, such as that of *Bormanus* and *Damona*, one could postulate that, as the female had a divine animal name, she may have been the original deity of the spring, and that she was usurped by a Celtic 'Apollo' type god, but this remains unproven.

While the derivation of river-names from specific groups of names with specific meanings is one factor that we need to consider, we also need to consider the association with ancestry and folk-group origins. The idea that groups of people claimed descent from deities was implied in the texts of Tacitus (Hutton, Ogilvie *et al.* 1970, *Germania* 2):

> *'Their ancient hymns – the only style of record or history which they possess – celebrate a god Tuisto, a scion of the soil. To him they ascribe a son Mannus, the beginning of their race, and to Mannus three sons, its founders; from whose names the tribes nearest the*

Ocean are to be known as Ingaevones, the central tribes as Herminones, and the rest as Istaevones.'

It is clear that the tribes perceived themselves as descending from the god, and that the tribes took their name from characters in this divine descent. This idea seems to have been embedded in the Germanic cultures from at least the first century AD. We are in more speculative territory with the statement concerning *Viridomix*, a third century AD descendent of *Rhenus* (Saint Clair Baddeley 1924, 27), because the source data has not been located. The Gaulish personal name *Viridovix* was recorded by Dio Cassius (Ellis Evans 1967, 126); however we are told that he was a leader of the *Venelli* in 56 BC, during the time of the *Gallic War* (Cary 1969, xxxix.45). A further group of Gaulish leaders also claimed descent from gods, became the personification of local rivers, and took their names from animals, plants, or mineral deposits. These include: *Camulogenus*, the descendents or son of the god *Camulos* (Ellis Evans 1967, 60–61, 203–207); *Caprigenus*, the children of the goat; *Boduogenus*, the sons of the Royston crow; *Vernogenus*, the offspring of the alder; *Matugenus*, those begat by a bear; and *Isanogenus*, who claimed an origin from mineral deposits. We find similar cases in the Welsh Marches and in the West Country of Britain; for example the place *Branogenium* referred to the descendants of the raven (Rivet and Smith 1979, 275). This means that in Gaul and Britain there were groups called the Bear People, the Raven People, and the Alder People, among others. It is only when we start looking at local folk-names that it becomes apparent that the folk-groups used river-names or spring-names to give themselves their local identity.

BRITAIN AND IRELAND

In the surviving myths of Wales and Ireland it is possible to glean a view of how British and West European traditions may have contained ideas similar to those discussed for Australia and Greece. In some of the tales, for example, there are mythical journeys associated with rivers or hills. It is not apparent, however, how these traditions developed; was it a way of explaining the name of the river, or was it part of the story which was associated with the naming of the river? There are also concerns about the antiquity of some of the component parts of these stories. Could the mythological tales have been a means of expressing knowledge for human survival? Many of the main books written on 'Celtic' religion deal with certain aspects of flora and fauna cults, for example Ross's (Ross 1967), but the main synthesis in more recent times was carried out by Aldhouse-Green (Green 1992, 162–195). Though general synthesis of the textual sources is important we still have to reach the point at which we can contextualise these ideas at a local level, be that tribal or non-tribal. This can be achieved through the combination of archaeological material and an analysis of the surviving onomastics.

IRELAND

A number of Irish rivers were recorded by Ptolomy (Ptolemaeus 1966). These included: the *Dabrona*, the *Iverne*, the *Dur*, the *Senos* (Shannon), the *Ausoba*, the *Libnios*, the *Ravios*, the *Vidva*, the *Argita*, the *Logia*, the *Vinderis*, the *Buvinda* (Boyne), the *Oboca*, and the *Modonnos*. Amongst these names a number have animal or plant associations, and some of the names may be equated with names found in Wales.

Boann

In Irish mythology, both the Shannon and the Boyne were associated with mythical journeys concerning their respective deities. The river-name Boyne, originally recorded as *Buvinda*, has been associated with the Gaelic *Boann* or *Boand*, the etymology of which is she of the **white cattle** (Ross 1967, 47; Green 1992, 44). She was the wife of *Nechtan* and was not allowed to visit his sacred well (the well of *Segais*); nevertheless she went there contemptuously and walked around the well, from which the waters rose up and chased her to the sea. The water's course became the river which now bears her name; in various versions of the tale she is either drowned at the source of the river or survived. There are a number of features in the tale which one can also find in the earlier Greek traditions, especially the river being associated with a specific animal, in this case a white cow. There is also the association with an individual being killed in the river, and the river taking the name of that individual. In this case, unlike in Greece, the name is firmly part of the animal traditions of river-names.

Sionan

The name Shannon, originally recorded as *Senos*, was derived from *Sionan* the daughter of *Lodan* (Ross 1967, 47). She ventured to the well of knowledge at the source of the river (the well of *Coelrind*) where the waters rose up and chased her to the sea, where she was drowned.

Conclusion

These two river stories are obviously very similar; the fact that one of the names means the **white cow** indicates that there was at one time a tradition which saw certain animals enact mythical journeys across the landscape which accounted for the rivers' creation and course. These rivers each had a sacred spring at their source, in both cases associated with knowledge. The source was where the goddess of the river transgressed, and the end was where the river terminated and the transgressor died. In the case of both of these rivers this was in the estuary when the rivers reached the sea.

BRITAIN

In western Britain Welsh traditions also have stories describing mythical creatures travelling across the landscape, although how and when they originated is not known. Interpretations of these stories can be found in *Celtic Folklore: Welsh and Manx* by John Rhys. One of these creatures was a sow called *Henwen*, who was with litter at a place called Kernyw (Rhys 1901, 503–508). It had been foretold that the island of Britain would be the worse for her brood and that it should be destroyed. She then took to the sea off the headland of Hawstin, before returning to land, where she dropped a grain of wheat and a bee at Maes Gwenith in Gwent. This place thus became the most renowned in Wales for the production of wheat and honey. At *Llonyon* she dropped a grain of wheat and a grain of barley. On *Rhiw Gyferthwch*, in *Afron*, *Henwen* then dropped a wolf-cub and an eagle chick, while at Llanfair, in *Arfon* below *Maen Du*, she dropped a kitten, which became the *Cath Paluc* a giant cat which terrorised the land. The mythical sow produced both beneficial and malevolent offspring, and deposited her offspring at specific locations. Why these sites were chosen is not now apparent, and there is nothing to suggest that this mythical journey was associated specifically with a river. There is also no obvious date at which this tale evolved; was it associated with a purely medieval take on the landscape and its fertility or did it descend from earlier traditions? If the latter was the case then one wonders whether it would be possible to find evidence for pre-Christian shrines.

Other examples of mythical journeys in the Welsh traditions can be found in the Mabinogion; for example, the tale of *Twrch Trwyth*, a boar, which ranged across Wales at the head of its offspring (Rhys 1901, 509–542). The boar had three objects placed between its ears, which needed to be secured: a comb, a razor, and a pair of shears. We are first told that the boar resided at a place called *Esgeir Oervel* in Ireland, by *Menw* a magician who tried to grab one of the treasures but just removed a bristle. Arthur went to Ireland with a host; the ensuing hunt laid waste to a fifth of the country. One of the offspring of *Twrch* is claimed to have been killed in Ireland. *Gwrhyr*, the interpreter of tongues, was then sent to communicate with *Twrch Trwyth* to find out if it would speak with Arthur. The boar *Grugyn Gwrych Ereint* (silver bristles) answered and refused; as a result the boar promised that its group would set out for Arthur's country and do all the harm they could there. The boars came ashore in Wales at *Porth Clais*; from where they travelled on to *Deugleðyf*, and then to Precelly. Arthur's men started hunting them along the banks of the Nevern. The *Twrch* then moved on to the *Cwm Kerwyn*, and then to a region called *Peuliniauc*. He then crossed from Ginst Point to the Towy Mouth, and from there to Clyn Ystyn. There was a tremendous battle in the valley of the *Loughor* where *Grugyn* and *Llwydawc Gouynnyat* did much damage. From there the boars continued on to *Wynyð Amanw*, where one of them, *Banw*, was killed. Two others were also killed in the area, *Twrch Llawin*, and *Gwys*. *Twrch Trwyth* then went to the vale of the Amman and lost another boar and a sow; with two remaining offspring Twrch headed for *Llwch Ewin*, the pool of Ewin, from where he travelled to *Llwch Tawi*. *Grugyn* then split away from the herd and headed for Towy Fort, before heading to Keredigion where he was killed, at *Garth Grugyn*. *Llwydawc* headed for Ystrad Yw, near Cwm Du, where he was also killed. The *Twrch* then headed towards the mouth of the river Severn. In this tale the Welsh landscape is filled with a mythical narrative and some of the creatures described have left their names behind. Rhys believed that *Twrch Trwyth* was associated with the Irish Orc or *Torc Tréith*, the name meaning king's boar. He also noted that the story was designed to account for certain place-names. *Grugyn* and *Garth Grugyn* were associated, *Gwys* was the name of a tributary of the Twrch; then there is *Twrch Llawin* who was associated with the river Twrch. Rhys also believed that *Llwydawc Gouynnyat* should account for a place-name, and that the name *Amanw* or *Amman* is also masked in this tale. He assumed, therefore, that the story was constructed to account for the names in this particular district of South Wales. At that time, Rhys was not aware how rivers in Europe came to be named, and that there may have been underlying traditions associating the rivers with mythical animals and genealogies.

In the rest of Britain there is evidence that the rivers were deified in a similar way, an idea which will be returned to later. Even though these are early medieval tales, parts of the stories are possibly far older; the fragmentary pieces being brought together in the early medieval period in the currently-known form. This process could explain the dispersed nature of some of the sites in the tale, although the river systems around the Glamorganshire and Carmarthenshire borders are the central core around which the tale was constructed. Of the river-names identified in this tale, the name *Twrch* has the etymology of **boar**, and *Gwys* means **sow**.

There are also other medieval traditions which discuss animals in a sacred or mythological context, many in the context of the foundation of religious establishments. They also contain creatures enacting mythical journeys, their mission to determine where a sacred site was to be located. Some of the earliest tales concerned the foundations of early Christian churches in South Wales. The churches of Saint *Gwynllyw* and Saint *Cadoc* were founded by a white boar and a white ox respectively (Knight 1971, 30). The church of Llandogo was dedicated to Saint *Oudoceus*, claimed as the third bishop of Llandaff; the miracle story associated with it refers to a stag taking refuge on the cloak of *Oudoceus*, on the banks of the *Caletan* (Cleddon) brook (Knight 2004, 275). Besides these there was also a magical horse in the tradition of the foundation of the new royal site at Portskewett (Knight 2004, 282–283).

How and when these flora and fauna legends arose, and when the cult formed around a river or a particular spring is unknown, but even in Britain we can start to identify some of the deities who presided over specific rivers. Sometimes these are known divinities, sometimes the names of animals which may previously have been regarded as divinities. At this stage it may be appropriate to give some of the known Brittonic animal and plant river-names from around Britain.

Aeron

The river *Aeron*, in Cardiganshire, is considered to take its name from a goddess who was a personification of battle (Owen and Morgan 2007, 1).

Alaw

In Anglesey there is a river Alaw, of which the etymology is *water lily* (Owen and Morgan 2007, 13). The name fits into the wider group of river-names associated with plants and animals which are evident in the Brittonic tongue. At a later date the river was called the Aber Glaslyn.

Arnemetia

The goddess *Arnemetia* was revered at the Derbyshire sanctuary of *Aquae Arnemetiae*, now called Buxton (Ross 1967, 57). The name of the goddess is considered to mean **before the sacred grove** (Rivet and Smith 1979, 254–255).

Artro

The Artro is a river-name found in Merionethshire which was initially interpreted as winding river; it has now, however, been decided that this is inappropriate and that it must be derived from *Arthro*, **bear** (Owen and Morgan 2007, 18). The *Helvetti* goddess *Artio* and the Gaulish *Mercury Artaios*, are both names derived from the same root word.

Aventia

The river Ewenni is probably associated with the recorded British river-name *Auentios*, which can be associated with the continental river names Avance and Avenza (Rivet and Smith 1979, 260–261; Owen and Morgan 2007, 143). The name of the goddess was probably *Aventia* and was probably a spring goddess; the name is usually interpreted as meaning **to moisten**, or **to flow**.

Banw

There are a number of rivers called Banw in Wales (Owen and Morgan 2007); an account of the story of *Twrch* in the Mabinogion, and its interpretation by Rhys, was given above.

Bran

The river Brân, which has an etymology **crow** (Owen and Morgan 2007, 44, 46), is a tributary of the river Usk in Brecknockshire, while Brenig, a lake in Denbighshire, represents a variation of this name. The deity turned up as a character in the Mabinogion. The name is attested as being used in the Roman period in the examples of *Branodunum* and *Branogenium* (descendants of the Raven) (Rivet and Smith 1979, 274–275).

Brigantia

Brigantia is a recognised divine tribal name and is associated with the rivers Brent and Braint (Ross 1967, 47; Rivet and Smith 1979, 278–280). A number of altars have dedications to this goddess in various guises: *Caelestis Brigantia* at Corbridge (RIB(I) 1995, no.1131), the *Nympa Brigantia* at Castlesteads (RIB(I) 1995, no.2066), *Brigantia Augusta*, and *Victoria Brigantia* at Castleford and Greetland (RIB(I) 1995, nos.627, 628). The fact that the goddess was recorded as a nymph indicates that the river-name association with her is correct. The name has been interpreted as meaning high (Ekwall 1928, 51–52), although it is also associated with the Welsh words *brenin*, **king**, and *braint*, **status** (Owen and Morgan 2007, 44).

Cannaid

The river-name Cannaid is considered to go back to a root-word meaning **bright** or **shining** (Owen and Morgan 2007, 2).

Cano-

The Roman fort of *Canovium* was located at Caerhun, and seems to contain an ancient river-name (Owen and Morgan 2007, 96). There was a similar Roman name in Essex, England, at *Canonium*, which referred to the Roman settlement on the River Blackwater

(Rivet and Smith 1979, 296–297); one could surmise that this is the older name of the Blackwater. The name is believed to be associated with the Welsh word *cawn*, **reeds**, derived from the British **cāno-*, of a similar meaning.

Cegir

The interpretation of Cegir is that it comes from a Welsh word which has the etymology of **hemlock** (Owen and Morgan 2007, 3).

Cennen

It has been suggested that the River Cennen takes its name from the word *cen*, **lichen** (Owen and Morgan 2007, 81), which is frequently found on the limestone rocks from where the river rises. A further possibility is that the name contains *[I]ceno-* which lies at the root of the tribal name *Iceni* and the *Cenimagni*, a variation in the spelling of the *Iceni* tribal name (Rivet and Smith 1979, 374).

Chwilog

The river-name Chwilog seems to be derived from **beetle** (Owen and Morgan 2007, 84).

Clota

The river Clyde was revered in Roman times as the *Clota* (Ross 1967, 47). The name could have derived from Gaulish personal name elements *clouto*, *cloto* and *cluto*, interpreted as meaning **to hear** (Ellis Evans 1967, 180–181). Rivet and Smith (1979, 310), however, recognised *Clota* as a river-goddess and suggested the word meant **the washer** or **the strong flowing one**.

Coventina

The nymph venerated at Carrawburgh was called *Coventina* (RIB(I) 1995, nos.1522–1525, 1528–1530, 1532–1535). Her shrine is a *nymphaeum*, with a spring rising from inside a square structure.

Craf

Craf is derived from a word which means **garlic** (Owen and Morgan 2007, 3), the river is a tributary of the Conwy.

Cywarch

The river-name Cywarch has the etymology **hemp** (Owen and Morgan 2007, 4).

Dar

A number of rivers in Wales take their name from the word *dâr*, **oak** (Owen and Morgan 2007, 4). The word must have derived from the Celtic **daru-*, **oak** (Rivet and Smith 1979, 353).

Deva

The river-name Dee originated as *Deva*, from the Celtic **dēuā*, **goddess** or **holy river** (Ekwall 1928, 117–118; Ross 1967, 47; Rivet and Smith 1979, 336). References to three such rivers are known from the Roman period: at Chester, in Kirkcudbright, and one in Aberdeenshire, as well as some six other rivers from north-west Britain. The river-name also occurred in Ireland, France and Spain. The name of the deity is derived from the same root word as Zeus and Jupiter, and thus fitted into a wider and more ancient linguistic tradition (see Chapter 2).

Eburos

The river Vernwy, or Efyrnwy, in Montgomeryshire is considered to have taken its name from **Ebur* with the suffix *-nwy* (Owen and Morgan 2007, 137); it is a tributary of the Severn. The name is similar to the Roman name of York, *Eboracum*, and *Eburo Castellum*, a fort near the Scottish-English border. The same element turns up as a common component of place-names of the Roman period (Rivet and Smith 1979, 355–357), in both Britain and on the Continent.

Elain-

The river-name Elan is associated with the Welsh word *elain*, a **hind** or **fawn** (Owen and Morgan 2007, 140).

Gwennol

There is a river Gynolwyn which is considered, from its earliest recorded names, to contain part of the word *gwennol*, a **swallow** or a **swift** (Owen and Morgan 2007, 9).

Leucaro-

The Roman fort at Loughor took its name from the river; the fort was called *Leucara* or *Leucarum* in *c.* 300 AD (Rivet and Smith 1979, 388–389; Owen and Morgan 2007, 302). The name is presently interpreted as having the meaning **daylight** or **light**. The *-ar* suffix is believed to be a common river-name component which means **great river.** It is possible that the name is associated with the Greek word *leukerodios* or *leucorodia*, which is the name of the **spoonbill** (Pollard 1977, 71), a bird with white plumage. This species breeds in a number of European locations, the nearest of which to Britain is the Netherlands; it is, however, a frequent visitor to the North Sea coast to feed. It could be that its range was once much larger than it is today. The association with a bird whose name means light has been noted elsewhere (see *Lugus*).

Nido

The remains of a Roman fortification, called in texts *Nido* (Owen and Morgan 2007, 342), have been found at Neath. The fort took its name from the river on which it stood, hence *Nidum*; as yet no satisfactory derivation of the name has been suggested. The name is associated with the Yorkshire Nidd, and the two German rivers Nidda and Nied. It is possible that these names may be extremely old and associated with the Greek river-name *Neda*.

Sentona

The name of a river-goddess is concealed in the names of the following rivers: Tarrant in Devon; Trent, an earlier name of the river Arun; Trannon in Montgomeryshire (Owen and Morgan 2007, 462); Trent, in Worcestershire; a Tarrant and a possible Trent, in Dorset; and a possible Trent in Somerset (Rivet and Smith 1979, 476–478). The river name has the prefix *Tri-*, **three**, which can be explained as a development from the way in which rivers were deified and the means by which the identity and sense of belonging were developed by the communities who lived along those rivers. From examples on the continent, at Glanum and Nîmes, it is apparent that springs were deified individually, and that there was a group of *matres*, or mothers, who were worshipped at those sites. These factors then became related to the genealogy of the groups living around the rivers. This happened amongst both the continental and British tribes (Yeates 2006v, 57–66); but in addition to this we can say that if you had a goddess, *Sentona*, and a group of *Matres* you would have *Tri-Sentona* or three *Sentona*. The name is just another means of expressing the trinity of the divine *matres*.

Soch-

The Irish river-name *Soch-* has the Welsh form *hwch* the etymology of which is **sow** (Owen and Morgan 2007, 11).

Tanad-

In North Wales there is a river Tanat believed to be derived from the Brittonic word *tân*, **bright**, plus the suffix *-ad* (Owen and Morgan 2007, 456). The same root word was used for *Tanatis* or *Tanatus*, the name of the Isle of Thanet (Rivet and Smith 1979, 468–469), showing that both names are ancient but not necessarily Britonnic.

Conclusions

There is evidence that north-west European rivers had, like the rivers of southern Europe, associations with animals or plants. This is also evident through our understanding of Brittonic river-names. Onomastics can help in our understanding of what exactly the ancient river-names were, and what we could expect to find depicted on religious inscriptions and reliefs, if any were recovered. Other potential river names are hinted at by some of the recorded place-names for Roman Britain: *Aballava* (**apple-tree**), *Anas* (**duck**), *Bovium* (**cow**), *Caereni* (**sheep**), *Calacum* (**the caller** or **cock**), *Carvetii* (**deer, stag**), *Concangis* (**horse**), *Derventio* (**oak**), *Durovernum* (**alder**), *Epidii/Epidium/Eposessa* (**horse**), *Gabrantovices* (**horse/goat**), *Lugi* (**raven**), *Manduessedum* (**pony-chariot** or **chariot-pony**), *Marcotaxum* (**horse**), *Matovium* (**bear**), *Oleracum*(?) (**swan**), *Onna* (**ash**), *Orcades* (*boar*), *Saponis* (**pine**), *Spinis* (**black-thorn**), and *Tarvedunum* (**bull**) (Rivet and Smith 1979, 238, 249, 273–274, 286, 288, 296, 301, 314, 333–336, 353, 363, 401, 411–412, 414, 431, 433, 452, 462, 469).

DOBUNNIC SACRED ANIMALS, TREES, RIVERS AND SPRINGS

In both Irish and Welsh traditions there are tales which explained the cultural importance of natural features and associated them with divine or supernatural beings. In many cases these supernatural beings shared their names with rivers and hills. Known examples of Brittonic river and hill names focus on flora and fauna names, besides others. This means that we will be able to determine many more names of *Dobunnic* and British divinities than had previously been considered, due simply to understanding the onomastics and linguistic developments. The understanding of river-name formation is essential if we are to start assessing which river-names are of antiquity and which are more recent, hence which could have been divine names. In an earlier work (Yeates 2006b, 63–81) I showed that, in the medieval period, it was invariably the case that rivers had two names, one of which was ancient (Celtic), the other a more recent development (Old English); for example, the Windrush and the Dickler, and the Bladon and the Evenlode. It was evident that one set of names had probably been used since the Iron Age at least, with the other set being introduced in the post-migration Anglo-Saxon period. It may seem obvious that the changes, in part, occurred due to language change or population replacement, as envisaged previously, but this has now been questioned and new names probably occurred more due to changes in ideology, which may in some cases have occurred with the introduction of new languages. When considering river-names in the *Dobunni-Hwicce* territory and in the adjacent part of Wales, the *Silures-Glywysinga*, it becomes evident that name changes in the early medieval period were comparable, even though Wales was affected far less by the Anglo-Saxon migration. The place-name changes were probably caused by a number of factors. Settlements have a life span; they are founded, lived in, and then abandoned. Once abandoned the name of the settlement may be wholly or partially recognised for numerous years, and it may become altered philologically, or corrupted, before finally being lost. Certain names used by communities were not specific to settlements; for example the toponyms of the landscape or names of folk-groups. These names will have developed differently and would probably have survived far longer than the settlement names. Coupled to these ideas it is also possible to detect another type of name change that occurred in South Wales. This is most notable in the introduction of names using llan (an enclosure and later church), church and basilica. In such cases the name change did not relate to the change of people or the change of language but to the changing ideology resulting from the introduction of a new religion. Certain settlements in South Wales and the Marches developed more than one place-name. Examples of this include Caerleon, a hybrid name of Welsh and Latin origin, derived from the Roman period name (Owen and Morgan 2007, 64). The parish or ecclesiastical name for the area is Llangattock, which refers to the enclosure of **the church of Saint Cadog** (Owen and Morgan 2007, 255–256). The settlement has, therefore, two names; one using a settlement name developing from pre-Christian and Roman imperial times, and the latter, firmly entrenched in the new Christian ideology. The same development can be recognised at Hentland, in Herefordshire. In the thirteenth century AD, the village was called Archenfield (Matthews 1913, 129–130); the present name Hentland referring to the **Old Church** (Ekwall 1960, 255). Near Hentland was a hamlet called *Erchin Holm*, recorded in 1291 AD, which lay on the river Wye (Matthews 1912, 14). Due to the location of these medieval place-names it is more likely that the Roman period *Ariconium* lay in the Hentland area and not at Weston-under-Penyard, where it is claimed to have been located until now. This suggests that the Roman settlement name survived in a philologically altered form, with additions, but eventually succumbed to the name referring to the area's Christian monuments. All of this supports the idea that many settlements changed name not because of the language change but due to the ideological change; the change from a deified landscape into the Christian world. This process can also be recognised in the *Dobunnic-Hwiccian* example of Evesham and Bibury; and in France in the case of Saint Marcel, Berry, and others. In the case of Evesham (discussed below) and Bibury it is evident, from surviving church documents, that these settlements have names associated with the traditions of the foundation of the churches as the people are, currently, considered to be historically documented characters.

If there was an ideological change driving settlement name alteration, could it also have led to name changes for rivers and other landscape features, such as hill ranges and individual hills at an earlier date? In order to determine this we would need to obtain information on what type of ideologies existed at specific times and how names changed over time. Certain types of name can be defined as deriving from a pre-Christian mode of thought. Of river-names there are two types which stand out as having particular antiquity. The first includes the flora and fauna group. We can identify animal and plant names in the place-names that existed in north-west Europe prior to the arrival of, and during the time of, the Romans. Two examples are *Bibracte* (Edwards 1963, i.23, vii.55, 63, 90, viii.2, 4) or *Bibrax* (Edwards 1963, ii.6), derived from the word **bibro*, **a beaver**, and those names attributed to words for brightness, for example *Glevum* (Rivet and Smith 1979, 368–369). Other groups of spring and river-names are related specifically to the ideologies that were developing in Christianity; a good example of this are names derived from numbers of which **seven,** as a spring-name, was the most frequently used (Briggs 2007, 7–44). We can make a list of the known river gods, but finding relationships between them or understanding how different rivers were perceived if they had the same name will be more difficult. For a distribution of the divine river-names across the *Dobunnic* territories see Figures 27, 29, 31, 33–34, 36–39, and 41–42.

Alaun-

The river-name Alne occurs in Warwickshire, and was also the name of a significant Roman period settlement at the confluence of the Arrow and Alne. It occurs in various forms across Britain: Allan, Aln, Allen, Alne and Ellen, and has been associated with the Celtic divinity *Mercury Alaunos* (Owen and Morgan 2007, 15). The precise meaning of the name is unknown. In Welsh interpretations the present belief is that any river starting with **al*, is seen as a reference to **wandering**. Other interpretations of the name have been suggested, usually **very white**, but an alternative interpretation by Pokorny (Rivet and Smith 1979, 243–247) who associated the name with the Gaulish **alausa*, the **alose** or **shad**. It is not apparent how one explains the difference with the <s> and <n>, and it would probably be more acceptable to see the word as akin to the Latin word *alnus*, **an alder**; or, alternatively and more likely, it could be related to the Welsh river-name Elan, derived from Welsh *elain* or *alan*, and the Cornish **elen*, **a fawn** (Padel 1985, 92).

Amimonedos

Amman is a known Welsh river-name (Owen and Morgan 2007, 16) which turns up in Gloucestershire, in the form of Ampney Brook, in Worcestershire, and in Berkshire as the Amwell. There are problems with the suggestion that it is derived from *banw*, **pig** or **piglet** (see above). The altar from Siddington seems to contain the name *Amimonedos*

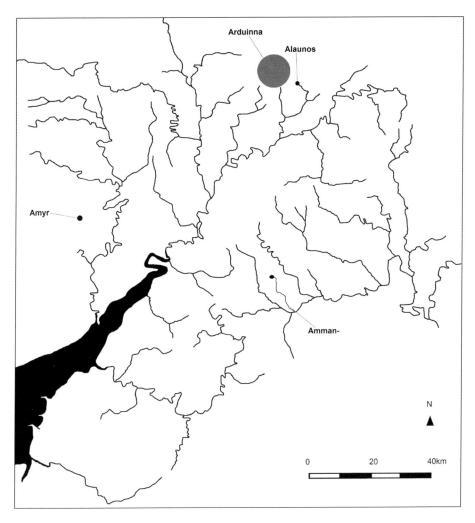

Figure 27: A map of the divine river-names in and around the Dobunnic territory starting with the letter A (drawing S. Yeates)

(under research, see Figure 28); if this is confirmed then it has parallels with the Ancient Greek river-name *Amymone*.

Arduinna

The goddess *Arduinna* is known on the continent where she was recognised as the presiding spirit of the *Arduenna Silva* (Derks 1998, 136–137). She was portrayed as a Diana-type huntress who rode on a wild boar. The reason for her inclusion here is that her name has been associated with the origins of the Forest of Arden, and it is evident from the linguistic association that some similar type of goddess must be envisaged,

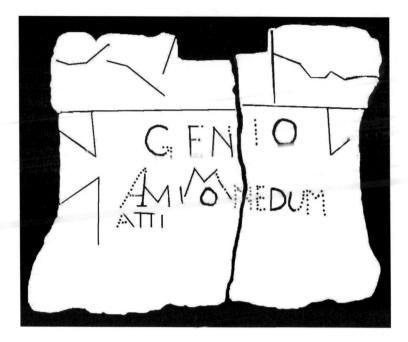

Figure 28: A drawing of the Roman altar from Siddington on which the name inscribed may have been Amimonedum (drawing S. Yeates)

even if we have not categorically demonstrated that her name has been found on a local inscription. The name is considered to contain *ardu-*, **high**, as its first component (Watts 2004, 17). The forest is discussed more fully elsewhere (Yeates 2006a; Yeates 2008b, 25–27). Certain aspects of folk tradition may have survived, been reworked or reinvented from archaeological material not now extant. The tale concerning the foundation of the abbey at Evesham, in about AD 700 (Macray 1863), may contain allusions to this goddess. The three divine females are undoubtedly a transformation of the *Dobunnic* mothers. *Eoves* (meaning **boar**) was the swine herder who followed the lost sow and came across the Virgin Mary. The question arises with respect to the identity of *Eoves*, whose name is associated with the foundation of Evesham abbey. Was he some mythical personification associated with older legends of the Forest of Arden or the local folk-group of Evesham? The name Evesham was also recorded as *Ecguines hamme* (840 x 852); in this the town was associated with Bishop *Ecgwine* of Worcester who founded the monastery and was buried there. Camden, in the sixteenth century AD, recorded that a boar was slain by Diana of the Woods in a place near Coventry. Only one textual source has been identified that gives an idea of how these topographical deities may have fitted into the local mythical tales which must have existed. This is the story of Plynlimon and his daughters, who were rivers that flowed from their mountain father. It is possible, but not provable, that *Arduinna*, and other topographical features, may have been perceived as the mother of the rivers which flowed from their rock strata.

Amyr

The river Gamber, in south-west Herefordshire, was originally recorded as *Amyr* in *c.* 1130 AD (Bannister 1916, 79). It was probably personified in the past as an eponymous god; as, in *The Wonders of Britain*, it was associated with a son of Arthur called *Amr*, whose tomb lay near the source of the river (Morris 1980, 42). He is mentioned once in the Mabinogion as *Amhar*, son of Arthur (Jones and Jones 1974, 231). This association between the name and the mythical character suggests strongly that he was a figure deified in the past. The river-name is also found on the continent in the form of: Amper, Emmer and Ammergau; while the name is associated with **ambr*, the suggested meaning of which is water (Ekwall 1928, 13). The interpretation of every river name by place-name experts as water must be suspect, so the origins of this particular name must be regarded as unresolved; it is possible, however, that the Brittonic name was related to the Old High German *amero*, **a yellow hammer** (Smith 1956, 9), or was associated with *emmer*, a type of **wheat**. In all of these cases there seems to have been an association with the colour yellow, or yellow-orange with respect to amber, the bird, and the ripened wheat field.

Bal-

The Grimley Brook, in Worcestershire, was, in the Anglo-Saxon charters of the area, referred to as the *Bæle* or *Bæles* in 851 AD (Mawer and Stenton 1927, 11); the name was also used for a tributary of the Arrow, at Alvechurch in the same county. The stream-name at Grimley, previously *Bæle*, survives in the name of Ball Mill, which lies on that brook. The word probably derived from a Celtic word, which occurred in Gallic personal names as *bal* or *ball*, equated with *bal(i)o*, white (Ellis Evans 1967, 147). The personal name part could be due to an origin as a divine-name and river-name of some antiquity. In Irish traditions there was a character called *Balar*, earlier *Bolar*, which was derived from the Celtic **Boleros*. The word means lightning, but at the time lightning was perceived as emanating from the sun (O'Rahilly 1946, 59). The deity was associated with a single eye and was probably a male representation of the sun. It has already been noted (Chapter 3) that there was probably a temple under the village of Grimley. Because of the way in which the Grimley Brook has been associated with potential religious activities it may mean that Ball may not be the old name.

Bebro-

The Barbourne Brook to the north of Worcester was recorded in AD 904 as *Beferburna*. This word is derived from *beofor*, **beaver**, although it may in turn have derived from the British **bebro*, also meaning **beaver**. On the opposite bank of the river Severn, in the Wyre Forest, there was a *Beferic*, which contains the word ***bebro** (Grundy 1927, 143–145; Ekwall 1928, 31–32). The ancient origin of these river-names, and their possible association with a *genius*, is perhaps inferred by the use of the name on the continent.

Beda

Beda is the name of a goddess recorded along with the name of another goddess, *Fimmilena*, on an altar found at Housteads (RIB(I) 1995, no.1593). The *Bædeswellan* was the name of a stream which flowed through Badsey in Worcestershire. The name is

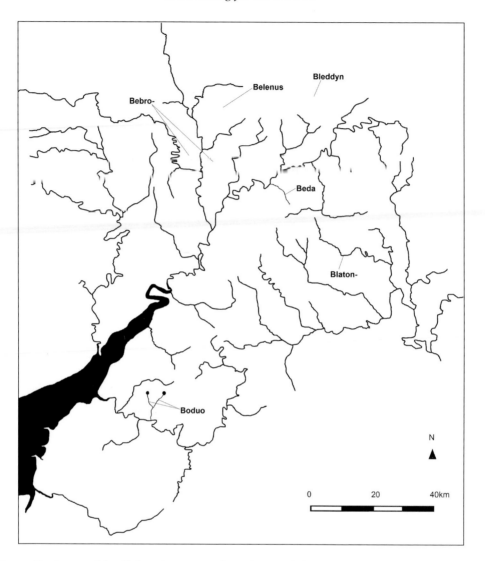

Figure 29: A map of the divine river-names in and around the Dobunnic territory starting with the letter B (drawing S. Yeates)

derived from *Bædda*, and gave its name to the folk-group the *Badsetena* (Mawer and Stenton 1927, 260–261), see Figure 30. The name can be associated with a recognised Welsh-river name *baedd*, **boar** or perhaps **wild pig** (Morgan and Powell 1999). The river-name also occurs in Aberbaiden, Brecknockshire.

Belenus

The Belbroughton brook was previously called the Bell (Mawer and Stenton 1927, 9, 274–275). The earliest known recording of its name is *Beolne*, in AD 817; it was recorded

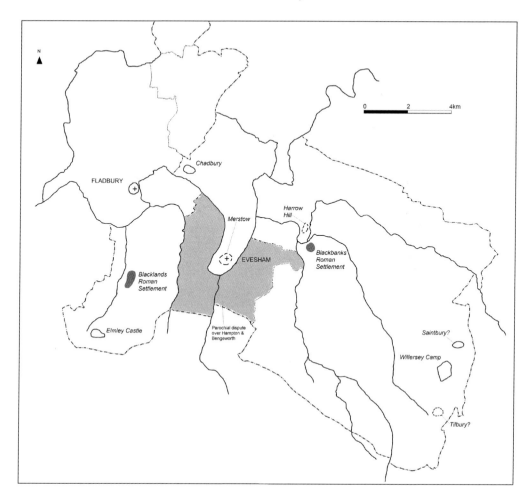

Figure 30: A map showing the parochiae of Evesham and Fladbury in Worcestershire. Evesham's territory was associated with the Badesæte (drawing S. Yeates)

as *Bellene* in AD 1275, and as *Bellenbrun* in AD 1280. It is possible that the name may be associated with the Celtic divinity *Belenus*. The god Belenus, **bright** or **brilliant**, was associated with Apollo and with healing cults in Aquitaine, Provence, and northern Italy (Green 1992, 30–31). He is associated with the festival of Beltane.

Blaton-

The river-name Bladen is recognised as being of British origin and comes from the British word *blatona* or *bladona* (Gelling 1953, 7). In an earlier work (Yeates 2006a, i.49; 2006b, 63–81; 2008b, 54) it was suggested that the name may be derived from the Welsh *blaidd*, **wolf**, but there are philological problems with this. The name could also be associated with the Welsh personal name *Blathaon*. *Blathaon* was the son of *Mwrheth*, and is regarded as one of Arthur's best and greatest knights (Jones and Jones 1974, 150). This may give a clue to the origin of *Blatonos;* if so then it is possible that the word is related to the Celtic/Brittonic **blato-*, **to bloom** (Rivet and Smith 1979, 268–269). This word is the recognised root of Roman period names in both Britain and the Continent.

Bleddyn-

The name *Bleddyn* has always been regarded as an early medieval Welsh personal-name, as the name was that of a king of Powys (Breeze 2000, 91). It is more probable, however, that it is more derived from the Welsh *bleidd*, **wolf**, whose final philological development in English would give the river-name Blyth, as found in Warwickshire and elsewhere in Britain. This group of river names have been discussed by Coates (2006, 23–29), where it was considered that, if of English origin, the name would have come from the Old English **blīðe*, blessed or happy. Alternatively this could have come from the Old English ***blīð*, derived in turn from the neo-Brittonic **bleið* (Yeates 2006b, 74–75).

Boduo

The river Boyd, in the south of Gloucestershire has confusing written forms. It was recorded as the river *byd* in a charter *c.* 950 AD (Smith 1964a, i.4), but has also occurred in a number of recorded names for Bitton; for example *Bettun c.* 1150, *Buttone c.* 1190, *Button c.* 1190, *Bitton'* or *Byton'* in 1248 and *Boyton* in 1275, using all possible vowel variations in the process (Smith 1964c, iii.75). It has been suggested that it is derived from the Old English *Byd*, which probably came from the Welsh *budd*, **profit, benefit**, or *budr*, **dirty** (Smith 1964a, i.4). Breeze (Breeze 2006, 111–112) suggested that it derived from the Celtic word **boud-*, meaning **victory** or **excellence**, and formed the first part of the name of Queen *Boudica*. The word has been associated with the Old Irish *búaid*, the Welsh *budd*, and the Breton *bud*. This river-name is also considered to show that there was a longer continuation of the Celtic or Brittonic derived language in the Gloucestershire area than had previously been believed. Ellis Evans (Ellis Evans 1967, 151, 156–158) noticed that *budd*, **profit** or **victory**, was a component part of a Gaulish personal name but that it was often confused with *Boduo*, a **Royston** or **hooded crow**. Thus, boduo is a further possibility and the name of this bird and **boud-* probably originated from an earlier common source. This name is significant because it is an animal name which would fit into the pre-Roman animal naming. It is also the name of an Irish goddess, written *Badbh* (Green 1992, 38), who, as the representation of a crow, was a symbol of war frenzy.

Caer-

The name Cherwell is recognised as being of pre-Old English origin (Ekwall 1928, 75–76), although the name has also been associated with the Old English *cear*, **a vessel**. The name is probably associated with the Gallic river-name Cher, and is also probably the first component of the tribal name *Carnutes*, the river name Carrant, and the Gallic names Charente and *Karantona*. There is also the Welsh river Ceiriog (Owen and Morgan 2007, 79). The first part of the name has also been associated with the Welsh *car*, **friend** (Smith 1964a, i.4–5) which has been associated with the Celtic words *carus*, **dear, friend** or **beloved one** or *caro*, **to love** (Ellis Evans 1967, 61, 162–165). If this derivation is correct certain connotations can be made. Evidence for this interpretation could be evident in the legendary traditions of Ireland in the story of *Oenghus* and *Caer* (Green 1995, 121–123). *Oenghus* was associated with birds, was the Irish god of love, and was the child of an illicit union between the *Dagdha* and *Boann*. The god of love, however, fell in love with a mortal woman called *Caer* who was under a shape shifting spell which made her change into a swan on every other Samhain for a year; she encapsulates many of the ideas which underlie this particular river-name. The name can be derived etymologically from love but, it also describes why the name was used. *Caer's* association with a mythical animal, a swan, may also be important and may conceal an older association, of the swan symbolising love. An alternative possibility is that the river's name is related to the British **caero-*, **a sheep**, especially **a ram** or **he-goat** (Rivet and Smith 1979, 286).

Camulos

Ekwall (1960, 271) suggested that the name Kemble was associated with the god *Camulos*. More recently this has become unfashionable and the tendency is to associate the name with *cyfyl*, **a border, brink or edge**. Breeze (2008, 255–256) considered Kemble to be an extremely ancient name; Watts (2004, 339) said that it lay in an area of fluctuating boundaries of the *Dobunni* territory. The name is probably ancient but, as seen in the discussions in Chapter 1, the area was not a location of fluctuating boundaries, as seen through the distribution of Iron-Age coinage and Roman sculptural reliefs, and even early medieval texts do not support this hypothesis. Potential archaeological evidence for the deification of the Upper Thames floodplain as *Camulos* was set out in an earlier work (Yeates 2006a; 2008b). Also relevant are the facts that Nennius used the name *Cafal*, Arthur's hound (Morris 1980, 42) and, in the Mabinogion *Cafall* was used as the name for a war horse (Jones and Jones 1974, 120). This is of interest as *Camulos* was seen by Aldhouse-Green (Green 1989, 113, 114), as being part of a horseman cult in his dedications at Reims, Rindern and Barhill.

Coll-

The river Cole takes its name from the Celtic **coll*, **hazel** (Ekwall 1928, 85); other rivers, including the Rea (née Cole) at Birmingham, the Colesbourne, and the Colwall also take their name from the same source. The only dedication found to a god associated with hazel trees is from Colchester where there was a shrine to *Silvanus Callirius* (Green 1992, 191); one interpretation of the name is **god of the hazel wood**. In the Colchester shrine there was a pit containing a small bronze plaque, with a dedication, and a small stag figurine. In Irish mythological traditions there was a character, *Mac Cuill* **son of the hazel** (Ross 1967, 54), which could be indicative of a mythical character called *Cuill* or *Coll*, **hazel**.

Corinius

The association between the river-name Churn and the Roman name, *Corinium*, for Cirencester suggests that *Corin-* > *Cerin*. The name Cerin has been associated with the Welsh *cern*, **a horn** (Ekwall 1928, 78–79), however, there are problems with this due to the previous association with the name *Durocornovium*. This has led to further suggestions

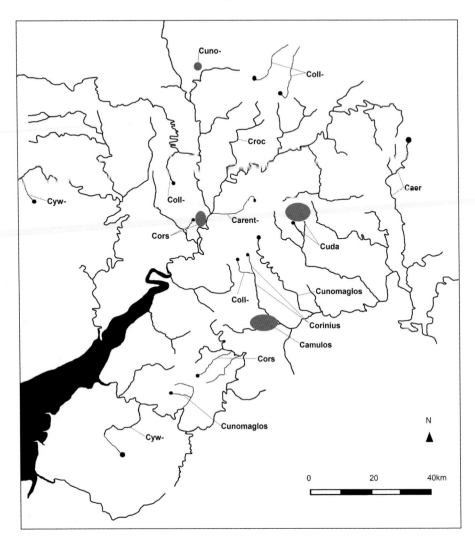

Figure 31: A map of the divine river-names in and around the Dobunnic territory starting with the letter C (drawing S. Yeates)

that the river-name used to be *Cornio* or *Cornia*, associated with the tribal-name *Cornovii*, but this derivation is not now accepted. Rivet and Smith (1979, 321) suggested that the name is associated with **ceri**, *medlartree*. There exists a carving of the sacred *genius* of Cirencester who, it can be argued due to the use of a mural crown, is *Corinius* (Yeates 2008b, 51, 59); it is feasible that the name is associated with the latin *Corin-*, a **crown**, referring to the head of the Thames. It is probably this character who appeared in the works of Geoffrey of Monmouth (see Chapter 3). However, a representation of a god claimed to be *Cernunos* (Henig 1993a, no.93) has also been found at Cirencester.

Cors

The name Corse is derived from the ancient British river-name *cors*, **reed** (Ekwall 1928, 95–96; Smith 1964c, iii.146). There are three locations in the *Dobunnic* territory where the name is known: in the Corse Forest is the Corswell Brook, a stream to the south of Malmesbury, now called the Gauze Brook (Watts 2004, 159), and the village of Corsham, which also probably derived its name from a brook called the *cors*. No dedication to a divinity of this topographical feature is known but the name fits well with the idea of areas having names of flora and fauna. This is also the known name for one of Arthur's knights in the Mabinogion, Cors Hundred Claws (Jones and Jones 1974, 101).

Croc-

In a charter for the estate of Crowle, from AD 840, the river-name *crohwællan* is recorded alongside the name of the local folk-group, the *crohhæma* (Grundy 1927, 66–68; Mawer and Stenton 1927, 315–316). The *crohwællan* was considered by Watts (2004, 172), to be the older name for the Bow Brook, but this has not been categorically confirmed. The *crohwællan*, being the primary name, determined the names of other features around it: the clearing by the river-*croh*, and the people who live on the *croh*. It was common for many early medieval folk-names to use ancient river-names as their prefix. The use of a plant-name as an old river-name indicates that the name was ancient. The Old English *croh* derived from the Latin *crocus* and it may have been the case that a Brittonic word derived from the same source. Of course, the date at which the crocus (Latin derived name), later called the saffron (Arabic derived name brought back by the Crusaders), was introduced into Britain is an important factor, and it is probable that it was used as a dye during the Roman period. British Roman villas are known to have had planned gardens into which a plant like this could have been introduced. It is now thought, however, that it may have died out and been reintroduced into Britain at the time of the crusades; this is all unproven.

Cuda

The name *Cuda* is inscribed on a relief from Daglingworth in the Cotswolds (Henig 1993a, no.102; RIB(I) 1995, no.129). Her cult has been discussed widely elsewhere (Yeates 2004, 1–8; 2006a, 9–27; 2006b, 63–83; 2007, 55–69; 2008b, 11–18). One new fact which has arisen since these debates is the recovery of a sculpture of this goddess from a site at Gill Mill (Henig pers. comm.) on the lee of the Cotswold dip slope. The name of the hills is shared by a river which is now called the Eye and the sculpture from her shrine at Lower Slaughter depicts images of a bird, which may be **a pigeon** (see Figure 32). Like the goddess of the Forest of Arden the mythological relationship which *Cuda* had with the rivers and other aspects of the Cotswolds is unknown.

Cuno-

The word *Cuno-* was used in a singular context in the place-name Kinver, in AD 736 as *Cynibre* (Watts 2004, 349); this was probably derived from British **Cunobriga*, **dog hill**. There is a recognisable group of Welsh river-names, some of which occurred with similar versions of the name in other parts of England, which contain the first component *cuno-*. These include: the Cynfal in Merionethshire, the Cynwrig in Brecknockshire, and the

Figure 32: The relief from a well at Lower Slaughter which shows the genii cucullati alongside a figure wearing a tunic, in the place of Cuda. In the pediment design of the relief are two birds, either side of a rosette, which are considered to be pigeons (photograph Gloucester City Museum and Art Gallery)

Cynan and Cynffig in Glamorganshire (Pierce 2002, 62–63). These were considered to be personal-names, but they may also mask associations with specific types of dogs, which may have been seen as personifications of the river.

Cunomaglos

The name *Cunomaglos* was recorded on an altar found at Nettleton Scrubb (Wedlake 1982, 53). It is highly likely that the name was used for two rivers in the Cotswold area; on the first, the Broadwater Brook, a temple of *Apollo Cunomaglos* stands; the second one is the Coln, for which the etymology remained unidentified until recently. With the early forms, *Cunuglae* or *Cunuglan* of AD 721–43, it is probable that the first part of the name is the Celtic *cuno*, **dog**. The latter part of the name may well be derived from *-maglos*, **lord** (Yeates 2006b, 63–83). This is supported by the oft-quoted case of the river **Cynfael**, described in the Mabinogion, where the hunter approached the river with his hounds and killed a stag (Jones and Jones 1974, 69). This river may be the one located in Merionethshire, but could also have been one of the Cotswold rivers in the land of the *Dobunni*, where this god's cult may have been focused.

Cyw-

The river Chew in Somerset takes its name from the Welsh *Cyw*, a **chicken** (Ekwall 1928, 77). There are no clear indications in the archaeology of Europe of an ancient divinity associated with this name. A second river of this name is at Cusop in Herefordshire, probably in the *Silurian* territory. The name Cusop seems to be derived from *Cyw-hope*, the **valley of the Cyw**, or **chicken river**, (Bannister 1916, 55; Coplestone-Crow 1989, 63; Watts 2004, 176). The stream now occupying that valley is called the Dulas Brook. The name Dulas is Welsh, with an etymology derived from the British *dubo-* and the Old Welsh *gleis*, hence **black stream** (Ekwall 1960, 138). Therefore, it seems that certain

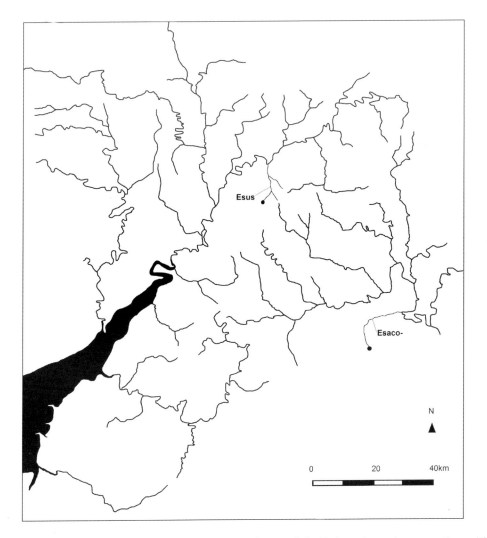

Figure 33: A map of the divine river-names in and around the Dobunnic territory starting with the letter E (drawing S. Yeates)

Welsh rivers also had two names; in this case the name Cyw fits into a recognisably older tradition than the Roman period, with the birds being introduced into north-west Europe in the Iron Age at least (see Chapter 5), and suggests that river names such as Dalch, Dulais, Dulas, Dawlish, Douglas and Dowlish, all come from an identical source, probably derived from names given out in the fifth to eighth century AD. The fifth century marked the advent of Christianity in South Wales, and the eighth century the time of the first recorded accounts. The name may not even refer to the colour of the water but to a river with particularly strong pagan traditions.

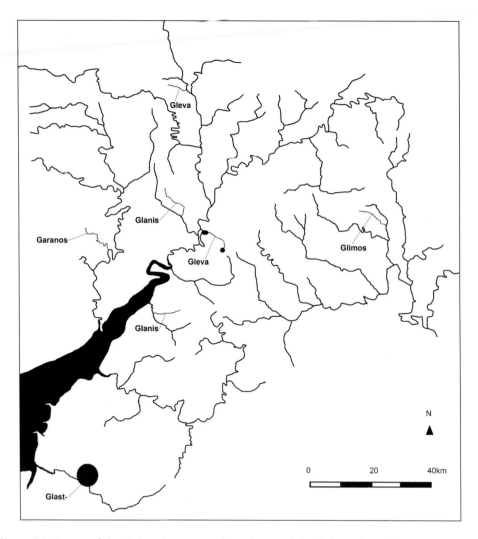

Figure 34: A map of the divine river-names in and around the Dobunnic territory starting with the letter G (drawing S. Yeates)

Esaco-

The river Ock, in Berkshire, has a name derived from the Celtic *esāco-*, **salmon** (Gelling 1973, 14–15). Originally Ekwall (1928, 306–307) suggested that the name derived from the Latin *esox*, **pike**. The shrine at Marcham-Frilford was probably associated with the worship of the river Ock.

Esus

The god *Esus* was mentioned, alongside *Taranis* and *Teutatis*, by the Roman poet Lucan in his *Pharsalia* (Duff 1967, i.444–446). His altars were described as wild and he was propitiated by human sacrifice. The god is only known from one inscription and another stone with similar imagery; the inscription was found in Paris in 1711 on the site of Nôtre-Dame, and the other image comes from Trier. In both cases *Esus* is depicted as cutting down a willow tree. This god and the willow tree, in Latin *Salix*, was important locally as the river Isbourne was the river of *Esa's* people (Ekwall 1928, 214; Smith 1964a, i.9), and one can surmise that the name *Esus* was the original association (Yeates 2008a, 44). This divine name has also been associated with the river *Aesius*, in Bithynia (Rivet and Smith 1979, 242). A tributary of the Isbourne is the Hailes Brook, whose old name is considered to have been derived from *Salia*, **salt** (Ekwall 1928, 188–189) but no chemical mineral association has yet been recognised. If it is correct that the Isbourne was associated with *Esus*, however, then the *Salia* name may have been associated with *Salix*, **willow**, and there may be a common allusion to the story seen on the continental reliefs.

Garanos

Two sculptured stones, one from Paris and one from Trier (discussed above), contain an image of *Tarvostrigaranos*, **the bull and the three cranes** (Green 1992, 207–208), but it is only the former that was inscribed with the name. It has been suggested that the birds shown on the relief are three egrets sat in a willow tree. Thus we have a triple form of the crane, possibly an allusion to the three fathers (as the name was recorded in a masculine form) a variation of what was discussed with *Tri-Sentona*. The name may also be associated with the god *Grannus*; who was worshipped on the continent at cult centres located at Grand, in the Vosges, and at Aachen or *Aquae Granni* (Green 1992, 32). The name is used in Herefordshire for a river now called the Garron (Ekwall 1928, 169). The antiquity of such names is demonstrated by the Roman period name *Gariennus*, the name of the Suffolk Yare (Rivet and Smith 1979, 366–367). The same river-name probably occurs in Cardiganshire with the Caron (Owen and Morgan 2007, 469).

Glanis

At *Glanum* in Gaul there is evidence for a spring shrine to the god *Glanis*, who presided over the sacred springs and gave his name to the settlement (Green 1992, 105–106). The *Glanicae* were also worshipped at the site, and seem to have been mothers of the local group who took their name from the springs and the river. Other rivers deriving their name from this source include two in Italy, others in the Ardennes and Spain, and in the Dordogne (Rivet and Smith 1979, 367–368). There is also a connection with two local rivers: the Glynch Brook, which rises in the southern part of the Malverns and feeds the

Leadon, and a tributary of the Little Avon in the *Dobunnic* territory near Berkeley. This river is now called the Doverle and was first recorded as the *dofer lan* in AD 940; the latter part of the name comes from **glano-* (Smith 1964a, i.6), derived from the British **glanīc-*, Welsh *glan*, **pure** (Smith 1964a, i.7–8).

Glast-

In the legendary story of the foundation of Glastonbury a figure called Glast discovered the abbey site by following a sow to the location of an apple tree under which she rested. He is seen as the eponymous ancestor of a people called the *Glasteningas* (Thornton 1991, 191 200). Thornton questioned the authenticity of this tradition, seeing it as a pseudo-historical invention of the medieval period, relying only on association between place-names. Problems arise, however, if we consider Thornton to be correct. In Roman period religion there were spirits of place; these personified, and resided in, natural features. 'Glass' is recognised from Gloucestershire as a Celtic name for a mere or pool; therefore, it is possible that Glastonbury took its name from Meare Pool. This would mean that Glastonbury contains the pre-Old English name of that feature. The word *glass* or *glast* has the etymology of **blue-green**, but is also associated with the plant **woad** (Ekwall 1960, 198; Watts 2004, 251–252).

Gleva

A mythical character called *Glywys* or *Gloiu* has been encountered in many of the traditions of South Wales, including in the works of Nennius and Geoffrey of Monmouth, as has been noted elsewhere (Chapter 3). The name means **bright**. In reliefs found at Gloucester the city seems to have been represented by a *Tyche*, wearing a mural crown (see Figure 35). The lake at Gloucester (see Chapter 6), was *Llyn Llyw* (*Glyw*), associated with the Severn salmon. One possibility is that the name of the city was derived from the animal, which seems to have been a personification of the lake; the use of the word meaning bright may be an allusion to the shining silver scales of the salmon. There is also a stream with the name Gladder, in Worcestershire (Mawer and Stenton 1927, 11; Ekwall 1928, 173), and another near Builth, in the territory of the *Silures*.

Glimos

The river Glyme, which takes its name from *Glime-*, bright (Ekwall 1928, 180–181), was probably associated with the god Jupiter, as suggested in the discussion of *interpretatio* (Yeates 2008a, 54–55) (Chapter 3). The word may also be connected in linguistic pre-history to the source of the Old Norse word *glámr*, **the moon** (Ekwall 1928, 180–181).

Icauna

In South Gloucestershire, the river Itchen is a tributary of the river Frome, and there is a further Itchen in Warwickshire (Ekwall 1928, 217–218). The name is derived from the sacred name *Icauna*. She was a goddess known in France where she personified the Yonne (see above).

Isca

The name Isca was used for a number of Roman settlements and, in all cases, was

Figure 35: A relief showing the images of two goddesses standing alongside Mercury. Mercury (see chapter 5) can be identified as the tribal god of the Dobunni, while the Fortuna figure replaces the tribal goddess. The central goddess, who wears a mural crown, may well be the city Tyche of Gloucester, Gleva (photograph by the late M. B. Cookson, Institute of Archaeology London, held at the Institute of Archaeology, Oxford)

derived from the name of a river (Ekwall 1928, 151–156; Rivet and Smith 1979, 376–379). Modern variations of this name include: Axe, Exe, and Usk, besides others. The name Axe is the only notable survival in *Dobunnic* territory. The name Isca has the meaning of **fish** (Rivet and Smith 1979, 376–377). The type of fish referred to is not known but thought to be a **trout**.

Lemana

The river Leam, in Warwickshire, derived its name from the ancient name **Lemanā*, **elm**. The oldest recorded example of this name in Britain is *Liminaea*, for Lympne, Sussex, in 697 AD (Ekwall 1928, 243–246). The name also occurred as a folk-name *Limenwaru* or *Lyminge* also with respect to Lympne. Rivet and Smith (1979, 385–386), however, suggested that the name meant **marsh**, although they admitted that **elm** was a possibility. On the continent Lucan mentioned Lake *Lemmano* (Duff 1967, i.395–400), now Leman, whose name probably derived from the same source. Traditionally, the elm was a tree associated with liminal space and burial customs. It is possible that the use of the name may indicate boundary areas; the name could also be associated with the Latin word *limes*, **boundary**.

Lovernius

Ekwall (1928, 238) suggested that the name of the Laughern Brook in Worcestershire was derived from the Welsh *llywarn*, **fox**. Breeze (1998, 251–252) expanded upon this interpretation and suggested that the word came from the much older Gallic *lowernius*, **fox**, which was recorded as the name of a chieftain in the Gallic War. This name is also considered to have been an earlier name of the river Troddi in Gwent.

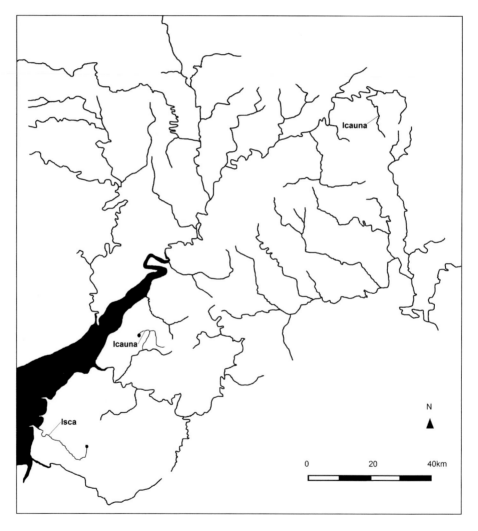

Figure 36: A map of the divine river-names in and around the Dobunnic territory starting with the letter I (drawing S. Yeates)

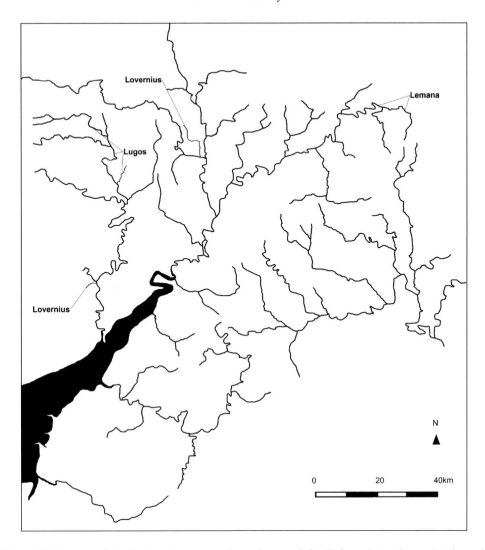

Figure 37: A map of the divine river-names in and around the Dobunnic territory starting with the letter L (drawing S. Yeates)

Lugus or Lugos

Lugos is associated with cities such as *Luguvalium*, now Carlisle (Rivet and Smith 1979, 402) and *Lugdunum*, now Lyon, in France. The etymology of the name is normally interpreted as **shining one** (Green 1992, 135) and that of the river-name as **leuk*, **brilliant white** (Ekwall 1928, 268–269). A further interpretation is that it is derived from *lugos*, **raven**, and is associated with the Greek word λούγεον (Ellis Evans 1967, 99). Here, we see again that some of the names interpreted as meaning light, shining or bright, may

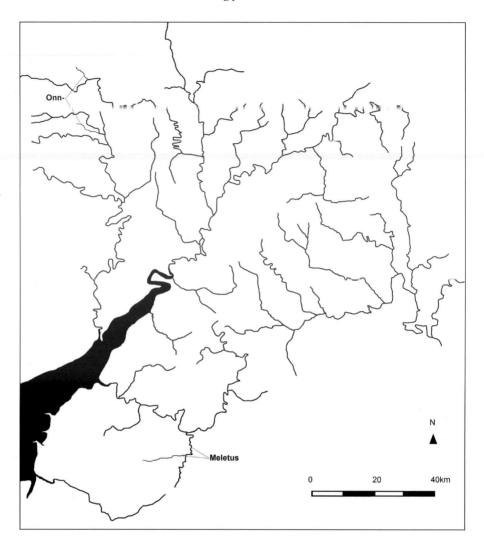

Figure 38: A map of the divine river-names in and around the Dobunnic territory starting with the letters M and O (drawing S. Yeates)

hide associations with the names of animals. *Lugos* has been equated with the later *Lugh*, of the Irish traditions, where he was portrayed as a craftsman, a warrior, and a wielder of a spear. In the later Welsh traditions he was known as *Lleu Llaw Gyffes* (Green 1992, 133). The name has also been associated with the river Lugg, in Herefordshire, and the river Llugwy, in Caernarvonshire.

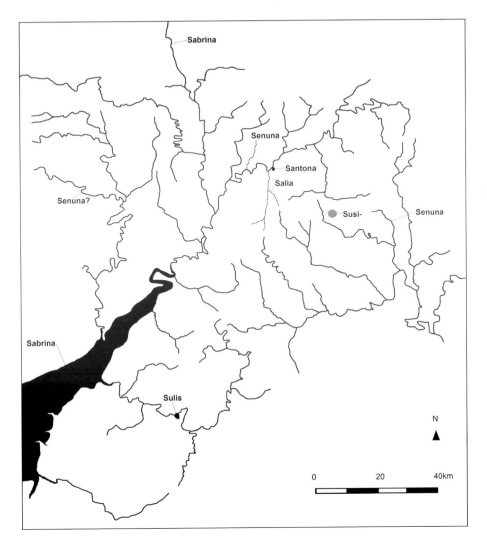

Figure 39: A map of the divine river-names in and around the Dobunnic territory starting with the letter S (drawing S. Yeates)

Meletus

The Latin *mel* or *mellis*, translates into English as **honey bee**. In Cornish it is *milin* and in Irish *mil*; it has also turned up as a component part of Gaulish personal names (Ellis Evans 1967, 115). The Welsh words *melys*, sweet, and *melyn*, yellow, are derived from the same source, indicating that an Old Welsh word, *milin* or *melyn*, must once have been used for the honey bee. Mells in Somerset, (*Milne* in AD 942, *Melnes* in AD 1196, and *Melles* in AD 1225) has been associated with the Old English *Myln*, a water mill (Watts 2004, 407), in the belief that a single water mill gave its name to the Mells Stream, on which Mells lies. In the *Ravenna Cosmography* the name *Meletium*, a place which lay in the southwest of Britain somewhere between Gloucester and Badbury, was recorded (Rivet and Smith 1979, 417); it has been associated with **melisso-*, **sweet**, the Old Irish *milis*, **sweet**, the Welsh *melys*, **sweet**, and the Latin and Welsh *mel*, **honey**, the interpretation being **honey-stream**. This could be a reference to the Mells stream which lies in the right location; there may also have been a Roman settlement somewhere in the Mells area. If there was an association with a mill, then it is possible that this device could have been used to hide the Celtic divine name. In Irish traditions there is a character known as *Míl* of Spain, *Míl Espáne*, or *Miles Hispaniae*, who was said to be an ancestor of the Irish Goidels (O'Rahilly 1946, 15, 195 199, 266 267).

Onn-

A small tributary of the Lugg, the Pinsley Brook in Herefordshire, was once called the Onny, recorded as *Onye* in 1250 (Bannister 1916, 145; Ekwall 1928, 310), like the Shropshire river. The name was derived from the Celtic word **onn*, **ash tree** (Padel 1985, 174), and was used for a number of Roman period towns.

Sabrina

The deification of the river Severn has been discussed elsewhere (Yeates 2008b, 31–35); it also turns up in a number of traditional tales. Along with the Wye she was considered one of three daughters of the mountain Plynlimon who all arose one morning to make their way to the sea by different routes (Palmer 1994, 24–27). Geoffrey of Monmouth described a princess, with a reduced form of the Severn river-name, who drowned in the shallows of the estuary, as discussed in Chapter 3. Folk-tradition has it that the Broadstone at Stroat is the grave marker of the river Severn. It seems that these two fragmentary tales may have been part of a far older tradition describing mythical journeys, in the same way as their Irish counterparts.

Salia

The Hailes brook is believed to have once been known as the *Salia* (Ekwall 1928, 188–189); if this is indeed the case then it is only natural to hypothesise that the *Salia* would have been personified as a nymph.

Salina

The ancient name of Droitwich is considered to be *Salina*; one can, therefore, hypothesise that there was a goddess *Salina* who presided over the town, the springs, and perhaps the Salty Brook (see Chapter 6).

Sapina

The name Sapey, as in Sapey Brook, is considered to be derived from an Old English word meaning **the sappy one** (Watts 2004, 528). Some of its earliest recorded forms, however, including *Sapina*, and a translation of a *Domesday Book* reference to the **fir wood** (Moore 1982, 1.11 and note) suggest that the name is an older flora name meaning the **pine tree** (Yeates 2006a, i.16).

Sargia

One of the streams of the Forest of Dean is known to have born the ancient name *Sarca*, a recognised Gallic river-name (Ekwall 1928, 353; Yeates 2006a, i.47). The name is probably ssociated with Sark, in the Channel Islands, for which the earliest recorded name was *Sargia*. The name is of unknown origin (Coates 1991, 73–76).

Senuna

At Ashwell, on the northern edge of the Chilterns in an area above a spring of the River Rhee, the remains of a shrine to the goddess *Senuna* were uncovered (Jackson and Burleigh 2007, 37–54; Tomlin 2008, 305–315). A number of plaques containing her name as *Senuna* were found, but also one which had the probable late Roman form *Siinia* (*Senia*), in which the central part of the name containing the <u> had gone. The river which flows from Ashwell was, in medieval times, called the river Henney (Reaney 1943, 2–3). *Siinia* (*Senia*) seems to have been an alternative Roman form for the goddess, with the intial <s> altering to <h>, a recognised linguistic process (Yeates forthcoming). The name is probably related to *Seno-*, **old**.

A number of rivers possibly share this name. The Anglo-Saxon charters for the estate at North Piddle mention the river-name *Hennuc* (Mawer and Stenton 1927, 222–223), which seems to have been an older name of the river Piddle or one of its tributaries. The name Hensington in Oxfordshire also seems to contain this name (Yeates 2008b, 86–88), in this instance being derived from a folk-name for a group living on the river. The river has not been identified but the name is probably the old name for the Dorn, which must also have included what is now the lower Glyme, below the two rivers' confluence. The name Wye is considered to have derived from the Welsh *Gwy*, **water** (Watts 2004, 706). If this was the case then it can not have been the original name of the river. Leland, in his itinerary, referred to it as the *Henewy(e)* (Smith and Kendrick 1964, 109), incorporating an apparently ancient river-name noun. Due to this name's late and unsubstantiated appearance, we should proceed with caution. It is, however, possible that the information was obtained from a local source. A relief of a Venus-type goddess has been found at Chepstow Castle (Figure 40), an ideal position for a shrine at the mouth of the Wye (see above).

Sulis

The cult of the goddess *Sulis* Minerva was well-represented and many altars and inscriptions have been found (RIB(I) 1995, nos.141, 143, 144, 146–150). The temple has been excavated and the layout of the sanctuary determined (Cunliffe and Davenport 1985). Here we are concerned primarily with the name of the goddess, which derived from a noun associated with the Welsh word *heol*, the **sun** (Rivet and Smith 1979, 255–256); her cult at Bath will be discussed further in Chapter 6. The name implies that, in the Roman period, some rivers may have been associated with celestial bodies; this was hinted at with *Sirona* (**star**), *Glimos* (**moon?**), and *Vandil* (**morning star** in Chapter 3). It is possible, from the evidence, to consider whether there was a series of Celtic deities similar to the Greek Titans, with male and female representations of the sun, moon and planets. Other river-names have been thought to mean bright or light, and it is possible that these may be so called because of this association. This may provide

Figure 40: Chepstow Castle, a site where a relief of Venus and the nymphs has been recognised re-set into the wall of the Norman great hall. The castle is in a location which would be ideal as a shrine for the mouth of the river Wye (photograph S. Yeates)

an insight into the names of the celestial bodies that were used in ancient Britain; how we would decipher this would, however, be extremely difficult.

Susi-

An Anglo-Saxon charter for Daylesford records the name *Susibre*, derived from *Susi*, and the Brittonic *briga*, a hill (Grundy 1936, 102). There is no known meaning for the first part of the name but the structure of the word is comparable to that of Kinver. It could be argued that the name was derived from either the divine name *Esus* or the female divine name *Isosa* (Batardy, Buchseuschutz *et al.* 2001, 89), or perhaps the name of some unidentified deity.

Tamesis

The deification of the Thames was investigated in an earlier work (Yeates 2008b, 49–51). The etymology of the name and other similar names is unknown. There are indications of a shrine at the source of the river near Hailey Wood, and another at Southwark. A relief from Bablock Hythe is thought to be a representation of a veiled *genius* of the Thames. Tradition has it that the Thames is 'old father'; this may derive from an older folk-tradition in the same way that *Rhenus* was a father to all his tributaries.

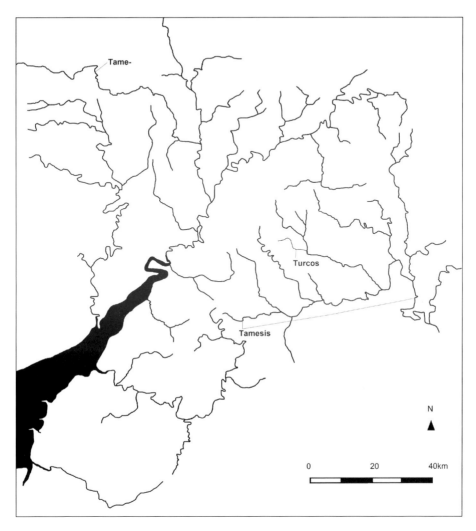

Figure 41: A map of the divine river-names in and around the Dobunnic territory starting with the letter T (drawing S. Yeates)

Turcos

No dedication to this god occurs, but it is evident in the Welsh legendary traditions of the Mabinogion, that there was a Welsh river that was personified as a boar. The name is used for a number of rivers in Wales the most notable of which is in Carmarthenshire (Owen and Morgan 2007, 479). The name also occurred as a tributary of the Windrush. It is derived from the Welsh *Turce*, **a boar** (Yeates 2006b, 63–81).

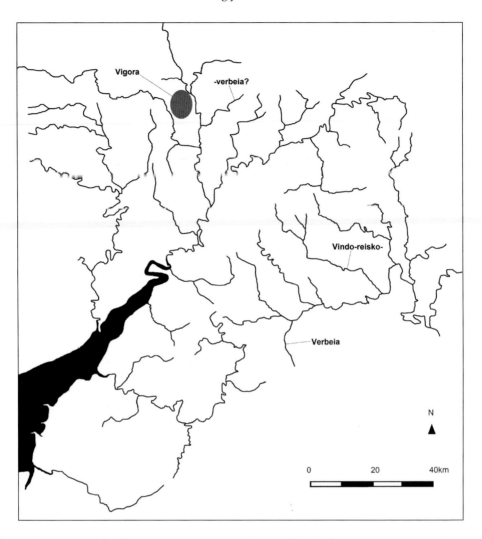

Figure 42: A map of the divine river-names in and around the Dobunnic territory starting with the letter V (drawing S. Yeates)

Verbeia

There is further evidence that rivers were deified in Yorkshire, from an inscription to the goddess *Verbeia*, found at Ilkley. She was the goddess of the river Wharf (RIB(I) 1995, no.635), but no representations of her have yet been identified. The river-name Wharf has usually been thought to mean twist or turn; an alternative is that it is named after **Verbeia**, goddess of the river, whose name was derived from the Old Irish *ferb*, *cattle* (Watts 2004, 525–526). There are many river Wharfs in the country, one in Shropshire, one in Wiltshire, while the Salwarpe in Worcestershire also derived the latter part of its name from this source.

Vigora

The Wyre Forest is known to have taken its name from the Celtic river-name *Vigora* (Yeates 2008b, 25), and there was probably an unidentified stream of this name in the area. Ekwall (1928, 170) noted that there was a stream called the *Gearnec* in AD 851 and the *Gearuec* in AD 961–70 (probably misreading *Gearnec*), which also provided the name *Gearriford* in AD 816 (probably *Gearniford*); all recordings are from the eleventh century. The name is that of a river between Hallow and Moseley. There is one small stream in the area but the reference is more likely to be to the lower course of the Laughern Brook, which has a bend between these two settlements. The name is probably a reduced corruption of (*Uueo*)*gernensis* in *c.* AD 736, (*Wio*)*goerna ceastre* in AD 825, or (*Wio*)*gerna ceastre* in AD 969, which are documented variations of the spelling of *Vigorna* (Mawer and Stenton 1927, 19–20). A Worcestershire charter for the parish of Ombersley leaves the initial part of the (*Sae*)*Firne* off (Grundy 1928, 22), indicating that this hypothesis is feasible. If this was the case then it is highly likely that the Fitcher, and what is now the lower Laughern Brook were the *Vigora* and that the river-name *Lowernicus* was only used above the confluence of the Fitcher. Once river-names stopped being used as the names of deities, they started to become confused (Yeates 2006b, 63–81). We can say, therefore, that the *Weogorena* were the people who lived on the *Vigora*, now the lower Laughern Brook (see Figure 43).

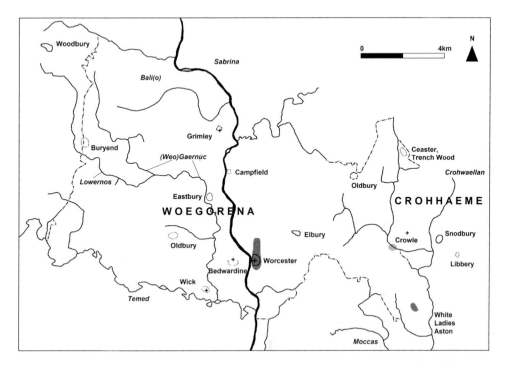

Figure 43: A map showing the parochia of Worcester and the territories of the folk-groups Crohhæme and Weogorena (drawing S. Yeates)

Vindo-reisko-

The Windrush is a river-name which has the Celtic etymology of *gwen reisko*, **the white rush** (Ekwall 1928, 461–462; Yeates 2006b, 63–81). As the name fits into the flora and fauna category we can consider this to be an ancient name and probably cognate with that of a divinity.

Conclusions on Dobunnic *deities*

Discussions on these river-names can be found in a series of place-name publications. These include: *River-names* by Ekwall (1928), *A dictionary of English place-names* by Ekwall (1960) or Watts (2004), and *The place-names of Roman Britain* by Rivet and Smith (1979). Besides this there is a series of county volumes: *The place-names of Worcestershire* by Mawer and Stenton (1927); *The place-names of Warwickshire* by Gover, Mawer and Stenton (1936); *The place-names of Oxfordshire* (Gelling 1953; 1954), and *The place-names of Berkshire* (Gelling 1973); and *The place-names of Gloucestershire* by Smith (1964a; 1964b; 1964c; 1965). Other works include *Herefordshire place-names*, by Copleston-Crow (1989) or by Bannister (1916). Increasingly, it has become evident that river-names of Brittonic origin, many of which can be identified in the bounds of Anglo-Saxon charters as discussed by Finberg, Grundy, Hooke, and Gelling, are actually named after plants and animals. This notion was noted in Wales some years ago (Thomas 1938) but the logic behind it has not been used fully for England, although there have been some localised attempts. By looking at these names we can start recognising a plethora of divinities amongst the *Dobunni*; the problem we have then is to understand how they fitted in to the *Dobunnic* pantheon and what stories were told about them.

We can now suggest that those names associated with floral and faunal names, or words meaning bright are of some antiquity. In Gaul they may go back beyond the first century BC, at least, in Greece they were almost certainly evident in the Classical period of the sixth century BC and probably go back to the Bronze Age. In Greek examples even when it is not possible to associate a flora or fauna name with the name of the river then quite often an animal or plant may be involved with the story of that river. In contrast to this it is evident that many more rivers in the *Dobunnic* territory contain these animal associated names even in the charters of the early Anglo-Saxon period. It is difficult to know precisely when these names were introduced, and there are problems with some of the names; not all of the known British names have been listed and some are named after species that were introduced into Britain. For example, some rivers are named after **wheat**, **wanott-*, which was introduced into Britain in the fourth millennium BC, while the chicken names can not be any earlier than the Bronze Age. Other names refer to the crocus which is not considered to have been imported into the islands until the Roman period. There are, however, certain caveats, as some of the names may have been used for a similar native species. If we take this naming process as part of a Europe-wide tradition existing in Greece at least from the seventh century BC, then it is possible that the tradition is extremely ancient.

Another group of names are those associated with light, bright and, possibly, pure. The name *Sulis,* and the continental *Sirona,* are references to the sun and a star. It is possible that other names, such as *Gleva,* and *Glimos* (moon) also derived from the names of heavenly bodies. The name *Vandil,* the morning star, may not be a Germanic introduction as is now thought. We have a problem associating these names with a specific time period and with an appropriate ideological context. If the Gallic 'Celts' (and Britons) wrote with Greek characters then it is quite possible that they could have heard of some of the Greeks religious traditions accounted in Hesiod. He described twelve Titans. In other accounts, such as the reconstructed Pelasgian creation myth, the Titans were associated with the planetary bodies being male and female. The Titans are listed below in Table 1; however, one should state that this is only extremely hypothetical.

	Greek Male	Celtic Male	Greek Female	Celtic Female
Sun	Hyperion	Bal(i)os (?)	Theia	Sulis
Moon	Atlas	Glimos?	Phoebe	
Mercury	Koeos	Vandil?	Metis	
Venus	Oceanos	Vandil?	Tethys	
Mars	Krios		Dione	
Jupiter	Eurymedon		Themis	
Saturn	Kronos		Rhae	

Table 1: The Greek titans along with their associated planet and the possible Celtic/Brittonic equivalents.

Rivers were often associated with tribal groups and tribal descent, as discussed in previous works (Yeates 2006a; 2007, 55–69; 2008b). In this work we can start adding to our understanding of the basic *Vicus* units. Most of the units take their name from a natural feature, many of which are drawn from specific groups of names: flora, fauna, heavenly bodies and others. The natural features were deified individually and were also represented as a divine triple mother, which in its basic form was the name of the local folk-group. The divine names would then have been installed at the start of a genealogy.

I also noted, in an earlier work, that *hæme*, *ingas* and *sæte* are all regarded as terms for dwellers on a river, the home of a group or community. These words are most frequently associated with river-names of Celtic or Brittonic origin. There are increasing problems with regarding the first of them as being of purely Germanic origin, and the context in which the word was used could be considered ambiguous. Tacitus stated (Hutton, Ogilvie *et al.* 1970, Germania 28):

> '*igitur inter Hercyniam silvam Rhenumque et Moenum amnes Helvetii, ulteriora Boii, Gallica utraque gens, tenuere. manet adhuc Boihaemi nomen sign(ific)atque loci veterem memoriam quamvis mutatis cultoribus.*'

The English translation of this is:

> '*accordingly the country between the Hercynian forest and the rivers Rhine and Moenus was occupied by the Helvetii, and the country beyond by the Boii, both Gallic races: the*

*name Boihaemum still subsists and testifies to the old tradition of the place, though there
has been a change of occupants.'*

Here, the word was used by a Latin author with respect to the homeland of a Celtic
tribe, for which the name persisted. The occupants of the land may have changed (if
only in name), but we should perhaps ask if it was the whole tribal group that had
changed or only the elite. This means that the origin of the word *hæme* could have been
either of Germanic or of Celtic origin.

CONCLUSIONS

In the Australian Dreaming, mythical creatures were responsible for the development of
landscape features. In both Greek and Roman traditions there was also an underlying
tradition that certain animals, or divine creatures, were responsible for the creation
of the landscape and were part of that landscape. There were also mythical animals
which wandered the landscape in Irish and Welsh traditions. Medieval documents are
full of these mythical creatures, but it is difficult to know whether each event refers to
a medieval pseudo-history, or whether it represents earlier surviving tales. To come to
terms with this tradition it is essential to amass as much religious material as possible
so that the survival of Celtic and Brittonic elements which survive in place-names can be
assessed. In doing this it is possible that we may come to know some of the characters
responsible for the creation of the landscape even if we can not put the whole picture
back together.

(Potential periods of ideological change in Britain affecting river-names can be
proposed from alterations in the archaeological pattern and also through suggested
periods of migration into Britain through DNA analysis (see Appendix 1)).

Chapter 5

The Divine Couple from the Shakespeare Inn

We have considered certain aspects of pre-Christian religion, including the potential development of the pantheon, the underlying principles behind cult, the question of how far beliefs could survive from one social system to another, and how animals and plant names were associated with river systems. It is now time to look at what is known about one of the principal aspects of any belief system within tribal or ethnic groups; the creation myth. First we must determine what survives in textual form, or in the place-names or folk tradition, in addition to archaeological evidence. Though the *Dobunnic* territory now lies in England, it was located in the province called *Britannia Prima* (White 2007), one of the provinces which gave rise to the traditions of continuity in Wales (see Figure 44). In these Welsh traditions we need to see if there are any references in medieval texts which hint at an earlier tradition, or may have come from an oral source. The *Dobunni* (later the *Hwicce*) was one tribe for which such information seems to exist; for other tribes, however, it is possible that we may never retrieve sufficient material to consider a creation myth. One of the main reasons for this is that the *Dobunni* tribal area was located at the heart of *Britannia Prima*. Cirencester and Gloucester have both been identified as potential capitals of this province, but in reviewing the traditions which are associated with Gloucester it would seem that it, rather than Cirencester, is the better candidate. Welsh traditions point to a main line of royal descent from Gloucester (Morris 1980, 33), possibly placing the divinity of that town at the head of their developing genealogies. Gloucester seems to have held a special place in *Britannia Prima* and it is for this reason that the town and the area around it appears in folklore and legends in the Welsh sources. This notion was touched upon in Chapter 3 with respect to the work of Geoffrey of Monmouth.

Very few European creation myths have survived; those which have are generally confined to the south of Europe, for example in the Greek and Roman worlds, or to the Germanic tribal groups of northern Europe. For the 'Celtic' World most of the information, from which creation myths could be inferred or reconstructed, has been lost. Of the myths which have survived it is probably the Greek ones which are the most important for our attempt to recreate the primal myth of the *Dobunni*. The surviving creation myths have been catalogued and reconstructed by numerous people, but the volume which will provide the basis for this discussion was brought together in Professor Barbara Sproul's *Primal Myths: Creating the World* (1979). With such accounts, one needs to display caution about the origin of the source and especially any over-elaborate interpretation.

GREEK CREATION MYTHS

The oldest of the known Greek creation myths is the *Pelasgian*; reconstructed, from fragmentary evidence, by Graves (1960, 1.27–30). The outline of the creation myth was followed by Sproul (1979, 156–157), which is considered to date as far back as *c.* 3500 BC. It has the goddess *Eurynome* (Goddess of **all things** or **wide-wanderer**) arising out of Chaos. She divided the sky and the sea, and created movement. The movement became *Ophion*, a great serpent, who was the north wind and was also called *Boreas*. *Eurynome* took on the form of a dove and laid the universal egg. *Ophion* coiled around this egg and fertilised it; from this egg all things were created. The objects which came

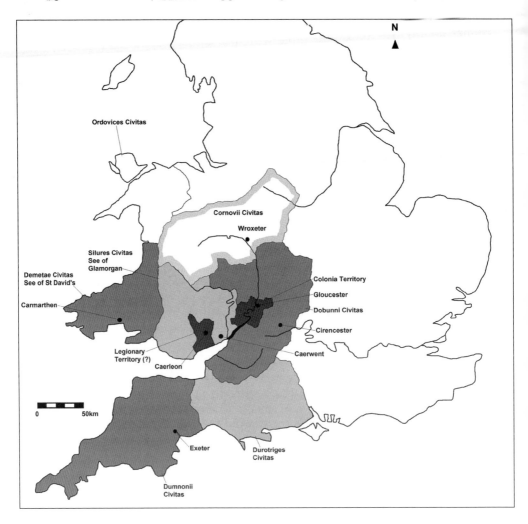

Figure 44: A map showing the civitates which almost certainly lay in the province of Britannia Prima; those which may have belonged to that territory are also shown (drawing S. Yeates)

from this egg were called her children and included: the sun, the moon, the planets, the stars, the earth, the mountains, the rivers, and all living things. *Eurynome* and *Ophion* took up residence on Mount Olympus where *Ophion* boasted, upset the goddess, and was banished. The goddess then set up a titan and a titaness to rule over each of the seven planetary powers. The three main works interpreting this myth are later, but there are problems with them. Although the characters *Ophion* and *Eurynome* appear in the *Argonautica* (Seaton 1912, I.496–511) they are not referred to there as the creative spirit. In the later traditions by Hesiod they are described as children of *Oceanos*. Another claim is that, prior to the rule of *Kronos* and *Rhea*, *Ophion* and *Eurynome* held sway on snowy Olympus; thus hinting at part of an earlier tradition. Appollodorus informs us that *Eurynome* was a child of *Oceanos* and *Tethys*, and also listed her children fathered by Zeus (Jackson 1921, 1.ii.1–5, 1.iii.1–12).

Homer spoke of the gods springing from the all-nurturing earth and *Oceanos*, along with his mother *Tethys* (Murray and Wyatt 1999, 14.195–210, 300–311). The actual phrasing of the Homeric texts indicates that *Oceanos* was once considered the father, but the relationship between the all-nurturing earth and *Tethys* is more open to conjecture. Thus, the Homeric creation myth saw *Oceanos* and *Tethys* as the creators of all things. *Oceanos* was the sea, or the universal waters, and was usually portrayed in Greek and Roman traditions alike, with a beard and wild hair, and a pair of crab claws extending from his forehead. The name *Tethys* is believed to mean **disposer**. The sources used come from two passages of the *Iliad*, a poem which talked of events in *c.* 1300 BC. From analysis of the texts it would seem to have remained oral and only written down in *c.* 800 BC (Sherratt 1992, 145–168). The *Iliad* comments on some of the later traditions recorded by Hesiod, so it is possible to take the idea of *Kronos* and the other titans and gods back further than the sixth century BC.

In the *Orphic* creation myth (Sproul 1979, 169), which was considered a development of the seventh or sixth centuries BC, there is an androgynous creator, Time, who lays an egg. Out of the egg came *Phanes-Dionysus* who was the first-born god. He was bisexual and from him was generated all things. His first daughter was Night (*Nyx*) and with her he created *Gaea*, *Uranus*, and *Kronos*.

The basis of the Olympian creation myth of the Greek world was recorded by Hesiod in his *Theogony* (Most 2006, xi–xxv). Hesiod is considered to have been born of emigrants from Asia Minor in the village of *Ascra* in Boeotia, on the Greek mainland, and to have worked as a shepherd in the mountains. One day, it is claimed, he started to produce poetry without any training; the works were recorded at the end of the eighth century or the beginning of the seventh century BC. The muses are attributed as having given him the ability to transform himself and initiated the ability to craft poetry. The *Theogony* is one of two poems which are credited to him, the other being *Works and Days*. Of these there is some debate as to whether they are by the same person or whether they were written by different poets. The *Theogony* was recorded in poetic form and, supposedly, imparted to the author straight from the nine muses. Some now suggest that Hesiod may not have been a real person at all but was the name for a specific type of poetry in the Greek world (Most 2006, xvii).

The *Theogony* laid out the origins of the gods and their descent, as seen in the Greek Classical period (Most 2006, 2–85). The title of the work, *Theogony*, literally means **the**

birth of the gods. The work starts with a long introductory hymn to the muses, and one is given the notion that the poem has been implanted or imparted to the poet by divine forces. Then there comes about the part of the work which is concerned with the creation myth proper. The first was Chaos, into which was born the Earth (*Gaia*). Amongst the earliest concepts to be given a form was Love (*Eros*), most beautiful of all the deathless gods. Also born of Chaos were Night (*Nyx*) and *Erebos*. Night gave birth to day and space; while Earth gave birth to starry Heaven, who was to be an equal to her. Then she gave birth to the deities of the land and sea. The next passage concerns, probably, the most important extract from the creation story. In it, Earth lay with Heaven (*Ouranos*) and bore the Titans: *Oceanos, Koius, Kreius, Iapetos, Hyperion, Theia, Rhea, Themis, Mnemosyne, Tethys, Phoebe, and Kronos*. There were also the Cyclopes: *Brontes* (**thunder**), *Steropes* (**lightning**), and *Arges* (**bright**), who were like the Titans but had but a single eye set in their head, and who produced lightning bolts for Zeus to throw. The other children of *Ouranos* and *Gaia* were *Kottos, Gyes*, and *Briareus*, each of whom had a hundred arms and fifty heads. *Ouranos* hid his children away from the light because he hated them and, in doing so, upset Earth; so she devised a plan, created a scythe and got *Kronos* to cut off his father's genitals as revenge for his shameful acts. The genitals of Heaven were thrown into the Sea and from the drops of blood sprang the Furies, the Giants, and *Meliae*. As the genitals floated in the Sea the goddess Aphrodite came into being, born in the foam of the waves. Her companions from the beginning were *Eros* (**love**), and Desire. The story then continues with further children of Night: Death, Sleep, and the tribe of Dreams. The climax of the tale is reached when Zeus defeated the monster *Typhoeos*. The *Theogony* is a wonderful and evocative piece full of primitive gods, big dark forces, sex, violence, and catastrophes portrayed in a tedious fashion. Having said this it is probably the single most important creation story surviving in Europe and all other re-creation stories, especially the Celtic or Brittonic ones, probably have some similarities with it.

In essence the same basic formula was being used in all of these creation cycles; a mother and father, the interaction between them, and the creation of offspring. There is then conflict between the father and son in an ever recurring cycle. This, at its most basic level, is based on certain aspects of human nature, a general knowledge of the natural relationship between male and female, the emotions of love and desire which exist between them, and the actions which bring about further creation. The underlying basis of the creation myths, which sociologists and anthropologists have long recognised in religious belief systems, reflected humanity and the societies created (Feuerbach 1957, 13–14; Marx and Engels 1957, 37–38; Durkheim 1964, 3, 35, 37; Geertz 1975, 90). At the heart of Ancient Greek society, was the idea of the couple as the basic unit. In the earliest myths the divine couple was not necessarily portrayed in human form and could also take on the form of animals. In the *Pelasgian* version, the female power took on the form of a dove, while the male power was represented by a serpent.

ROMAN CREATION MYTHS

Publius Ovidius Naso was born in *Sulmo* in 43 BC to parents of an equestrian rank (Miller and Goold 1977, ix–xiv). He was trained in law, but found it, and the public life that went with it, distasteful; instead he desired the life of a poet. He was banished to *Tomi* on the *Euxine* Sea for a misdemeanour, and died in AD 18 in exile. His best known work, the *Metamorphoses*, was finished in AD 7 just before his banishment; it is a work in which he tried to bring together all the classical Roman texts on mythology and the creation of the universe.

Ovid (Miller and Goold 1977, I.1–32), provided the only extant Roman creation myth (Sproul 1979, 169–171). In the prologue Ovid calls upon the gods of this ever changing world under their command. He then turns his attention to Chaos who was there in the beginning and is seen as a shapeless and discordant form which, nevertheless, has the potential to create. The power behind this chaos is not readily apparent but is considered to be Nature. This entity separated heaven from earth, and water from land and air. Each of these elements found their place and order. Fire was created, which claimed the highest realm in heaven above the air. This nameless deity is seen as the moulder of the earth, creating its zones and regions. In the air the creator brought about the winds of the cardinal points, *Eurus* in the East, *Zephyrus* in the West, *Boreas* in the North, and *Auster* to govern the South.

Though the above may be the oldest creation myth which survives in Roman literature, it is apparent that this poem combines many older traditions into a harmonious piece of literature. Ovid, unlike the Greeks, did not place the birth of the gods in a list of who begat who, but talked about the gods, whichever one, shaping and forming the earth (Miller and Goold 1977, I.32–35). This is probably the first example in which we come across this process and marks perhaps the period between classical Greece and Augustine Rome when the discussions of the creation of the Universe had moved forward; certain observations had been made which meant that some of the past beliefs were becoming redundant. The work continued and, even though of Italian origin, still drew heavily on Greek traditions. In the Greek traditions Zeus and Hera were fitted into a divine linage. In Ovid's version they were not, but there is something which is important and shows up constantly in the archaeological record of many Roman period towns and settlements across the empire. Jupiter and Juno can be seen as a divine couple and were often placed alongside the goddess Minerva. It is possible that the female in the divine couple was split and that the goddess Juno represented the mother with Minerva taking on the role of protector (as mentioned in Chapter 2). Many of the later traditions, which we can recognise from the north-west provinces, orientated towards this idea, but was this because they already had their tradition of the divine mother and consort or were these images and traditions being exported from the Roman Empire? There was almost certainly a temple of the Capitoline triad built in Cirencester to the south of the basilica-forum complex (see Figure 45).

GERMANIC CREATION MYTHS

Caesar (Edwards 1963, VI.21) provided one of the earliest accounts of Germanic belief systems. Though how much of this brief statement can be relied upon one must wonder:

> *"The Germans differ much from this manner of living. They have no Druids to regulate divine worship, no zeal for sacrifices. They reckon among the gods those only whom they*

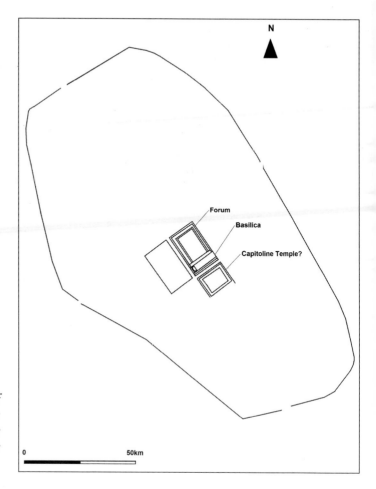

Figure 45: A plan of Cirencester showing the probable location of the temple of the Capitoline triad (drawing S. Yeates)

see and by whose offices they are openly assisted – to wit, the Sun, the Fire-god, and the Moon; of the rest they have learnt not even by report."

Reprinted by permission of the publishers and Trustees of the Loeb Classical Library from I. Caesar: The Gallic War, Loeb Classical Library Vol. 72, translated by H. J. Edwards, Cambridge, Mass.: Harvard University Press, © 1917, by the President and Fellows of Harvard College. The Loeb Classical Library ® is a registered trademark of the President and Fellows of Harvard College

This account over generalises and does not make any comment of a mother goddess for which there seems to be some evidence for the following century.

Tacitus (Hutton, Ogilvie *et al.* 1970, *Germania*, 40, 45) provided the second earliest account of the beliefs of the Germanic people. He spoke primarily about an earth-born god called *Tuisto*, the father of a god called *Mannus*. To *Mannus* were born a number of sons which gave their name to various tribal groups. Other gods worshipped amongst the Germans he compared to Mercury, Hercules and Mars. Of the cults employed within this religion the sacred grove and the sacrifice carried out within it are mentioned. Further on in the passage Tacitus mentions that the Germans worship a common mother called *Nerthus* or Mother Earth. He wrote about one of her main sanctuaries being located on an island on which there was a chariot. There was much ceremony at her festival after which slaves are ritually drowned. Further to this Tacitus informs us that the German tribe called the *Aestii* spoke a language which was very similar to that of the British. This tribal group is also known to have worshipped a divine mother goddess. In fact it is notable that the ancient Germanic peoples worshipped and revered the female form and the mother goddess; this could lead us to speculate about their creation myths and the possibility that the Germanic tribes had a series of earth-born genealogies like those of Hesiod (Campbell 1964, 473–477).

SCANDINAVIAN CREATION MYTHS

Surviving primal myths from northern Europe include the creation of the *Vala*, from the Germanic world, and the *Kalevala*, from the Finno-Urgic peoples. The first of these is accounted in the Poetic Edda, of *c.* 1200, which has been summarised by *Snorri Sturluson* (Ellis Davidson 1964, 27–28; Sproul 1979, 173–176). In the beginning there were two regions, *Muspella* a land of fire and brightness and a second place of snow and ice in the north. Between these two places there was a void called *Ginnungagap*. As the temperatures fluctuated between the two the frost giant *Ymir* was formed. The first man and woman formed under his left arm and the frost giants grew from his two legs. *Ymir* was nourished by the milk of a cow called *Auðhumla*, who licked the ice blocks and in so doing released a being called *Buri*. The son of *Buri* was called *Bor* and he fathered *Odin*, *Vili*, and *Ve*. These siblings in turn slew *Ymir*. From his body they formed the world and from his skull the vault of the sky. In this world the gods fashioned the earth, the sun, and the moon. This tradition seems to bring itself into line with that accounted by Ovid, where gods fashioned the earth and other objects and were not necessarily identified with specific aspects of the earth or universe.

The *Kalevala*, even though it contains much older material, was brought together by Elias Lonnrot in 1835 (Sproul 1979, 176–178). The story starts with the chaotic waters; the agent of creation being a teal who created a dry spot for her nest, on the knee of the mother of the waters. In the nest were laid seven eggs. When these eggs were dipped into the waters they were transformed into the material which created the universe. Six of the eggs were of gold while the seventh was of iron.

CELTIC AND BRITTONIC CREATION MYTHS

Finally, we come to what is known about the 'Celtic' creation myths, which is not a great deal. None of these oral traditions were, as far as we know, written down extensively by an impartial ethnographer. The tales which do survive represent, rather, an analysis and re-creation. John Rhys attempted the reconstruction or the inferred creed of the Celts in *Lectures on the Origin and Growth of Religion as Illustrated by Celtic Heathendom* (1862, 669–672; Sproul 1979, 172–173). This, in many ways, may be an over-simplification and drew heavily on Greek material. In the beginning there were two world giants who were the parents of numerous offspring. The children crowded in amongst their parents until one day one of the sons mutilated their father, Heaven. Out of the parts of his body they made various parts of the natural world. His skull formed the firmament and his blood caused a great flood, which settled in the hollows of the earth. The children of Heaven and Earth included gods, giants or titans, creatures of the air, and those of the earth. The titans came to the throne first but were driven from it by the gods. The king of the gods was the sky father, and as bright as day. From where this tradition is derived is not overly apparent (probably from Hesiod), but it probably also relied on Irish and Welsh medieval manuscripts, some of which may contain older oral traditions, and Gallo-Roman sculpture, which was first catalogued by Espérandieu. The divine couple do represent an important aspect of Celtic and British religious traditions (Green 1989, 45–73). In the *Dobunnic* pantheon it is possible to recognise a mother and father and Mabon their son, as mentioned previously.

One other source from which this tradition may be drawn is Caesar (Edwards 1963, vi. 17–18), who claimed that the Gauls were all descended from the common god *Dis*, or *Dispater*, as he was called (Chapter 2). However, this reference was from a context in which Caesar was probably using a process of *interpretatio* in which he equated the Gallic gods with Roman ones. These beliefs were said to have developed from the religion of the Druids; however, we do not know the extent to which Caesar was trying to impose his Roman views on the Celts and *Belgae*. *Dis* was also discussed by Rhys and Hubert, and the way he was used by these authors implies a common origin for 'Celtic' myths, in much the same way that the Greeks and Romans had. This may, of course, be due to modern interpretations of an homogenous 'Celtic' world.

Discussions of Celtic traditions invariably have their problems. Many draw too little information from too wide an area so that a narrative can be created. On the other hand such works can (and almost invariably do) wander off into the realm of fantasy, such as the recreation of Welsh Druidism by Iolo Morgannwyg.

Much has been written about Irish myth and sagas; their interpretation having changed much over time. Initially, Jackson (1964) insisted that they were a window on the Iron Age, but this has been challenged by the likes of Aitchison (1994) where they are seen as containing more contemporary early medieval attributes and material culture. Even though this is now believed to be a fair assessment there are, nevertheless, echoes of the earlier traditions and the texts are seen as stratified. For Ireland there are claims of a common descent in the invasion cycles (O'Rahilly 1946, 15); the common ancestor being *Míl* of Spain (Chapter 4). Although common descent is claimed the stories are not concerned with how Ireland came to exist and hence do not constitute a creation myth.

That there was a similar use of a divine couple amongst the tribes of north-west Europe, who are generally referred to as Celts, can be inferred by the use of this image on religious reliefs and altars. This was discussed primarily by Aldhouse-Green (nee Green) in *Symbol and Image in Celtic Religious Art* (Green 1989, 45–73), and in later works such as *Celtic Goddess* (Green 1995). The image was a common phenomenon with a wide distribution across Gaul and the German Rhineland, and although the individual gods or goddesses represented on these reliefs may have altered from area to area the underlying ideas were the same. These reliefs, to some extent, also inform us of certain values with regard to the family unit and other aspects of the so-called 'Celtic' societies.

How much this over-generalisation informs us of the traditions of local tribes is a moot point; *Religion, Community and Territory* (Yeates 2006a) attempted to ascertain details of the religion of the local tribal grouping known as the *Dobunni*; the tribe we are concerned with here, and which we encountered in the discussions on pantheons.

Normally, the divine couple consisted of a male divinity, represented in the guise of a Roman god, alongside a female deity, in a native guise and usually with a local name. With this scenario we might be expected to find Mercury paired with *Rosmerta*, as in one relief from Gaul, and Apollo paired with *Sirona* or *Damona*, sometimes with Apollo given a local name such as *Grannus* and *Moritasgus*. Mars was another Roman god whose image was often incorporated into the idea of the divine couple; one example is Mars *Loucetius* who resided alongside *Nemetona*. A further group of divine couples consisted of two divinities with Celtic names. These include: *Veraudinus* and *Inciona*, *Luxovius* and *Bricta*, and *Ucuetis* and *Bergusia*. In many cases all that can be ascertained about these deities is from the interpretation of the etymology of the name and the interpretation of the accompanying images. One of the most widely distributed images of the divine couple is of *Sucellus* and *Nantosuelta* (as mentioned in Chapter 4). The god is always shown holding a hammer and, although there is a common image on the reliefs, the names varied regionally, reflecting localised aspects of certain tribes. The distribution of this god and goddess pair was concentrated in: an area along the Rhône Valley, an area of Burgundy, and the Rhineland. It is of interest that a relief from Strasbourg, in the Rhineland, shows Mercury holding a hammer. He has thus been dubbed *Mercure-Sucellus* (Baudoux, Flotte *et al.* 2002, 292–293). It is possible that this relief points to a wider conflation of Mercury and *Sucellus* but, on the evidence of just one representation, this would be highly speculative. One of the problems which has arisen with respect to the divine couple is that only a few reliefs still contain inscriptions. This means that, although images from different parts of Gaul and Britain may appear similar, it is possible that different native deities may be represented and been conflated with the Roman deities. It is, however, only reasonable to equate similar images if they come from the same area, as seen in the material from the *Dobunnic* area.

Aldhouse-Green (Green 1989, 45–73) believed that the dominant image of the divine couple was to promote ideas of fertility and prosperity, but it is probably more complex and, in certain cases if not all, may provide evidence of the creation myth of the tribal group. This can be implied, to some extent, from ideas present in the Greek creation myths, as at the heart of each tale there is always a divine couple, whether *Eurynome* and *Ophion*, *Oceanos* and *Tethys*, or *Gaia* and *Ouranos*. As in the reference to *Dis* it is possible that the peoples of north-west Europe took a similar view to the Greeks of the world around them. Caesar, however, did not state explicitly whether *Dis* had a consort; though the presence of one can be presumed from his work.

The divine couple occurred in Greek, Roman, and Celto-Brittonnic traditions, but there are other aspects of the creation myths which show how these stories evolved. Some of these traditions saw the work reconfigured by poets and bards, a notable Roman example being the work of Ovid, who started to incorporate material from the rhetoric of scholars (above). There is some evidence that tribal groups from the north-west may also have altered the origin stories in accordance with the rhetorical debates emanating from Classical Greece.

The druids were recognised in the ancient literature as having had influence on the Celtic and *Belgae* tribal groups in Gaul and Britain. In fact, Caesar (Edwards 1963, VI.13–14) claimed that the cult and traditional beliefs associated with the Druids originated in Britain and were exported from there to Gaul. In the piece concerned, he discussed the physical constitution of the world, and gave the first indications that there was, perhaps, a pan north-west European religious system. It may have, on the other hand, been the case that they manipulated the ideas to fit into this belief system, some of which was presumably influenced, in various ways, by Greek and Roman traditions. Both Diodorus Siculus (Oldfather 1939, V.28) and Ammianus Marcellinus (Rolfe 1950, XV.9.8) believed that Celtic societies had a *Pythagorean* belief system.

Caesar was born in 100 BC, and became governor of *Gallia Cisalpina*, *Gallia Narbonensis*, and *Illyricum* in 59 BC. It was from 58 to 51 BC when he undertook military operations in Gaul, Germany, and Britain, which resulted in the defeat of *Vercingetorix* and the incorporation of Gaul into the Roman Empire. It was also during this campaign, and mainly at *Bibracte* or Mont Beauvray, that he compiled *The Gallic War*. He was murdered in 44 BC.

Caesar did not describe specifically the beliefs of the Britons, but he did describe briefly those of the Gauls in Book VI of *The Gallic Wars*. In his account of the Gauls Caesar gave indications of a stratified society with commoners treated on a par with slaves. The two classes above this were the druids and the knights. Following this distinction there are accounts of the religion of the druids: the performance of sacrifices, the interpretation of ritual questions, and the instruction of the young. The druids also acted as a type of judiciary in the settlement of disputes. Caesar also implied that the British had traditions similar to those of the Gauls and emphasised the British origin of the religious tenets (Edwards 1963, VI.13–14);

> *'These druids, at certain time of the year, meet within the borders of the Carnutes, whose territory is reckoned as the centre of all Gaul, and sit in conclave in the consecrated spot. Thither assemble from every side all that have disputes, and they obey decisions and judgements of the Druids. It is believed that their rule of life was discovered in Britain and transferred thence to Gaul; and to-day those who would study the subject more accurately journey, as a rule, to Britain to learn it.'*

> Reprinted by permission of the publishers and Trustees of the Loeb Classical Library from *I. Caesar: The Gallic War*, Loeb Classical Library Vol. 72, translated by H. J. Edwards, Cambridge, Mass.: Harvard University Press, © 1917, by the President and Fellows of Harvard College. The Loeb Classical Library ® is a registered trademark of the President and Fellows of Harvard College

The druids, he continued, were aloof from war and did not pay military taxes. Amongst the druids' schools the scholars learned a great number of verses. These were not, however, placed in a written form but retained in an oral tradition. This was done so that the minds of the druids were constantly cultivated in thought. The cardinal doctrine that they taught was that the soul did not die; further discussions centred on: the stars and their movements, the size of the universe and the earth, the order of nature, the strength and powers of the immortals, and the process of handing down their law to the young. When Caesar spoke of discussion on such things as the soul and the size of the universe, he touched on areas which Greek and Roman ethnographers would have seen as fitting into a *Pythagorean* belief system although he did not call it such himself. The inference that the druids' belief system was *Pythagorean* is supported by two texts, but it is not apparent what influence Greek or Roman ways of thinking had on the perceptions and views of these ethnographers.

Diodorus Siculus was a contemporary of Caesar and, as his name suggests, was born on the island of Sicily (Harvey 1984, 146). His work concerned Rome, from its mythical times to the conquest of Gaul in his own age. The work is considered to be an uncritical compilation plagiarising earlier sources. He suggested that many of the gods were derived from Egyptian traditions; in others, such as Apollo, Poseidon, and Dionysus, he sees mortals who had been given divine status. Besides discussing the Roman world he also addressed certain aspects of the religious belief systems of the north-west provinces.

The traditions described by Diodorus Siculus (Oldfather 1939, V.28) are not directly applicable to the Britons but, in the light of what *Caesar* said about the druidic traditions emanating from Britain, it is likely that they were similar. There is a reference to the feast, and the central cauldron on the embers of the fire, as will be returned to later; at such occasions duels often developed over trivial matters, and it is in this context that the following reference to Pythagoras was made:

> *"And it is their custom, even during the course of the meal, to seize upon any trivial matter as an occasion for keen disputation and then to challenge one another to single combat, without any regard for their lives; for the belief of Pythagoras prevails among them, that the souls are immortal and that after a prescribed number of years they commence upon a new life, the soul entering another body."*

The commentary on the lives of the Gauls continues with the deposition of letters on the flames of the pyres, suggesting a belief that communication could take place between the living and the dead. Perhaps we can see the results of this belief in the lead pipe burial practices, where a lead pipe was placed between the burial and the ground surface; for example at Welsford in Warwickshire (Booth 1994, 37–50). Diodorus Siculus inferred, however, that *Pythagorean* beliefs were not universal to all tribes. Burials such as that at Welsford Pasture may indicate that such a belief did exist in parts of the *Dobunnic* territory and probably all, but does not categorically prove it to be *Pythagorean*, only suggesting that there was a belief in communication between the living and the dead.

All that we know about the life of Ammianus Marcellinus comes from his own works (Rolfe 1950, ix–xlvii). He was born in Antioch, to a Greek family, in *c* AD 330; his historical writings thus belonging primarily to the second half of the fourth century. It was in the AD 350s that Ammianus gained first-hand knowledge of Gaul, as after AD 359 he was removed from it. His writings indicate that he did not consider himself to be a Christian, although there are references to Christian rites, ceremonies, and officials. He questioned the closing of the schools of rhetoric in favour of Christian teachings.

Ammianus Marcellinus (Rolfe 1950, XV.9.8) was a late Roman writer who also wrote predominantly about Gallic, as opposed to British, tradition. One could suggest that the context of what Caesar said about the British-Gaulish connections is relevant; however, the amount of time that elapsed between Caesar and Marcellinus makes the arguments less sustainable. Marcellinus's comments on *Pythagoras* need to be seen in a context of increasing liberal art, as encouraged by the bards, the *euhages*, and the druids. The bards, we are told, sang of famous men and their heroic deeds. The *euhages*, or vates, attempted to explain the secret rules and laws of nature. Of the druids we are told:

> *"The druids, being loftier than the rest in intellect, and bound together in fraternal organisations, as the authority of Pythagoras determined, were elevated by their investigation of the obscure and profound subjects, and scorning all things human, pronounced the soul immortal."*
>
> Reprinted by permission of the publishers and Trustees of the Loeb Classical Library from *I. Ammianus Marcellinus: History*, Loeb Classical Library Vol. 300, translated by J. C. Rolfe, Cambridge, Mass.: Harvard University Press, © 1935, rev. 1950, by the President and Fellows of Harvard College. The Loeb Classical Library ® is a registered trademark of the President and Fellows of Harvard College

Here again, we are informed that the association with *Pythagoras* was made because of the way the druids perceived the soul and its transmigration. With regard to the *euhages*, or vates, their discussion of the secrets of the universe could also, perhaps, be seen as part of this mathematical *Pythagorean* world view.

Pythagorean systems were described in a number of Greek works including Plato's *Timaeus* (Bury 1929, 3–253), and Aristotle's *Metaphysics* (Tredennick 1933, xiv–xix). In these works we find that *Pythagoras* of Samos, who lived in the sixth century BC (about 530 BC), practiced a form of Orphism; a system based on mysticism. This included: the doctrine of transmigration, the analogy of macrocosm and microcosm, a doctrine of universal unity, and an understanding of numerical ratios in mathematics. *Pythagoras* was the first to treat mathematics as an abstract science. It was only from later works, plagiarising *Pythagoras* to varying degrees, that we can reconstruct some of the lost ideas of *Pythagoras*.

Plato was born in *c.* 427 BC, in Athens (Harvey 1984, 331), and is known to us, primarily, as a poet. He turned his attention to philosophy after meeting Socrates in *c.* 407 BC. Socrates died in the same year and, following this, Plato moved to *Megara* and also travelled widely. It is believed that he visited Syracuse in *Magna Graecia*, on three different occasions, 389, 367, and 361 BC, where he met a number of *Pythagoreans*. After these visits he returned to Athens to teach philosophy at the Academy. Plato died in 348/7 BC.

The work *Timaeus*, regarded by later philosophers as the most important of Plato's texts, takes its name from *Timaeus* of *Locri*, who was considered to be a man of high social status and wide cultural ability; some later traditions made him the leader of the *Pythagorean* School (Bury 1929, 3–15). The work is, in essence, an attempt to explain the creation of the universe. It is, essentially, divided into three parts; the first of which includes the Atlantis legend as related by Solon. The second covers the making of the world soul, a doctrine of the elements, and the theory of matter; while the third covers the making of man, his soul, and his body, with commentaries on physiology and pathology. What we realise, in the association of Gallic traditions with *Pythagorean* beliefs, is that the Gauls, like the Greeks and the Romans, must have moved from a world in which creation or primal myths were laid down by poets and bards to one in which pseudo-scientific approaches evolved. The *Timaeus* contains an explanation of how the Cosmos was gradually built out of Chaos; and there are attempts to explain the cause of these events. In these discussions there are a number of developing traditions, including ideas on the demiurge, the world soul, the solar system, and the elements. Plato also drew a distinction between the idea of being, on that which was eternal; and the idea of becoming, that which was seen as ever-changing. There are also some accounts of a demiurge, not considered the creator but only as someone who imposed order on the world, maybe for divine reasons. Later, the gods become involved in the shaping of the world that we see. The idea of the World-Soul is a product of myth and mathematics; the underlying principle in this idea was to explain the function of the Solar System. To Plato, the soul was, in some way, bound to the idea of motion. The next significant debate concerned how the universe was constructed from the four elements: fire, air, water, and earth, a doctrine which was taken straight from Empedocles.

Aristotle was born in Stagira in Chalcidice, in 384 BC (Tredennick 1933, vii–ix), into a clan called the *Asclepiadae* in which the medical profession was hereditary. When 18 he went to the Academy to study, where he was influenced by Plato. When Plato died Aristotle left Athens for *Atarneus*, to live with a fellow pupil called *Hermias*. He spent time on Lesbos before going to the Macedonian court in 343 BC. In 336 BC he returned to Athens where he established the Lyceum. The main features of *Pythagoras's* doctrine, as accounted by Aristotle, can be listed as follows (Tredennick 1933, xiv–xix, I.viii.17–ix.36). Firstly, the transmigration of the soul; in which each individual soul came from the divine being and later returned to it. Second, there was an analogy drawn between god and the human soul, using a macrocosm and microcosm interpretation, and the perception that the universe was a living organism. Third, it was considered that the living entity must be finite or limited, thus enabling ideas of the universe to be reproduced in the individual. These notions implied that the principle order forming the universe was restricted, and that disorder (the opposing power to the principle of order) was unlimited. Fourth, to create unity between order and disorder there were specific ratios; this last aspect being identifiable through *Pythagoras's* study of mathematics. The incorporation of mathematics, and the idea of even and odd numbers, started division in the original unique entity of creation, and a duality in the elements of creation. Could such a statement be seen as hinting at the presence of a divine couple in the act of creation rather than a single acrogenous entity? *Pythagorean* traditions in Greece later became united with other schools of thought, namely the Eleatic schools, from which *Leucippus* of *Miletus* and *Democritus* of *Abdera* obtained their philosophies.

The problem with quoting the later historical works directly is that their authors lived after the time they were trying to describe. Caesar's commentary was, however, very political. He may have been trying to imply that the Gauls were more unified, and so more of a threat, than they really were, for political ends. Caesar may also have implied that the degree of contact between the tribes was greater than it was, for the same purpose. It is not clear in the texts which tribes were using a *Pythagorean* druidic ideological framework and even to what degree we can actually believe that one existed. Historically, it is known that *Diviciacus* was a Druid who lived amongst the *Aedui*, and that there was an annual gathering of these priests in the land of the *Carnutes*. For Britain, it is known that druids were killed at a gathering on the Isle of Anglesey in the land of the *Ordovices*, for other tribes we assume they existed as a priesthood.

Having recognised that certain Roman and Greek ethnographers believed that there was an association between the beliefs of the druids (as developed by the vates and druids) in Britain and those in Gaul, one has to wonder how this arose. If there was a *Pythagorean* tradition then it may be considered more likely that these beliefs developed through interaction with the Greek and Roman worlds (perhaps through Marseilles). *Pythagorean* traditions had apparently spread to Rome by the fourth century BC, when *Numa* is accounted as one of his pupils (Wiseman 2008, 158). There are suggestions that texts amongst the Gauls and the Britons were written in Greek (Edwards 1963, I.29, V.48, VI.14). This has to be weighed against the comments of Caesar about the religious belief systems of the druids being developed in Britain (Edwards 1963, VI.13). What these Classical authors do suggest, however, is that any tribal primal myth was influenced by the rhetoric of the Classical world to a greater or lesser extent.

THE DIVINE COUPLE OF THE *DOBUNNI*

Most 'Celtic' representations of the divine marriage and couple have come down to us from Gaulish sources rather than British ones. There exists, however, a representation of the divine couple found in Nottinghamshire which shows the image of a hammer-god alongside a female. Most British images of the divine couple, however, come from the *Dobunni* territory, in the lands of the Severn Vale and Cotswold Hills (see Chapter 1). In these images a deity, portrayed as Mercury, is accompanied by a native goddess, always accompanied by a **sacred vessel**, called the *Mater*, or *Modron* in the singular form. The information appertaining to this subject has been assessed elsewhere (Yeates 2006a; 2007, 55–69), but there are two basic arguments. The first concerns the physical representation of the goddess on the Roman reliefs; the second the linguistic arguments.

Of the images of this divine couple two came from the *colonia* of Gloucester: a complete example, found in the middle of the nineteenth century (the better preserved piece) (Henig 1993a, no.78), and a partial relief which was recovered near the cross in excavations in the 1960s (Henig 1993a, no.79). The nineteenth century find, of 1857, came from the Shakespeare Inn in London Road. Initially, it was believed that it came from near a Roman period shrine site, but it is equally plausible that the piece was taken from central Gloucester (see Figures 46). The name of the public house should remind us of one of the bard's better known plays in which Macbeth met three witches. These have previously been seen as a symbol of Germanic origin, but the reference by Shakespeare, himself a *Hwiccian* lad, may derive from local folk-tradition in his youth concerning the three mothers. The 1960s piece is incomplete and was recovered during excavations in the area north-east of the forum (see Figure 47). A third, terracotta, image of the goddess was recovered near the Cross (Medland 1895, 142–158; Fullbrook-Leggatt 1933, 73–74).

Figure 46: The relief of Mercury and the mother, found in 1857, from Northgate Street, Gloucester. This has the best surviving image of the mother goddess of the Dobunni. In it she holds a ladle above a bucket or circular vessel (photograph used by kind permission of Gloucester City Museum and Art Gallery)

For a map of the location of the finds from Gloucester, and probable temple locations in the city (see Figure 48).

Images of the divine couple are also found on a stone carving from Cirencester recovered in 1862 at the Leauses (Henig 1993a, no.81). This is one of a larger group of reliefs, recovered at the same time, associated with the cult of the goddess and her consort (see Figures 49–51). These include images of Mercury on his own (Henig 1993a, no.70), and parts of what may have been a cult statue. Images of the goddess occur also in triple form (Henig 1993a, no.118). The recovery of these reliefs from the same area implies that they came from the same temple site and that the variation on the reliefs fits into a wider cult present amongst the *Dobunnic* people. Antiquaries describe the remains of a possible circular temple in the Ashcroft area of Cirencester.

Other reliefs have been recovered from towns and rural locations in the south of the *Dobunnic* territory (see Figures 52–53); including a relief of the divine couple at

Figure 47: The relief of Mercury and the mother, found in 1960, in excavations at the Cross, Gloucester (photograph used by kind permission of Gloucester City Museum and Art Gallery)

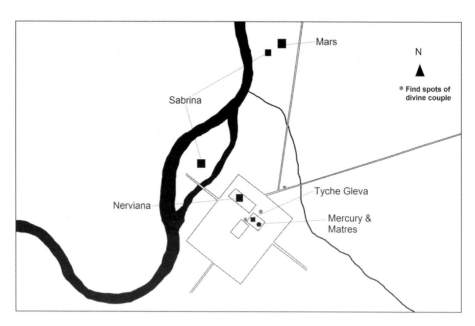

Figure 48: A map showing the location of the main shrines in the Gloucester environs (drawing S. Yeates)

Figure 49: The relief showing Mercury and the mother from the Leauses site in Cirencester (photograph by the late M. B. Cookson, photograph held by the Institute of Archaeology, Oxford)

Bath (Cunliffe and Fulford 1982, no.39) and a further relief of Mercury on his own from excavations on the great bath at Bath (Cunliffe and Fulford 1982, no.24). These seem to represent the same cult which was identified in Gloucester and Cirencester. A relief of three mothers has also been found at Bathwick, but it is insufficiently detailed to indicate which group of *Matres* are represented (Cunliffe and Fulford 1982, no.38). The cult temple at Bath (see Figure 54), which these reliefs lay nearest to, was circular in design (Cunliffe 1989, 59–86). A similar circular temple has been described in the Ashcroft area of Cirencester, which is where the reliefs of Mercury and the *Matres* were recovered.

At the small Roman town of Nettleton Scrubb in Wiltshire a similar but fragmentary

Figure 50: The relief of Mercury recovered from the Leauses in Cirencester in 1862 (photograph by the late M. B. Cookson, photograph held by the Institute of Archaeology, Oxford).

relief of the goddess and consort (see Figure 55) was also recovered (Cunliffe and Fulford 1982, no.117). The nature of the building where this sculpture originated is more difficult to ascertain. The object depicted alongside the goddess is taller and may represent a churn rather than a cauldron.

Another relief of the divine couple was uncovered at Wellow in Somerset (Cunliffe and Fulford 1982, no.116), but in this case the couple is portrayed flanking a further female goddess (see Figure 56). The mother goddess is on the left and is accompanied by a churn type vessel. A stone panel with a similar image was also recovered from within the

Figure 51: The relief showing the Matres from the Leauses site in Cirencester. This shows the consort of Mercury in a triple representation. (photograph by the late M. B. Cookson, photograph held by the Institute of Archaeology, Oxford)

Figure 52: The relief of Mercury and the Mater recovered at Bath from excavations at the Great Bath (photograph used by kind permission of The Roman Baths, Bath and North East Somerset Council)

Figure 53: The relief of Mercury recovered in Bath from excavations at the Great Bath (photograph used by kind permission of The Roman Baths, Bath and North East Somerset Council)

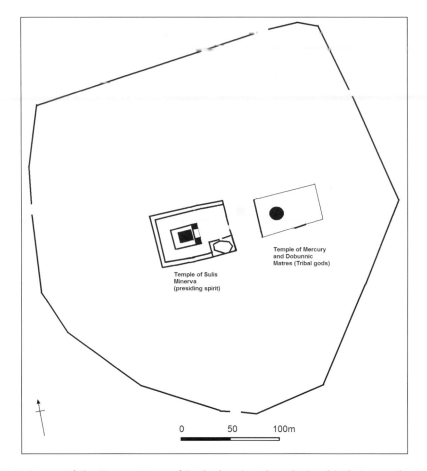

Figure 54: A map of the Roman town of Bath showing the relationship between the temple of Sulis Minerva, who personified the springs and the town, and the probable shrine of Mercury and Mater (drawing S. Yeates)

Colonia walls at Gloucester (Henig 1993a, no.80) (see Figure 35). In this one the goddess usually sculptured with the cauldron is portrayed as Fortuna while the central goddess wears, what seems to be, a mural crown and is thus, probably, a representation of the deity which resided over the city of Gloucester (see Chapters 3 and 4).

A further relief of the divine couple has come from Aldsworth in the Cotswolds (Henig, Cleary *et al.* 2000, 362–363); however, on this relief the image of Minerva stands alongside that of Mercury. In this case it is possible that the mother was being identified not only as the parent of the tribe but also as the protectress (see Figure 57).

There is one further image that we can mention with respect to Mercury and the *Mater* of the *Dobunni* and that is a fresco described by Aubrey on his travels in 1665–93. He mentioned the painting, presumed medieval, of an image in Worcester Cathedral of two giants, one of which was male, the other female. Both were described as being

Figure 55: A sketch of the relief of Mercury and the Mater recovered from Nettleton in 1912 (drawing S. Yeates)

naked but the female was described as holding two javelins of a Roman design (Fowles 1980, 476). Although the image can not be linked precisely to that of the group of sculptures, certain similarities to the Aldsworth relief, where the female is portrayed as the protector, may be drawn. Why this image should be depicted in the *Cathedral of the Witches* can only be surmised. Excavations have been carried out in the vicinity of the cathedral, especially in recent years, around the chapter house. The circular shape of this building is considered to have developed from an earlier rotunda; the church of Saint Mary (Crawford and Guy 1997, 7; Crawford 2000, 345–348), which was part of the dual church foundation at Worcester. The date of the foundations has, however, not been proven categorically. It is known from analysis and comments concerning Bath and Cirencester that the tribal deities were probably worshipped in a circular temple or tholos (Yeates 2008b, 137–146).

Figure 56: A sketch of the relief of Mercury with two goddesses, from Wellow in Somerset (drawing S. Yeates)

That this divine couple represents the father and mother of the *Dobunni* people is implied by the persistent use of the image in the *Dobunnic* towns and in the key locations in those towns from which they were recovered. It is apparent, from the archaeology of Bath and Cirencester, that the temples of the mother and father were circular in shape and that they were probably designed to align with the temple of the presiding deity of the town in which their temple stood. The distribution of these reliefs is also an indication that the territory of the *Dobunni* extended into Somerset and Wiltshire. There are further indications in the form of an inscription that the territory also extended into Herefordshire, as discussed in more depth in Chapter 1. This would have meant that Gloucester and the Vale of Gloucester comprised only the central part of the territory.

Now that the divine couple has been identified it is possible to show how the cult

Figure 57: The relief of Mercury and consort from Aldsworth, in which the goddess is portrayed as Minerva and is, in this guise perhaps, a representation of the goddess as protector (photograph Robert Wilkins, Institute of Archaeology archive, source Martin Henig)

survived for over a thousand years, and that it was focussed on a specific area of the territory. This has previously been discussed elsewhere, but it is necessary to repeat the idea here in more depth. The royalty of the *Dobunni* are represented, presumably, by the richest known burials identified from this time; these burials were located on the hills of Birdlip and Crickley as described in *The Birdlip Cemetery* (Stealens 1982, 19–31) (see Figures 58 and 59). Objects from the burials survive and are located in Gloucester Museum. There was also a further large cemetery, described by antiquaries, on Leckhampton Hill. The burials on Crickley and Birdlip contained buckets or cauldrons which were placed over the heads of the deceased. This action may be seen as a ritual act of feeding from the **sacred vessel**, which would have held an elixir of life. It is also apparent that the buckets or bowls symbolised of an aspect of the landscape as the burials were located at Barrow Wake and on Crickley Hill on the brow of the Cotswold escarpment. Anyone standing on these sites would have a view out over a large circular valley. The circular valley lies between the hills of Cleeve, Cooper's, Corsewood and Bredon (see Figures 60 and 61), and is some 12 miles in diameter (see Figure 62). There was a parallel between the objects placed in the Iron-Age tombs and the nature of the surrounding landscape. The dead were presumably feeding from both vessels on their journey into the otherworld.

Numerous depictions of mothers have also been found on the continent, especially

Figure 58: The burial goods from the Birdlip Cemetery, including basin and mirror (photogaph used by permission of the Gloucester City Museum and Art Gallery)

in the Rhineland area, so it is apparent that the tradition of the *Matres, Matronae,* or *Mater* was widespread (Green 1989, 188–204). The various forms of the name seem to have been interchangeable. In the *Dobunni* territory the Cirencester inscription refers to the *Matres* (Wright and Hassall 1973, 324 no.1), but in the Mabinogion (Jones and Jones 1974, 125) the goddess is referred to as *Modron,* derived from *Matrona,* or plural *Matronae.* It is apparent, from the representations of the mothers found in Gaul and the German provinces that the qualifying designation of the mother is always the tribal or folk-group name for example: *Aufaniae, Gesahenae, Gavadiae, Vacallinehae, Boudunneihae, Nemausicae* and *Glanicae* (Green 1989, 194–198). The name *Suleviae* (RIB(I) 1995, nos.105, 106, 151) is recorded on some triple mother sculptures, but this representation is distinctly different in certain aspects, such as hairstyle, from the group which accompanies Mercury and is known as the *Matres.* The *Suleviae* sculpture also came from a different location in Cirencester to that of Mercury and the *Matres.* The cult of the *Matres* was not associated with just a local folk-group amongst the *Dobunni* as evident from the distribution of reliefs of this goddess. They have been found spread right across the *Dobunnic* territory. We can thus hypothesise, if not yet prove, that the mother goddess on these reliefs would have been known as *Mater Dobunna* (singular) or *Matronae Dobunnae* (plural).

The 'Celtic' and 'Germannic' *Matres* are by some considered to be derived from the

Figure 59: The skyline of Barrow Wake, on Birdlip Hill, the major recognised burial place of the Dobunni elite (photograph S. Yeates)

Figure 60: The major hill-fort on Bredon Hill, Worcestershire (photograph S. J. Yeates)

Figure 61: The line of the hills which lie around the north-east edge of the Vale of Gloucester (photograph S. Yeates)

Roman *Iunones*, a development of the goddess Juno (Green 1992, 126). These were considered to have been the essential spirit of a female: an earth deity who protected women during pregnancy and childbirth. The format of mother, triple mother, and tribal descent has been recognised in Irish traditions outside the Roman Empire and seem, therefore, to have been part of an indigenous Celtic, Brittonic, and Germannic tradition (Chapter 2).

The etymology of the name *Dobunni* has, to a large extent, been shrouded in mystery and because of that the meaning has been officially regarded as unknown (Rivet and Smith 1979, 339–340). Having said that, various suggestions have been put forward, for example Guest associated the name with *dubn*, a **valley**, **chasm** or **deep** (Guest 1862, 193–218). A further suggestion, discussed elsewhere, is that it refers to the black ash tree, *dub-onni* (Rudd 2003, 7–14), the **ash tree** was sacred to the *Dobunni* but there seems to be a problem with the location of the <u> and the <o> in this interpretation. One further possibility is that it is associated with the Old English *buna*, also written *bune*, which has an etymology of **cup** (Ekwall 1928, 56–57; Coplestone-Crow 1989, 35). In Oxfordshire and Buckinghamshire the word seems to be the root of the river-name Bune, recorded *Bunon* or *Bunan* in AD 995, which rises at Somerton on a hill on the east side of the river Cherwell. On the western borders of the *Dobunni* territory is the name Bunhill, thought to derive from the same source. The word may have occurred first in Old English but it is also possible that there was a pre-Old English Brittonic form of this word which is the final component of the *Dobunni* name. This would tie in with the cult of the mother and her recognised symbol. The prefix *Do-* may be some type of honorific addition in the same way that *To-* was added to saint names in the early medieval period; or it may have the meaning **to give** or **goddess**. This would mean that the name refers to a **cup** or some type of **sacred vessel**.

The goddess of the *Dobunni* provided the reason why this tribe was given their Old English name *Hwicce* (Gelling 1982, 59–78; Yeates 2008b), meaning the **sacred vessel**. The word *Hwicce*, as a folk-name, may be one of three, or perhaps four, words that are probably derived from a common English source. *Hwicce* also sometimes referred to a box or chest (Northcote Toller and Campbell 1921, 581). The other words are *wicca*, a wizard, and *wicce*, a witch (Northcote Toller 1898, 1213). The latter part of the name in each case is philologically the same; variations in the name occurring with the <hw> or <w>. Hooke (Hillaby 2008, 20–21) suggested that the <h> was dropped from *Hwicce* in Middle English and that these names could not have been related as the bishops of Worcester were styled *episcope Hwicciorum* as late as the tenth century. Her argument, however, has a number of problems if we consider what is stated in the Anglo-Saxon dictionaries for the various dialects and translations from Old English dialects into Latin. In certain English dialects, such as Northumbrian, it is uncertain if the initial silent <h> ever existed (Northcote Toller 1898, 496); examples noted for this are <hl>, <hn>, and <hr>. The phrase and inference is 'especially in respect to these combinations' but there are obviously others besides. Thus the tribal name *Wicce*, *wicce* a **sacred vessel**, and *wicce*, a **witch** could all have been spelled the same way. In a list of territorial tribal-names, known as the tribal hidage, the folk-name *Hicca* is recorded, the name has already been associated with the *Hwicce*, but is now known to be a small group in the East Midlands; it is evident, from a Latin version of the text, that the name was recorded as *Wicca* (Northcote Toller and Campbell 1921, 581). Thus we can determine that in an eleventh century version of an eighth century document there was confusion between Old English pronunciation and Latin with the initial <h>. Even the spelling of the tribal name *Hwicce* has been confused as *Hicna*. The word *hwicce* (not the kingdom), **a sacred vessel**, **box**, or **chest** is recorded on several occasions in the Anglo-Saxon dictionary; the first two of which contain the <h> while all later cases are spelled with a <w>, for example *whichche* and *whyche* (Northcote Toller and Campbell 1921, 581). In the case of the *whichche* spelling there are brackets containing the words 'the ark' so one would naturally assume that this was taken from an ecclesiastical text and was referring to the Biblical Ark of the Covenant. We should also remember that, in all of these cases, the <h> is relatively silent and, therefore, should not affect the philology but only the written form. However, when one looks at these names the tribal territory seems to have been singled out as an important religious landscape within the British Isles, and it is extremely difficult to separate all these words philologically. In some instances we can actually see how some of the changes in the tribal name and the associated place-names occurred. *Mons Huuicciorum*, in AD 780 (Smith 1964b, ii.8, xi), had, in AD 964, become *Monte Wiccisca*. It is plausible that in certain cases where texts had been transcribed from earlier sources the <hw> may have occurred late, as in the case of Wychwood, where *Hwichewod* occurred in 1230 (Gelling 1954, ii.386), and in other names of the fourteenth century which occurred a long-time after <w> forms dominated. Thus one could argue that, due to local circumstances, archaic forms of the name persisted, maybe in elite circles when transcribed from earlier documents. It is even feasible that, if the ecclesiastics at Worcester were aware of an association between *Hwicce* and *wicce*, then they would perhaps have wanted to separate the two and may have deliberately maintained the <h> even though it had become philologically redundant some time before. There should also be no problem with seeing the name of a religion or a religious practitioner being associated with an ethnic group, for example Jew and Judaism represents a well known example. Rather than the linguistic arguments being problematic, they can often enhance the visual argument. The vessel of the goddess and the Severn Valley at Gloucester were one and the same. Their mother goddess was portrayed alongside a bucket, cauldron or churn; as well as in triple form, as discussed previously, and there was a process of Germanic *interpretatio* leading to an association with the Germanic Norns or Wyrd sisters who lived at the root of the world tree, and watered that tree from the well of life.

The goddess, and her priestesses, were also referred to, or rather implied, in the tale of *Peredur* in the Mabinogion (Jones and Jones 1974, 198). In it, we are informed of the mother and father and the nine witches of Gloucester. The nine witches, hags, mothers, or maidens are usually seen as a reference to the nine women who looked after the sacred cauldron, mentioned in the poem of Taliesin, called *the spoils of Annwn* (Nash 1858, 210–216). The Welsh word *gwidonot* was used in the red book or Mabinogion, which translates into English as **witch**. The historical authenticity of this group of priestesses is apparently confirmed by a second source. In the Breton *Life of Saint Samson of Dol*, written in Latin, there is a passage where the saint was chased by a *theomacha* with a trident (Chadwick 1970, 72). The *theomacha* confessed to being one of nine sisters, all of whom possessed supernatural powers. Chadwick believed that the passage related to Samson's British visit and that the group of sisters were the nine witches of Gloucester. The word *theomacha* translates as **witch**. Other groups of nine priests/priestesses were referred to in continental Celtic and Irish traditions. In the *Book of Armagh* there were nine druid-prophets of *Brega* who lived on the great plain (Bieler 1979, I.14 (13).2). The nine hags of Gloucester can be equated with the cult of the cauldron or **sacred vessel**, identified as being focused on Gloucester and evident in the temple reliefs from the city. These were the priestesses of the divine mother and father who looked after the cult object. In the tale of *Culhwch and Olwen* the goddess was specifically called *Modron* (as mentioned in Chapter 2 and elsewhere).

It is probable that, in this tradition, there are clues to part of the creation myth of the *Dobunni*. The traditional myth in the Mabinogion, the information observed in the images on reliefs, the burial practices of the *Dobunni*, and the interpretation of the name of the tribal group *Hwicce* which followed, all imply that it was the Vale of Gloucester that was the **sacred vessel**, the cauldron of the mother goddess of the tribe. It would have been the site from which life came and the place where the *Dobunni* believed they had their origin. The valley was the focus for the cult of presumed royal or elite burials in the Iron Age, and was the image which gave the tribe their English name.

We have no recognised name for the tribal goddess but it is apparent that one of the two figures would or could have shared their name with the tribe *Dobunni*. That the term *Matres* was used in the area may imply that, as with her continental or Germanic equivalents, the title of mother was followed by the name of the tribe, *Dobunni*, and that there was probably a folk suffix as an ending.

A FATHER FOR THE DOBUNNI

Much can be determined about the goddess but little can be said about the identity of the father of the tribe, as the sculptors of the Roman period have chosen to portray this deity in a wholly Roman guise. Conventionally, Mercury with his caduceus, ram, cockerel and purse represents a god of prosperity and well-being. That this may have been a significant factor may be underlined by the large and wealthy villas which scattered the Cotswold area and Severn Valley. However, Caesar's comment and coin analysis may enable us to glimpse the remains of a divinity that was pre-Roman; not a deity paired with a Celtic consort, but a god in his own right who had been given a Roman image or veneer. Caesar (Edwards 1963, VI.15) said about the Gauls, but not the British:

> *"Among the gods, they most worship Mercury. There are numerous images of him; they declare him the inventor of all arts, the guide for every road and journey, and they deem him to have the greatest influence for all money-making and traffic."*
>
> Reprinted by permission of the publishers and Trustees of the Loeb Classical Library from *I. Caesar: The Gallic War*, Loeb Classical Library Vol. 72, translated by H. J. Edwards, Cambridge, Mass.: Harvard University Press, © 1917, by the President and Fellows of Harvard College. The Loeb Classical Library ® is a registered trademark of the President and Fellows of Harvard College

The reason that this statement is important for the *Dobunni* is because the father was portrayed as Mercury. This means that he was probably part of a widespread cultural tradition amongst the peoples of the north-west provinces. Caesar (Edwards 1963, V.12) stated, in an account of one of his incursions into the island that:

> *"They account it wrong to eat of hare, fowl/chicken, and goose."*
>
> Reprinted by permission of the publishers and Trustees of the Loeb Classical Library from *I. Caesar: The Gallic War*, Loeb Classical Library Vol. 72, translated by H. J. Edwards, Cambridge, Mass.: Harvard University Press, © 1917, by the President and Fellows of Harvard College. The Loeb Classical Library ® is a registered trademark of the President and Fellows of Harvard College

The reference to a fowl or chicken, the word used by Caesar is *gallinam*, which undoubtedly led to the word Gallic and the symbol of Gaul as the cockerel. These two passages probably sum up some of the underlying ideas about Gallic, and possibly British, religion, that the cockerel was revered, yet Mercury was accounted as the most important god amongst the Gauls, and a god whose symbol was the cockerel. Mercury was one of the most common divinities to have been incorporated into the Gallic religious system; this surely must have been because of an association with underlying beliefs.

On the *Dobunnic* sculptural reliefs, specifically associated with the divine couple, Mercury is portrayed only with the cockerel and not the ram. This is of interest as there are two Iron-Age coins of the *Dobunni* which depict the head of a cockerel below the legs of their sacred horse. The two coin types (see Figures 63 and 64), are known as the Cotswold Cock and the Cotswold Eagle types (Yeates 2008a, 2–4). Both show clearly the cockerel's head and we can surely see the forerunner of the image which turns up alongside the tribal god portrayed as Mercury. This interpretation questions some of the previous beliefs about the divine couple in the traditions of *Interpretatio Romana* and indicates that a deity associated with a cockerel was known amongst the *Dobunni* and that he was used symbolically on their coins before being portrayed on the reliefs.

The cockerel may have been the underlying reason why Mercury was associated with the father figure of the *Dobunni* tribe so it is perhaps essential to identify when this species was brought into Britain. There are clear indications that this animal, a native species of India or Burma, was in Gaul and Britain in the late Iron Age. Indeed the name Gaul seems to be associated with the name *gallinam* used for the chicken. Normally, domestic fowl would be expected to show up in the flora and fauna remains of refuse pits, which it does in some of the later Iron Age deposits from Danebury, Hampshire (Serjeantson 1991, 479–481), but if the animal was revered in such a way that it was taboo to eat, as Caesar implied, then it would not have been eaten and would not have ended up in these pits. In southern Asia the chicken is believed to have been domesticated around 1000 BC (Davis 1987, 127, 134, 152), though some have claimed its domestication in China as early as 6000 BC. From textual sources it is apparent that the cockerel had been introduced to Greece by the seventh century BC (Pollard 1977, 88–89). One can assume that it reached Western Europe between 1000 BC and 100 BC. Chicken bones have been recovered from the Heuneberg in Germany which date to the sixth century BC, and are known to have been common in the Mediterranean world from this date (Green 1992, 22–24, 82). In Gaul they turn up in burials, for example the tomb of La Gorge Meillet in Marne uncovered in 1876, where a skeleton of a chicken and eggs were placed as food for the afterlife. A small silver model has been recovered from the sanctuary of Estrées-Saint-Denis, Oise, while at Reinheim a hen depicted on a brooch was deposited as a grave good.

It is, therefore, possible to assume that the cockerel was brought into Europe through contact with India and Persia. In Zoroastrian traditions this bird was considered to be particularly sacred. Aldhouse-Green (Green 1992, 125–127) suggested that bird burials turn up at sanctuary sites because the birds may represent spirits or the souls of the dead. That the chicken could be used in this context in the north-west provinces is of particular interest when we start associating the cockerel, Mercury, his *interpretatio* with Hermes, as guide to the souls of the dead, and ideas of *Pythagorean* mysticism involving the transmigration of the soul. From this we may be looking at some of the important traditions associated with the *Dobunnic* father.

Frazer (1922, 447–464), in discussing aspects of European folklore, determined that various animals were associated with the cutting of the last sheaf of corn, for example: a dog, a wolf, a cockerel, a hare, a cat, a goat, a bull, a cow or ox, a horse, and a boar or sow. These traditions vary from place to place, but it is evident that there was a widespread tradition that the cockerel played this role in parts of Germany, Hungary, Poland, France, Romania, Austria, and Spain. It was the case in certain circumstances to sacrifice the cock. This may have resulted in the chicken being buried and its head chopped off while still in the ground. One could argue that the cockerel represented the spirit of the corn and that he was associated with the transmigration of its spirit from one year to the next. It should also be noted that the goat also appeared in the list, another animal associated with Mercury.

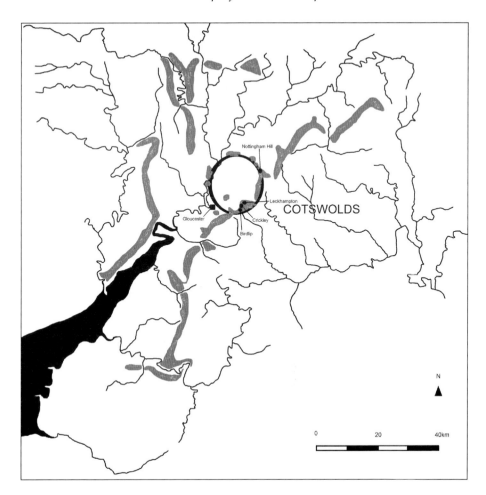

Figure 62: A map of the Severn valley showing the location of the rich late Iron-Age burials at Crickley and Birdlip, and the other unusual but undated burials at Leckhampton Hill and Nottingham Hill. The grey areas indicate the lines of scarp slope along the Cotswold Edge and outliers, the Forest of Dean, Malverns, Mendips, and Wyre Forest. The enclosed circular valley lies to the north-east of Gloucester and is highlighted in black (drawing S. Yeates)

At the shrine of Uley it was found that chickens and goats were buried at the sanctuary; it is believed that this was because they were particularly associated with Mercury, who was worshipped at the site (Woodward and Leach 1993, 272–300). Some of the bones turn up in small ritual pits so it has been suggested that these small discrete deposits were votive in nature. In phase 4 building structure IV, there were deposits of goats and fowl, for which there was no evidence of butchery on the bones, thus indicating that they were not killed for domestic consumption but had been killed for some ritual purpose. These specific activities are most noted in structures I and IV. The time of year

Figure 63: An image of the cockerel can be seen on this Dobunnic silver coin unit, called today the Cotswold Cock. On one side the coin has a female head with moon symbolism and a small horse; on the other is a triple tailed horse, with the hooked beak of a bird above and the cockerel's head between the legs of the horse (photograph courtesy of Chris Rudd and Liz Cottam)

for this apparent slaughter was placed in August-September, around harvest time; it is discernable that these animals are predominantly male, especially noted in phase 5. It should be noted that there was a tradition of burying animals in the ground which, it could be claimed, fit in with the corn traditions as described by Frazer. What we do not know as yet about Mercury is if this representation of him was associated with the tribal deity. One could imply that the sacrifice of these animals at Uley represented a recognisable archaeological representation of the activities which Frazer was revealing about the folk-traditions of Europe. In the case of Uley it is apparent that the goat, sheep, and cockerel were being used for similar purposes. Although most of the folklore publications are quiet about the significance of the cockerel in the *Dobunni* territory it was mentioned by Harvey Bloom (1930, 84) that, in the Stour valley, Warwickshire, certain traditions concerning the cockerel may have survived or be derived from the type of Roman period traditions which can be detected at Uley.

> *"From the neighbourhood of Brailes hill come the traces of what looks like the survival of the sacrifice to the corn spirit. A cock was brought into the field and fastened by a string to a stake, while the men stood at a distance and shot at it, the lucky sportsman receiving the bird as his reward. On one occasion the wily fowl was too quick for his enemies, and dodged the shots until a gamekeeper charged his piece with a silver sixpence. There is no such tale told at Whitchurch, but the last strands of corn were knotted to represent a cock's head and thrown at with sickles."*
>
> From *Folk-lore, Old Customs and Superstitions in Shakespeare Land* by J. Harvey Bloom

This indeed does seem to fit into a cohesive pattern of beliefs which, it can be argued, may have been evident in the Roman period. Uley may, therefore, give an indication that the cockerel had become associated with the spirit of the corn. As yet there are no indications that the Mercury who can be identified as the tribal divinity and the Mercury worshipped at the Uley Shrine were the same native deity.

Figure 64: An image of the cockerel can be seen on this Dobunnic silver coin unit, now called the Cotswold Eagle. The coin has a female head with moon symbolism on one side, and the triple tailed horse, with the cockerel's head between the horse's legs on the other (photograph courtesy of Chris Rudd and Liz Cottam)

CONCLUSIONS

Amongst the *Dobunni* it is possible to recognise a divine couple, the female of which is simply known to us as *Mater* and *Modron* (singular), and *Matres* (plural). Such dedications are known, from continental examples, to be associated with the tribal group. The cult can be seen emerging in the late Iron Age in what was, presumably, the royal burial practice amongst the *Dobunni* and it was this that gave the Iron-Age and early medieval people their folk-name. The association of a specific topographical feature associated with the name and tradition, now called the Vale of Gloucester, also seems apparent from the specific location of the Iron-Age burials, and the later indications in the Mabinogion that Gloucester was the focus of this cult. Here we have the image of a goddess whose cult vessel represented a specific part of the Gloucestershire and Worcestershire landscape. The implications of this are quite profound, if the *Matres* were the head of the tribal or genealogical tradition then the origin of the *Dobunni* tribe, later known as the *Hwicce*, must have been based in the Vale of Gloucester. This topographical feature was sacred, to which there are vague references in medieval texts (this will be explored further in the next chapter). This goddess and her cult, as we will see later, were the foundation onto which much of Britain's early medieval mythical traditions were built.

The father of the Dobunni has long remained the more obscure of the two figures due to his representation in Roman guise. It is now possible, due to the recognition of certain Mercurial images on the *Dobunnic* coinage, to suggest that he was not a Roman period invention and that he was probably worshipped prior to their acculturation of British traditions. The cockerel seems to have been his emblem, but this still leaves us in a position where there is more speculation than fact.

Chapter 6

Sacred Places

In modern neo-paganism there is a sense that certain places are sacred; consequently there has been much focus on sites such as Stonehenge and Avebury. The reasons why these are regarded as important have often been subsumed into the beliefs of the new-age religionists who claim antiquity for their rites when most of them are recent inventions. Even so the importance of such sites has been recognised in archaeology and has given rise to such works as *A phenomenology of landscape: places, paths and monuments* (Tilley 1994), which considers the specific locations of monuments and the impact that they must have had on the landscape; considering views from the monument and the visibility of the site from other locations. The study looked at the landscape of south-west Wales, the Black Mountains, and the Dorset Downlands. Archaeologists have also realised that, for any structure, there are certain ways in which its internal space can be used. General theories about the use of space can be found in *Architecture and Order* (Parker Pearson and Richards 1994). Besides the analysis of structural remains and the phenomenology of their location, there are also surviving references in texts which indicate that some places in the British landscape were considered more important, or more sacred, than others. How and why these places became sacred may have a simple explanation or the reasons may have been extremely complex and have been the result of peculiar natural attributes, or the site at which specific events took place. The reason for these sites' use may also have altered over time.

That certain places were considered to have been more sacred than others is evident in some of the surviving creation myths; it is also relevant that some of these sites were seen as places where divinities lived or were born. In the Greek world there was a focus on Mount Olympus, which was considered initially to be the home of *Eurynome* and *Ophion*, in the *Pelasgian* creation myth, and of the Olympian gods, in the *Theogony* of Hesiod. Olympus, a crag-topped mountain often obscured by banks of clouds, is an atmospheric location and it was the feeling of mystery generated by it which enabled Greek culture to treat the site as holy. Thus Zeus, god of the sky and daylight, and Hera, his queen, ruled the realm of the gods, and that of man, from Olympus. While Stonehenge relies on its construction and subsequent cultural connections in the minds of man, Olympus derives its sanctity from its natural grandeur. In Britain we can still appreciate the natural beauty of much of our countryside, but to a great extent, through the development of Christianity, we have lost the meaningful stories which explained these locations' cultural importance; the only exceptions to this being when saints were adopted to take on the mantle of an ancient god and the sacred place.

Besides being associated with Olympus many of the deities of the Greek world had relationships with other places, and their tales were entwined with the sacred geography and topography of the everyday landscape. Delphi, another sacred Greek site (Tomlinson 1976, 64–71; Harvey 1984, 137–138), was considered to have been the location of the omphalos (the naval of creation), a highly significant cultural centre. It was here that *Python* resided, until he was replaced by Apollo, and where his worshipers communed with the gods, through an oracle. In the Peloponnes, Olympia, a sanctuary for the god Zeus, was established; a cultural centre grew up around the Altis, and as at other sanctuaries athletic competitions took place. These three sites were sacred to all Greeks, fitting into a wider cultural tradition in which the various city states could all participate. It can be noted that at Delphi and Olympia there are archaeological remains, at Mount Olympus these are not so apparent. The mythological realm of Olympus was inhabited by Gods, Titans, Giants, Cyclops, gods, and *genii*; in it the *Aloeids*, the *Ephialtes*, and *Otus*, assaulted the mountain home of the gods and created a mound by piling Mount Pelion upon Mount Ossa to achieve this. These traditions helped to create a cultural tradition for the landscape and oriented man's perceptions of the landscape, as considered in previous chapters. However, they also allowed an ordered sanctification of the landscape to be created. A further mythical battle took place at Athens on the Acropolis, where Athena fought over the rocky hill with Poseidon, god of the sea. In this battle the goddess Athena was victorious and so the site became sacred to her. It seems that there was a process of ranking sites in terms of their religious importance. Olympus, Delphi, and Olympia, because of their pan-Hellenic associations, were ranked above other sites, such as the Acropolis in Athens, or the mountains of Ossa and Pelion. Locally, however, the Acropolis at Athens was an extremely important site. Not surprisingly, in Britain there are often problems in identifying which sites are significant and which ones are not. Often this can only be determined when cultural activity survives to indicate that a site was sacred. Many of the traditions associated with the land may have disappeared. If Greece had gone through a similar process as Britain, Mount Olympus would have been an example of this, and if the tales had not survived then archaeologists and historians would not have been able to recognise the significance of the sites there.

The ranking of sacred sites was not peculiar to the Mediterranean world but it provides a good example of how and why this occurred. Further examples can be identified in northern Europe, in Germany, and in Gaul. The *Irminsul* was a post which stood at the centre of Saxon territory in Germany. It was cut down by Charlemagne in *c.* AD 800 (Ellis Davidson 1964, 196). For France, Caesar mentioned that the centre of Gaul lay in the land of the *Carnutes* (Edwards 1963, vi.13); the actual site is not known but underneath the cathedral of Chartres there is some evidence of a pagan sanctuary (1966–68, d38). In the middle ages there was a double cult of the Virgin Mary, which became a prophetic cult by the fourteenth century. The focus of the cult was a spring, beneath the crypt, which flowed from a cave or grotto. Its waters were considered miraculous and were used to heal the sick. The focus of veneration was a wooden statue, claimed to be pre-Christian in origin, which was burned in 1793 during the revolution. In Ireland Tara was elevated to a place of extreme importance as the centre from which the high kings ruled all of Ireland (Raftery 1994, 64–70). The significance and ranking of religious sites seems to have been, to some extent, part of a process associated with the development of larger cultural identities. This was certainly the case in the Greek world, as the religious sites were seen to be significant in a pan-Hellenic context. By applying this model to Gaul, the references by Caesar to the centre of Gaul, even if more symbolic than literal, implied that there was a recognition that the Celtic tribes of Gaul had some form of common cultural identity which predated the Roman invasion.

Britain was, presumably, no different from other European territories at this time and, from the Iron Age to the medieval period, must have had some sort of ranking system for its religious sites. There are certain medieval texts, primarily of a Welsh origin, which give indications of some of the sacred sites in the land of the *Dobunni* and Wales generally. The first of these is the work of a Welsh monk called Nennius, who described *The Wonders of Britain* and Ireland, while the second is in the Mabinogion especially the texts of *Peredur* and *How Culhwch won Olwen*. These sources will be returned to later. One can also presume that there was a form of ranking of religious sites in the Roman period where the foundation of a number of imperial temples to deified emperors were built: to Claudius in the *Colonia* of Colchester (Toynbee 1964, 46–47; Drury 1984, 7–50; Simpson 1993, 1–6), the marble head of a statue from London is claimed to be of *Nero* (Toynbee 1964, 50) who was never deified, Hadrian's head may also have come from a cult statue (Toynbee 1964, 50–51) but more likely stood in a public space; presumably there was a temple to Nerva or *Nerviana* in the *Colonia* of Gloucester, where the temple stood in the north-west quarter (Heighway and Garrod 1980, 73–114). During Boudica's revolt, in AD 60, the views of the *Iceni* and *Trinovantes*, but not necessarily of the other tribes, on the Imperial cult became very evident with the attack on Colchester. This involved slaughter in the Imperial temple, and the cutting off of the head of a statue of Claudius and its deposition in the river Alde (Huskinson 1994, no.23) The head was recovered from the river in 1907, and was presumably deposited as a votive offering to the deity of this *Iceni* river. Presumably there were two other imperial temples at the other two *Coloniae,* Lincoln and York. These sacred sites were imposed by the external force of Roman legislation and the requirement to sacrifice to the deified Emperor (*Divus*). Henig (1999, 419–425) has suggested that the temple at Bath which was dedicated to *Sulis Minerva* was also possibly dedicated to Vespasian (*Divus Vespasianus*) under the reign of Domitian.

After the Imperial temples the next most important would presumably have been the *Capitolia* sites at which Jupiter, Juno and Minerva were worshipped (see Chapter 2). Analysis of the religious sculpture from Cirencester tends to indicate that one of these temples lay to the south-east of the basilica there, as mentioned previously. Other significant temples of the Roman Empire were Pantheons, are temples to the twelve gods, an idea which the Romans borrowed directly from the Greeks. Although there are columns dedicated to multiple gods the inscriptions surviving for such temples are lacking. Excavations have identified a circular or oval building in the centre of the Roman Legionary base at Chester which is believed to have been one of these temples (Mason 2000, 404–413). Besides these sites, which are all located in urban areas, there are the rural shrines remained active much longer and were a focus for tradition and folklore. It is possible that one could obtain a better understanding of the significance of sacred sites, their nature and design, and the ways in which cult centres, (amongst them Bath, Lydney Park, Marcham-Frilford, and Woodeaton) were developed. The association of earlier activity with some of these sites may show that the significance of religious centres extended back into the Iron Age.

NENNIUS

To return to the early Middle Ages Nennius, in *c.* 800 AD, provided an account of a number of important and sacred places in Britain and Ireland, called *The Wonders*. *The Wonders* were initially classed as first, second, third and so on; towards the end, however, they were simply listed. The *Wonders* were listed in the following order: the first was Loch Leven; the second the estuary of the *Trahannon*; the third the hot lake of *Badon* in the *Hwicce*; the fourth the salt spring in the *Hwicce*; the fifth the Severn Bore; the sixth the mouth of *Llyn Lliwan*; the seventh the Fount of *Gorheli*; the eighth a sacred tree near the estuary of the river Wye; the ninth Windblow, in Gwent; the tenth the altar of *Llwynarth*; the eleventh the spring in the Severn estuary, at *Pydew Meurig*; the twelfth the *Carn Cafal*; the thirteenth the tomb of *Llygad Amr* in *Ergyng*; and the fourteenth the tomb on *Crug Mawr* (see Figure 65). There is clearly, in this account, a bias towards places in Wales, which one would expect, but some of the cases are clearly not in Wales, but in the land of the *Hwicce*. The Welsh bias continues with a listing of four wonders on the island of Mona (Anglesey). The first is the shore with no sea; the second the hill which turns around; the third a ford flooded by the sea; while the fourth is a moving stone in a valley. This is followed by the account of two wonders in Ireland; *Loch Lein*, with its natural resources; and *Loch Echach*, with its petrifying properties. The bias to sites in south-east Wales and in the adjacent parts of England is not readily explainable, but one possibility is that Nennius came from this area and was, therefore, more likely to know sites in this region. Of the sites which were further away it is possible that their fame, or reputation for sanctity, went far beyond their immediate vicinity. The account of Anglesey's wonders may be due to Nennius's association with Bangor, where he is considered to have lived as a monk. Alternatively, if Nennius did not come from the Gwent area then it hints at the possibility that, from a British perspective, this area was considered to have been extremely important. It is also noticeable that none of the sites are located in eastern or northern England. This indicates either that these areas were not culturally and geologically important enough or simply that in the early medieval period the cultural connections between the east and the west of Britain were not significant enough. It is possible that, in Roman times, the *Dobunnic* territory was seen as central and had a cultural importance in Britain far beyond the tribal area.

The first two sites mentioned do not lie anywhere near the region with which we are concerned. The first, Loch Leven, is in Scotland. In fact there are two Loch Levens, one on the Argyll-Inverness border, the other in east central Scotland, and the place where Mary Queen of Scots was later imprisoned. *Trahannoni* was a river-name, originating as *Trisentona* (see chapter 4), and which has been associated with the river names Trent, Tarrant and other variations of which there are some seven possible examples in Britain. Which of these rivers Nennius was referring to is not apparent. Due to Nennius's association with Bangor it may be the one in North Wales.

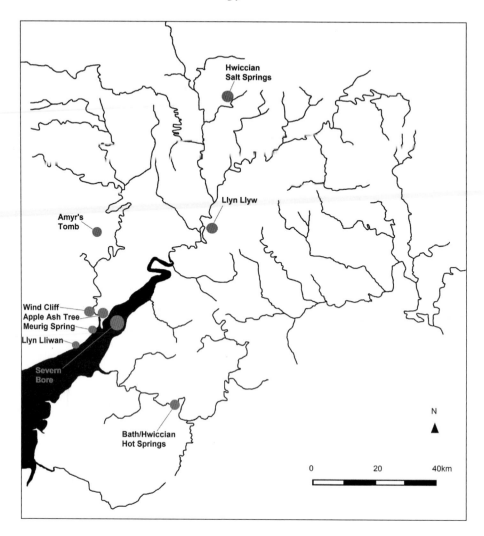

Figure 65: A map showing the locations of The Wonders of Britain *as listed by Nennius (drawing S. Yeates)*

THE THERMAL SPRINGS

Of the sites mentioned by Nennius a number of them can be located positively or at least approximately; some of them can be shown to have been in specific locations in the early medieval territories of the *Hwicce,* or in the neighbouring territory of the *Glywysinga.* The third site, and the first within the territory of the *Hwicce,* is the hot springs. The spring referred to is Bath *(Badon)* although there are a number of hot springs in the Avon valley, in the southern part of the *Hwicce* territory (see Figure 66). There are three springs at Bath, and a further one at Hotwells in the Avon Gorge near Clifton in Bristol;

a fifth one has been claimed to exist at Freshford in Somerset, although its existence needs to be confirmed. It is possible that there are other hot springs, in the *Hwicce* or beyond, that we are not aware of. A warm well has been described at Ruardean, in the Forest of Dean, and another at Builth Wells, in Brecknockshire. The site of Saint Anthony's Well, near Devizes, is another site at which the waters may be thermal. The hot spring *Aquae Calidae*, which Ptolemy identified as being in the polis of the *Belgae*, may not even be at Bath, as generally assumed, but at another, unrecognised, site in the Hampshire region. Others still regard *Aquae Calidae* as being located at Bath, as they are the major thermal springs in Britain (Rivet and Smith 1979, 255–256; Henig 1999, 419–425). The text from Nennius reads as follows (Morris 1980, 40):

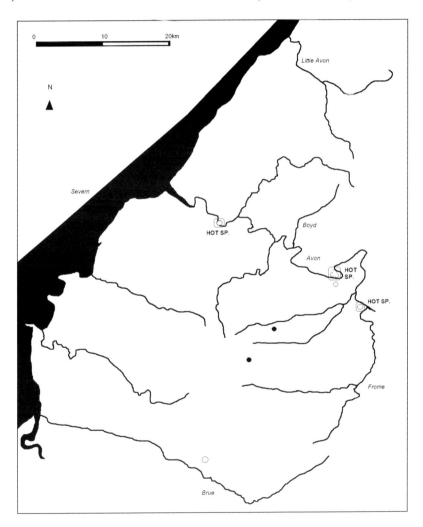

Figure 66: A map of the known thermal springs in the area around the Bristol Avon (drawing S. Yeates)

> *'The third wonder is the Hot Lake, where the Baths of Badon are, in the country of the*
> *Hwicce. It is surrounded by a wall, made of brick and stone, and men may go there to*
> *bathe at any time, and every man can have the kind of bath he likes. If he wants, it will*
> *be a cold bath; and if he wants a hot bath, it will be hot.'*
>
> From *Nennius: British History and The Welsh Annals*, translated by John Morris © Phillimore,
> used by kind permission

The name *Badon* is a reference to the present place-name, Bath. The site is described
as being surrounded by brick and stone so that men can go there and bathe any time,
in hot or cold water. This clear reference describes aspects of the major Roman temple
site, with its sacred springs and bath complex. It is, however, a remarkable description
considering that it dates some 400 years after the Roman period. Much investigative
work by Barry Cunliffe and others has been published in *The Temple of Sulis Minerva
at Bath* (Cunliffe and Davenport 1985). Excavations in and around Bath have shown
that extensive deposits have survived from the first century and later (see Figure 67).
How the springs were venerated in the pre-Roman period is not known, and it is now
not possible to say that the Iron-Age coins found at the site were deposited in the pre-
Roman period, as we know that they were still in circulation in early Roman times.
Underneath the bath complex excavations have identified the remains of an enclosure
which contained the post-holes of a number of standing posts. It is not apparent if these
posts all stood together or replaced each other over time. These may provide evidence
for earlier religious activity at the site.

The largest and the most powerful spring lay in the corner of a major temple complex
in which the deity of the springs, *Sulis Minerva*, was venerated. The dedication to this
goddess is affirmed by Roman altars found in each of the springs, the bath complex,
and at other locations around the town (as mentioned in Chapter 4). The dedications
confirm that this was the place called *Aquae Sulis* as mentioned in later textual sources.
Excavations and assessment of the style of the temple have shown that the temple
complex evolved in the first two centuries AD. The temple was tetrastyle in design and
stood on an east-facing podium. The columns were Corinthian in style and the pediment
highly decorated, with a central feature of a male gorgon's head surrounded by a wreath
of oak leaves (Cunliffe and Davenport 1985). Along the axis of the temple, there were
a number of monuments placed in a row; these included an altar and, probably, a
votive column. The spring in the temple enclosure had a stone wall around it built on
timber pile foundations and was covered by a building which had images of the four
seasons, *Sol*, and *Luna*. The other two springs, the Hot and Cross wells, also had stone
walls around the springs forming a cistern, into which the warm water could rise. The
temple and major spring were also enclosed by a *temenos* boundary wall. To the south
of the temple complex, and between the three springs, was a large and prestigious
bath complex which, one can infer from the writing of Nennius, was still operational
at the start of the ninth century. This is not what is implied by the excavation report,
but there is no datable material in the post-Roman phases, something which has been
noted by others, and which Gerrard (2007, 148–164) has recently tried to clarify. Nennius
may have been correct in saying that the temple complex was still in use in some way
in his day, or he may have been using oral accounts of what the complex looked like.

Figure 67: The sacred spring at Bath being excavated under the auspices of Prof. Barry Cunliffe. The walls that surround the spring were described by Nennius in the eighth century AD (photograph Robert Wilkins, Institute of Archaeology archive, source Barry Cunliffe)

One possibility may be that the temple, or parts of it, was still being used as a church, dedicated to Saint Mary. The temple precinct is known to have affected the layout of the burgh in *c.* 900 AD, while Scarth thought that the temple was only taken down in the high medieval period. It has been argued that the *temenos* around the temple complex was not the only religious boundary around Bath. The city walls of Bath surround all three of the hot springs which formed the major focus of this religious complex. Dark (1993, 254–255) argued that the whole area of the Roman town was sacred and that the outer wall of the town was the *temenos* boundary. Such a claim is worth making due to the location of the three springs in the town, but this could probably never be proved.

The goddess worshipped on the site was called *Sulis* (RIB(I) 1995, nos.141, 143–144, 146–150), as mentioned above, and it was only in the Roman period that she obtained the name Minerva also. She was originally a personification of the springs, but later became associated with the town and was undoubtedly associated with the identity of the people of that place. Her name is a noun, the Celtic word for the **sun** (Rivet and Smith 1979, 255–256), but here portrayed in a female form. In Chapter 4 it was suggested that this goddess may have been a titanness of the sun. Only the head of the gilt-bronze cult statue now survives (Cunliffe and Fulford 1982, no.26). On the pediment of the temple is what is normally described as a male gorgon's head, but it is feasible that this representation may be of the sun, with the wavy hair representing the rays of light; another suggestion is that the wings in the hair mean that the image is a conflation of a river deity with Medusa (Henig 1999, 419–425). The folklore which was associated with the temple and the springs is no longer known, and we are left only with a tale which shows that the healing properties of the spring were recognised in prehistory.

Now we can consider the other known hot springs in the Avon valley. These sites would also have been given special treatment, but their renown was, in the time of Nennius, less than Bath's. The Hotwells spring, in Bristol, now lies below the waters of the Avon; in historic times, however, it is known to have been above the level of the river and only covered by extremely high tides (Rudder 1779, 377–378). It is possible that platforms of oak were built around the spring, as antiquaries' descriptions of the dredging of huge oak trunks from the Avon are described in the *Bath section* of the *Somerset Archaeology and Natural History Society* volumes. These structures may have been designed to protect the spring from high river levels. The fact that whole oak trunks are described may indicate that the structure may be late prehistoric in date as the use of uncut trunks is known in Bronze-Age sites, for example at Seahenge in Norfolk. The old name of the hill on which Clifton Camp lies was Ghyston Rock (Worcestre 1969, 263; Worcestre and Neale 2000, nos.55–56, 64); Ghyst was the name of a local giant. Who or what Ghyst was, and how he originated is not altogether clear. It is known, however, that the hill above the spring was the location of an Iron-Age encampment, where there is much evidence of Roman period activity. The site was also occupied by a later medieval chapel dedicated to Saint Vincent. The association between the Iron-Age and Roman material and religious activity is highly plausible if not yet proven. If a temple was, at some time, located in the area an excavation of the site would elucidate some of these questions. The camp at Clifton may have been the boundary of a sacred enclosure. As the second major hot spring site in Britain the location needs more attention and recognition than has hitherto been given to it. It would be appropriate to not mention Bath as the only hot spring site of the British Isles, as is often the case.

If there is a hot spring at Freshford then further investigation is necessary; there is also some evidence that another hot spring lies in the vicinity of Chippenham, associated with scatters of Roman period material. The hot springs at Builth Wells should also be considered as a potential site of religious devotion and it is possible that earlier human activity remains to be discovered underneath the castle, which lies on a spur between the River Wye and the Gloew Brook. The name Gloew, used for a spring or a stream, is attested elsewhere, for example in an early medieval account from north-west Worcestershire (see Chapter 4).

THE SALT SPRINGS

The reference to the salt springs of the *Hwicce* is more ambiguous, as many of them are located throughout the Cotswolds and the Severn and Avon valleys. The evidence for their existence can be found in the scientific analysis of the water; their past importance can be ascertained from place-name evidence. In some cases it is possible to identify the past use of a spring through the remaining archaeology around the spring. Such activity may be elaborated, as witnessed at Bath, or may simply be in the form of a pottery or artefact scatter. It is highly likely that the springs being referred to as the fourth wonder of Britain are, however, those of Droitwich, which are probably the most powerful and salt-laden waters in the whole of the territory, and probably in the British Isles. There are indications of at least two temples in the area of Droitwich; one is initially described in the Bays Meadow complex (Rahtz 1971, 18–19), which was only partially revealed (but now not included in the final report); the other a probable temple site at Upwich, which is a large wooden cruciform structure (Frere 1992, 283). The Bays Meadow complex is usually described as a villa site but the fact that it seems to have contained four buildings means that the assumption that the villa was the key component is not completely assured. The early interpretation of the site in an interim report claimed that one corner of a central building was uncovered; which seemed to be part of the central cella and part of an ambulatory of a Romano-Celtic style building. To the north is the villa, while to the east and west are two long buildings, one of which has been described as a basilica type structure, the other as a granary. Both this site and the large cruciform building which lies close to the major Upwich Salt Spring were constructed over earlier brine pits and salt workings. On top of the hill is the location of a minster church in an enclosure, claimed as the site of a Roman military camp or fort on account of its square nature and the profile of one of the ditches. However, earlier Iron-Age material has also been recovered from the site. In other parts of the territory it is apparent that salt springs were often sites by which hill-forts or hill-enclosures were constructed. It is possible that the site was reused and that there was a similar one on the hill above Droitwich. So, if it was a Roman camp then it may have just been reused. Henig (2004, 11–28) has noted that the Roman site at Bewcastle operated as a sanctuary and a fort. Much of Droitwich and Dodderhill is now masked by the post-medieval industrial town, which may hide the past importance of the Roman shrines and the significance paid to the site by Nennius. The name of the deity who was worshiped at Droitwich is not known but the name of the town is considered to have been *Salinae*, meaning **salt**. It is possible to hypothesise that there would have been a goddess called *Salina*, who presided over the town and the salt springs in much the same way that *Sulis* did for Bath, as suggested by Haverfield, which was confirmed by the recovery of artefacts.

Of other salt springs in the area a number are located by Iron Age hill-forts, as mentioned above. These include Little Solsbury, originally called *Saltbury*, a large triangular camp lying to the north-east of Bath. The enclosure on Langley Hill, near Winchcombe, the nature of which has been much-discussed to the point where its use as a hill-fort site has been questioned, was also probably a *Salbury*. This can be ascertained from medieval documentation as it lies above a site called Sawcombe or Salt Valley. Last, the hill-fort at Iccombe was located near a salt spring, which was described in an Anglo-Saxon charter. In all of these cases it is apparent that the salt spring would have acted as a focus for the Iron-Age enclosure. How these sites were perceived spiritually, and how they were ranked in an ordered and structured sacred landscape, is not known. But one of them, almost certainly Droitwich, ranked very highly in the early medieval period. When considering the evidence from some of these hill-forts it is also apparent that there was very little internal activity, which suggests that the enclosures were being used at a specific time in the year for a specific social gathering.

THE SEVERN BORE

The fifth of *The Wonders of Britain* was the Severn Bore or *'the two kings fighting'*, as the Welsh name implies. This clearly refers to the struggle of the fresh and the salt water in the estuary and may hint at some of the legends which once surrounded this stretch of water. The length of the estuary makes it impossible to pinpoint an exact location along the course of the river for a sacred site, but a number of locations could be considered as contenders. On the island of Steepholm there are two hill forts, one of which has produced a stone head believed to be of a Roman date (Green 1993, 241–242); the other contains a circular Roman building of unknown use. The building has been interpreted as a Roman watch-tower, but on present evidence could easily have been a shrine or cult centre located on the more prominent of the two islands. There is also evidence of a religious site on the cliff top at Aust, above the estuary, where a small bronze of a late Iron-Age goddess was recovered. The object was at one time thought to have been an import from Iberia, but now Henig (2007, 11, fig.1) is of the impression that it is of local manufacture and probably late Iron Age in date. It is difficult to determine, however, whether these features are associated with the river in general or with the phenomenon of the bore specifically. It may, however, also be possible that the two can not be disentangled as the bore is an integral part of the river. The word bore, normally interpreted as Germannic, may be of a Celtic origin as there is a Gallic word *bor*, found in personal names, which has a meaning of **swelling** (Ellis Evans 1967, 154), which may be cognate with certain Germanic words.

A further sacred site may have existed halfway between the mouth of the Wye and *Llyn Lliwan*, as it was here the mythical beast *Twrch Twrth* entered the river (Jones and Jones 1974, 134). In the passage there are indications of ritual activity, with the body of Arthur's champion and a sword being thrown into the river. The deposition of weaponry in this fashion is a recognised Bronze Age activity, as discussed earlier, while the deposition of humans in watery contexts is more associated with the Iron Age and early Roman periods. Perhaps, in this case, we have an indication of an older folk memory. Bog bodies are generally considered to have been ritual sacrifices, but this idea has more recently been challenged by Ronald Hutton, who has suggested an alternative theory for the Lindow Man case. The area around the confluence of the Wye is associated with a mythical beast which was chased across south Wales and entered the Severn near that point, before continuing back down the other side of the Severn Sea to Cornwall. The story may have something to do with the bore, or the tidal flows in the Severn Estuary and Bristol Channel. The journey of *Twrch* across the south Wales landscape, as described in Chapter 4, was plotted by Rhys. At Beachley is *Saint Twrog's* Chapel; the significance of the name *Twrog* has not been identified but it is possible that it is an English corruption of the Welsh *Twrch*, a boar, despite the fact that no old spellings of this have been found to clearly attest this development. There are indications, in Welsh charters, that there was a Roman period settlement that may have been known by the name *Sabrina*; in *c.* 700 AD, a church was founded in the Tidenham area at *Istrat Hafren* (Davies 1979, nos.174b, 229b). This site can probably be equated with Oldbury, near Stroat, with the former part of the name surviving to form the modern name. The Broadstone at Stroat is considered by local folk tradition to be the grave marker of *Sabrina*, so it is interesting that there are indications of surviving traditions which do associate the early medieval place-names, the river, and the stone.

The temple of *Nodens* is often associated with the Severn Bore, but it is not clear why as, even though the temple has a good view across the estuary, the activities at the site seem to be more concerned with the traditions of the Forest of Dean. The creatures described as Tritons, on a priestly crown from the temple, may simply be chthonic creatures rising from the earth and the claimed anchors in their hands may simply be pickaxes. The existence of further, as yet undiscovered, sites associated with the Severn Bore, this unusual natural phenomenon, is highly probable. One would expect a temple to have been located at the highest limit of the bore.

THE SACRED LAKE

The sixth wonder was a lake called *Lliwan*, which lay next to the Severn Estuary. Nennius wrote quite a long extract on this site; and described it as a Llyn or lake, scourged by the flow of the Severn Bore (Morris 1980, 40–41). The descriptions are vague but the references could possibly be to a river estuary or a lake on or near the river. The power of the bore would have been adsorbed by such a lake. In a recent study carried out into the location of this wondrous lake (Evans, Nettleship *et al.* 2008, 295–318), a number of possible sites were put forward: Caerleon, Chepstow, Gloucester, the mouth of the Taff, Goldcliff, Lymon Brook, Ystrad Havren, Carmarthen Bay, Caldicot, or alternatively a lost site in the estuary. Only two lakes, known to have existed in the Severn estuary, could be associated with the references in the Welsh tales. Some of the confusion surrounding the identification of this site may be the insistence that *Llyn Lliwan* (*in the wonders*) and *Llyn Llyw* (in the Mabinogion) are one and the same place and that their philology could be connected (Jackson 1982, 17). It is possible that there were a number of lakes that are now silted up and no references to them survive. Here, it will be suggested that this connection is misleading and that the two texts may be referring to two different features. Much has been said of the philology and there have been attempts to associate the names with *Li*, **flow** or *Liu*, **clear** or **shiny**. More recently it has been noted that the name *Lliwan* is a homonym of *L(l)uan*, a daughter of *Brychan* (Evans, Nettleship *et al.* 2008, 297). The first of the known lakes was at Portskewett, or Sudbrook; this one can perhaps be identified with *Llyn Lliwan*, although place-name evidence is lacking. A second one was to the north of Gloucester, near Longford, and it is this one which can be associated with *Llyn Llyw*.

The possible location of *Llyn Lliwan* at Portskewett (Evans, Nettleship *et al.* 2008, 295–318), or rather Sudbrook, is where there are features called the whirlyholes or whirlpools. There are some three of these features identifiable in the valley of the Troggy, two of which are too far upstream to be associated with the site while the third lies at Portskewett, or rather Sudbrook (see Figure 68). The site seems to fit the description of *the Wonder*, with a spring or sink hole above an area of marsh which on occasions was transformed into a lake. The forceful spring and sudden sinkholes are a classic feature

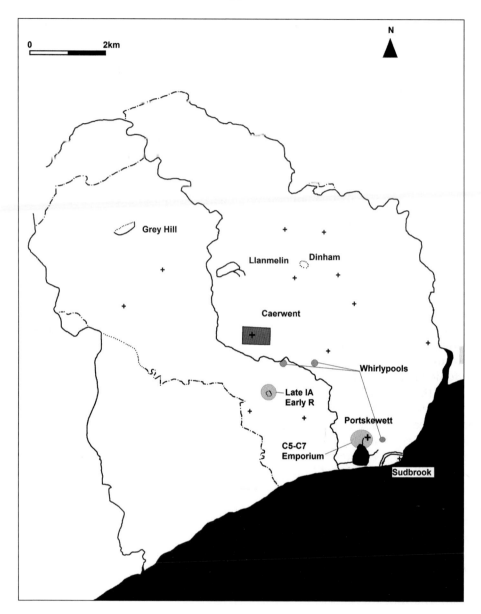

Figure 68: A map showing the parochia of Caerwent and the location of the Whirlypools along the River Troggy (drawing S. Yeates)

of a siphoning spring, whose ebb and flow would be tied to the tidal flows in the river Severn. Antiquaries describe a copious spring at Portskewett, just below the church, which produced a rill, with a mighty flow, and then formed a large lake which drained into the Severn Estuary (Walker 1891). It is said that Portskewett was the third largest port in Britain during the early medieval period. The antiquarian sources explained why this would have been the case, and also provides a context for why the royal court moved from Caerwent to the estuary in the *Vita Tatheus* (Bradney 1933, 128; Campbell and MacDonald 1993, 90; Howell 2004, 244; Knight 2004, 279–280); to a place where ships could beach and trade, and which would have been an ideal location for a major wic or trading emporium. Other traditions connected with the site have been incorporated into the tale of *Saint Tatheus*. In it the king left *Tatheus* at Caerwent and then rode his horse to what would be the location of his new palace. The new site was decided by a horse stamping his hoof on the ground and releasing a spring from which water gushed. So, this spring was another natural feature associated with a specific mythical animal, in this case a horse. The tale may spring from older mythology as in Greece the *Hippou Krene* (**Horse Spring**) sprang from the ground when it was struck by a hoof, and horses were drowned in the whirlpool of Argos in honour of Poseidon (Burkert 1985, 138). There is evidence for a Roman site on the hilltop and there has been some speculation that this was also a temple site (Brewer 2004, 225). This has, however, not yet been confirmed and the site is generally referred to as a villa. During the Anglo-Saxon period the site on the top of the hill became the location of a royal hunting lodge for Harold II. A spring rises near the church, and as this seems to have been the location of an early royal church, it is possible that this was also the probable location of the suspected temple, if indeed one existed. This would agree with the building of early churches on earlier sacred sites. However, the Welsh name of Portskewett means **the harbour of the Elder-tree**; it is probable that the name contains the ancient Celtic or Brittonic name, as rivers and lakes were often named after plants or animals, as we have seen (Morgan 2005, 180–181) (see Chapter 4). The three river-names associated with the area are *Aber Tarogi*, Portskewett, and Sudbrook, all of which may refer to different streams in the area. The name of *Llyn Lliwan* is not recorded in the area in earlier surviving texts, but this does not mean that it was not used as an earlier name in the area. It has been suggested that the Sudbrook marks the location of *Llyn Lliwan* (Evans, Nettleship *et al.* 2008, 306–310), and as the only known names for the Sudbrook are of English derivation it is highly feasible that the Brittonic name is the name which we seek.

The springs in this area no longer flow as they did as the hydrology was upset by the construction of the Severn railway tunnel in the 1870s. The building of the tunnel was described in a contemporary work by Thomas A. Walker (1891), called *The Severn Tunnel*, and in a more recent assessment *The making of the Severn railway tunnel* by Roger Cowles (1989). The construction of the tunnel was stopped twice when two springs were hit. The first was called the Great Spring and, even now, it provides enough water for the town of Caldicot. This spring broke into the tunnel in 1879 and rapidly filled it. The consequence of the alterations to the hydrology was that all springs in a five square mile area dried up (Evans, Nettleship *et al.* 2008, 309–310). The spring at Sudbrook originally lay on a hillside above the Nedern Brook and would have been one of the features that was obliterated by the railway's construction. This event has made it difficult to understand how the landscape in the Portskewett area appeared in the past, although the persistent references to a powerful spring, as well as indications of an early royal church, are indicative of the reuse of sacred space.

The second lake which we can identify along the Severn was at Gloucester, and is probably the lake referred to as *Llyn Llyw*. Place-name evidence indicates that there was a Mere in the course of the Severn (see Figure 69), or adjacent to it, which in the 1400s was called the *Oldmere* (Smith 1964b, ii.150). It was located at Longford, near Gloucester. In the Mabinogion tale an ancient Salmon, who swam on the Severn tide up to Gloucester, resided in a lake called *Llyn Llyw* (Jones and Jones 1974, 125). The etymology of *Lliwan* was mentioned above, but that of *Llyw* is probably different; it could be related to the name *Glevum* and Gloucester as in the same text Gloucester is called *Caer Loyw* with the initial *-g-* being lost. This suggestion agrees with the speculation by Ekwall (1928, 173) that Gloucester derived its name from that of a river, which was probably the earlier name for the Horsebere Brook (Yeates 2008b, 38–39). It is along the Horsebere Brook where most of the early settlement of the Gloucestershire *parochia* lay; the name *Glevenses* (of which *Glywysinga* is a derivation) referring to the people dwelling along the river *Gleva*. The Salmon in the tale was considered to be the oldest living creature in the world and was, according to the tale, attacked by an eagle, who attempted to drag him from the water in his talons. The eagle was known by the name *Llew*. This tale seems to provide the motif for an image on a penannular brooch which was recovered from the sacred springs at Bath (Henig, Brown *et al.* 1988, 23). In it a

Figure 69: A picture of the Severn in flood during the 1980s near Wainlode, with the Malvern Hills in the background (photograph S. Yeates)

Figure 70: The penannular brooch (of Irish type) recovered from the sacred spring at Bath. The images depicted represent local mythological tales found in the The Mabinogion associated with Gloucester. The salmon being pulled from the water was thought to be the oldest living creature in the world (photographs Robert Wilkins, Institute of Archaeology archive, source Barry Cunliffe)

bird of prey perches on the back of a fish which has the fin formation of a salmon (see Figure 70). This lake silted up during the medieval period; the effect that it would have had on the bore has not been determined. Geologically, the area between Maisemore and Longford, with a further extension of alluvium up to Twigworth, could provide the location of a lake in the channel of the Severn or in the channel of the Horsebere Brook. Two brooks would have entered this lake from the east, the Horsebere, previously probably the *Glev-*, and the Hatherley or Broadboard Brook. On the spur at Sandhurst, above the lowland into which this mere lay, there are field-names which indicate the presence of a fortification or enclosure, while at Walham there are surviving earthworks. Nothing about these sites is known beyond the place-names but it is possible that one or both may have been associated with a mere in the river.

THE APPLE ASH TREE

The eighth wonder of Britain is recorded as having been located on a hillside overlooking the estuary of the river Wye (Morris 1980, 41). The information given is sparse but its general location, to the south of Wentwood or the Forest of Dean, should be noted. The site is difficult to pin down but the references to apples growing on an ash-tree may point to a site on the Gloucestershire side, such as Ashbury. This is, of course, only hypothetical. The Wye valley, at this point, is flowing through one of the more spectacular parts of its valley, with sheer limestone cliffs dropping into the Wye estuary. The site of Chepstow Castle is spectacular, on a narrow spur of land above the cliffs, as mentioned previously (see Figure 40). The remains of a piece of votive Roman sculpture has been found built into the castle (Brewer 1986, no.51), as mentioned in Chapter 4.

What Nennius states about the location of this sacred tree may be slightly misleading, because it has been noted that the Ash-tree, with its specific type of coal-black bud, is a tribal emblem found on *Dobunnic* coins (Rudd 2003, 7–14). The ash as displayed on the coinage

Figure 71: The image of a pollard Ash tree used as a tribal emblem on the Dobunnic gold coinage unit of Anted Rig. The pollard ash-tree is shown on one side, while the triple tailed horse is seen on the other below the legend of Anted and a wheel below (photograph courtesy of Chris Rudd and Liz Cottam)

has been pollarded (see Figure 71). The coinage of the *Dobunni* and Nennius's works, therefore, point to a common origin or source, but from Nennius's inference there may simply have been one tree that was considered more significant than any other. The coinage would hint that the site Nennius referred to was possibly in *Dobunnic* territory, either on the east bank of the Wye or perhaps even on the east bank of the Severn (although the *Silures* religion has not been fully analysed and probably produce further surprises).

The most noted Ash tree in European traditions was the Yggdrasil, of which the first element *yggr* has come from Greek hydra, meaning the **sea** or **water**. A local history book discussing Chepstow and its association with the rivers Severn and Wye stated that one local name for the Severn Bore was the *Hygre*, and that Davies in 1783 stated that it was used by William of Malmesbury in *De Gestis Pontificum* of *c.* 1140 (Waters 1952, 87–88). The association of these names, however, may be misleading because the two sources originate from potentially different cultures and do not necessary prove anything.

THE WINDBLOW

The next wonder, the ninth, was also in this area. The best clue to its location is that it was in the country called Gwent. There is a reference to a cleft in the rocks 'from which the wind constantly blows', even in the summertime when the winds were normally quiet. The reason it was described as a wonder was because it blew from within the earth. In British the site was known as *Chwyth Gwynt*, and in English translation *Windblow*. From researching the religious sites of the land of Gwent it becomes apparent that this place must have been located in the upland region between the rivers Wye and Usk. The most likely location is that known as the Windcliff, which lies to the north of Chepstow, on the plateau of Gwent wood. The Windcliff is a cliff standing above the Wye gorge. Within its face is the entrance to one of the largest natural caverns in the

British Isles, now only approachable when the tides of the Wye are low enough. With rising river levels in the Severn Estuary, as noted with Hotwells, it is possible that the entrance to the cavern may at one time have been permanently above the level of the river Wye. On the cliff above the Windcliff, and above the cave in the rock, are the probable remains of a Roman temple (Shoesmith 1991, 157), as buildings show up on aerial photographs and a well carved Roman finial has been recovered from the site along with other material of that date. The present name hints at the tradition recorded in Nennius, the Wind-cliff, as does the possible presence of the Roman temple. The name Gwent is considered to have derived from a Latin word for town or market place (Rivet and Smith 1979, 492–493); however, this has been doubted (Morgan 2005, 57).

THE MEURIG STREAM

The tenth wonder was in Gower, but the eleventh wonder was back in the territory of Gwent. This was a spring called *Pydew Meurig*, which had a plank in it which was affected by the Severn bore, rising and turning on the tide. The *Meurig* is still the name of a stream which flows into the Severn to the west of Chepstow. One of the springs to the south-west of *Pwllmeyric* is reckoned to be the spring in question. Maybe the bore once penetrated the lower reaches of this small stream, rising up over the marshy ground to the south and travelling inland, or it may be a spring like that of *Llyn Lliwan*. Little evidence has been found for the veneration of this particular river, and its spring, but that is not to say that they were never venerated. The inclusion of this stream and spring in the list may indicate that Nennius did have some local knowledge of the Caerwent, Portskewett, and Chepstow area. Alternatively, the sanctity of this area may have been such that it was considered to be an extremely numinous landscape.

THE TOMB OF AMR

The thirteenth wonder was also in the border lands between the *Silures* and *Dobunni*; in the territory of Ergyng, or Archenfield. This was a tomb, near a spring, where *Amr*, a son of Arthur, was buried; he was mentioned as a possible reduced river deity in Chapter 4. The son was killed by Arthur, but the important point about the feature was that it was continuously changing size. The site was listed in the Herefordshire Sites and Monuments Record as lying on the Gamber, in the parish of Llanwarne. However, this is situated below the village of Wormlow Tump, which is in the parish of Much Birch. It is feasible, if not at present provable, that the site is the Tump of Wormlow which would have straddled the watershed between the river Gamber (*Amr*) and the Worm; it is known to have been the location where the courts for the sessions of the hundred of Wormlow were held. Alternatively, there may have been two mounds in the area, as Wormlow means **the mound of the river Worm**, while the information in Nennius's work implied that there was a mound by the Gamber (*Amr*). Certain Antiquarian sources situate the site at a different location but there is no known indication that the river *Amr* or Gamber was correctly located.

The fact that there was a whole series of natural features in the area, which were perceived as having special properties, may have meant that the area was special, or regarded as such; on the other hand it may have been no more special than other parts of Britain, and Nennius was simply more familiar with this landscape. It may be that he only had vague knowledge of the legendary hot springs of the Avon valley or the saline springs of the *Hwicce*, but based on the description given this would seem unlikely. One of the other wonders mentioned was *Carn Cafal*, in the territory of Builth, because it contained the footprint of *Cafal*, the hound of Arthur. The Wye must have been a special river for Nennius, but, as discussed in Chapter 4, it is a river for which the old name is not known. The paw print of *Cafal* and the claimed suspended sacred altar on the South Wales coast are believed to derive from early medieval traditions. The sacred altar is Christian in origin; while the former was associated with the legendary traditions associated with King Arthur and, presumably, likewise early medieval in date. What should be recognised is that the list of sacred sites, as recorded by Nennius, may well have been due to a process of temporal stratification. For some of these sites there is some evidence of Roman period sanctuaries; for the others it can not be assumed that each site had a religious history going back further than the eighth century AD. Certain aspects of the tomb of *Amr* hint at a much older history, as *Amr* shared his name with the river. The source of the river, presumably, was the location of a shrine to the river's deity, and the wonder could have been perhaps a podium and not a tomb.

Nennius's wonders indicate that the land around the Roman town of *Venta Silurum* was considered sacred; it could have chosen by the Romans and the *Silures* because it incorporated important traditions from the past. If this was the case it is possible that other *Civitas* towns, or even *Colonia*, were also located at the centres of traditional landscapes; suggesting that attempts to define such a site as being at the node of a catchment area are incorrect. Thus, we should consider why the *Civitas* of the *Dobunni*, at Cirencester, and the *Colonia* of Gloucester, were both established in that same tribal area and so close together; would they also have been seen as residing in more sacred landscapes than other settlements in the area?

This could have meant that there were two sacred landscapes in the *Dobunni* territory which may have contained a higher than normal number of sacred sites. Gloucester's site, at the lowest crossing point of the Severn, has already been much discussed. It resided in the valley associated with the mother goddess of the *Dobunni* (Yeates 2008b, 137–146), and was close to an important lake or mere, to the north of the town, in which the oldest living creature in the world resided.

THE CIRENCESTER LANDSCAPE

Cirencester, the tribal capital of the *Dobunni*, is close to the source of the river Thames; and to a known religious complex in Hailey Wood. The area around Cirencester has also produced the largest late Bronze-Age gold hoard recovered in Britain. It was perhaps a votive deposit, initially deposited in a natural feature which has now, due to agriculture or low water tables, lost its previous prominence. What is known of the water levels at the head of the Thames would support this notion. A Roman sanctuary, constructed at the source of the Thames, at a site now called Hailey Wood in Sapperton, was presumably known as *Aquae*, or *Fontes Tamesa* or *Thamesis*. The Thames no longer rises near this site, due to a drop in the level of the water table in the Cotswolds generally, but in the past it is known to have risen further up the valley. There are indications that the area around the Thames's upper feeder springs and streams may have been important in the late Bronze Age, due to the gold hoard mentioned. The hoard came from Poulton, which means the farmstead or town by the pool (Smith 1964a, i.79–80). The pool can no longer be identified, but the village is also the source of an unusual legend which concerned a beautiful maiden, or queen, a pool, and a serpent. The date of the tradition is not known but it is possible that there was a larger pool in the area, now silted up, which may have been the focus for ritual activity and provided the inspiration for the name of the village.

The remains of a significant hill-fort are hinted at by early post-medieval place-names to the west of the Roman town, which seems closer and more appropriate as a prehistoric forerunner to *Corinium* than the *oppidum* at Bagendon. Due to the development of the park in that area, it is not, however, possible to confirm that such a site existed.

THE TALE OF PEREDUR

Earlier, the two works of Nennius and the Mabinogion were acknowledged as being key sourcs for understanding the folk traditions around the natural landscape of the Gloucester area. The tale of Peredur is an unusual tale which mentions the mother and father and the nine witches, an allusion to the cult of the father and mother goddess the latter of whom had a **sacred vessel**. Discussion of these subjects clearly indicates that the city at which this cult was centred was Gloucester (Yeates 2008b, 137–146). There are also other references to certain sites not far from Caerleon which may be referring in some way to Gloucester and its environs. In a number of places in the text there is a reference to the **round valley** (Jones and Jones 1974, 203–204), which lay upon the other side of a forest from Caerleon in which there stands a castle. Gloucester lies in a large circular valley which has already been discussed. There are also references to a *Castle of Wonders* which lay on the banks of a lake (Jones and Jones 1974, 224), where there was a magical *gwyddbwyll* on which the gaming pieces played themselves. Peredur became angry with the board and threw it into the lake. At the end of the tale (Jones and Jones 1974, 227);

> *'Then Arthur and his household fell upon the sorceresses and slew the sorceresses of Gloucester every one. And thus it is related concerning the Castle of Wonders.'*
>
>   From *The Mabinogion* (1838) translated by Lady Charlotte Guest, p. 370

The tale also implies that *Caer Loyw* and the *Castle of Wonders* were one and the same place.

THE GLOUCESTER LANDSCAPE AND THE VALE OF GLOUCESTER

A number of shrines or temples have been discussed in this chapter and some of these can be shown to have lain in the immediate vicinity of Gloucester (see Figures 48 and 72). The possible imperial temple was located in the north-west of the town under the ecclesiastical area of medieval Gloucester. The temples associated with the divinity of Gloucester and the tribal deities were probably in the north-east area of the town. There was also a war temple to Mars in the area of a late Anglo-Saxon palace. Under Saint Mary de Lode there are indications of a shrine which was probably associated with the worship of the River Severn. In the hinterland around Gloucester other shrines can also be recognised.

As was said, the *Colonia* of Gloucester was sited in an important religious landscape, the associated significant natural feature of which was discussed earlier (see Chapter 5). Earlier in this chapter it was determined that there had been a probable sacred lake to the north of Gloucester which was associated with Welsh legendary traditions. Gloucester was also situated in a large circular valley, now called the Vale of Gloucester. From Iron-Age burial practices, the Iron-Age tribal name, Roman period votive reliefs, the tribal name of the *Hwicce*, and the texts of the Mabinogion (see Figures 8, 58, and 62), it can be stated with confidence that there was a cult somehow associated with this feature. The valley was probably perceived as the womb of the *Dobunnic* mother goddess, the place from where creation had sprung. By looking at general trends in European creation myths it could be surmised that there was an egg, laid by a mother

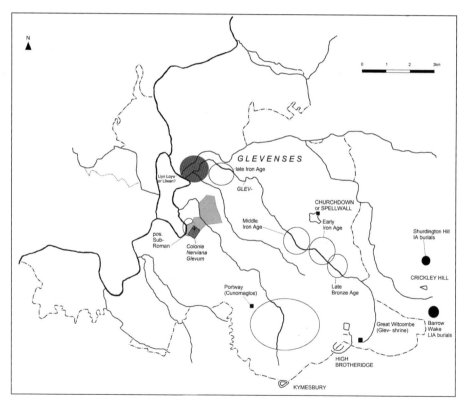

Figure 72: The parochia of Gloucester, showing the locations of Roman Gloucester and the minster, along with the four Iron-Age hill-forts located in and around the parochia (drawing S. Yeates)

goddess in the darkness of the womb. From that egg all life was generated. There are a number of peculiar sites in the vicinity of Gloucester, the strangest of which are two hills, which stand out because of their topography, and their folk-lore. These are Cooper's Hill, located on the rim of the circular valley at its southern end, and Churchdown Hill, within the valley (see Figure 62). The Old Mere, recorded in Welsh tradition as *Llyn Llyw*, was possibly located in the Severn Estuary, near the city of Gloucester and, therefore, to the west of Churchdown Hill. The extent of the lake can not, at present, be determined but the name Innsworth, located between Churchdown Hill and the lake, means **the enclosure on the island**, thus indicating that it was once a raised area of land in a marsh.

Cooper's Hill is the location of the annual Cheese Rolling event (Jefferies 2007), which people attend from far and wide. The antiquity of this event is not known but it is generally ascribed a Roman or medieval origin although it was not attested prior to the 1800s. One suggestion is that the event developed to protect commoner's rights upon the hill in the medieval period as other wakes did. The hill contains the probable remains of an Iron-Age Camp and an Iron-Age enclosure. Other woodland banks, which are essentially undated, could have been part of a *nemeton*, the presence of which is indicated by a probable shrine to the god *Cunomaglos*, at Portway, in the Twyver Valley (Rawes 1984, 23–72; Yeates 2008b, 114).

Despite the fact that the Cheese Rolling itself may only have been attested in the post-medieval period there are unusual features which indicate that there may be a connection between the tradition, the hill, and key aspects of the sun's seasonal cycle. Jefferies (2007, 15–17) noted that the hill is in shadow for certain times of the year, but this had been discussed in the family long before that publication. The hill lies on the southern side of the large circular valley; that is the Vale of Gloucester. The north end of the hill projects out from the Cotswold scarp, with a small coomb on its north face, referred to on early maps by an Old English name Howcombe. This means **a small valley in an extended headland**, an apt description. The angle of the slope, within the coomb, is some 33°, an angle which allows light to fall on the slope between the vernal and autumnal equinoxes over the summer months (see Figure 73). Jefferies speculated that the tradition may have had something to do with the summer solstice, but it is the equinoxes, which the sun itself seems to mark, that are significant. This being the case it was possible to use it as a reasonable indicator of the passing seasons. It is not known if there has been any intervention to alter the slope or if past peoples were aware of this. There are, however, some circumstantial reasons, that have to do with the names Gloucester and Horsebere Brook, for believing that this was the case. It has long been recognised that the name Gloucester, originally *Glevum*, was derived from a probable river-name. It has been suggested that it was probably derived from the original name of the Horsebere Brook (Yeates 2008b, 38–39). In the Roman period, the brook was identified as rising from a spring on the north-east side of Cooper's Hill, near Witcombe Roman villa. A shrine, identified at this site, survives as an earthwork and has not, as yet, been excavated (Holbrook 2003, 179–200) (see Figures 74, 75 and 76). The name Gloucester is derived from a British word the etymology of which is **glow**. This cannot be explained from our current understanding of the topography of the city, but it may become more understandable if there was a connection between the city and the river which flowed from Cooper's Hill and on which were possibly held solar festivals. It was on the Horsebere Brook where all of the oldest settlements in the area were situated and which could well have given rise to the name *Glevenses*, the dwellers on the **bright river** (Yeates 2000b, 63–66).

The other peculiar site is the hill-fort of Churchdown Hill (Baker 1821, 161–175). The name was traditionally seen as having an etymology derived from the British **crouco-*, a hill or mound, associated with the Pre-Welsh **crŭc* which was interpreted as a reference to the prominent hill sticking out in the valley (Smith 1964b, ii.119–120). However, later

Figure 73: The sunlight shining on the face of Cooper's Hill in the period just after the Vernal Equinox (photograph S. Yeates)

Figure 74: The earthworks and buildings at Witcombe Roman Villa which lie above a spring, the probable source of the Gleva (Horsebere). This stream and the mythical lake gave their name to the city and people of Gloucester (photograph S. Yeates)

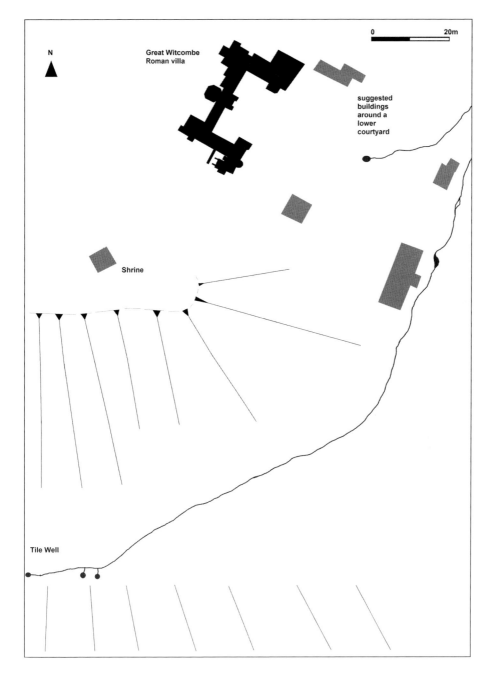

Figure 75: A sketch plan of Witcombe Roman Villa and shrine above the spring of the Gleva (drawing S. Yeates)

Figure 76: The mound which is considered to be the location of a temple set above the Tile Well at the source of the Horsebere Brook (photograph S. Yeates)

interpretations claimed that this hill was not the correct shape to receive such a name, and that it must refer to the **church**, the origin being the Old English *ċiriċe* (Watts 2004, 138). Both explanations could be correct as the church stands on an artificial mound and it is this mound which could derive its name from the Pre-Welsh **crūc* rather than the whole hill (see Figure 77).

Early antiquaries described the hill-fort on Churchdown, but there was some doubt over its authenticity as the hill is made of lias clay which is liable to slump naturally. It was only in the 1960s and 1970s, when excavations for the construction of a second reservoir and water pipes identified the remains of a constructed rampart, and a pit which contained a piece of middle Iron-Age pot (Hurst 1977, 5–10). Medieval texts referred to a site in the parish of Churchdown in *c.* 1340 as the *Spelewalle*. This is a reference to the rampart where people came to speak, and is evidently a reference to the Iron-Age hill-fort. Figure 78 shows a plan of the Iron Age hill-fort before it was severely damaged by the construction of reservoirs in the Second World War and in the 1960s, and shows some of the important locations. There are three important cultural locations on the hill, the hill-fort entrance, the church of Saint Bartholomew, and the site of a great Oak Tree which stood on the south-east side of the hill, now gone. The

Figure 77: The artificial mound, forming part of the Iron Age rampart or built over the rampart, which is claimed by tradition (and supported by the surviving evidence) to have been the location of an important pre-Christian shrine (photograph S. Yeates)

entrance to the hill-fort is a complex affair with a large saddle-like earthwork in its middle with paths extending on either side; it is known locally as Saddle Hill, and lies beside a well called Mussel Well (see Figure 79). Part of the hill in this area is called the Roman Steps, which must refer to the approaches to the hill-fort. There is a folk-tradition concerned with this part of the hill that it is the place where a fairy funeral (Swift 1905, 84–85), that disappeared at an ash tree, has been seen. The disappearance at an ash tree is of interest as there was a Gospel Ash in the village (Swift 1905, 86), a peculiar designation as trees chosen for this tradition were usually oak trees. This type of tale, rare in England, seems more Irish in nature, as seen in the stories surrounding Cruachan (Raftery 1994, 70–71), where a significant site was recognised as a passageway between two worlds, this one and the one of the gods or fairy folk.

The second important location on the hill is where the church of Saint Bartholomew now stands, on the line of the Iron-Age rampart and at a point where there is a large mound or platform. This feature is either contemporary with the rampart or a later addition; (at present there is no way of knowing which), which was claimed, by Lysons, to be the location of a temple dedicated to Thor (Swift 1905, 6–7); this is perhaps an exaggeration or misinterpretation, but one which may contain a kernel of truth. Lysons's claims were based on a text in which he identified Churchdown with a place

Figure 78: A plan of the Iron-Age hill-fort on Churchdown Hill, which shows the main locations where there are mythical traditions (drawing S. Yeates)

called *Thorsdown* in an earlier text. The place-name evidence for Churchdown does not refer to the reference by Lysons and this may have originated as a misreading of the later recordings, such as *Chorsdown* of 1719 (Smith 1964b, ii.119–120). However, some stonework in the church is believed to have survived from a pagan shrine or earlier church or chapel (Waters 1999, 9–12, 18, 20). The importance of the church's location

Figure 79: A photograph of the Saddle Hill, which is the major horn-work of the Iron-Age entrance way into the fort. It is through this gate that the fairy funeral was claimed to enter into the depths of the hill (photograph S. Yeates)

is indicated by the legend that the stones of the church were cast down by the devil each night, while a further tradition indicates that the Saint himself carried the church to the hilltop. The church is also known to have contained medieval wall paintings depicting grotesque demons which were only whitewashed over at a late date. The site is, therefore, associated with many ideas of supernatural, or non-Christian, origin, which is further evidence that the site was used for an Iron-Age or Roman shrine. Church traditions may explain why this place was called the *Spelewalle* (Smith 1964b, ii.123); on Rogation Sunday it was traditional to give the sermon from the Mount on the rampart of the hill-fort.

There are further implications or possible insights concerning Lysons's claim. A further twist to this, which is difficult to explain satisfactorily, is that on the south side of the hill is the suburb of Gloucester called Hucclecote. Initially this settlement was a hamlet in the extensive parish of Churchdown. The site is most readily known in archaeological circles as being the location of a Roman villa (Clifford 1933, 323–376). The name is interpreted as being derived from the Old English **Hucela's cote** or **cottage** (Smith 1964b, ii.147). The name is associated with just two other names in the country; Hockleton in Shropshire and Hugglescote in Leicestershire. The name is considered to be Old English yet there is a Celtic divine name *Sucellus* (Green 1992, 200), a divinity mentioned earlier (see Chapter 4), which can be variously spelt from its inscriptions with one or two <c>s and <l>s, for example *Succelus* from the spring at the source of the river Arroux. It was recognised by Jackson that an initial <s> in Brittonic would invariably change to an <h> (Jackson 1953, 517–521), thus a form *Sucel-* would become *Hucel-*. The name has now been given an etymology of '**the good striker**' or '**he who strikes to good effect**'. If these names are connected then the reference is to the villa or the ruins of the Roman villa. A connection with the god *Sucellus* leads to unusual implications although these can at present be only speculative. The first is the symbol of the hammer used by *Sucellus*, which is interesting when we think of Lysons's claim that the pagan site on Churchdown Hill was associated with Thor (Swift 1905, 6–7; Cooke 1939, 12), whose symbol was also the hammer. *Sucellus* and Mercury were also the two main deities associated with the divine couple (Green 1989, 45–73). In some of the images of *Sucellus* and Mercury, Mercury holds a purse, while *Sucellus* holds a pot. The last thing to note here is an interesting suggestion made by Aldhouse-Green with respect to the god (Green 1992, 240):

> '*The symbolism of the hammer is not easy to interpret. The implement is a noisy, striking tool: it may be a weapon, a fencing mallet or a cooper's hammer. But it can also be perceived as an instrument of power – a wand of authority, like a sceptre. In view of the known affinity between Sucellus and fertility symbolism, especially the grape harvest (symbolized by the Hammer-god's pot and barrel), it could be that the hammer may reflect the striking of earth, awakening it after the death of winter.*'
>
> From the *Dictionary of Celtic Myth and Legend* by Miranda J. Green © Thames and Hudson Ltd., London

The hammer is important for waking up the mother goddess after winter and is important. This is at present extremely speculative, but the folk-tradition, the probable pagan-shrine, and the place-name Hucclecote make this point worth saying. It is also worth noting that, with respect to Grimstock, formerly Grimscot, that the word cote or cottage has been associated with a divine name and refers to a Roman building, in this case a temple (see earlier discussion on Grim in Chapter 3).

The third site of importance on the hill was that on which stood a large and ancient oak tree. The location was on the south-east side of the hill where a reservoir was built in the 1960s. The tree was called the Devil's Oak and was associated with the tale of a large fox that took refuge in the tree after being chased by hounds, and the fact that the hounds would not go anywhere near the tree (Cooke 1939, 11). This and other places in the parish were claimed to be haunted by his Satanic majesty (Swift 1905, 85), a terminology born from the Victorian and Edwardian period language which should not be seen as literal. These are just some of the folk traditions associated with the hill and, it is claimed, there are more legends and folk-traditions concerning this hill than any other in Gloucestershire. Previous discussions have considered that Iron-Age hill-forts were the location of pagan shrines, or were, in themselves, pagan sanctuaries. Churchdown Hill Fort certainly supports this idea; with the sanctuary and a possible Roman shrine in the north-east corner. The surviving legends mirror what is known of earlier Irish traditions although they have no known antiquity; there is, however, no

Figure 80: A glass intaglio depicting two deities, Hera (Juno) and Tyche (Fortuna) closely associated with a sacrilised mountain, Mount Argaeus, in Asia Minor. The horse below must also be associated with the Mount Argaeus cult. From Gadar in Jordon (photograph Robert Wilkins, Institute of Archaeology Oxford)

easy way of dating the origin of these legends. Hills are known to have been venerated throughout the Roman Empire, for example Mount Argaeus in Asia Minor (see Figure 80).

Interestingly, Churchdown Hill has also ended up with the corrupted name Chosen Hill (Bigland 1989, 345); could this name have developed because of the special significance the hill had to the people that lived around it. Geographically, the site is important, but it is only one of two hills that lie within the circular valley bounded by Cleeve Hill on the east, Bredon Hill on the north, Cooper's Hill on the south, and the Corsewood Hills on the West. It is, however, the more centrally sited of these two. If the valley represented the cauldron of the mother goddess, the symbolic womb of creation, then the hill that stands proud in the valley could be interpreted as the egg of creation in the middle of the womb, or as the navel (*omphelos*) in the centre of the body. Its role as the central point in this gigantic scheme may explain the elaborate hill-fort on Churchdown Hill and the significance of the pre-Christian shrine which stood proud on the north-east rampart. Primal myths often contain images of a mother goddess and an egg of creation from which all life emerged; it is feasible, therefore, Churchdown Hill was very important, perhaps the most important site in the pre-Christian *Dobunnic* world and played a vital part in its cosmology.

CONCLUSION

Although the Welsh tales and chronicles are much despised and poorly understood it is evident that in Nennius and even within some texts of the Mabinogion (*Peredur* and *How Culhwch won Olwen*) there are allusions to folk traditions which indicate that certain parts of the landscape were more sacred than others and can point to certain traditions about the sanctity of the landscape. It has been possible to pinpoint some of the sacred sites listed in *The Wonders* and explain why they are there and point back to a sanctity which extended back into the Roman period if not earlier. It was evident around the civitas of the Silures that there were a cluster of sacred sites which were intriguing. They were either a product of Nennius's local knowledge or had renown that spread over a large part of Britain. Although Cirencester had the potential for being a focus for religious activity it was Gloucester and the Vale of Gloucester which seems to be referred to in the Welsh texts. The persistent allusion to the Gloucester area may be understandable, in the context of the Roman province of *Britannia Prima,* as recently White (2007, 97–101) alluded to the possibility that Gloucester was the capital of the province. If this was the case then allusion to the lost capital and fortress of wonders would be more expected. In the area of Gloucester there is the circular valley, the sacred lake, and the Severn Bore all of which are described in the ancient Welsh traditions. Coupled to this there are two unusual hills in the Gloucester area which seem to have folk-traditions which seem important but which can not be dated. Other aspects such as place-names give some credibility to this. At present much of this is speculation but it is interesting to wonder.

Chapter 7

Tribal Legends and the Holy Grail

A number of factors have been discussed which may help determine how some of the archaeological aspects and folk-traditions, which survive regarding the *Dobunni* and *Hwicce*, could be put together in a more coherent way. Although much of what has been discussed can not be proven, it is possible to raise ideas that further archaeological and onomastic studies can get to grips with in properly referenced works. There has been some consideration of how anthropologists study tribes and identify aspects of their religious belief systems, including how any pantheon would have come about, and also of aspects of the underlying religious principles (Chapter 2). Lurking behind all such discussions is the work of Frazer, *The Golden Bough* (1922), which suggests that one can reconstruct past belief systems with examples from all around the world. Consideration has also been given (in Chapter 3) to the process of *interpretatio*, an important process of acculturation described by Tacitus, but clearly evident in earlier works. The rivers and hills of Europe were once named from, or gave their names to, animals and plants (Chapter 4). The importance of Brittonic river-names was shown to be a significant factor around which traditions, long gone and unnoticed by archaeologists but not by onomasticists, could be identified. The idea that every tribe in the north-west provinces of Europe once had a creation myth was also taken as a starting point (Chapter 5). The ranking and context of sacred sites has also been discussed (Chapter 6). Some of these ideas are not current in present archaeological debates, and the evidence often lies outside archaeological tradition.

A REPRISE

Anthropological and ethnographical investigations have determined, across the globe, that each ethnic group produced a cosmology or set of religious beliefs and practices unique to itself. The tribes of north-west Europe would have been no different. The idea that these tribes tied themselves into a pan-'Celtic' group, with a uniform set of religious principles and beliefs, has to be further explored and discussed, as there are casual references by Caesar and others which suggest that this may have been the case. Such discussions focus on the druids as a priesthood residing among the Celtic and British tribes. It may be true that certain aspects of tribal religion were shared, or similar, between the various groups. Vague names were used by early authors and ethnographers to describe the peoples concerned, and this lack of clarity has enabled the terms and concepts to be manipulated by various scholars old and new through time. Now we can start looking at the evidence for the religion of each tribal group individually; and assess what was occurring in each tribal territory and *civitas*, assuming the evidence allows this. The emerging evidence from the study of the *Dobunni* supports the idea that each group should be looked at individually, each having its own creation myth and pantheon, its own set of ritual practices, and different qualities for divinities within the pantheons.

The definition of tribal territories can be achieved in Gaul, but is more difficult in Britain. Also for Gaul, Iron-Age coinage distribution gives us the most reliable basis, it has been claimed that this method is also useful for south-east Britain. Also for Gaul it is known that the early bishoprics, formed at the end of the Roman period, were based predominantly on tribal territories; only in a couple of cases in Brittany has this method been questioned (Giot, Guigon *et al.* 2003, 107–113). This was perhaps also the case for Britain, but in contrast to Gaul, the territorial hierarchy soon broke down and knowledge of its formation was lost.

In ancient European religious belief systems there is evidence that tribal groups worshipped a pantheon of gods. The pantheons that we have some knowledge of can be best understood in a pan-Greco or pan-Roman context, or maybe in pan-Irish, pan-Germanic, or Scandinavian contexts. Whether the pan-Irish group formed part of the larger pan-Celtic pantheon of gods is difficult to determine; further studies of tribal groups through ancient ethnographies may eventually determine this. We can even determine the localised origins of certain deities if we are lucky in finding shrines and assessing onomastics.

One of Caesar's statements concerning the beliefs of the peoples of the north-west provinces was that religious ideas were exported from Britain to the continent and that there may have been a common underlying set of beliefs. These beliefs may have had *Pythagorean* undertones but there is other evidence which emphasises the differences between the religious beliefs of separate groups. The fact that there are only two references to these traditions is a drawback; it is also the case that they were stated after the events under investigation. However, one further possibility is that the later references to these religious beliefs indicate that native traditions may have been more durable than previously thought, with the Gauls and Britons holding onto their underlying cosmological views.

There are also indications that the process of *interpretatio* which, in the documentation, is seen exclusively as a Roman invention and was only first recognised with the arrival of the Romans. This process had probably occurred many times before the Romans' arrival, just as it did after their influence waned, as evident in the changing faces of the Romano-British deities. This process of cultural interaction and acculturation can be recognised elsewhere in the world, but is denied by some to have occurred at the time of the alleged migration period in Britain. Radical reinterpretations of the genetic database of Britain (Oppenheimer 2006), placing this in its European context, has enabled a new interpretation of the data. The migration period is considered to be responsible for only 5.5% of the present gene pool of that group but has had far more influence than any other. A number of examples of continuing *interpretatio*, from the Iron Age into the early medieval period, can also be found. Examples including the *Dobunnic Matres* or *Modron*, and *Cunomaglos*, demonstrate a process of deities being re-invented or reworked (Yeates 2006a; 2008b). In this study it has also been suggested that similar processes were occurring with the *Dobunnic* father as he is probably evident on their coins. There are further examples of name pairing for example *Sulis Minerva*. In the migration period *interpretatio* can be demonstrated in the *Dobunnic* world, and it almost certainly occurred in other parts of Britain. It is also extremely unlikely that Christianity managed to filter out all forms of earlier religions, especially from what is known from other regions. *Interpretatio* must, therefore, be seen as an ongoing process of re-evaluation and adaptation.

Comparisons of surviving legends from places as diverse as Greece and Ireland are giving us a number of new insights: the associations between rivers and animals, mythical genealogical descent, accounts of persons or mythical characters dying in the estuaries or confluences of rivers. If such components are found in medieval writings it is possible that they represent some form of survival of an older oral tradition. Some of these components may be evident for the goddess of the Severn (Chapter 4). A study of ancient river-names and land toponyms indicates that land forms were associated with the names of plants, animals, minerals and heavenly bodies. Welsh texts, like the oral traditions of Australia, talk about ancestral or mythical animals which wandered the landscape. Were the rivers named first in accordance with their usefulness to man, or was it that the rivers were named because of some perceived relationship with mythological situations? And when did rivers first become personified? When looking at the broader landscape there seems to be a language of hidden meaning and association, a sacred topography. This could help explain why certain temple sites were developed on locations which are not obviously significant in any other way.

THE GRAIL QUEST

Throughout many parts of the world it is recognised that tribal groups produced the cultural stories which are known as creation or primal myths. Some European examples have survived, in Greece, Italy, and Scandinavia. Most, or all, of these stories involved a divine couple, as seen in the Greek myths as accounted by Hesiod. This may well have been a common theme in the north-west provinces. The religious sculpture and accompanying traditions suggest that for the *Dobunni,* at least, this was the case. The names of the deities involved varied from tribe to tribe as can be seen for the *Brigantes* and *Luci* tribes. How these deities' names evolved and to what extent they were homonyms of the tribal name will only be shown with the recovery of more Roman-period inscriptions. The goddess of the *Dobunni* can be recognised through the use of the cauldron in a religious context, which led to the tribe being called the *Hwicce* by the incoming Anglo-Saxon culture. The use of the cauldron, seen in the legend of *Peredur,* is significant and hints at the durability of the cult and the goddess's association with the tribe over long periods and through chaotic times. The significance of *Peredur* will be considered later.

The fifth and sixth centuries AD are referred to as the Dark Ages, as it was a period of very little textual evidence in Britain. What there is is sometimes contradictory and few assessments blend Welsh and English sources, *The Age of Arthur* (Morris 1973), a reliable interpretation of the British past, is one which does. It is in this era for which some of the most enigmatic and world renowned traditions to come out of Britain arrive in the form of Arthur and the legends of the grail quest. It has been recognised that these are derived from a fusion of ideas, Christianity cemented onto a bedrock of pre-Christian beliefs (Loomis 1963). For legends to be accepted in the medieval period there had to be an acceptance of these stories by the Church. In the case of the grail quest legends there was an acceptance of this tradition like no other group of romantic tales. The two principle knights of these stories are known as Percival and Galahad and the recounting of and rewriting of these tales in the medieval period was considerable. Versions of these stories were developed on the continent, in Champagne by Chrétien de Troyes called *Conte del Graal or Perceval* (Owen 1987) with its subsequent re-workings by Manessier and de Montreuil; in Barvaria by Wolfram von Eschenbach in *Parzival* (Hatto 1980); there was also the French prose *The Didot Perceval*; the Burgundian version by de Boron called *Joseph d'Arimathie*; and the French or Belgian prose *Perlesvaus* translated as the *High History of the Holy Grail*. Much of this grail tradition was brought together in England in specific chapters on the *Book of King Arthur*, which concerned *Lancelot* and the *Grail Quest*. To these we should also add the Welsh version of *Peredur* (Jones and Jones 1974, 183–227), as it is this version which may represent the oldest of these tales, not necessarily in written form but perhaps from an oral source, indeed Loomis (Loomis 1963, 6) stated:

> *"There can be no doubt that the French men of letters who told of these astonishing adventures regarded them as inseparably connected in time and place with Arthur's reign and Arthur's realm."*
>
> From *The Grail: from Celtic myth to Christian symbol* by R. S. Loomis (1963), © 1991 Princeton University Press reprinted by permission

This being the case it is to the Romano-British province of *Britannia Prima*, which was Arthur's realm, where we should look for the underlying pre-Christian traditions of the legends, and why the Welsh version of these tales should lie at the heart of understanding Britain's pagan past. Although the textual data about Arthur is sparse, it is apparent that the reign of a king of Britain or a part of Britain can be placed around the year *c.* 470 to *c.* 515 AD (Morris 1973, 103, 140). Arthur is considered to have ruled from the site of Camalot, but in the Welsh versions of *Peredur* he is associated with the legionary base of Caerleon in South Wales (Jones and Jones 1974, 203, 207). There are other medieval authors: Geoffrey of Monmouth (Thorpe 1966, 202–203) and Layamon (Mason 1962, 223–227), besides others who considered Caerleon the seat of Arthur's power (Kennerley 1971, 30–41; Olding 1987, 23–29; Knight 2001, 47–57) (see Figures 81 and 82). Loomis stated further (1963, 20):

> *"It is apparent that, since the stories of the grail belong to the Arthurian cycle, the most likely regions in which to look for their origin and their pristine meaning is Wales and Ireland."*
>
> From *The Grail: from Celtic myth to Christian symbol* by R. S. Loomis (1963), © 1991 Princeton University Press reprinted by permission

We can recognise that these traditions were wrapped up in traditions of mythical cycles. However, there was a tradition, within the Arthurian discourse, of direct comparisons

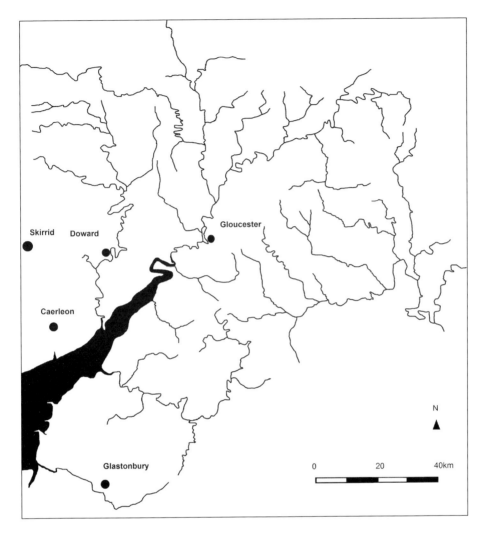

Figure 81: A map showing the most significant Arthurian sites located in the West Country and Wales (drawing S. Yeates)

between texts and with other Irish and Welsh traditions. Problems arose in that these legendary traditions should be based on our knowledge of the religion of the Romano-British world, where there was a tradition of local spirits, animal totems, and major cult stories. Our knowledge of that Romano-British world is, however, not well founded. *Peredur* can be linked into the Roman period religious traditions through the tribe of the *Dobunni* and his association with place and myth within their territory (Yeates 2006a; 2008b).

The town of Glastonbury was a medieval focus of these folk-traditions and was

Figure 82: A view of Caerleon a site claimed in the majority of British medieval tales as Arthur's seat of power; the legionary amphitheatre was known as Arthur's Round Table (photograph S. Yeates)

consequently claimed as the location of the mythical Isle of Avalon (Loomis 1963, 249–250). Much of this tradition is, however, pseudo medieval historical construction. This was claimed as the mythical burial place of Arthur, yet this is evidently a tale spun by a medieval abbey and its attempt to gain power and influence by controlling the past. This past was no ordinary past, but was a sacred grail past which the Christian church had allowed to develop; not only did they wish it to develop they also wanted to control it (Figure 83). Glastonbury was probably not the only site associated with Arthur's death, as on the Skirrid there is a cairn known as Arthur's Chest (Olding 1987, 23–29) (see Figure 84). However, that Glastonbury probably had older associations with this pagan past is almost certain as we can assume from the place that Glastonbury occupies in the landscape of Iron Age and Roman Britain. Glastonbury lies on the edge of an ancient British tribal area of the *Dobunni*; it is a liminal place. The motherland of the *Dobunni* lay to the north extending to the Forest of Arden. At the heart of this tribe's ancient religion was a mother goddess with a **sacred vessel**, a cauldron of rebirth and regeneration. It is this folk-goddess and her **sacred vessel** (the *Hwicce*) which is the bedrock for all of the Christian mythology of the grail quest.

Peredur is considered the Welsh name of Percival, who played an important role in the grail traditions of Malory, and the oldest surviving tale concerning his origins and attributes. It is in these stories that we come across the large circular valley with a castle (Gloucester – the fortress of Marvels) sat within. It was at that fortress where *Peredur* met the father and mother (Mercury and *Mater*) and also the nine witches

Figure 83: The abbey of Glastonbury, Somerset; the claimed burial site of King Arthur. The Tor, considered the location of the Isle of Avalon, can be seen framed by the abbey ruins (photograph S. Yeates)

(priestesses) who warmed the cauldron. That these stories can be projected out onto the landscape, not in an archaeological way which can be dug up, but in a spiritual view of the topography of the world rests on a raft of circumstantial Welsh medieval textual sources coupled to the physical reliefs and the inference of cult activity as portrayed . At present it is not known what other parts of the *Peredur* story may have been lifted from the mythological or historical tradition of the *Dobunni*, but there may be other elements within it which will eventually be noted.

Some locations and sites were considered to be more sacred than others, such as henges and hill-forts. Temples were regarded as the dwelling places of the gods; often, the reasons behind the locations chosen were to do with a natural feature which was regarded as having some importance. In Nennius's *The Wonders of Britain*, in *c.* AD 800, there are indications that such ideas persisted into the post-Roman period. Many of the sites chosen by Nennius, such as Bath and Droitwich, had their origins in the Roman or Iron Age periods. There were often Roman temples at these sites and some of the information recorded in the eighth century must have been derived from an earlier period. It is also clear that Nennius put a great deal of emphasis on one area near the confluence of the Severn and the Wye; this may have been because he originated from that region or that the sites in that area had a greater renown because of the traditions of

Figure 84: The Skirrid (Ysgyryd Fawr) and the Sugar Loaf on the eastern edge of the Black Mountains. On the former is a cairn known as Arthur's Chest (photograph S. Yeates)

the area in which they found themselves. The Roman town of *Venta Silurum* was situated in a landscape which may have been dotted with temples. This raises the question of how and why other towns were established, and whether they, also, formed part of extensive religious landscapes. Could the significance of the *colonia* at Gloucester and the *civitas* at Cirencester be thought of in these terms? Probably underpinning the *Dobunnic* creation myth was the shape of the landscape, the large cauldron and the prominent hill within it, Churchdown Hill. The imagery of the goddess and her specific association with the cult centre at Gloucester probably led to the ranking of this site as a *Colonia* in the Roman period and the granting, to this group of people serving its important religious sites, of Roman citizenship at an early date. Churchdown Hill seems to have had a special place in this tradition but what its role was exactly can not, at present, be confirmed. It is possible to recognize the goddess of the **sacred vessel** who ruled over the *Dobunni* and haunted that tribe for over 1,000 years, but it is also possible to consider that she and her cult were the bedrock onto which the later Arthurian grail myths were grafted.

Appendix

Potential Periods of River-name Changes

Periods when there were major ideological changes in the Archaeological record and in DNA migration patterns are as follows. In Mesolithic Britain a hunter-gatherer system was in operation; the types of river-name used in this period are unknown. It has been suggested that the initial Mesolithic immigrants account for some 24% of the modern British population and that later Mesolithic arrivals push the percentage coming from the Iberian ice retreat to 45% (Oppenheimer 2006, 173, 193); while the arrival from the Balkan ice retreat accounts for only 3% of the British population. Linguistic language splits in prehistory are often difficult to determine but there has been much debate about a culture called the Kurgen culture, which is claimed to have helped the spread of agriculture and the Indo-European languages (Clackson 2007, 15–19). In the early Neolithic a new way of life was being introduced into Britain, hence ideological change, and it may be that some of the flora and fauna names were introduced at this time. It has been suggested from DNA analysis that some 10–30% of the modern inhabitants of Britain are descended from Neolithic immigrants coming from places such as the Near East and the Balkans (Oppenheimer 2006, 243–244). The figures vary regionally indicating that patterns of local identity had commenced. In the later Neolithic and the early Bronze Age there is evidence of further change with the construction of henges, cursii, and tombs showing astronomical alignments. If springs and rivers were named after celestial objects then one would expect these names to have been given in this period. In the middle Bronze Age a further change happened as the great ceremonial monuments ceased to be important and settlements became more important. The Bronze Age saw small amounts of migration from Scandinavia, with a slightly higher than average recording of these DNA types in the Severn valley area (Oppenheimer 2006, 276–280), although not significantly higher than 3–4.5% of the population. Other migrants from what is now Germany are found at 4–5% in the east of Britain. From the later Bronze Age there is increasing evidence of river worship in the forms of major votive deposition. This carried on into the Iron Age, the Roman period, and the early medieval period. The Iron Age saw a level of migration into Britain estimated at 3% of the modern population (Oppenheimer 2006, 309). The next period of major ideological change followed the arrival of Christianity. Certain names then became lost or went into secondary use. River-names associated with this period include those associated with numbers (for example Seven Springs), some Welsh descriptive names (for example possibly Dulas), English descriptive names (the Dikler or the Evenlode), and moves to words meaning river: Wye, Wey, Dore, and Dover in Welsh, and Ea, Rea in English. There is increasing evidence from England and Wales that the early medieval period was a time when many names changed due to Christian ideology. The alleged Anglo-Saxon migration during the time in which Christianity was introduced into the British Isles has been assessed, using DNA analysis, to contribute only 5.5% of the population, while the Viking migrations is considered to account for a similar amount (Oppenheimer 2006, 443, 462–463). The last ideological change was the introduction of maps; it is this final phase which froze the river-name landscape of Britain and it is from this period that many English names were imposed over other earlier names in England.

Bibliography

Aitchison, N. (1994) *Armagh and the royal centres in early medieval Ireland*, Glasgow, Cruithne Press.

Aldhouse-Green, M. J. (1999) Introduction, In M. J. Aldhouse-Green (ed.) *Pilgrims in stone: stone images from the Gallo-Roman sanctuary of Fontes Sequanae*, 1–9, Oxford, British Archaeological Reports International Series 754.

Allen, D. (1944) The *Belgic* dynasties of Britain and their coins, *Archaeologia* **90**, 1–46.

Anonymous (1935) Roman Britain in 1934, *Journal of Roman Studies* **25**, 201–227.

Anonymous (1956) Roman Britain in 1955, *Journal of Roman Studies* **46**, 119–152.

Anonymous (1966–68) *Dictionnaire des eglises de France: France Ouest, Ile-de-France, part iv*, Paris, CPB.

Anonymous (1994) *Vercingetorix et Alesia*, Paris, Musee des Antiquites nationales.

Austin, R. (1934) Proceedings at the spring meeting 7th May 1934, *Transactions of the Bristol and Gloucestershire Archaeological Society* **56**, 1–8.

Bailey, K. (1989) The Middle Saxons, In S. Bassett (ed.) *The origins of Anglo-Saxon kingdoms*, 108–122, Leicester, Leicester University Press.

Baker, T. J. L. (1821) An account of a chain of ancient fortresses, extending through the south western part of Gloucestershire, *Archaeologia* **19**, 161–175.

Bannister, A. T. (1916) *The place-names of Herefordshire: the origin and development*, Cambridge, privately printed at the University Press.

Barber, M. (2003) *Bronze and the Bronze Age: metalwork and society in Britain c 2500–800 BC*, Stroud, Tempus.

Barclay, A., A. Boyle, and G. D. Keevil (2001) A prehistoric enclosure at Eynsham Abbey, Oxfordshire, *Oxoniensia* **66**, 105–162.

Barker, P. P. and G. F. Ranity (2003) *A report for the friends of Leominster Priory on a geophysical survey carried out at Leominster Priory*, Leominster, The friends of Leominster Priory.

Bassett, S. (2000) How the west was won: the Anglo-Saxon takeover of the west midlands, *Anglo-Saxon Studies in Archaeology and History* **11**, 107–118.

Batardy, C., O. Buchseuschutz and F. Durnasy (2001) *Le Berry antique, atlas 2000*, Paris, Archeologies d'Orient et d'Occident.

Bately, J. M. (1986) *The Anglo-Saxon Chronicle, volume 3: ms A*, Cambridge, D. S. Brewer.

Baudoux, J., P. Flotte, M. Fuchs and M.-D. Waton (2002) *Strasbourg*, Paris, Carte Archeologique de la Gaule 67/2.

Bayley, H. (1919) *Archaic England: an essay in deciphering prehistory from megalithic monuments, earthworks, customs, coins, place-names, and faerie superstitions*, London, Chapman and Hall.

Bennett, J. (1985) *The Roman town of Abonae: Excavations at Nazareth House, Sea Mills, 1972*, Bristol, City of Bristol Museum and Art Gallery Monograph 3.

Bieler, L. (1979) *The Patrician texts in the book of Armagh*, Dublin, Institute of Advanced Studies, Scriptures Latini Hiberniae vol.10.

Bigland, R. (1989) *Historical, monumental and genealogical collections, relative to the county of Gloucester; printed from original papers of the late Ralph Bigland Esq. garter principal king of arms: part 1: Abbenhall-Cromhall, Gloucester*, Gloucestershire record series 2.

Blair, J. (1994) *Anglo-Saxon Oxfordshire*, Stroud, Sutton Publishing.

Bloom, J. H. (1930) *Folk lore, old customs and superstitions in Shakespear land*, London, Mitchell Hughes and Clarke.

Booth, P. M. (1994) A Roman burial near Welford-on-Avon, Warwickshire, *Transactions of the Birmingham and Warwickshire Archaeological Society* **98**, 37–50.

Bradbury, J. and R. A. Croft (1989) Somerset archaeology, 1989, *Proceedings of the Somersetshire Archaeological and Natural History Society* **133**, 157–185.

Bradley, R. (1988) Hoarding, recycling and consumption of prehistoric metalwork: technological change in western Europe, *World Archaeology* **20 (2)**, 249–260.

Bradley, R. (1990) *The passage of arms: an archaeological analysis of prehistoric hoards and votive deposits*, Cambridge, Cambridge University Press.

Bradley, R., R. Entwistle, and R. Frances (1994). *Prehistoric land divisions on Salisbury Plain: the work of the Wessex linear ditches project.* London, English Heritage Archaeological Report 2.

Bradney, J. A. (1923) *A history of Monmouthshire: from the coming of the Normans into Wales down to the present time, volume 3 part 2: The hundred of Usk (Cantref Brynbuga) with indices of names and places, addenda and corrigenda*, London, Mitchell Hughes and Clarke.

Bradney, J. A. (1933) *A history of Monmouthshire: from the coming of the Normans into Wales down to the present time, Volume 4 (part 1): The hundred of Caldicot (Gwent Iscoed) with title, indices of names and places, addenda and corrigenda*, London, Mitchell Hughes and Clarke.

Branston, B. (1957) *The lost gods of England*, London, Thames and Hudson.

Breeze, A. (1998) The name of Laughern Brook, near Worcester, *Transactions of the Worcestershire Archaeological Society (Third Series)* **16**, 251–252.

Breeze, A. (2000) Doulting, near Wells, Somerset, In R. Coates and A. Breeze (eds) *English places, Celtic Voices: studies of the Celtic impact on place-names in England*, Stamford, Shaun Tyas.

Breeze, A. (2006). The rivers Boyd of Gloucestershire and Bude of Cornwall, *Transactions of the Bristol and Gloucestershire Archaeological Society* **124**, 111–112.

Breeze, A. (2008) Kemble and the Britons, *Wiltshire Archaeological and Natural History Magazine* **101**, 255–256.

Brewster, H. (1997) *The river gods of Greece: myths and mountain waters in the Hellenic world*, London, I B Tauris Publishers.

Brewer, R. J. (1986) *Corpus of sculpture of the Roman World, Great Britain volume I fascicule 5: Roman sculpture from Wales*, Oxford, British Academy: Oxford University Press.

Brewer, R. J. (2004) The Romans in Gwent. In M. J. Aldhouse-Green and R. Howells (eds) *The Gwent county history: volume 1, Gwent in prehistory and early history*, 204–243, Cardiff, University of Wales Press.

Briggs, K. (2007) Seven wells, *Journal of the English Place-name Society* **39**, 7–44.

Brossler, A., M. Gocher, G. Laws and M. Roberts (2002) Shorncote Quarry: excavations of a late prehistoric landscape in the upper Thames Valley, *Transactions of the Bristol and Gloucestershire Archaeological Society* **120**, 37–87.

Brown, P. (1981) *The cult of the saints: its rise and function in Latin Christianity*, Chicargo, University of Chicargo Press.

Brück, J. (1995) A place for the dead: the role of human remains in Late Bronze Age Britain, *Proceedings of the Prehistoric Society* **61**, 245–277.

Brunaux, J.-L. (1988) *The Celtic Gauls: gods, rites and sanctuaries*, London, Seaby.

Bryant, R. and C. M. Heighway (2003) Excavations at Saint Mary de Lode church, Gloucestershire, 1978–9, *Transactions of the Bristol and Gloucestershire Archaeological Society* **121**, 97–178.

Burkert, W. (1985) *Greek religion*, Oxford, Blackwell.

Burne, C. S. (1917) Witchcraft in Great Britain, *Folk-lore* **28**, 453.

Bury, R. G. (1929) *Plato: Timaeus, Critias, Cleitophon, Menexenus, Epistles*, London, Loeb Classic Library.

Caley, J. and J. Hunter (1817), *Valor ecclesiasticus: Temp. Henr. VIII, auctoritate regia institutus, part III*, London, Record Commission.

Camp, J. M. (1986) *The Athenian Agora: excavations in the heart of Classical Athens*, London, Thames and Hudson.

Campbell, E. and P. MacDonald (1993) Excavations at Caerwent Vicarge Orchard Garden 1973: an extra-mural post-Roman cemetery, *Archaeologia Cambrensis* **142**, 74–98.

Campbell, J. (1964) *The mask of God: occidental mythology*, Harmondsworth, Penguin Books.

Carley, J. P. (1988) *Glastonbury Abbey: the holy house at the head of the moors adventurous*, Woodbridge, The Boydell Press.

Cary, E. (1924) *Dio Cassius: Roman history (VII), books lvi–lx*, London, Leob Classical Library.

Cary, E. (1969) *Dio Cassius: Roman history (III), books xxxvi–xl*, London, Loeb Classical Library.

Casey, P. J. and B. Hoffman (1999) Excavations at the Roman temple in Lydney Park, Gloucestershire in 1980 and 1981 *The Antiquaries Journal* **79**, 81–143.

Chadwick, J. (1976) *The Mycenaean world*, Cambridge, Cambridge University Press.

Chadwick, N. K. (1970) Early literary contacts between Wales and Ireland, In D. Moore (ed.) *The Irish Sea province*, 66–77, Cardiff, Cambrian Archaeological Association

Charlton, D. B. and M. M. Mitcheson (1983) Yardhope: a shrine to Cocidius, *Britannia* **14**, 143–153.

CIL (1908), *Inscriptiones trium Galliarum et Germaniarum Latinae, voluminis decimi, parties secundae, fasciculus 11*, Berlin, Georgium Reimerum.

Clackson, J. (2007) *Indo-European linguistics: an introduction*, Cambridge, Cambridge University Press.

Clarke, D. L. (1972) A provisional model of an Iron Age society and its settlement system, In D. L. Clarke (eds) *Models in archaeology*, 801–869, London, Cambridge University Press.

Clifford, E. M. (1933) The Roman villa, Hucclecote near Gloucester, *Transactions of the Bristol and Gloucestershire Archaeological Society* **55**, 323–376.

Coates, R. (1991) *The ancient and modern names of the Channel Islands: a linguistic history*, Stamford, Paul Watkins.

Coates, R. (2006) Stour and Blyth as English river-names, *English language and linguistics* **10**, 23–29.

Colgrave, B. and R. A. B. Mynors (1969) *Bede: Ecclesiastical history of the English people*, Oxford, Clarendon Press.

Collis, J. R. (2003) *The Celts: origins, myths, and inventions*, Stroud, Tempus.

Colt Hoare, R. (1819) *The ancient history of North Wiltshire*, London, Lackington, Hughes, Harding, Mavor and Jones.

Cook, M. (1996) The work of the Hereford and Worcester County Council Archaeological Service, 1994–1995, *Transactions of the Worcestershire Archaeological Society (Third Series)* **15**, 347–356.

Cooke, J. J. D. (1939) *Churchdown through the ages*, Gloucester, Privately Published.

Coplestone-Crow, B. (1989) *Herefordshire place-names*, Oxford, British Archaeological Report British Series 214.

Cowan, J. (1989) *Mysteries of the Dream-time*, Bridport, Prism Press.

Cowles, R. (1989) *The making of the Severn railway tunnel*, Stroud, Sutton Publishing.

Coxe, W. (1801) *An historical tour in Monmouthshire: illustrated with views by Sir R. C. Hoare, a new map of the county and other engravings, part 2*, London, T. Cadell and W. Davies.

Crawford, S. (2000), A late Anglo-Saxon sculptural fragment from Worcester Cathedral, *Transactions of the Worcestershire Archaeological Society (Third Series)* **17**, 345–348.

Crawford, S. and C. Guy (1997) As Normans tore down Saxon cathedrals, *British Archaeology* **29**, 7.

Cunliffe, B. (1989) The Roman tholos from the sanctuary of Sulis Minerva at Bath, England, In R. I. Curtis (ed.) *Stvdia pompeiana and classica, in honour of Wilhelima F. Jashemski, volume II: Classica*, New York, Aristide D. Caratzas, Orpheus Press, 59–86.

Cunliffe, B. (1991) *Iron Age communities in Britain (third edition)*, London, Routledge.

Cunliffe, B. and P. Davenport (1985) *The temple of Sulis Minerva at Bath, volume 1(I) the site*, Oxford, Oxford University Committee for Archaeology Monograph 7.

Cunliffe, B., W. and M. G. Fulford (1982) *Corpus of sculpture of the Roman World, volume I fascicule 2: Great Britain, Bath and the rest of Wessex*, Oxford, British Academy.

Dark, K. R. (1993) Town or temenos? A reinterpretation of the walled area of Aquae Sulis, *Britannia* **24**, 254–255.

Dark, K. R. (1994) *Civitas to Kingdom: British political continuity 300–800*, Leicester, Leicester University Press.

Darlington, R. R. and P. McGurk (1995) *The Chronicle of John of Worcester*, Oxford, Clarendon Press.

Darvill, T. (1987) *Prehistoric Britain*, London, Batsford.

Davis, S. J. M. (1987) *The archaeology of animals*, London, Batsford.

Davies, W. (1979) *The Llandaff charters*, Aberystwyth, The National Library of Wales.

de Vries, J. (1963) *La religion des Celts*, Paris, Payot.

Derks, T. (1998) *Gods, temples and ritual practices: the transformation of religious ideas and values in Roman Gaul*, Amsterdam, Amsterdam University Press.

Dickinson, O. (1994) *The Aegean Bronze Age*, Cambridge, Cambridge University Press.

Doig, A. (2008) *Liturgy and architecture: from early church to the middle ages*, Aldershot, Ashgate.

Donovan, H. E. (1933) Excavations at Bourton-on-the-Water, *Transactions of the Bristol and Gloucester Archaeological Society* **55**, 377–381.

Donovan, H. E. (1934a) Excavation of a Romano-British building at Bourton-on-the-Water, Gloucestershire, 1934, *Transactions of the Bristol and Gloucester Archaeological Society* **56**, 99–128.

Donovan, H. E. (1934b) A Roman oven at Bourton-on-the-Water, Gloucestershire, *Transactions of the Bristol and Gloucester Archaeological Society* **56**, 260–265.

Donovan, H. E. (1935) Roman finds in Bourton-on-the-Water, Gloucestershire, *Transactions of the Bristol and Gloucester Archaeological Society* **57**, 234–259.

Drury, P. J. (1984) The temple of Claudius at Colchester reconsidered, *Britannia* **15**, 7–50.

Duff, J. D. (1967) *The civil war, books i–x*, London, Loeb Classical Library.

Durkheim, E. (1964) *The elementary forms of religious life*, London, Allen and Unwin.

Edmonds, M. (1999) *Ancestral geographies of the Neolithic: landscapes, monuments and memory*, London, Routledge.

Edwards, H. J. (1963) *Julius Caesar: The Gallic War*, London, Loeb Classical Press.

Ekwall, E. (1928) *English river-names*, Oxford, Oxford University Press.

Ekwall, E. (1960) *The Oxford dictionary of English place-names (fourth edition)*, Oxford, Oxford University Press.

Ellis Davidson, H. R. (1964) *Gods and myths of Northern Europe*, Harmondsworth, Penguin Books.

Ellis Davidson, H. R. and P. Fisher (1996) *Saxo Grammaticus: The history of the Danes, books I–IX*, Woodbridge, Boydell and Brewer.

Ellis Evans, D. (1967) *Gaulish personal names: a study of some continental Celtic formations*, Oxford, Oxford University Press.

Espérandieu, É. (1907) *Recueil Général des bas-reliefs, statues, et bustes de la Gaule Romaine (tome première): Aquitaine*, Paris, Imprimerie nationale.

Espérandieu, É. (1908) *Recueil Général des bas-reliefs, statues, et bustes de la Gaule Romaine (tome deuxière): Aquitaine*, Paris, Imprimerie nationale.

Espérandieu, É. (1910) *Recueil Général des bas-reliefs, statues, et bustes de la Gaule Romaine (tome troisième): Lyonnaise, première partie*, Paris, Imprimerie Nationale.

Espérandieu, É. (1911) *Recueil Général des bas-reliefs, statues, et bustes de la Gaule Romaine (tome qualtrième): Lyonnaise, deuxième partie*, Paris, Imprimerie Nationale.

Espérandieu, É. (1915) *Recueil Général des bas-reliefs, statues, et bustes de la Gaule Romaine (tome sixième): Belgique, deuxième partie*, Paris, Imprimerie Nationale.

Espérandieu, É. (1918) *Recueil Général des bas-reliefs, statues, et bustes de la Gaule Romaine (tome huitième): Germanie Supérieure*, Paris, Imprimerie Nationale.

Espérandieu, É. (1922) *Recueil Général des bas-reliefs, statues, et bustes de la Gaule Romaine (tome huitième): Gaule Germanique, deuxième partie*, Paris, Imprimerie Nationale.

Espérandieu, É. (1925) *Recueil Général des bas-reliefs, statues, et bustes de la Gaule Romaine (tome neuvième): Gaule Germanique, troisième partie*, Paris, Imprimerie Nationale.

Espérandieu, É. (1928) *Recueil Général des bas-reliefs, statues, et bustes de la Gaule Romaine (tome dixième): suppléments*, Paris, Imprimerie Nationale.

Espérandieu, É. (1938) *Recueil Général des bas-reliefs, statues, et bustes de la Gaule Romaine (tome onzième): suppléments*, Paris, Imprimerie Nationale.

Evans, A. J., J. Nettleship and S. Perry (2008) Linn Liuan/Llynn Llyw: The Wonderous Lake of the Historia Brittonum's de Mirabilibus Britanniae and Culhwch as Olwen, *Folk-lore* **119**, 295–318.

Evelyn-White, H. G. (1919) *Ausonius Decimus Magnus (I)*, London, Loeb Classical Library.

Evelyn-White, H. G. (1921) *Ausonius Decimus Magnus (II)*, London, Loeb Classical Library.

Evelyn-White, H. G. (1982) *Hesiod: The Homeric hymns and Homerica*, London, Loeb Classical Library.

Feuerbach, L. (1957) *The essence of Christianity*, New York, Harper.

Finberg, H. P. R. (1955) *Roman and Saxon Withington: a study in continuity*, Leicester, Leicester University Press.

Finberg, H. P. R. (1964) *The early charters of Wessex*, Leicester, Leicester University Press.

Finberg, H. P. R. (1972) *The early charters of the West Midlands*, Leicester, Leicester University Press.

Fisher (1926) The Welsh Celtic bells, *Archaeologia Cambrensis* **81**, 324–334.

Forcey, C. (1998) Whatever happened to the heroes? Ancestral cults and enigma of Romano-Celtic temples *Theoretical Roman Archaeology Conference* 97, 87–98.

Foster, B. O. (1924) *Livy: History of Rome, books v–vii*, London, Loeb Classical Library.

Foster, B. O. (1984) *Livy: History (III), books v–vii*, London, Loeb Classical Library.

Forster, P., T. Polzin, and A. Röhl (2006) Evolution of English basic vocabulary within the network of Germanic languages. In P. Forster and C. Renfrew (eds) *Phylogenetic methods and the prehistory of languages*, Cambridge, McDonald Institute Monograph Series.

Fowles, J. (1980) *Monumenta Britannica: John Aubrey (1626–97), parts 1 and 2*, Milborne Port, Dorset Publishing Co.

Fowler, P. J. and H. Miles (1971) Excavation, fieldwork and finds, *Archaeological Review* **6**, 11–49.

Frazer, J. G. (1921) *Apollodorus: the library (I), books i–iii*, London, Leob Classical Library.

Frazer, J. G. (1922) *The golden bough (abridged version)*, London, Macmillan Press.

Frazer, J. G. (1989) *Ovid: Fasti*, London, Loeb Classical Library.

Frend, W. H. C. (1955) Relgion in Roman Britain in the fourth century AD, *Journal of the British Archaeological Association* **18**, 1–18.

Frend, W. H. C. (1992) Pagans, Christians and the 'barbarian conspiracy' of AD 367 in Roman Britain, *Britannia* **23**, 121–131.

Frere, S. S. (1992) Roman Britain in 1991: 1, sites explored, *Britannia* **23**, 256–308.

Fullbrook-Leggatt, L. E. W. O. (1933) Glevum, *Transactions of the Bristol and Gloucestershire Archaeological Society* **55**, 55–104.

Gardner, R. (1958), *Cicero: the speeches: Pro Caelio – de Provinciis, con sularibus – pro balbo*, London, Loeb Classical Library.

Geertz, C. (1975) *The interpretation of cultures*, London, Hutchinson.

GEK (1978) *An intermediate Greek-English lexicon founded upon the seventh edition of Liddell and Scott's Greek-English lexicon*, Oxford, Oxford University Press.

Gelling, M. (1953) *The place-names of Oxfordshire: part 1*, Cambridge, Cambridge University Press.

Gelling, M. (1954) *The place-names of Oxfordshire: part 2*, Cambridge, Cambridge University Press.

Gelling, M. (1973) *The place-names of Berkshire: part 1*, Cambridge, Cambridge University Press.

Gelling, M. (1979) *The early charters of the Thames Valley*, Leicester, Leicester University Press.

Gelling, M. (1987) Further thoughts on pagan place-names, In K. Cameron (ed.) *Place-name evidence for the Anglo-Saxon invasion and Scandinavian settlement*, 99–114, Nottingham, English Place-Name Society.

Gelling, M. (1982) The place-name volumes for Worcestershire and Warwickshire, In T. R. Slater and P. J. Jarvis (eds) *Field and forest: an historical geography of Warwickshire and Worcestershire*, 59–78, Norwich, Geo-Books.

Gelling, M. (2006) The place-name Grimstock (earlier Grimscot), *Transactions of the Birmingham and Warwickshire Archaeological Society* **110**, 5–7.

Gerrard, J. (2007) The temple of Sulis Minerva at Bath and the end of Roman Britain, *The Antiquaries Journal* **87**, 148–164.

Giot, P.-R., P. Guigon, and B. Merdrignac (2003) *The British settlement of Brittany: the first Bretons in Armorica*, Stroud, Tempus.

Godley, A. D. (1922) *Herodotus: The Persian wars (III), libri v–vii*, London, Loeb Classical Library.

Godley, A. D. (1926) *Herodotus: The Persian wars (I), libri i–ii*, London, Loeb Classical Library.

Godley, A. D. (1938) *Herodotus: The Persian wars (II), libri iii–iv*, London, Loeb Classical Library.

Goodburn, R. (1979) *The Roman villa Chedworth*, London, The National Trust.

Goold, G. P. (1999) *Virgil: Eclogues, Georgics and Aeneid libri i–vi*, London, Leob Classical Library.

Gover, J. E. B., A. Mawer, and F. Stenton (1934) *The place-names of Surrey*, Cambridge, Cambridge University Press.

Gover, J. E. B., A. Mawer, and F. Stenton (1936) *The place-names of Warwickshire*, Cambridge, Cambridge University Press.

Gover, J. E. B., A. Mawer, and F. Stenton (1939) *The place-names of Wiltshire*, Cambridge, Cambridge University Press.

Graves, R. (1960) *The Greek myths*, London, Penguin.

Gray, M. (1998) Settlement and land use in the Man-moel district of Gwent: monastic and post-monastic evidence, *The Monmouthshire Antiquary* **14**, 14–24.

Green, M. J. (1989) *Symbol and image in Celtic religious art*, London, Routledge.

Green, M. J. (1992) *Animals in Celtic life and myth*, London, Routledge.

Green, M. J. (1992) *Dictionary of Celtic myth and legend*, London, Thames and Hudson.

Green, M. J. (1993) A carved stone head from Steep Holm, *Britannia* **24**, 241–242.

Green, M. J. (1995) *Celtic goddesses: warriors, virgins and mothers*, London, British Museum Press.

Grundy, G. B. (1927) Saxon charters of Worcestershire, *Transactions of the Birmingham Archaeological Society* **52**, 1–183.

Grundy, G. B. (1928) Saxon charters of Worcestershire *Transactions of the Birmingham Archaeological Society* **53**, 18–131.

Grundy, G. B. (1936) *Saxon charters and field names of Gloucestershire*, Gloucester, Bristol and Gloucester Archaeological Society.

Guest, C. (1838) *The Mabinogion from the Llyfr Coch o Hergest, and other ancient Welsh manuscripts, with an English translation and notes, vol. 1*, London, Longman, Brown, Green and Longmans

Guest, C. (1844) *The Mabinogion from the Llyfr Coch o Hergest, and other ancient Welsh manuscripts, with an English translation and notes, vol. 2*, London, Longman, Brown, Green and Longmans

Guest, E. (1862) On the English conquest of the Severn valley, *The Archaeological Journal* **19**, 193–218.

Gwilt, A. (2004) Late Bronze Age societies (1150–600 BC) tools and weapons, In M. J. Aldhouse-Green and R. Howell (eds) *The Gwent county history: volume 1, Gwent in prehistory and early history*, 111–139, Cardiff, University of Wales Press.

Haeussler, R. (2007) The dynamics and contradictions of religious change in Gallia *Narbonensis*, In R. Haeussler and A. C. King (eds) *Continuity and innovation in religion in the Roman West, volume 1*, 81–102, Portsmouth (RI), Journal of Roman Studies Supplement 67.

Harvey, P. (1984) *The Oxford companion to Classical literature*, Oxford, Oxford University Press.

Hatto, A. T. (1980) *Wolfram von Eschenbach: Parzival*, Harmondsworth, Penguin Books.

Hawkes, C. F. C. (1954) Archaeological theory and method: some suggestions from the Old World, *American Anthropologist* **56**, 155–168.

Heighway, C. and A. P. Garrod (1980) Excavations at Nos. 1 and 30 Westgate Street, Gloucester: the Roman levels, *Britannia* **11**, 73–114.

Henig, M. (1984) *Religion in Roman Britain*, London, Batsford.

Henig, M. (1993a) *Corpus of sculpture of the Roman World, Great Britain volume I fascicule 7: Roman sculpture from the Cotswold Region with Devon and Cornwall*, Oxford, British Academy: Oxford University Press.

Henig, M. (1993b) Sculpture in Stone, In A. Woodward and P. Leach (eds) *The Uley shrines: excavation of a ritual complex on West Hill, Uley, Gloucestershire: 1977–9*, 89–101, London, English Heritage Archaeological Report 17.

Henig, M. (1999) A new star shining over Bath, *Oxford Journal of Archaeology* **18 (4)**, 419–425.

Henig, M. (2002) *The heirs of King Verica*, Stroud, Tempus.

Henig, M. (2004) *Corpus of sculpture of the Roman World, Great Britain volume I fascicule 9: Roman sculpture from the North West Midlands*, Oxford, British Academy: Oxford University Press.

Henig, M. (2004) *Murum civitatis, et fontem in ea a Romanis olim constructum*: the arts of Rome in Carlisle and the *civitates* of the *Carvetii* and their influence, In M. R. McCarthey and D. Weston (eds) *Carlile and Cumbria: Roman and medieval architecture, art, and archaeology*, 11–28, British Archaeological Association Conference Transactions at Carlisle 2004.

Henig, M. (2007) Statuettes and figurines in Roman Britain, *The Bulletin of the Association for Roman Archaeology (ARA)* **18**, 11–17.

Henig, M. (2008) 'And did those feet in ancient times': Christian churches and pagan shrines in South-east Britain, In D. Ruding (ed.) *Ritual landscapes of Roman South-east England*, 188–204, Oxford, Oxbow.

Henig, M., D. Brown, D. Baatz, N. Sunter and L. Allason-Jones (1988) Objects from the sacred spring, In B. Cunliffe (ed.) *The temple of Sulis Minerva at Bath, volume 2: the finds from the sacred spring*, 5–35, Oxford, Oxford University Committee for Archaeology monograph 16.

Henig, M., R. Cleary, and P. Purser (2000) A relief of Mercury and Minerva from Aldsworth, Gloucestershire, *Britannia* **31**, 362–363.

Hill, J. S. (1914) *The place-names of Somerset*, Bristol, Saint Stephen's Printing Works.

Hillaby, J. (2008) Book review: the Tribe of Witches: the religion of the Dobunni and Hwicce by Stephen Yeates *Worcestershire Recorder* **78**, 20–21.

Hingley, R. (1984) Towards a social analysis in archaeology: Celtic society in the Iron Age of the Upper Thames Valley, In B. Cunliffe and D. Miles (eds) *Aspects of the Iron Age in central southern Britain*, 72–88, Oxford, Oxford University Committee of Archaeology Monograph 2.

Holbrook, N. (2003) Great Witcombe Roman villa, Gloucestershire: field surveys of its fabric and environs, 1999–2000, *Transactions of the Bristol and Gloucestershire Archaeological Society* **121**, 179–200.

Howell, R. (2004) From the fifth to the seventh century, In M. J. Aldhouse-Green and R. Howell (eds) *The Gwent county history: volume 1, Gwent in prehistory and early history*, 244–268, Cardiff, University of Wales Press.

Hooper, W. D. and H. B. Ash (1934) *Marcus Porcius Cato: On agriculture; and Marcus Terentius Varro: On agriculture*, London, Loeb Classical Library.

Hornblower, S. and A. Spawforth (1996) *The Oxford classical dictionary (3rd edition)*, Oxford, Oxford University Press.

Hurst, H. (1977) The prehistoric occupation on Churchdown Hill, *Transactions of the Bristol and Gloucestershire Archaeological Society* **95**, 5–10.

Hurst, J. D., E. A. Pearson and S. Ratkai (1995) *Salvage recording at the Wagon Wheel, Grimley, Worcestershire*, Worcester, Archaeological Services, Hereford and Worcester County Council Report 380.

Huskinson, J. (1994) *Corpus of sculpture of the Roman world, Great Britain: volume I fascicule 8: Roman sculpture from Eastern England*, Oxford, Oxford University Press.

Hutton, M., R. M. Ogilvie, E. H. Warmington, W. Peterson, and M. Winterbottom (1970) *Tacitus: Agricola, Germania, Dialogus*, London, Loeb Classical Library.

Hutton, R. B. (1991) *The pagan religions of the ancient British Isles: their nature and legacy*, Oxford, Blackwell.

Hutton, R. B. (1996) *The stations of the Sun: a history of the ritual year in Britain*, Oxford, Oxford University Press.

Jackson, H. (1921) *Appollodorus: The library*, London, Loeb Classical Library.

Jackson, J. E. (1864) Malmesbury, *Wiltshire Archaeological and Natural History Magazine* **8**, 14–50.

Jackson, K. H. (1953) *Language and history in early Britain: a chronological survey of the Brittonic languages first to twelfth centuries AD*, Edinburgh, Edinburgh University Press.

Jackson, K. H. (1964) *The oldest Irish tradition: a window on the Iron Age*, Cambridge, Cambridge University Press.

Jackson, K. H. (1982) Rhal Sylwadau ar Kulhwch ac Olwen, *Ysgrifau Beirniadol* **12**, 12–23.

Jackson, R. and G. Burleigh (2007) The Senuna treasure and shrine at Ashwell (Herts), In R. Haeussler and A. C. King (eds) *Continuity and innovation in religion in the Roman West, volume 1*, 37–54, Portsmouth, Journal of Roman Archaeology Supplementary Series 67.

Jefferies, J. (2007) *Cheese rolling in Gloucestershire*, Stroud, Tempus.

Jones, G. and T. Jones (1974) *The Mabinogion*, London, Dent.

Jones, H. L. (1923) *Strabo: The geography (II), libri iii–v*, London, Leob Classical Library.

Jones, W. H. S. (1935) *Pausanias: Description of Greece (IV): libri vii(22)–x*, London, Loeb Classical Library.

Kennerley, E. (1971) Caerleon in literature, *Presenting Monmouthshire: The Journal of the Monmouthshire Local History Council* **32**, 30–41.

Kerényi, K. (1979) *Goddesses of sun and moon*, Dallas, Spring Publication.

Kerényi, K. (1986) *Hermes guide of souls*, Dallas, Spring Publication.

Knight, J., K. (1971) Saint Tatheus of Caerwent: an analysis of the Vespasian life, *The Monmouthshire Antiquary* **3 (1)**, 29–36.

Knight, J., K. (1993) The early church in Gwent, II: the early medieval church, *The Monmouthshire Antiquary* **9**, 1–17.

Knight, J., K. (2001) City of Arthur, city of the legions: Antiquaries and writers at Caerleon, *The Monmouthshire Antiquary* **17**, 47–54.

Knight, J., K. (2004) Society and religion in the early middle ages, In M. J. Aldhouse-Green and R.

Howell (eds) *The Gwent county history: volume 1, Gwent in prehistory and early history*, 269–286, Cardiff, University of Wales Press.

Kovacs, D. (1999) *Euripides: Trojan Women, Iphigenia among the Taurians, and Ion*, London, Loeb Classical Library.

Loomis, R. S. (1963) *The grail: from Celtic myth to Christian symbol*, New York, Columbia University Press.

Macray, W. D. (1863) *Chronicon Abbatiæ de Evesham*, London, Chronicles and memorials of Great Britain and Ireland during the Middle Ages.

Magilton, J. R. (2006) A Romano-Celtic temple and settlement at Grimstock Hill, Coleshill, Warwickshire *Transactions of the Birmingham and Warwickshire Archaeological Society* **110**, 1–231.

Mahon (1848) Thursday, May 11th, 1848, *Proceedings of the Society of Antiquaries of London* **1 (13)**, 262–264.

Mallory, J. P. (1989) *In search of the Indo-Europeans*, London, Thames and Hudson.

Marsden, P. (1987) *The Roman Forum site in London: discoveries before 1985*, London, HMSO.

Mason, D. (2000) Chester: the elliptical building, *Current Archaeology* **167**, 404–413.

Mason, E. (1962) *Wace and Layamon: Arthurian chronicles*, London, Dent and Sons.

Matthews, J. H. (1912) *Collections towards the history and antiquities of the County of Hereford: in continuation of Duncumb's history, Hundred of Wormelow (upper division part 1)*, Hereford, Jakeman and Carver.

Matthews, J. H. (1913) *Collections towards the history and antiquaries of the county of Hereford in continuation of Duncumb's history: Hundred of Wormlow (Lower Division part 1)*, Hereford, Jakeman and Carver, Hightown.

Mawer, A. and F. M. Stenton (1926) *The place-names of Bedfordshire and Huntingdonshire*, Cambridge, Cambridge University Press.

Mawer, A. and F. M. Stenton (1927) *The place-names of Worcestershire*, Cambridge, Cambridge University Press.

Mawer, C. F. (1995) *Evidence for Christianity in Roman Britain: the small-finds*, Oxford, British Archaeological Report British Series 243.

Maltwood, K. E. (1964) *A guide to Glastonbury temple of the stars*, Cambridge, James Clarke and Co.

Maltwood, K. E. (1982) *Enchantments of Britain*, Cambridge, James Clarke and Co.

Marx, K. and F. Engels (1957) *On religion*, Moscow, Progress.

Medland, M. H. (1895) An account of Roman and medieval remains found on the site of the Tolsey at Gloucester, *Transactions of the Bristol and Gloucestershire Archaeological Society* **19**, 142–158.

Miller, F. J. (1984) *Ovid: Metamorphoses (II), books ix–xv*, London, Leob Classical Library.

Miller, F. J. and G. P. Goold (1977) *Ovid: Metamorphoses (I), books i–viii*, London, Loeb Classical Library.

Miller, W. G. (1965) *The Red Horse of Tysoe*, K. A. Carrdus.

Millett, M. (1990) *The Romanization of Britain: an essay in archaeological interpretation*, Cambridge, Cambridge University Press.

Moffatt, J. M. (1805), *The history of the town of Malmesbury and its ancient abbey*, Tetbury, J. G. Goodwyn.

Moore, J., S. (1982), *Domesday Book: Gloucestershire*, Chichester, Phillimore.

Moore, T. (2006) *Iron Age societies in the Severn-Cotswolds: developing narratives of social and landscape change*, Oxford, British Archaeological Report British Series 421.

Morris, B. (1987) *Anthropological studies of religion: an introductory text*, Cambridge, Cambridge: University Press.

Morris, J. (1973) *The age of Arthur: a history of the British Isles from 350 to 650*, London, Weidenfeld.

Morris, J. (1980) *Nennius: British History and the Welsh Annals*, Chichester, Phillimore.

Morgan, R. (2005) *Place-names of Gwent*, Llanrwst, Gwasg Carreg Gwalch.

Morgan, R. and R. F. P. Powell (1999) *A study of Breconshire place-names*, Llanwrst, Gwasg Carreg Gwalch.

Most, G. W. (2006) *Hesiod: Theogony, Works and Days, Testimonia*, London, Loeb Classical Library.

Müller, F. M. (1889) *Natural religion*, London, Longmans.

Mullin, D. (2003) *The Bronze Age landscape of the northern English Midlands*, Oxford, British Archaeological Report British Series 351.

Murray, A. T. and W. F. Wyatt (1999) *Homer. Iliad (I), libri xiii–xxiv*, London, Loeb Classical Library.

Murray, M. A. (1921) *The witch-cult in Western Europe*, Oxford, Oxford University Press.

Nash, D. W. (1858) *Taliesin; or the bards and druids of Britain, a translation of the remains of the earliest Welsh bards, and an examination of the bardic mysteries*, London, John Russell Smith.

Northcote Toller, T. (1898) *An Anglo-Saxon dictionary based on the manuscript collections of Joseph Bosworth*, Oxford, Oxford University Press.

Northcote Toller, T. and A. Campbell (1921) *An Anglo-Saxon dictionary based on the manuscript collections of Joseph Bosworth: a supplement, revised and enlarged*, Oxford, Oxford University Press.

Neuerburg, N. (1975) *Herculaneum to Malibu: a companion to the visit of the J. Paul Getty Museum building: a description and explanatory guide to the re-created ancient Roman villa of the Papyri built at the wishes of J. Paul Getty in Malibu, California, 1970–1974*, Malibu, J. Paul Getty Museum.

O'Duinn, S. (2005) *The rites of Brigid: goddess and saint*, Dublin, The Columba press.

Oldfather, C. H. (1939) *Diodorus Siculus: library of history, libri iv.59–viii*, London, Loeb Classical Library.

Olding, F. (1987) Gwent and the Arthurian legend, *Gwent Local History: Journal of the Gwent Local History Council* **63**, 23–29.

Olding, F. (2000) *The prehistoric landscapes of the Eastern Black Mountains*, Oxford, British Archaeological Report Britsih Series 297.

Oppenheimer, S. (2006) *The origins of the British*, London, Robinson.

O'Rahilly, T. F. (1946) *Early Irish history and mythology*, Dublin, Dublin Institute for Advanced Studies.

Otto, W. F. (1981) *Dionysus: Myth and Cult*, Dallas, Spring Publications.

Owen, D. D. R. (1987) *Chretien de Troyes: Arthurian romances*, London, Dent and Son.

Owen, H. W. and R. Morgan (2007) *Dictionary of the place-names of Wales*, Ceredigion, Gomer Press.

Owen-Crocker, G. R. (1981) *Rites and religions of the Anglo-Saxons*, Newton Abbots, David and Charles Publishers.

Padel, O. J. (1985) *Cornish place-name elements*, Nottingham, English Place-Name Society.

Palmer, R. (1994) *The folklore of Gloucestershire*, Tiverton, Westcountry Books.

Parker Pearson, M. (1996) Food, fertility and front doors in the first millennium BC, In T. Champion and J. R. Collis (eds) *The Iron-Age in Britain and Ireland: recent trends*, 117–132, Sheffield, Sheffield University Press.

Parker Pearson, M. and C. Richards (1994) *Architecture and order: approaches to social space*, London, Routledge.

Paton (1922) *Polybius: The histories, books i–ii*, London, Loeb Classical Library.

Paton (1922) *Polybius: The histories, books iii–iv*, London, Loeb Classical Library.

Pearson, M. K. (1909) *Chipping Norton in bygone days: a brief sketch of the history of the town from pre-historic times to the close of the nineteenth century*, Chipping Norton, W. C. Hayes.

Petrie, W. M. F. (1926) *The hill figures of England*, London, Royal Anthropological Institute of Great Britain and Ireland.

Petts, D. (2003) *Christianity in Roman Britain*, Stroud, Tempus.

Pierce, G. O. (2002) *Place-names in Glamorganshire*, Cardiff, Merton Priory Press.

Pike, A. (1992) A review: South Midlands archaeology, *South Midlands Archaeology* 22, 4–76.

Pollard, J. (1977) *Birds in Greek life and myth*, London, Thames and Hudson.

Pretty, K. (1989) Defining the Magonsæte, In S. Bassett (ed.) *The origins of Anglo-Saxon kingdoms*, 171–183, Leicester, Leicester University Press.

Pryor, F. M. M. (1991) *The English Heritage book of Flag Fen: prehistoric Fenland centre*, London, Batsford.

Ptolemaeus, C. (1966) *Geographia*, Amsterdam, Theatrum Orbis Terrarvm Ltd.

Rackham, H. (1938) *Pliny the Elder: Natural history (I), libri. i–ii*, London, Loeb Classical Library.

Raftery, B. (1994) *Pagan Celtic Ireland: the enigma of the Irish Iron Age*, London, Thames and Hudson.

Rahtz, P. A. (1971) West Midlands archaeology: fieldwork, *West Midlands Archaeological News Sheet* 14, 6–38.

Rahtz, P. A. (1991) Pagan and Christian by the Severn Sea, In L. Abrams and J. P. Carley (eds) *The archaeology and history of Glastonbury abbey: essays in honour of the ninetieth birthday of C. A. Raleigh Radford*, 3–37, Woodbridge, Boydell Press.

Rahtz, P. A. and L. Watts (1976) The end of the temples in the West of Britain, In K. Branigan and P. J. Fowler (eds) *The Roman West Country: Classical culture and Celtic society*, 183–210, Newton Abbot, David and Charles.

Ralston, I. (2006) *Celtic Fortifications*, Stroud, Tempus.

Rankin, D. (1987) *Celts and the Classical World*, London, Routledge.

Rawes, B. (1984) The Romano-British site on the Portway, near Gloucester, *Transactions of the Bristol and Gloucester Archaeological Society* 102, 23–72.

Reaney, P. H. (1943) *The place-names of Cambridgeshire and the Isle of Ely*, Cambridge, Cambridge University Press.

Rhys, J. (1862) *Lectures on the origin and growth of religion as illustrated by Celtic heathendom*, London, Williams and Norgate.

Rhys, J. (1901) *Celtic Folklore: Welsh and Manx*, Oxford, Oxford University Press.

Rhys, J. (1910) *The Coligny calendar*, London, British Academy.

RIB(I) (1995) *The Roman inscriptions of Britain I: inscriptions on stone*, Stroud, Alan Sutton.

Rivet, A. L. F. and C. Smith (1979) *The place-names of Roman Britain*, London, B. T. Batsford.

Rolfe, J. C. (1931) *Sallust: Catiline, Jugurtha, and Histories*, London, Loeb Classical Library.

Rolfe, J. C. (1950) *Ammianus Marcellinus: History, books xiv–xix*, London, Loeb Classical Library.

Roscher, H. H. (1897–1909) *Ausführliches lexikon der Griechischen und Römischen mythologie, vol. 3*, Leipzig, B. G. Teubner.

Ross, A. (1967) *Pagan Celtic Britain*, London, Routledge and Keegan Paul.

Ross, A. (1968) Shafts, pits, wells – sanctuaries of the Belgic Britons? In J. M. Coles and D. D. A. Simpson (eds) *Studies in ancient Europe: essays presented to Stuart Piggott*, 255–285, Leicester, Leicester University Press.

Rudd, C. (2003) Ash and the Dobunnic tree, *Chris Rudd List* 72, 7–14.

Rudder, S. (1779) *A new history of Gloucestershire (comprising the topography antiquities, curiosities, produce, trade, and manufactures of the that county)*, Cirencester, Samuel Rudder.

Rushton Fairclough, H. (1999) *Virgil: Eclogues, Georgics, Aeneid i–vi*, London, Loeb Classical Library.

Saint Clair Baddeley, W. (1924) *History of Cirencester. Cirencester*, Cirencester Newspaper Co. Ltd.

Savory, H. N. (1984) *Glamorgan county history II: early Glamorgan, pre-history and early history*, Cardiff, Glamorgan County History Trust.

Seaton, R. C. (1912) *Apollonius Rhodius: Argonautica*, London, Loeb Classical Library.

Serjeantson, D. (1991) The bird bones, In B. Cunliffe and C. Poole (eds) *Danebury, an Iron Age hillfort in Hampshire, volume 5: the excavations 1979–1988: the finds*, 479–481, York, Council for British Archaeology Research Report 73.

Sherratt, E. S. (1992) Reading the texts': archaeology and the Homeric question, In C. Emlyn-Jones, L. Hardwick and J. Purkis (eds) *Homer: readings and images*, 145–165, London, Duckworth.

Shipley, G., J. Vanderspoel, D. Mattingly and L. Foxhall (2006) *The Cambridge dictionary of Classical civilization*, Cambridge, Cambridge University Press.

Shoesmith, R. (1991) *Excavations at Chepstow 1973–1974*, Bangor, Cambrian Archaeological Monograph 4.

Simpson, C. J. (1993) Once again, Claudius and the temple at Colchester, *Britannia* **24**, 1–6.

Simpson, J. (1994) Margaret Murray: who believed her, and why? *Folk-lore* **105**, 89–96.

Sims-Williams, P. (1983) The settlement of England in Bede and the Chronicle, *Anglo-Saxon England* **12**, 1–41.

Sims-Williams, P. (1990) *Religion and literature in Western England 600–800*, Cambridge, Cambridge University Press.

Smith, A. H. (1956) *English place-name elements: part 1*, Cambridge, Cambridge University Press.

Smith, A. H. (1964a) *The place-names of Gloucestershire: part 1, the rivers and road names, the East Cotswolds*, Cambridge, Cambridge University Press.

Smith, A. H. (1964b) *The place-names of Gloucestershire: part 2, the North and West Cotswolds*, Cambridge, Cambridge University Press.

Smith, A. H. (1964c) *The place-names of Gloucestershire: part 3, the lower Severn Valley, the Forest of Dean*, Cambridge, Cambridge University Press.

Smith, A. H. (1965) *The place-names of Gloucestershire: part 4, introduction, bibliography, analyses, index, maps*, Cambridge, Cambridge University Press.

Smith, C. R. and T. Wright (1847) On certain mythic personages mentioned on Roman altars found in England and on the Rhine, *Journal of the British Archaeological Association* **2**, 239–255.

Smith, L. T. and T. Kendrick (1964) *The itinerary of John Leland in or about the yeas 1536–1539, part vi, volume 3*, London, Centaur Press.

Spence, L. (1931) *The mysteries of Britain or the secret rites and traditions of ancient Britain restored*, London, Rider.

Spencer, H. (1876) *The principles of sociology (3 volumes)*, London, Williams and Morgate.

Sproul, B. C. (1979) *Primal Myths: creating the world*, London, Rider.

Stealens, Y. J. E. (1982) The Birdlip cemetery, *Transactions of the Bristol and Gloucestershire Archaeological Society* **100**, 19–31.

Swift, W. T. (1905) *Some account of the history of Churchdown*, Gloucester, Wellington and Co.

Taylor, C. S. (1900) Bath: Mercian and West Saxon, *Transactions of the Bristol and Gloucester Archaeological Society* **23**, 129–161.

Terry, W. N. (1953) A bronze spearhead from Moreton-in-Marsh, *Transactions of the Bristol and Gloucestershire Archaeological Society* **72**, 150.

Thomas, C. (1981) *Christianity in Roman Britain to AD 500*, London, Batsford.

Thomas, R. (1989) The bronze-iron transition in southern England, In M. L. S. Sorensen and R. Thomas (eds) *The Bronze Age–Iron Age transition in Europe*, 263–286, Oxford, British Archaeological Report International Series 483.

Thomas, R. J. (1938) *Enwau afonydd a nentydd Cymru*, Cardiff, Gwasg Prifysgol Cymru.

Thorn, C. and F. Thorn (1979) *Domesday Book: Wiltshire*, Chichester, Phillimore.

Thornton, D. E. (1991) Glastonbury and the *Glastening*, In L. Abrams and J. P. Carley (eds) *The *archaeology and history of Glastonbury abbey: essays in honour of the ninetieth birthday of C. A. Raleigh Radford*, 191–203, Woodbridge, Boydell Press.

Thorpe, L. (1966) *Geoffrey of Monmouth: The history of the kings of Britain*, London, The Folio Society.

Tierney, J. J. (1960) The Celts ethnography of Poseidonius, *Proceedings of the Royal Irish Academy* **60**, 189–275.

Tilley, C. (1994) *A phenomenology of landscape: places, paths and monuments*, Oxford, Berg.

Tolkien, J. R. R. (1932) The name 'Nodens', In R.E. M. Wheeler and T. V. Wheeler (eds) *Report on the excavation of the prehistoric, Roman, and post-Roman site in Lydney Park, Gloucestershire*, 132–137, Oxford, The Society of Antiquaries.

Tomlin, R. S. O. (1993) The inscribed lead tablets: an interim report, In A. Woodward and P. Leach (eds) *The Uley Shrines: excavation of a ritual complex on West Hill, Uley, Gloucestershire: 1977–9*, 113–130, London, English Heritage Archaeological Report 17.

Tomlin, R. S. O. (2008) *Dea Senuna*: a new goddess from Britain, *Instrumenta Inscripta Latina* II, 305–315.

Tomlin, R. S. O. and M. W. C. Hassall (2003) Roman Britain in 2002: 2, inscriptions *Britannia* **34**, 361–382.

Tomlinson, R. A. (1976) *Greek Sanctuaries*, London, Book Club Association.

Toynbee, J. M. C. (1964) *Art in Britain under the Romans*, Oxford, Clarendon Press.

Tredennick, H. (1933) *Aristotle: Metaphysics (I), books i–ix*, London, Loeb Classical Library.

Tylor, E. B. (1913) *Primitive culture*, London, Murray.

Underwood, G. (1969) *The pattern of the past*, London, Museum Press.

van Arsdell, R. D. and P. de Jersey (1994) *The coinage of the Dobunni: money supply and coin circulation in Dobunnic territory with a gazetteer of findspots*, Oxford, Oxford University Committe for Archaeology.

VCH(Ox1) (1939) *The Victoria history of the counties of England: a history of Oxford 1*, London, Oxford University Press.

VCH(Wo1) (1901) *The Victoria history of the counties of England: a history of Worcestershire 1*, Haymarket, James Street.

von Däniken, E. (1969) *Chariots of the gods: unsolved mysteries of the past*, London, Souvenir.

Wade-Evans, A. W. (1920) Saint Paulinus of Wales, *Archaeologia Cambrensis (Sixth Series)* **20**, 159–178.

Walker, T. A. (1891) *The Severn tunnel: its construction and difficulties 1872–1887 (third edition)*, Bath, Kingsmead Reprints.

Waters, G. (1999) *The story of Churchdown*, King's Stanley, Past Histories.

Waters, I. (1952) *About Chepstow*, Chepstow, The Newport and Monmouth branch of the Historical Association and Chepstow Society.

Watkins, A. (1918–20) Archaeology, *Transactions of the Woolhope Naturalists' Field Club* **23**, 129–131.

Watkins, A. (1923) Archaeology, *Transactions of the Woolhope Naturalists' Field Club* **24 (3)**, 286–289.

Watkins, A. (1924) Archaeology, *Transactions of the Woolhope Naturalists' Field Club* **25 (1)**, 80–82.

Watkins, A. (1925) *The old straight track*, London, Methuen and Co.

Watkins, A. (1928) Archaeology, *Transactions of the Woolhope Naturalists' Field Club* **26**, 228–231.

Watkins, A. (1931) Archaeology, 1931, *Transactions of the Woolhope Naturalists' Field Club* **27 (2)**, 134–135.

Watkins, A. (1931) A Romano-British pottery in Hereford, *Transactions of the Woolhope Naturalists' Field Club* **27 (2)**, 110–112.

Watkins, A. (1932) Archaeology 1932, *Transactions of the Woolhope Naturalists' Field Club* **27 (3)**, 184–191.

Watts, D. J. (1991) *Christians and pagans in Roman Britain*, London, Routledge.

Watts, D. J. (1998) *Religion in late Roman Britain*, London, Routledge.

Watts, V. (2004) *The Cambridge dictionary of English place-names*, Cambridge, Cambridge University Press.

Webster, J. (1995a) *Interpretatio*: Roman word power and the Celtic gods, *Britannia* **26**, 153–161.

Webster, J. (1995b), Translation and subjection: Interpretatio and the Celtic gods, In J. D. Hill and C. G. Cumberpatch (eds) *Different Iron Ages: studies on the Iron Age of temperate Europe*, 175–183, Oxford, British Archaeological Report International Series 602.

Wedlake, W. J. (1982) *The excavation of the shrine of Apollo at Nettleton, Wiltshire, 1956–1971*, London, The Society of Antiquaries of London.

Weir, A. and J. Jerman (1986), *Images of lust: Sexual carvings in medieval churches*, London, Batsford.

Weir Smyth, H. (1922), *Aeschylus (I): Suppliant maidens, Persians, Prometheus, and Seven against Thebes*, London, Loeb Classical Library.

Wells, P. S. (2003) *The battle that stopped Rome: Emperor Augustus, Arminius, and the slaughter of the legions in the Teutoburg Forest*, New York, W. W. Norton.

Westwood, J. O. (1849) On the ancient portable hand-bells of the British and Irish churches, *Archaeologia Cambrensis* **4**, 167–176.

Wheeler, R. E. M. and T. V. Wheeler (1932) *Report on the excavation of the prehistoric, Roman, and post-Roman site in Lydney Park, Gloucestershire*, Oxford, The Society of Antiquaries.

White, R. (2007), *Britannia Prima*, Stroud, Tempus.

Whittaker, C. R. (1970) *Herodian: History of the Empire from the time of Marcus Aurelius (II), books v–viii*, London, Loeb Classical Library.

Wiseman, T. P. (2004) *The myths of Rome*. Exeter, University of Exeter Press.

Wiseman, T. P. (2008) *Unwritten Rome*, Exeter, Exeter University Press.

Woodward, A. (1992) *English Heritage book of Shrines and sacrifice*. London, Batsford.

Woodward, A. (1993) The cult of relics in prehistoric Britain, In M. Carver (ed.) *In search of cult*, 1–7, Woodbridge, Boydell Press.

Woodward, A. and P. Leach (1993) *The Uley Shrines: excavations of a ritual complex on West Hill, Uley, Gloucestershire: 1977–9*, London, English Heritage Archaeological Report 17.

Worcestre, W. (1969) *William Worcestre itineraries: edited from the unique ms Corpus Christi College, Cambridge, 210*, Oxford, Clarendon Press.

Worcestre, W. and F. Neale (2000) William Worcestre: the topography of medieval Bristol *Bristol Record Society Series* **51**.

Wright, N. (1985) *The historia regum Britannie of Geoffrey of Monmouth, I, Bern, Burgerbibliothek, MS. 568*, Woodbridge, Boydell and Brewer.

Wright, R. P. and M. W. C. Hassall (1973) Roman Britain in 1972: 2, inscriptions, *Britannia* **4**, 324–337.

White, R. (2007) *Britannia Prima*, Stroud, Tempus.

Yeates, S. J. (2004) The Cotswolds, the *Codeswellan*, and the goddess Cuda, *Glevensis* **37**, 2–8.

Yeates, S. J. (2005) *Religion, community, and territory: defining religion in the Severn valley and adjacent hills from the Iron Age to the early medieval period*, D.Phil. thesis Institute of Archaeology. Oxford, University of Oxford.

Yeates, S. J. (2006a) *Religion, community and territory: defining religion in the Severn Valley and adjacent hill from the Iron Age to the early medieval period (3 volumes)*, British Archaeological Report British Series 411 (i–ii–iii).

Yeates, S. J. (2006b) River-names, Celtic and Old English: their dual medieval and post-medieval personalities, *Journal of the English Place-name Society* **38**, 63–81.

Yeates, S. J. (2007). Religion and tribe in the Northwest Provinces: a goddess for the *Dobunni*, In R. Haussler and A. C. King (eds) *Continuity and innovation in religion in the Roman West, volume*

1, 55–69, Portsmouth (RI), Journal of Roman Studies Supplement 67.

Yeates, S. J. (2008a) The religion of the Dobunni with some clues from their coins, *Chris Rudd List* **101**, 2–4.

Yeates, S. J. (2008b) *The tribe of witches: the religion of the* Dobunni *and* Hwicce, Oxford, Oxbow Books.

Yeates, S. J. (forthcoming) Senuna, goddess of the river Rhee or Henney, *Proceedings of the Cambridgeshire Antiquarian Society*.

Index

Aachen (Germany) 121
Aberbaidon (Breconshire) 112
Aberdeenshire (Scotland) 105
Abergavenny (Gwent) 75
Academy, Athens (Greece) 148–149
Achelous/Aspropotamus (River) 78
Acheron (River) 34, 85, 89
Achilles 90
Acropolis, Athens (Greece) 36, 84
Aedui/Haedui (Gallic tribe) 5–7, 93, 150
Aegean 37, 40
Aegesta 92
Aegina (Greece) 32, 87
Aeolos/Aeolic (Greece) 33–34
Aeron (River) 102
Aeschylus 5
Aesepus (River) 78
Aesir 50–51
Aesius (River) 121
Aestii (Germanic tribe) 80, 143
Africa 2, 4–5
Akragas (Italy) 32
Akrisos (King) 88
Alaun-/Alne (River) 108
Alaunos, Mercury 108
Alaw (River) 102
Albanactus 73
Albula 92
Alci 57
Alde (River) 24, 172
Alder 99, 106, 108
Aldescus (River) 78
Aldhouse-Green, Miranda 3, 99, 115, 144–145, 166, 198
Aldsworth (Gloucestershire) 16, 156–157, 159
Alexandria (Egypt) 5

Alfred the Great 21
All Hallows/All Souls 4
Allen, Derek 7
Allerey (France) 94
Allobroges (Gallic tribe) 7
Aloeids 171
Alne (River), see Alaun-
Alpheios (River) 78, 85–86
Alor (Brook) 60
Alose/shad 108
Alps 5, 7
Amalthea 31
Amathus 39
Ambarri (Gallic tribe) 6
Amber 98
Ambigatus (King) 53
Ambrosius Aurelius 26
Amimonedos/Amimonedum (River) 108, 110
America 2, 4–5
Amman (River) 101–102, 108
Ammergau (River) 111
Ammianus Marcellinus (Historian) 29, 146–147
Amnisos, cave (Greece) 41
Amper (River) 111
Amphitrite 33
Ampney (Brook) 108
Amwell (Brook) 108
Amyklai (Cyprus) 38
Amymone (River) 86, 92, 109
Amyr/Amr (River) 111, 173, 187–188
Ancamna (Spring) 93
Angles 26, 81
Anglesey/Mona 150, 173
Anglian 64
Anglo-Saxon 17–18, 20, 58, 64, 66–68, 70–71, 77, 107, 111, 129–130, 163, 179, 183, 190, 203, 210

Anglo-Saxon Charters 134
Anthropology 2, 4
Antioch-on-the-Orontes 79, 147
Apam Napat 45
Apennines (Italy) 92
Aphrodite 35–37, 39–41, 48, 90, 92
Apollo 37–39, 42, 56–57, 75, 84–85, 88, 90, 93–94, 97–98, 113, 118, 147
Apollo Moritasgus 145
Apollodorus 6, 139
Apple-tree 106
Aquae Calidae 175
Aquitaine (France) 113
Arcadia (Greece) 89
Archbishopric(s) 12
Archenfield/Ergyng (Herefordshire) 107, 173, 187
Arden, Forest of (Warwickshire) 14, 63–64, 109–110, 206
Ardennes (Belgium/France) 121
Arduinna/Arduenna (Forest) 110–111
Ares 36–37, 87
Arethusa 86
Aretium 92
Arfon (Wales) 101
Arges 140
Argita (River) 100
Argive(s) (Greece) 33, 50, 84, 88, 92
Argonautica 139
Argos, whirlpool (Greece) 33, 86
Argyll 173
Argyra 90
Ariadne 41
Aristotle 5, 30, 148–149
Aroanios (River) 86, 90
Arnemetia (Spring) 102
Arroux (Spring) 97
Arrow (River) 108
Artaios 98, 103
Artemis 38, 46, 84, 86, 88, 91
Arthur/Arthurian 72, 76, 101, 111, 114, 117, 188–189, 203–206, 208
Arthur's Chest (Gwent) 206, 208
Artio (River) 98, 103
Arverni (Gallic tribe) 5–7
Asclepiadae 149
Ascones (Iberian tribe) 7
Ascra (Greece) 139
Ash tree 98, 106, 128, 162, 185–186, 195

Ashcroft, Cirencester (Gloucestershire) 74, 151, 153
Ashwell (Hertfordshire) 129
Asia 4–5, 166
Asia Minor 84, 139, 199
Askalaphos 85
Asopos (River) 86–87
Astarte 39
Asterion 88
Astley (Worcestershire) 23
Atalanta 88
Atarneus 149
Atepomarus 93
Athelstan (Bishop) 18
Athena 31, 35–36, 38, 40, 42, 44, 56, 84, 91
Athens/Athenian (Greece) 33, 36, 40, 40, 42, 148
Atlantic 5
Atlantis 149
Atlas 135
Atrebates (British tribe) 8, 19
Attica/Attic (Greece) 38, 41
Aubrey, John (Antiquarian) 156
Auðhumla 143
Aufaniae 160
Augean Stables (Greece) 86
Augustus 4
Aulerci (Gallic tribe) 6
Aurivandala 65
Ausoba (River) 100
Ausonius 75
Aust (Gloucestershire) 59
Auster 141
Australia/Australian 1–2, 81, 84, 86, 99, 136, 203
Austria 166
Avalon, Isle of 206
Avebury (Wiltshire) 170
Aventia/Ewenni (River) 103
Aventine Hill, Rome 42, 45
Avignon (France) 13
Avon-Bristol (River) 21, 24, 174, 178, 188
Axe (River), 123

Bablock Hythe (Oxfordshire) 130
Bacchus 41, 49
Baco 98
Badbury (Dorset) 128
Badmardi (Australian tribe) 84

Badsey (Worcestershire) 111
Badsæta (Folk-group) 112–113
Bagendon (Gloucestershire) 189
Bal- (River) 111, 135
Balder 51
Balkan/Balkans 93, 209
Baltic 80
Bampton (Oxfordshire) 19
Bangor (Gwynedd) 173
Banw (River) 101, 103
Barbourne (Brook) 111
Barley 101
Barhill (Scotland) 115
Barrow Wake, see Birdlip
Barvaria 204
Bassaleg (Gwent) 68
Bath/Badon (Somerset) 21, 66–67, 71, 75, 129, 151,
    153, 155–158, 173–174, 176, 178–179, 184, 207
Bathwick (Somerset) 153
Batsford (Gloucestershire) 24
Bayley, Harold 2, 4
Beane (River) 72
Bear 38, 86, 99, 103, 106
Beaver 108, 111
Bebro- (River) 111
Beda (River) 111, 112
Bede (Historian) 20, 26, 67
Bedfordshire 65
Beech tree 94
Beehive 95
Beetle 104
Beferic (Brook) 111
Beire-le-Châtel (France) 94
Belgae/Belgic 6–8, 53, 81, 144, 146
Belgae (British tribe) 8
Belgian 204
Belinus/Belenus 75, 112, 113
Bell/Belbroughton (Brook) 112
Belinstock (Gwent) 75
Beltene 4, 61, 113
Beningas (Folk-group) 72
Bergusia 145
Berkeley (Gloucestershire) 122
Berkshire 8, 65, 108, 121
Berry (France) 53, 108
Besançon (France) 97
Bibracte/Mont Beauvray (France) 108, 146
Bibrax (France) 108
Bibury (Gloucestershire) 108

Birdlip Burials (Gloucestershire) 159–161, 167
Bishopric(s)/Episcopal Sees 9, 12
Bishop's Cleeve (Gloucestershire) 64–65
Bishop's Frome (Herefordshire) 69
Bisley (Gloucestershire) 71
Bitburg (Germany) 97
Bithynia (Turkey) 121
Bitton (Gloucestershire) 114
Bituriges Cubi (Gallic tribe) 6–7
Black Mountains (South Wales) 170, 208
Black-thorn 106
Blackwater (River) 103
Bladon/Blathaon/Blatonos (River) 24, 55, 107,
    113–114, 209
Bladud 73, 75
Bleddyn/Blyth (River) 114
Bloom, Harvey 168
Boar 87, 101–102, 109–110, 112, 131, 166
Boduo-/Boyd (River) 114
Boeotia (Greece) 33, 87–88, 139
Bohemia 135–136
Boii (Tribe) 135
Bolands (France) 96
Bonus 75
Book of Armagh 164
Bor 143
Boreas 138, 141
Bormanus (Spring) 93, 98
Boudica (Queen) 24, 114
Boudunneihae (Folk-group) 160
Bourbonne-les-Bans (France) 93
Bourges 6, 53
Bourton-on-the-Water (Gloucestershire) 66–67
Bow (Brook), see Croc-
Boyne (River) See Buvinda
Bradford-on-Avon (Wiltshire) 20
Bragi 51
Brailes Hill (Warwickshire) 168
Bran (River) 103
Bran/Brennus 75
Breconshire/Brecknockshire 103, 112, 117
Bredon Hill (Worcestershire) 159, 161, 199
Brenig (River) 103
Bres 52
Breton 114
Brian 52
Briareus 140
Bricta 95, 145
Brigantes (British tribe) 8, 203

Brigantes (Irish tribe) 7
Brigantia/Braint (River) 103
Brigantia/Brent (River) 70, 103
Bristol (Gloucestershire) 174, 178, 180
Britannia/Britain/British/Pritannic Isles 1, 4–8,
    11, 13–14, 20, 22, 25, 27–28, 30, 42–43, 45, 45,
    52, 59, 67, 69, 72–73, 75–76, 78–80, 86, 92,
    94, 96, 99–104, 106–107, 113–114, 117, 130,
    134, 135–136, 143, 145–146, 150, 165–166,
    169, 170–172, 179, 183, 186, 200, 201–203,
    206, 209–210
Britannia Prima (British Province) 28, 137,
    200, 204
British Mothers 72–73
Brittonic 140, 143, 145, 162
Broadboard/Hatherley (Brook) 185
Broadstone, Stroat (Gloucestershire) 128
Broadwater (Brook) 60, 118
Brompton (Antiquarian) 20
Brontes 140
Bronze Age 4, 7, 22–24, 30–33, 36–38, 55–56, 71,
    80, 89, 91, 134, 188–189, 209
Brooches 185
Brouron (Greece) 38
Brue (River) 14
Brutus 72–73
Buckinghamshire 162
Builth Wells (Breconshire) 122, 175, 178, 188
Bull 33, 85, 88, 91, 98, 106, 121, 166
Bune/Bunon (River) 162
Bunhill (Herefordshire) 162
Burford (Oxfordshire) 19
Burgundy/Burgundian 96, 98, 145, 204
Buri 143
Burma 166
Buvinda/Boann/Boyne (River) 73, 100
Buxton (Derbyshire) 102

Caer- (River) 114–115
Caduceus 165
Caelin Hill, Rome 92
Caereni (British tribe) 7
Caerhun (Wales) 103
Caerleon (Gwent) 75, 107, 181, 189, 204, 206, 208
Caernarvonshire 126
Caerwent/Venta Silurum (Gwent) 67, 182,
    187–188, 201–202
Caesar 5–7, 14, 29, 53, 57, 73, 79, 141, 144–146,
    148–149, 165–166, 171

Caicus (River) 78
Caldicote (Gwent) 181, 183
Caledones (British tribal grouping) 8, 11
Camden, William 110
Camelot 204
Campania (Italy) 46
Camulos, see Mars Camulos
Candlemass 4
Cannaid (River) 103
Cano- (River) 103–104
Canterbury (Kent) 27
Cantiaci (British tribe) 8, 13, 27
Cape Sunium (Greece) 34
Capitoline Hill, Rome 50, 141
Capua (Italy) 46
Cardiganshire/Keredigion 101–102, 121
Carlisle (Cumbria) 125
Carmarthen Bay 181
Carmarthen 102
Carmarthenshire 131
Carn Cafal 173, 188
Carna (Spring) 91
Carnoacae (British tribe) 8
Carnutes (Gallic tribe) 6–7, 114, 146, 150, 171
Caron (River) 121
Carrant (River) 114
Carrawburgh 104
Carvetti (British tribe) 8, 52
Cassivellauni 6–7
Castleford (Yorkshire) 101
Castor 57
Cat 101, 166
Cath Paluc 101
Cathedral of the Witches 156–157
Catholic hierarchy 13
Cato 5, 46
Catuvellauni (British tribe) 6–8, 19
Cauci (Irish tribe) 7
Cauldron, see sacred vessel
Causewayed camps 21
Cegir (River) 104
Cella 67
Celtiberia/Celtiberian 5, 7
Celtic bell 68
Celto-Brittonic 145
Celto-Ligurian 96
Celts/Celtic 3, 5–6, 26, 29, 52–53, 58–59, 61, 64,
    73, 80–81, 93, 96, 98–99, 100, 107, 111, 114,
    128, 133, 135–137, 1410, 143–144, 146, 160, 162

Cenimagni (Tribe) 104
Cennen (River) 104
Cenomani (Italian tribe) 5
Cereālia (Festival) 45
Ceres 45
Cernunos 53, 98, 116
Cerretes (Iberian tribe) 7
Chalcidice 149
Chalon-sur-Saône (France) 97
Channel Islands 129
Chaos 138, 140–141, 149
Charante (River) 93
Chariot-pony 98, 106
Charlemagne (Emperor) 171
Charon 85
Chartes (France) 171
Châtillon-sur-Seine (France) 98
Chedworth Roman Villa (Gloucestershire) 66–67
Cheese Rolling 191
Chelmsford (Essex) 73
Chepstow (Gwent) 129–130, 181, 185, 187
Cherwell (River) 14, 114
Chester 105, 172
Chew 119
Chi-rho 66
Chicken 106, 119, 165–168
Chilterns 7, 129
China 166
Chippenham (Wiltshire) 20, 178
Chrétien de Troyes 204
Christian(s)/Christianity 4, 13, 25, 56, 63–64, 66–68, 70, 72, 76, 107–108, 120, 148, 203–204, 206, 209–210
Christmas 70
Church 12–13, 67–69, 70, 71, 107, 194, 197, 204
Churchdown Hill (Gloucestershire) 191–192, 194–199, 208
Churn (River), see Corinius
Chwilog (River) 104
Cicero 6
Cirencester (Gloucestershire) 67, 73–74, 115, 137, 141, 151, 153–155, 157–160, 188–189, 208
Civitas/Civitates (Political units) 9, 12–13, 17, 21, 188
Classical World/period 2, 31, 34, 38, 52, 140, 145, 150
Claudius 24, 75, 172

Cleddon (Brook) 102
Cleeve Hill (Gloucestershire) 65, 159, 199
Clifton, Bristol (Gloucestershire) 174, 178
Clota/Clyde (River) 104
Clyn Ystyn (Wales) 101
Cnebba 71
Cocca 54
Cocidius 52, 57
Cockerel, see chicken
Colchester/Camulodunum (Essex) 24, 48, 52, 115
Cole (River) 115
Colesbourne (River) 115
Coleshill (Warwickshire) 65
Coligny Calendar 4
Colinjnsplaat (Netherlands) 96
Coll- (River) 115
Coln (River) 118
Colwall (River) 115
Concord 75
Connaught 7
Continent, see Europe
Conwy 104
Cooper's Hill (Gloucestershire) 159, 191–192, 199
Corbridge (Northumberland) 103
Corieltauvi (British tribe) 8
Corineus 73
Corinius/Churn (River) 24, 74, 115
Corinth (Greece) 34
Cornovii/Cornovian (British tribe) 7–8, 21
Cornucopia 85
Cornwall/Cornish 127
Cors (River) 55, 117
Cors Hundred Claws 117
Corse (Gloucestershire) 117
Corse, Forest 117
Corsham (Wiltshire) 117
Corswell (River) 117
Côte d'Or (France) 94
Cotswold Cock 165, 168
Cotswold Eagle 165, 169
Cotswolds 19, 23, 54, 60–61, 63, 117, 150, 156, 159, 165, 167, 178
Corsewood Hills (Gloucestershire) 159, 199
Cosmos 149
Coughton (Brook) 19
Coventina (Spring) 104
Coventry (Warwickshire) 69, 110

Cows/cattle 32, 88, 83, 100, 106, 132, 166
Craf (River) 104
Cranes 121
Creation Myth/Primal Myth 1, 25–26, 78, 137–138, 140–141, 143, 145, 199
Credne 52
Creones (British tribe) 8
Crete/Cretan (Greece) 31, 37, 89
Cricklade (Wiltshire) 20
Crickley (Gloucestershire) 159, 167
Crida 71
Crimissus (River) 92
Croc/Bow Brook (River) 117
Crocus 117
Crohhæme (Folk-group) 117
Crow 89, 103
Crowle (Worcestershire) 117
Crown 116, 123, 156
Cruachan (Connaught) 195
Crunnchu 53
Crug Mawr (Wales) 173
Crusaders 117
Cuckoo 32
Cuda/Codes 54, 63, 117, 118
Culhwch 54, 172, 164, 200
Cullymurra Waterhole (Australia) 84
Cumberland 8
Cunliffe, Barry 176
Cuno-/Cynan (River) 117–118
Cunomaglos (Cynfael-River) 54–55, 60–61, 63, 70, 72, 117–118, 191, 202
Cusop (Herefordshire) 119
Cwm Du (Breconshire) 101
Cwm Kerwyn (Wales) 101
Cyclades (Greece) 38
Cyclopes 140, 171
Cynewald 71
Cynffrig (River) 118
Cynwrig (River) 117
Cyparissus 48–49
Cyprus 38–39
Cyw (River) 119–120
Cywarch (River) 104

Dabrona (River) 100
Daedala (Festival) 33
Dagda 52
Daglingworth (Gloucestershire) 117
Damnonii (British tribe) 8

Damona (Spring) 93, 98
Danaos (King) 86
Danebury (Hampshire) 166
Danube 5
Daphne 90
Daphnephhoria (Festival) 38
Dar (River) 104
Dark Ages 203
Darni (Irish tribe) 7
Darwin, Charles 2
Daylesford (Gloucestershire) 69
Dean, Forest (Gloucestershire) 14, 18–19, 59, 129, 167, 175, 185
Decangli (British tribe) 8
Decantae (British tribe) 8
Deer 98
Deimos 36
Deiri (Australian tribe) 84
Delbaeth 52
Delos (Greece) 37–38, 84
Delphi (Greece) 35, 37–38, 90, 171
Demetae (British tribe) 8, 13, 27, 71, 75
Demeter 31, 33–35
Democritus of Abdera 149
Denbeighshire 103
Denmark 26
Derbyshire 102
Derybraces (Iberian tribe) 7
Desire 140
Deugleðyfi (Wales) 101
Deva/Dee (River) 104
Devil/Hob 70
Devizes (Wiltshire) 175
Devon 13, 27, 105
Dian Cécht 52
Diana 2, 46, 109–110
Didyma (Greece) 37
Dikler (River), see Windrush
Dimet 71
Dinann 52
Dio Cassius 5–6, 99
Diodorus Siculus 5–6, 29, 146–147
Dione 39, 135
Dionysos 49, 56, 147
Dis 53, 144–145
Divine Couple 16, 25, 58, 95, 137, 140–141, 145, 150–151, 158, 154, 165
Diviciacus 150
Diwija 30–31, 34

Djuwarr Lagoon (Australia) 84
DNA 18, 26–27, 80, 136, 209–210
Dobunni/Dobunnic (British tribe) 1, 4, 6–8, 13–15, 17–18, 21, 23, 25, 27–28, 54–55, 58–59, 63, 66, 70, 72, 76, 78, 94, 106–110, 112, 115–120, 122–127, 131–132, 137, 144–145, 147, 150–151, 156, 158–160, 162–165, 168–169, 172, 186, 188, 190, 199, 201–203, 205–206, 208
Dobunnic coinage 13–14, 169, 186
Dobunni etymology 162–163
Dobunni father, see Mercury also 165–169
Dobunnic Mater/Matres 16, 21, 190, 54–55, 156, 160, 202–203, 206
Dobunnic tribal gods 16–21, 54, 70, 202–203
Dodderhill (Worcestershire) 179
Dodonna (Greece) 32
Dog 61, 117–118, 166
Domburg (Germany) 95
Domitian 172
Don 52
Donon, Le (France) 98
Dorchester-on-Thames (Oxfordshire) 19, 81
Dordogne (France) 97, 121
Dore/Dover (River) 209
Dorian/Doric 33–34, 37–38
Dorn (River) 129
Dorset 106, 170
Doverle (River) 122
Dreaming/Dreamtime 1, 81–84, 136
Dreams 140
Drimios 55
Droitwich (Worcestershire) 128, 179, 207
Druids 53, 55, 141, 144, 146, 148, 150
Duck/teal 106, 143
Dulas (River) 120, 209
Dumnonii (British tribe) 8, 13, 21
Dumnonii (Irish tribe) 7
Dur (River) 100
Durocornovium/Wanborough (Wiltshire) 115
Durotriges (British tribe) 8, 19, 20
Dyfed (Kingdom) 13, 27, 71
Dyrham (Gloucestershire), Battle of 19

Ea/Rea/Rhee (River) 209
Eagle 101
Earith (Huntingdonshire) 47
Earth 34, 140, 143–144
East Anglia (Kingdom) 8
East Midlands 8, 163
East Riding 8
Easter 70
Ebraucus/Eboraci (Genius) 73
Eburos/Vernwy (River) 105
Eburones (Gallic tribe) 7, 12
Ecgwine 110
Eccles (Brook) 69
Eccleswall (Herefordshire) 68
Edwardian 2, 198
Egg 138, 143, 190–191, 199
Eggleton (Herefordshire) 69
Egyptology/Egyptian 3, 147
Eign (River) 23
Eileithyia 41
Elain (River) 105
Eleatic School 149
Eleusis (Greece) 35
Elm 123–124
Elysium Fields 34
Emhain Macha (Ireland) 53–54
Emmer (River) 111
Empedocles 149
England/English 2–3, 7–8, 15, 18, 25–26, 63, 66, 70, 75, 80, 103, 107, 114, 117, 127–128, 137, 162, 203, 209–210
Entraines-sur-Nohain (France) 94
Eoves 110
Ephesus 38
Ephialtes 171
Ephorus 5
Epona 52–53, 93, 94
Erasinos (River) 87
Erebos 140
Erechtheos/Erichthonios 33, 36, 40
Eridanus (River) 78
Erigone 41
Eros/Love 140
Erymanthos (River) 86–87
Esaco-/Ock (River) 121
Esgeir Oervel (Ireland) 101
Espérandieu 144
Esquiline Hill, Rome 42
Essarois 97
Essex 81, 103
Estrées-Saint-Denis (Oise-France) 166
Esus/Isbourne (River) 121, 130
Eteokles 88
Ethnographies/Ethnography 2, 4, 6, 80

Etruscans (Italian tribe) 42, 44, 48, 50
Etrymon (River) 78
Eubouleus 34
Euhages 148
Euenus (River) 78
Euripides 88
Europe 1, 5–7, 26, 29–30, 52, 73, 78–79, 81, 86, 88, 90–93, 99, 105–106, 108, 119–120, 137, 143–144, 166, 171, 201–203
Eurotas (River) 87
Eurus 141
Eurymedon 135
Eurynome 87, 89, 91, 138, 145
Euxine Sea (Black Sea) 141
Evenlode (River), see Bladon
Evenos (River) 87
Evesham (Worcestershire) 69–70, 108, 110, 113
Exe (River) 123
Exhall (Warwickshire) 69
Eye (River) 117
Eynsham (Oxfordshire) 19, 22

Fagus 94
Faliscans (Italian tribe) 44
Fasti 91–92
Fawn 105, 108
Fen 7
Fimmilena 111
Finberg, H. P. R. 134
Fire god 142
Fladbury (Worcestershire) 113
Flag Fenn (Cambridgeshire) 23
Flamines/Flamen, see priests
Foederati 26
Folklore/Folk-tradition 2–3, 78, 128, 130, 166, 168, 172
Fontes Sequanea (France) 97
Fortuna 123, 156, 199
Foss Dyke (Lincolnshire) 47
Fount of Gorheli (Wales) 173
Fox 124
France/French 5, 78, 105, 108, 122, 125, 166, 171, 204
Frazer, James George 2, 81, 166, 168, 201
French Revolution 13
Freshford (Somerset) 175, 178
Freyja 51
Freyr 51

Frigg 51
Frome (River) 122

Gaea/Gaia 139–140, 145
Galahad 204
Gallia Cisalpina (Province) 146
Gallia Narbonensis (Province) 146
Gallic War 73, 99, 146
Gamber (River) 111, 187
Gangani (Irish tribe) 7
Garanos (River) 121
Garlic 104
Garron (River) 19, 121
Garth Grugyn (Wales) 101
Gaul/Gallia/Gallic 1, 4–7, 9, 12–13, 25, 27, 30, 42–45, 52–53, 55, 70, 78–80, 93–94, 98–99, 104, 115, 134–135, 144, 146–150, 165–166, 171–172, 202
Gauze (Brook) 117
Gavadiae 160
Ge 33
Genius 73, 171
Geoffrey of Monmouth (Historian) 66, 72–73, 75–76, 116, 122, 128, 137
Georgopotamos (River) 90
Germania/Germany/Germanic 6, 12, 25–27, 30, 50–52, 56–58, 63–65, 78–79, 80–83, 93–94, 98–99, 105, 134, 136–137, 141–144, 146, 150, 160, 162, 164, 166, 171, 202, 209
Germanistaion 80
Gesahenae 160
Gewisse/West Saxon 20 81
Ghyst 178
Giants 65–66, 70, 140, 143, 156, 171
Gildas (Historian) 26
Gill Mill (Oxfordshire) 117
Ginnungagap 143
Gladder (River) 122
Glamorgan 7, 18–19, 102, 118
Glamorgan, See of 13, 19
Glanicae 98, 121, 160
Glanis 98, 121
Glanum (France) 106, 121
Glast- (River)
Glasteningas (Folk-group) 122
Glastonbury (Somerset) 21, 68, 122, 205–207
Glastonbury Lake Village (Somerset) 23
Gleva/Horsebere (Brook) 58, 76, 122–123, 134, 184–185, 191–193

Glevenses 72, 75
Gloew (Brook) 178
Gloucester 54, 58, 67–68, 71, 75–76, 122, 137, 150–153, 156, 158–159, 164, 167, 169, 172, 181, 184, 188–191, 197, 200, 206, 208
Gloucester Museum 159
Gloucestershire 4, 20, 23, 62, 64, 114, 122, 128
Glyme/Glimos (River) 61, 64, 122, 129, 134–135
Glynch (Brook) 121
Glywysinga 18, 67, 107, 174
Glywys/Gloiu/Gloius 71, 75, 122
Goats 91, 99, 106, 115, 166–168
Goibnia/Govannon/Gorbonanus/Govannon 52–53, 75
Goldcliffe 181
Gorge Meillet, La (Marne-France) 166
Gold 143
Golden Bough, The 2, 46, 201
Goose 165
Gorgyra 85
Gorgon 60
Gothic Bible 81
Gournay-sur-Aronde (France) 25
Graeco Major 32
Grail/Grail Quest 76, 203–204, 208
Grand 121
Granicus (River) 78
Grannus 121, 145
Greek/Greece 5–6, 29–46, 49–51, 55–57, 66, 78–79, 84–87, 89–92, 96, 99–100, 105, 134–135, 137–138, 140, 143, 145–147, 149–150, 160, 172, 203
Green man/Jack-in-the-Green 3
Greetland (Yorkshire) 103
Grim 63–66, 198
Grimley (Worcestershire) 65–66, 111
Grim's Dyke (Oxfordshire) 63
Grimsetne (Folk-name) 65
Grimstock (Warwickshire) 65, 198
Grugyn Gwrych Ereint 101
Guma 72
Gumeninga (Folk-group) 72
Gware 55
Gwennol/Gynolwyn (River) 105
Gwent 7, 18, 68–69, 75, 101, 124, 186
Gwidonot 164
Gwrhyr 101
Gwys 101

Gyes 140

Habren, see Sabrina
Hades 34–35, 89–90
Hadrian 172
Hadrian's Wall (England) 52
Hæme 135
Hago 89
Hagondange 94
Hailes (Brook) 58
Hailey Wood (Gloucestershire) 130, 188
Haliacmon (River) 78
Hallow (Worcestershire) 65
Hammer/Hammer god, see Sucellus also 150, 198
Hampshire 166, 175
Hanbury (Worcestershire) 68
Hare 61, 165–166
Harii (Germanic tribe) 57
Harmonia 37
Harrow (Middlesex) 72
Harvington (Worcestershire) 23
Hawk 98
Hawkes, Christopher 21, 28
Hawstin (Wales) 101
Hawthorn 92
Hayling Island (Hampshire) 25
Hazel 115
Heaven 140, 144
Hecatus 5
Heimdaill 51
Hellenic/Hellenistic 31, 33, 36, 38, 41–42, 50, 90
Helgakviða Hundingsbana 65
Helisii (Germanic tribe) 57
Helvecones (Germanic tribe) 57
Helvetti (Gallic tribe) 6–7, 103, 135
Helvii (Gallic tribe) 6
Hemlock 104
Hemp 104
Henig, Martin 117
Henley Wood (Somerset) 59, 67
Henney (River) 129
Hennuc (River) 129
Hensington (Oxfordshire) 129
Hentland (Herefordshire) 18, 107
Henwen 100–101
Hephaistos 36, 40–41
Heptaporus (River) 78

Hera 31–34, 40, 42, 55, 56, 84, 88, 91, 141, 170, 199
Heracles/Herakles 50, 86–87, 142
Heraclides of Pontus 5
Herculaneum (Italy) 6
Hercynian Forest (Germany) 135
Hereford 14, 18
Herefordshire 23, 68–69, 107, 111, 119, 121, 126, 128, 158, 187
Hermes 38–39, 85, 166
Hermias 149
Hermiones (Germanic tribal grouping) 99
Hermus (River) 78
Herodian 75
Herodotus 5
Hertfordshire 65
Hesiod 5, 39, 78, 85, 89, 135, 139–140, 143–144, 203
Hesiod's Creation Myth/Theogony 139–140
Hesperides 85
Hestia 35, 46
Heuneberg (Germany) 166
Hicca (Folk-group) 163
Hill-fort 22, 59, 64–65, 71, 90, 194–195, 197–198, 207
Himlico 5
Hittite 30–31, 35, 37
Hoards 14, 23, 67
Hob Ditch Causeway (Warwickshire) 63
Hoder 51
Hoenir 51
Homer/Homeric 31, 33–36, 39, 56, 88–90, 139
Honey Bee/Honey 98, 101, 127
Horses 33, 37, 45, 47, 53–54, 85, 93, 95, 98, 106, 115, 166
Horse Racing 33
Horse Spring (Greece) 33, 183
Hotwells, Bristol (Gloucestershire) 174, 178, 187
Housesteads (Northumberland) 111
Hucclecote (Gloucestershire) 197
Humber (River) 73
Hungary 166
Hunter God, see Cunomaglos
Hutton, Ronald 2, 4, 180
Hwicce/Hwiccian 4, 13, 15, 17–18, 20, 27–28, 63–64, 67–68, 72, 107–108, 137, 163–164, 150, 173–174, 178, 190, 201, 203
Hwiccian etymology 163
Hwicce (Sacred vessel) 163

Hyllikos (River) 88
Hyperboreans 5
Hyperion 135, 140

Ianuaria (River) 93–94
Iapetos 140
Iberia/Iberian 8, 180, 209
Icauna/Yonne (River) 94, 122
Icel 71–72
Icelandic 51
Icelingas (Folk-group) 72
Iceni (British tribe) 8, 104, 172
Icovellauna (River) 94
Idas 87
Idun 51
Ilergetes (Iberian tribe) 7
Ikarios 41
Iliad 34, 88, 91, 139
Ilkley (Yorkshire) 132
Illyrian/Illyrium 30, 146
Imbolc 4, 70
Imbrasos (River) 32
Imperial Cult 4, 71
Inachos (River) 88
Inciona 145
India/Indic 2, 30, 45, 166
Indicetes (Iberian tribe) 7
Indo-European(s) 30, 80, 209
Ingaevones (Germanic tribal grouping) 99
Interpretatio 27, 56–77, 201, 203
Interpretatio (Christiania) 66–76
Interpretatio (Germania) 63–66, 164
Interpretatio (Graeca) 56–57
Interpretatio (Romana) 57–62, 166
Inverness 173
Io 88
Iolo Morganwg 2, 144
Ionia/Ionian 35, 38
Ireland/Irish/Hibernia 4, 7, 10, 22, 26, 52–53, 55, 56, 68, 70, 73, 78, 86, 94, 99, 100–101, 105, 115, 128, 136, 144, 166, 171, 173, 203–205
Irish quarter days 4
Iron Age 4, 9–10, 12–15, 22–24, 28, 40, 42, 51, 58–59, 63, 68, 71, 84, 91, 97, 120, 144, 159, 164, 167, 169, 173, 178–180, 190–191, 194, 197–198, 207, 209
Iron-Age coinage 6–7, 12–13, 15, 25, 115, 176, 186, 165, 202
Iron-Age currency bars 13–15

Iron-Age round houses/spatial use 22–23
Iron ores/iron 14, 59, 143
Isbourne (River) 23
Isca (River) 122
Ishtar/Ister 39, 78
Island Germanic 81
Ismenius (River) 87, 92
Isosa 130
Istaevones (Germanic tribal grouping) 99
Iothmia (Greece) 34
Istrat Hafren (Gloucestershire) 18, 180
Italy/Italian 5, 7, 32, 43 46, 49–50, 57, 78, 80,
    91–92, 203
Itchen (River) 122
Ithome 89
Iuchar 52
Iucharba 52
Iunones 162
Iverne (River) 100
Iverni (Irish tribe) 7

Jackson, Kenneth 3, 26
Janus 49, 91
Jewish 29
John of Worcester 18
Jordan 199
Joseph of Arimathea 76
Julian-Augustan line 47–48
Juno 43–44, 141, 162, 199
Jupiter (Jove) 42–44, 47, 50, 53, 57, 61–62, 64,
    67, 96, 122, 141
Jupiter Glimos 62
Julian (Emperor) 67
Jutes 26

Kadmos 37
Kalevala 143
Kalkreise (Germany) 79
Kalydonian (Greece) 88
Kangeroo 84
Kamber 73
Karneia Hyakinthia (Festival) 38
Kemble (Gloucestershire) 20, 115
Kempsey (Worcestershire) 23
Kempsford (Gloucestershire) 20
Kenchester (Herefordshire) 16, 18
Kent/Cantwara 13, 27, 81
Keos 41
Kephisos (River) 88

Kernyw (Wales) 101
King's Norton (Worcestershire) 64
Kingswood (Forest) 14
Kinver (Staffordshire) 117, 130
Kirkcudbright (Scotland) 105
Kition (Cyprus) 39
Kladeos (River) 86
Klymenos 34
Knossos, Crete (Greece) 31, 36
Koios/Koeos 135, 140
Kokytos (River) 34, 89
Kolakola 84
Komawentia 30
Kore 34–35, 45
Kottos 140
Kreius/Kreios 135, 140
Kronos 31–32, 34–35, 42, 50, 89, 91, 135, 139–140
Kunia (Australian tribe) 81–83
Kurgen culture 209

La Tène 24
Ladder of Inference 21
Ladon (River) 78, 86, 89
Lammas 4
Latin(s) 6, 44, 45, 50, 136, 163–164
Latium (Italy) 46, 50
Laughern (Brook) 124, 133
Leadon (River) 122
Leam (River) 123
Leauses, Cirencester (Gloucestershire) 151,
    153–155
Leckhampton Hill (Gloucestershire) 159, 167
Leda 87
Leicester 75
Leicestershire 197
Leinster 7
Leir 75
Leland (Antiquarian) 129
Lemana (River) 123–124
Lemmano (Lake) 98
Lenus 93
Leominster (Herefordshire) 71
Lepontii (Italian tribe) 5
Lepraucorn 70
Lesbos (Greece) 40, 149
Lethe (River) 34
Leto 31, 38, 84
Leucaro- (River), 105
Leucippus of Miletus 149

Liber Pater 45, 49
Libera 45
Liberalia (Festival) 49
Libnios (River) 100
Lichen 104
Lilara 88
Lincoln 172
Lindow Man (Cheshire) 180
Lingones (Gallic tribe) 93, 95
Linear B 30–34, 36–38, 41–42, 56
Linton (Herefordshire) 68
Liriope 88
Liru (Australian tribe) 81–83
Little Solsbury (Somerset) 179
Livy 6, 42, 53
Llandaff, See of 19, 102
Llandaff Charters/Book of Llandaff 18–19
Llandogo (Gwent) 102
Llanfair (Wales) 101
Llangors (Breconshire) 68
Llonyon (Wales) 101
LLugwg (River) 126
Llwydawc Gouynnyat (Wales) 101
Llyn Lliwan 173, 181–184
Llyn Llyw (Lake) 54, 122, 181, 184. 191
Llyon 70
Loch Echach (Ireland) 173
Loch Lein (Ireland) 173
Loch Leven (Scotland) 173
Locri 148
Locrinus 73
Lodan (River) 100
Lodge Hill Camp (Gwent) 75
Loeb Classical Library 80, 91
Loegria 75
Logia 100
Loki 51
London 24, 48, 73, 75, 172
Long Newton (Gloucestershire) 20
Longford (Gloucestershire) 185
Loomis, Roger Sherman 76, 204
Loucetius (Spring) 94, 145
Loughor (River) 101, 105
Lovernius/Laughern (River) 124
Lower Slaughter (Gloucestershire) 118
Lucan 121
Luci (Gallic-Tribe) 203
Luchta 52
Lugg (River) 126, 128

Lughnasad 4, 61
Lugos/Lug/Lugh 4, 52, 125, 126
Luna 176
Luxeuil (France) 95
Luxovius (Spring) 95, 145
Lyceum, Athens (Greece) 149
Lydia (Turkey) 41
Lydney Park (Gloucestershire) 67, 173
Lykormas (River) 87, 91
Lymax 89
Lymon (Brook) 181
Lympne (Sussex) 123
Lyon/Lugdunum (France) 4, 124
Lysons, Samuel 195–196

Mabon/Maponus 54–55, 72
Mabinogion 26, 54–55, 63, 66, 72, 103, 111, 117,
    118, 131, 164, 169, 184, 189–190, 200
Macbeth 150
Macha 53–54, 94, 96
Macedonia (Greece) 149
Maen Du (Wales) 101
Maes Gwenith (Wales) 101
Magic 2
Magna Graecia 148
Magonsæte (Kingdom) 18, 21, 68
Maia 31, 39
Malmesbury (Wiltshire) 20, 68, 117
Malverns (Herefordshire/Worcestershire) 121,
    167
Manimi (Germanic tribe) 57
Mannus 98, 142
Mantua 7
Marcham-Frilford (Oxfordshire) 173
Marches 107
Marden (Herefordshire) 68, 69
Marineus 30
Marpassa 87
Mars 30, 37, 43–44, 46–47, 57–59, 61, 94, 96–97,
    142, 145
Mars Camulos 52, 99, 115
Mars Nodens, see Nodens
Marseille/Massalia (France) 5
Mary Queen of Scots 173
Mater/Mothers 63, 76, 93–94, 106, 142–144,
    150–153, 155–156, 160, 164, 169
Mater Dobunna/Matronae Dobunnae, see
    Dobunnic mother goddess
Matres Britannae 72

Matrona/Marne (River) 95
Mauron 75
May Day 4, 61
Meander (River) 78
Meare Heath (Somerset) 23
Meare Pool (Somerset) 122
Meath (Ireland) 70
Medieval, see Middle Ages
Mediomatrici (Gallic tribe) 7, 93
Mediterranean 91, 92, 171
Medlartree 116
Medusa 33, 178
Megara 148
Meletus 127–128
Melksham (Wiltshire) 24
Mells (Somerset) 127–128
Mellt 55
Mempricius 73
Menapii (Ireland) 7
Mendips 20, 59, 167
Menw (Wales) 101
Meonware 81
Mercia/Mercian 18–20, 64, 72
Mercury 48–49, 55, 61, 95, 98, 103, 123, 142, 145,
    150–156, 158–160, 165–166, 168, 198, 206
Mercury (Dobunnic) 16, 21, 198, 206
Merionethshire 103, 117–118
Mesolithic 209
Mesopotamia (Iraq) 31
Messenia 90
Metamorphoses 141
Metaphysics 148
Metis 31, 36, 135
Metope 87
Metz (France) 94, 97
Meurig (Brook) 173, 187
Meuse (River) 96
Middle Ages 13, 25–26, 75, 136, 169, 178, 194,
    205, 206
Middle Anglia 19
Middle East 30, 70, 78
Middlesex 72
Midlands 22–24
Midsummer 4
Midwinter 4
Míl of Spain 128, 144
Milletus (Bishop) 70
Minerva, see Sulis Minerva also 16, 44–45, 57,
    59, 141, 156, 159, 177

Minerva Medica 59
Minoa/Minoan 31
Mirarr (Australian tribe) 84
Mirebaeu (France) 25
Mnemosyne 140
Moccus (River) 95
Modonnos (River) 100
Modron 54–55, 63, 150, 160, 164, 169
Moenus 136
Möhn (Germany) 93
Monaigh (Irish tribe) 7
Monmouth (Gwent) 18
Monnow (River) 18
Mons Huuicciorum (Gloucestershire) 163
Montgomeryshire 105
Moon 122, 129, 142, 168
Morini (Gallic tribe) 96
Morning Star 129
Mórrígan 52
Mossell (River) 94
Mother Goddess, see Mater
Mount Argaeus (Near East) 199
Mount Aroanios (Greece) 86, 90
Mount Artemisius (Greece) 86, 88
Mount Cyllēne (Greece) 39
Mount Ida (Turkey) 32
Mount Kithairon (Greece) 86
Mont Lampeia (Greece) 87
Mount Lykaion (Greece) 32, 89
Mount Olympus (Greece) 32, 90, 139, 170
Mount Ossa (Greece) 171
Mount Pelion (Greece) 171
Mount Tifata (Italy) 46
Mouse 98
Much Marcle (Herefordshire) 18
Müller 2
Mullo 95
Munster 7
Murry, Margaret 3
Muspella 143
Mwrheth 114
Mycalē (Greece) 34
Mycenae/Mycenaean 31–33, 38–39, 41–42, 88

Naharvali (Germanic tribe) 57
Nanna 51
Nantosuelta (River) 95, 145
Navan Fort (Ireland) 54
Narcissus 88

Naxians 38
Nechtain 45
Neda (River) 89
Nehalennia 52, 95
Neidaldorf (Germany) 97
Nemausicae 96, 160
Nemausus (River) 96
Nemea (Greece) 32
Nemedh 53
Nemetona 94, 145
Nemeton, see Sacred grove
Nemi (Italy) 2
Nene (River) 23
Nennius 66, 72, 75, 115, 122, 172–173, 175–176, 181, 186–188, 200, 207
Neolithic 4, 21–22, 209
Neo-paganism 170
Nepos 6
Neptune 45
Nero 24
Nerthus 51, 143
Nerva/Nerviana 172
Nessus (River) 78
Netherlands 95
Nettleton Scrubb (Wiltshire) 60, 118, 153, 157
Neuchâtel (Lake) (Switzerland) 24
New Year 46
New Zealand Indo-European Tree 80
Newport (Gwent) 68
Nido/Neath (River) 105
Night (Nyx) 139, 140
Nile (River) 78
Nîmes (France) 96, 106
Njord 51
Nodens/Nuadha/Nudd 45, 52, 54–55, 59, 181
Noricum 75
Norman 130
Norns, see Wyrd
North Piddle (Worcestershire) 129
North Sea 95–96
North-west provinces 6
Notitia Dignitatum 80
Nôtre-Dame, Paris 121
Nottingham Hill (Gloucestershire) 167
Nottinghamshire 150
Novantae (British tribe) 8
Nuits Saint Georges (France) 96
Numa 42, 150
Numerian (Emperor) 18

Nymph(s) 38, 90, 103–104, 127
Nymphaeum 97

Oak 59–60, 98, 104, 106, 194
Oboca (River) 100
Oceania 4–5
Oceanos 78, 84–87, 90, 135, 139–140, 145
Odin, see Woden also 51, 72, 143
Oenghus 115
Offa (King) 19
Ogma 52
Old Oswestry (Shropshire) 22
Oldbury, Stroat (Gloucestershire) 181
Olwen 54, 172, 164, 200
Olympia (Greece) 86, 89, 171
Ombersley (Worcestershire) 133
Omphelos 199
Onn-/Pinsley (River)128
Onomastics 1, 4, 202
Ophion 145, 170
Ops 50
Orchomenos 88
Orcus (River) 89–90
Ordovices (British tribe) 8, 150
Orphic Creation Myth 139
Orphic/Orphism 138–139, 148, 170
Oros (Greece) 32
Orvandill 65
Oscans (Italian tribe) 44
Ostia (Italy) 92
Osteria dell'Osa (Italy) 42
Ouranos 39, 140, 145, 137
Ouse (River) 73
Ovid 42, 45, 50, 61, 85, 91–92, 140, 143, 145
Owl 91
Ox 47, 166
Oxfordshire 14, 19, 64, 129, 162

Pactolus (River) 92
Padus/Po (River) 96
Pagan revival 67
Paiawon 37
Palatine Hill, Rome 50
Palla 90
Pamisos (River) 90
Panentheism 79
Pantheon(s) 29–55, 93, 144–145, 202
Pantheon 'Celtic' 51–54
Pantheon Dobunnic 54–55

Pantheon Germanic 50–51
Pantheon Greek 30–42
Pantheon Romana 42–50
Paphos 39
Paris (France) 121
Parisi (British tribe) 8
Parochia/Parochiae 18–19, 69, 184
Partheism 79
Parthenius (River) 32, 78
Parthenon (Greece) 04
Patroklos 90
Paul 75
Pausanias 86–87
Pagai (Greece) 86
Pelagon (Greece) 87
Pelasgian Creation Myth 138, 140, 170
Peloponnese (Greece) 85
Penda 71
Peneios/peneus (River) 78, 89–90
Pennsylvania Indo-European Tree 80
Perachora 32
Percival 204, 206
Peredur 164, 172, 189, 200, 203–206
Periplus text 5
Pero 87
Persephone 34–35
Persia 166
Phanes-Dionysus 139
Phasis (River) 78
Penean Lake (Greece) 89
Phigalians 89
Philyra (Greece) 89
Phlegethon (River) 34
Phobos 36
Phoebe 135, 140
Phoenician 39
Phoenodamas 92
Phrygia/Phrygian Cap 41, 61
Pictes (Irish tribe) 7
Picts (Scotland) 26
Picus 50
Pig(s) 47, 95, 98, 108, 112
Pigeon 117–118
Pike 121
Pillars of Hercules 5
Pine 106, 128
Pitjandjara (Australian tribe) 81, 83
Plataea (Greece) 33, 86
Plato 5, 148
Plouton 34

Pluto 45
Plutos 34
Plynlimon (Wales) 128
Poland 166
Pollux 57
Polybius 5–6
Poppy 35
Porth Clais (Wales) 101
Portskewett (Gwent) 60, 102, 181–183, 187
Poseidon 33–34, 36, 84, 86–88, 147
Poseidonius of Apameia 6
Poulton (Gloucestershire) 189
Powys (Kingdom) 114
Priests/Priestesses 43, 45, 54, 164
Ptolemy 6, 10, 100, 175
Pypba 71
Pylos (Greece) 34, 41
Pyrennes (France/Spain) 94
Pytheas 5
Pythagoras/Pythagorean 30, 146–150, 166, 202
Python 38

Quinquatrus 44
Quirinus 43, 47

Rainbow serpent 84
Ram 165
Raven 75, 95, 99, 125
Ravenna Cosmography (Text) 128
Ravios (River) 100
Redwald (King) 70
Reed(s) 104, 117
Regni (British tribe) 8
Reims (France) 115
Reinheim (Germany) 166
Religion 2, 4, 42, 51, 58, 66–67, 165
Remi (Gallic tribe) 7, 52
Remus 47
Rešep 37–38
Rex Nemorensis 46
Rhea 34–35, 89, 135, 139–140
Rhenus/Rhine (River) 88, 96, 99, 130, 135
Rhesus (River) 78
Rindern (Germany) 115
Rhineland 144, 160
Rhiw Gyfertlwch (Wales) 101
Rhodius/Rhône (River) 5, 78, 145
Rhys, John 3, 100–103, 143, 180
Ribemont-sur-Ancre (France) 25
Rogation Sunday 197

Roman(s) 5–6, 9, 12–13, 24–25, 28, 29–30, 37, 42–52, 55, 56–59, 61, 63–65, 67–68, 71–74, 76–77, 79–85, 93, 96, 103, 105, 107, 115, 120–122, 128, 134, 137, 139–140, 144–147, 149–150, 156, 160, 165, 168, 176, 179–180, 188, 191, 195, 197, 199, 202, 205, 207–208
Roman Empire 7, 26, 49, 55, 77, 78, 88, 92–94, 96, 141, 199
Romania 166
Romanisation 79–80
Rome 5, 7, 42, 44, 46–50, 57, 70, 92, 141, 147, 150
Romulus 47
Rosmerta 145
Ross-on-Wye (Herefordshire) 18–19, 68, 69
Royston crow 99, 114
Ruardean (Gloucestershire) 175
Rudhall (Brook) 19
Rumon (River), see Tiberinus 90
Rura (River) 96
Rush(es) 134

Sabines (Italian tribe) 44, 46
Sablon (France) 94
Sabrina/Severn (River) 23, 54, 59, 71, 73, 75–76, 96, 105, 108, 111, 122, 128, 133, 173, 178, 180, 181–182, 184, 186–187, 190, 200, 203, 207
Sacred groves/Nemetons 54, 63, 71, 102
Sacred lake(s) 24, 181–185
Sacred vessel 15, 63, 76, 147, 150, 154, 156–157, 159, 163–164, 169, 206, 208
Saefes (Iberian tribe) 7
Saint Asaph (Gwynedd) 72
Saint Bartholomew 194–195
Saint Bride 70
Saint Cadoc102, 107
Saint David's 13
Saint Dogmael's (Dyfed) 71
Saint Dubricus 19
Saint Gwynllyw 102
Saint Marcel (Berry-France) 108
Saint-Maur (France) 25
Saint Mary de Lode (Gloucestershire) 68, 190
Saint Mary de Stalls, Bath (Somerset) 71, 177
Saint Mary's, Worcester (Worcestershire) 157
Saint Oudoceus 102
Saint Patrick 70
Saint Paulinus 68
Saint Samson of Dol, Life of 164
Saint Tatheus 67, 183

Saint Teliau 72
Saint Twrog 180
Sainte-Fontaine (France) 94, 97
Salassi (Italian tribe) 5
Salenses (Folk-group) 58, 72
Salford Priors (Warwickshire) 69
Salia/Hailes (Brook) 121, 128
Salii (Festival) 47
Salina (River) 128
Sallust 6
Salmon 54, 121, 122
Salt 121
Salty (brook) 128
Salwarpe (River) 132
Samhain 4
Samos (Greece) 32, 148
Sangarius (River) 78
Sapina/Sapey (River) 128
Sardis 5
Sargia (River) 129
Sark (Island) 129
Saturnālia (Festival) 50
Saturnus 49–50
Saxo Gramaticus 72
Saxon(s) 19, 26, 81–82, 171
Scamander (River) 78, 78
Scandinavia 29, 63, 79, 143, 202–203, 209
Scandinavian Eddas 29, 143
Scheldt (River) 96
Schleider's Indo-European Tree 80
Science 2
Scotland 8
Sea Mills (Gloucestershire) 67
Sedge 98
Sedgeberrow (Worcestershire) 23
Segelocum 96
Segomo (River) 96
Segontium 96
Sele (River) 32
Selemnos (River) 90
Selgovae (British tribe) 8, 52
Semetic 39
Senones (Gallic tribe) 6
Senos/Sionan/Shannon (River) 73, 100, 102
Senuna 129
Sentona (River) 105
Sequana/Seine (River) 97
Sequani (Gallic tribe) 7
Seven Springs (Spring) 209
Severn (River), see Sabrina

Severn Tunnel 183
Severn Vale/Valley 8, 150, 164–165, 167, 209
Shakespeare, William
Shakespeare Inn, Gloucester 137, 150
Shannon (River), see Senos
Sheela na gigs 3
Sheep 47, 106, 115, 140, 168
Sherston (Wiltshire) 20
Shipton-under-Wychwood (Oxfordshire) 19
Shorncote Quarry (Gloucestershire) 20
Shropshire 23, 128, 132, 197
Siciliy 32, 92
Siddington (Gloucestershire) 110
Silchester (Hampshire) 81
Silures (British tribe) 7, 13, 18, 67, 107, 119,
    122, 188, 200
Silvanus 46, 49, 58
Silvanus Callirius 115
Simois (River) 78
Sirens 85
Sirona 94, 97, 134
Skadi 51
Skirrid (Gwent) 206, 208
Sky father 144
Sleep 140
Smeritrius 96
Snak(es)/serpent 85, 138
Snettisham (Norfolk) 46
Snorri Sturluson 51, 143
Soch- (River) 106
Socrates 148
Sol 176
Sol Invictus 70
Solon 149
Somerford Keynes (Gloucestershire) 20
Somerset 20–21, 106, 119, 127, 175, 154, 158,
    207
Somerset Levels 23
Somerton (Oxfordshire) 162
Souconna (River) 97
South Mercia 19
South Wales 59, 63, 67, 75, 122
Southwark (Surrey) 130
Sow 101, 106, 166
Spain/Spanish 5–7, 105, 121, 166
Sparta (Greece) 86–87
Spence, Lewis 2
Spencer 2
Spercheios (River) 90
Spoils of Annwn 164

Spoonbill 105
Stag 61, 102, 106, 115
Stagira 149
Stanna 97
Star 97, 129
Stanton Harcourt (Oxfordshire) 24
Steepholm 180
Steropes 140
Stonehenge (Wiltshire) 170
Strasbourg (France) 96, 145
Stroat (Gloucestershire) 181
Stour Valley (Warwickshire) 168
Strymon (River) 78
Stymphalos Lake (Greece) 87
Styx (River) 89–90
Sucellus 53, 97, 145, 198
Sudbrook (Gwent) 181, 183
Sugar Loaf (Gwent) 208
Suffolk 24
Sugambri (Germanic tribe) 7
Suleviae (Folk-group) 160
Sulis Minerva 58, 60, 71, 129, 134–135, 156,
    176–177
Sulmo (Italy) 140
Sumerian-Babylonian 35
Sun 70, 129, 142, 177–178
Suovetaulia (Festival) 47
Susi- 130
Sussex 81, 123
Sutton (Herefordshire) 68–69
Swallow/Swift 105
Swan 106
Swedish 71
Switzerland 24
Syracuse 148

Tacitus 11, 50–51, 56–57, 72, 79–80, 82–83, 98,
    142–143, 201
Taezali (British tribe) 8
Taff (River) 181
Tainaron (Greece) 34
Taliesin 164
Tamesis/Thames (River) 19–20, 22–24, 48, 96,
    115, 129–130, 188
Tamworth (Warwickshire) 64
Tanad- (River) 106
Tanais (River) 92
Tara (Meath) 70, 171
Taranis 121
Tarquin 49

Tartarus 34, 90
Tarvostrigaranos 121
Tellus 45
Telo (Spring) 97
Temples/Sanctuaries/Shrines 24, 31–36, 38, 40,
    45–48, 54, 59–61, 65–67, 70–71, 80, 92, 97, 172,
    176, 179, 187, 189, 191, 196, 198, 202, 207
Tetbury (Gloucestershire) 20
Tethys 78, 85–87, 90, 135, 139–140, 145
Teutatis 121
Tews (Oxfordshire) 63–64
Thames (River) see Tamesis
Thebes (Greece) 41
Theia 135, 140
Theisoa 89
Themis 135, 140
Theomacha 164
Theopompus 5
Thessaly 41, 56
Thetis 31
Tholos 157
Thomas, Charles 13, 66
Thor 51, 196
Thrace 41, 88
Thrush 86
Tiberinus (River) 92
Tidenham (Gloucestershire) 180
Timaeus 148
Titans 140, 144, 171
Tiw/Tye 30, 51, 64
Tomi 140
Torc Tréith 101
Tortoise 39
Toulon (France) 97
Toulouse (France) 24
Towy Fort (Wales) 101
Tragos (River) 91
Transalpine Gaul 6
Transmigration of the soul (see Pythagoras)
Treveri (Gallic tribe) 7, 93
Trier (Germany) 93–94, 98, 121
Trinovantes (British tribe) 6, 8, 52, 73
Trisantona/Trehannon/Trent (River) 105–106,
    173
Troddi (River) 124
Troggy/Nedern (River) 182–183
Trout 91, 123
Troy 32
Tuatha de Danann 52
Tuirill deo Danonni 52

Tuisto 98, 142
Turcos (River) 131
Turmus 48
Twrch Llawain 101
Twrch Trwyth 101, 180
Twyver (River) 191
Tyche 75
Tylor 2
Typhoeos 140
Tysoe (Warwickshire) 64

Ubii (Germanic tribe) 7
Ucuetis 145
Uley Shrines (Gloucestershire) 25, 61–62, 67,
    70, 167–168
Ull 51
Ulster/Ulstermen 7, 53
Uluru (Australia) 81–84
Umbrians (Italian tribe) 42, 44
Underwood, Guy 1
Usk (River) 103, 123

Vacallinehae 160
Vacomagi (British tribe) 8
Vala 143
Vale of Gloucester 65, 158, 162, 164, 169,
    190–191
Vale of Tempe (Greece) 89
Vandil/Vandilo 65, 134–135
Vanir 50–51
Varro 42
Vates 148
Ve 51, 143
Vedic Scriptures 2
Vendel 65
Veneti (Gallic tribe) 7
Venus 48
Veraudinus 145
Verbeia/Wharf (River) 132
Vercingetorix 7, 146
Vesontius 97
Vespasian 172
Vesta 45–46, 70
Vestals 46, 92
Vicus/Vici 9, 135
Victorian 2, 20, 26–27, 198
Vidva (River) 100
Vigora/Wyre (Forest) 111, 133, 167
Viking(s) 210
Vili 51, 143

Villa of the Papyri (Italy) 6
Vinderis (River) 100
Vindonnus 97–98
Vindo-reisko (River) 134
Virgil 45, 73
Virgin Mary 70, 109, 171
Viribus 46
Viridomix 99
Vitalinus 75
Volcae (Gallic tribe) 5
Von Daniken, Eric 1
Vosegus/Vosges (Forest, River) 98, 121
Votadini (British tribe) 8
Votive deposition 23–24

Wales/Welsh 1, 3, 8, 18, 20, 22, 25–26, 28, 51,
    55, 59, 64, 71, 73, 75–76, 99–102, 104, 107,
    113–114, 127–128, 131, 136–137, 144, 170,
    173, 200, 204–207
Wændelescumb (Berkshire) 65
Walcheren (Netherlands) 96
Wandsworth (Surrey) 65
Warwickshire 64, 108, 114, 122–123, 147, 168
Watkins, Alfred 1
Water Lily 102
Wednesbury (Staffordshire) 64
Well of Coelrind (Ireland) 100
Well of Segais (Ireland) 100
Wellow (Somerset) 16, 21, 154
Welsford (Warwickshire) 147
Wendel 65
Wendlesbiri (Hertfordshire) 65
Wendle's Cliff (Gloucestershire) 64–65
Wensdon (Bedfordshire) 65
Wentwood (Gwent) 185
Wessex (Kingdom) 81, 20, 22
West Saxon 19–20
Westbury-on-Trym (Gloucestershire) 23
Western Germanic 81
Western Hecana (tribe) 18, 68
Weston-under-Penyard (Herefordshire) 107
Weogorena (Folk-group) 58, 133
Wheat 101, 111, 134, 166
Whitchurch (Herefordshire) 18–19
Whitchurch (Warwickshire) 168
White poplar 85
Wicce/witches 63, 163–164
Widia 64
Wiggington Roman Villa (Oxfordshire) 66

William of Malmesbury 186
Willow 121
Wiltshire 20–21, 132, 153, 158
Winchcombe (Gloucestershire) 58
Winchester (Hampshire) 72, 81
Windblow/Windcliff (Gwent) 173, 186–187
Windrush/Dickler (River) 107, 131, 134
Witcombe Roman Villa (Gloucestershire) 191–
    194
Witham (River) 23
Withington (Gloucestershire) 64
Woad 122
Woden, see Odin also 63–64, 71
Wolf 91, 101, 113–114, 160
Wolfram von Eschenbach 204
Woodeaton (Oxfordshire) 173
Woolhope-cum-Fownhope (Parochia) 19
Woolhope Naturalists' Field Club 1
Worcester 19, 68–69, 157, 163–164
Worcestershire 4, 23, 65, 68, 106, 108, 111, 124,
    132–133, 178
Worm (River) 187
Wotton (Gloucestershire) 20
Wychwood (Oxfordshire) 19, 21, 63, 163
Wye (River) 18, 128, 173, 178, 185, 207, 209
Wynyd Amanw (Wales) 101, 129
Wyrd Sisters 63, 164
Wyre (Forest), see Vigora

Xanten (Germany) 72
Xanthus (River) 92
Xenophon 5
Xulsigia (Springs) 98

Yare (River) 121
Yellow hammer 111
Yew 98
Yggdrasil 186
Ymir 79, 143, 145
Yonne, see Icauna
York 73, 105, 172
Yorkshire 7–8, 105, 132
Ystrad Yw (Wales) 101

Zephyrus 141
Zeus 30–36, 38–39, 41–43, 52, 55, 87, 89, 91,
    139–141
Zodiac Circles 1
Zoroastrian 166